PUBLICATIONS OF THE FINNISH SOCIETY
OF CHURCH HISTORY, NO. 174

SUOMEN KIRKKOHISTORIALLISEN SEURAN
TOIMITUKSIA 174

STORY OF A STORM

*The Ecumenical Student Movement
in the Turmoil of Revolution,
1968 to 1973*

Risto Lehtonen

WILLIAM B. EERDMANS PUBLISHING COMPANY
GRAND RAPIDS, MICHIGAN / CAMBRIDGE, U.K.

HELSINKI 1998
SUOMEN KIRKKOHISTORIALLINEN SEURA
FINNISH SOCIETY OF CHURCH HISTORY
SOCIETAS HISTORIAE ECCLESIASTICAE FENNICA

The manuscript has been examined on behalf of the Finnish Society of Church History by Dr. Mikko Juva and Docent Martti Lindqvist.

Suomen kirkkohistoriallinen seura
P.O. Box 33 (Aleksanterinkatu 7)
FIN-00014 University of Helsinki
Finland
Fax +358 9 1912 3033

Bookstore Tiedekirja
Kirkkokatu 14, FIN-00170 Helsinki
Tel. +358 9 635 177, fax +358 9 635 017

Printed in the United States of America

03 02 01 00 99 98   7 6 5 4 3 2 1

Library of Congress Cataloging-in-Publication Data

Lehtonen, Risto.
Story of a storm: the ecumenical student movement in the
turmoil of revolution, 1968-1973 / Risto Lehtonen.
p.   cm.
"This book recounts the experiences of the
World Student Christian Federation" — Introd.
Includes bibliographical references.
ISBN 0-8028-4429-4 (pbk.: alk. paper)
1. World Student Christian Federation — History.
I. Title.
BV970.W8L44   1998
267'.13 — dc21   97-44688
                                           CIP

ISBN 952-5031-06-3
ISSN 0356-0759

Contents

v

*To my colleagues
on both sides of the barricades
of the revolutionary years,
with gratitude*

Foreword

As I am writing this Foreword, a massive ice storm, such as happens once in a century, has just struck northeastern Canada and the United States. Its effect on the forests of that region has been devastating. Rain, wind, ice, and snow, all good forces in the balance of nature, became in their excess instruments of destruction. The ground is littered with branches stripped from vigorous healthy trees. Others are bent or flattened by the weight of ice. The storm has already subsided; its fury was ephemeral; the ice will melt. But its influence is lasting. Some trees will die. Some will be permanently bent or scarred. Others will gradually grow new limbs and foliage. It will take fifty years and a new generation for the forest to restore itself.

In this book Risto Lehtonen tells the story of a socio-political storm of similar ferocity. It struck the youth and students of the world, and with it the student movement of the Christian churches, some thirty years ago. The agencies were human, not natural, but they still were good forces in themselves. Rebellion against injustice and the will to transform the church and the world were their ice, wind, and rain. But, as in a natural storm, these forces, driven to unchecked excess, have produced results just as devastating, and as lasting. Lehtonen, as General Secretary of the World Student Christian Federation, was in the middle of this tempest, trying to keep an organization together and on course. Most of this book is the event-by-event account of this struggle, of the clashing convictions, the power plays, the loss of faith, community, and trust that at last left the Federation as stripped and broken as an ice-crushed grove of trees.

What is the meaning of this storm for us a generation later, when brambled underbrush has already grown up over the fallen forest? Why should we read about it today? To answer these questions we need to place it, as Lehtonen does in his first chapter, in the context of the history that it invaded, and, as he attempts in his conclusion, in the light of the work of the Holy Spirit in the whole ecumenical life and witness of the churches in this century.

The World Student Christian Federation was the seedbed of the twentieth-century ecumenical movement. Already in 1886 a group of students had come together in Mount Hermon, Massachusetts, to found the Student Volunteer Movement for Foreign Mission and to take its famous pledge: "It is my purpose, if God permit, to become a foreign missionary." The movement spread like wildfire, especially in the U.S.A., Britain, and the British Dominions. One of the participants, John R. Mott, became its leader and inspiration. In 1895 he presided over a conference of Student Christian groups from several countries in Vadstena, Sweden, which formed the World Student Christian Federation. He became chairman of this association. Then he sailed around the world, beginning with Sweden and Britain, and going as far as India, China, and Australia, meeting, praying, and planning with student Christian groups. The result was a world movement for mission and evangelism that caught the imagination and challenged the minds of youth leaders in churches everywhere.

Meanwhile, under the stimulus of the World YMCA, evangelical mission conferences were being held around the world. They brought together Christians from many churches. The largest of them, in 1900 in New York, which took as its theme the challenge formulated and expounded by Mott, "The Evangelisation of the World in This Generation," called itself explicitly ecumenical. There followed the World Mission Conference in Edinburgh in 1910, where the twentieth-century ecumenical movement first took form. Mott was the Conference chairman, and he went on to form the International Missionary Council, which he chaired as well. At the same time, also inspired by Edinburgh, the world Faith and Order Movement was formed to explore the problems of centuries-old church division and to seek ways to restore the unity of all believers that was given in

Christ. It was followed a decade later by the Life and Work Movement, which brought churches together to seek the form of Christian social witness in a divided world. These three movements — for mission, for unity, and for witness in society — joined after World War II to form the World Council of Churches.

Through all of these events the World Student Christian Federation served both as school and as challenge. In its member associations on campuses everywhere, Christian minds and hearts were formed in ecumenical fellowship and inspired toward mission and unity. National Student Christian Movements cultivated leaders — their number is legion — who later would teach and lead their churches into the communion of the Spirit which the World Council of Churches aspires to be and represents. Asian, African, Middle Eastern, and later Latin American leaders arose out of these movements to guide the ecumenical community into a new understanding of the church's mission, no longer centered in the Euro-American world. In short, the WSCF and its member movements were base nourishing communities in and alongside the churches, where the ecumenical vision of the church of Jesus Christ in mission to the world of the twentieth century flourished and grew.

At the same time this Student Christian Movement was a pioneer, a critic, and a goad in the ecumenical process. It bred responsible prophets. It was the WSCF that developed a new approach to Bible study, as an immediate interaction between the student in his society and the Word of God. It was students who moved first, often against resistance, to promote the world mission of the church and supply its corps of missionaries. It was also students, working together in the WSCF from every land and continent, who worked to reform and transform mission into a calling of the whole church in every place, not just an enterprise of some churches toward pagans in other cultures. Local Christian Associations in their schools and colleges, and the World Student Christian Federation on the international stage, as they gathered Christians of various communions in their fellowship and in dialogue, constantly confronted the churches with the unfaithfulness, the sin, of their divisions and with the urgency of seeking unity. Finally, it was the Student Christian Movement everywhere that pushed social witness not just as an activity of the church but as itself a form of the church's confession of Jesus Christ as Lord and Savior.

All of this was the substance of lively theological debate, ardent prayer, earnest searching of the Scriptures, and committed action in student circles long before ecumenical awareness penetrated church councils. The publications of the WSCF, most notably *The Student World* during its four decades of publication, were the only forum fully devoted to ecumenical dialogue before the World Council of Churches was formed and continued their prophetic role thereafter. The great themes of church doctrine and practice were discussed in this forum by the major theologians of the day. Orthodoxy and Protestantism encountered one another, and Roman Catholics entered the deliberations when they could. "First" and "third" world Christians, to use the anachronistic terms, confronted each other about imperialism, nationalism, and the mission of the church. The confession of the church faced with Nazism/Fascism was debated, along with the theological issues of revelation versus culture Christianity, and Christian responsibility toward the Jews, that underlay it. Marxism and Christianity was a continuing theme. So was encounter with humanist philosophies from existentialism to positivism. Even more important, life was shared, between student Christian groups, often with radically different experiences, convictions, and problems, sometimes from nations at war with each other, in all parts of the world. In short, here, among students around the world under the WSCF umbrella, was where ecumenical awareness was cultivated and where the ecumenical vision challenged the churches in at least the first sixty years of this century. It held evangelical motivation and social involvement in creative tension. It was a vision of church renewal in mission, in and for the world.

Then, in the sixties, something happened among youth and students. Lehtonen calls it a change of mood. If so, the mood was global. The post–World War II social consensus was torn apart. Young people with little memory of the struggles and forces that produced that consensus were cold to the balance of power between the Soviet world and the West, to the problem of combining freedom with justice that had produced mixed economies everywhere, and to the tentative steps toward limiting conflict and producing relative peace that the United Nations was facilitating. They were anti-war (though not always anti-violence), anti-imperialist, anti–traditional values, and anti-authority. The word "revolution" expressed their spirit and their hope. In America, provoked by the Vietnam War and betrayed by the liberal-conservative establishment that waged it, campus demonstrations broke out from Maine to California. Their theme was not only peace but dismantling of traditional authority structures and curricula in college and university, and power to the people against all the economic and political powers that oppress them. In Europe the rebellion tended to be ideologically Marxist, though radical and anarchist to a degree that made the standard Communist Parties look like defenders of the status quo. The Maoism of China's Cultural Revolution was the ideal, not the ordered movement of a socialist state toward communism. In Asia and Africa nationalism was the theme, and with it profound suspicion of European-American principles and ideals.

Student Christian Movements participated in all of this to some degree, but they also had their own dynamic. It started already in 1960, when the World Student Christian Federation held what they advertised as a world teaching conference on the life and mission of the church in Strasbourg, France. The leaders of the ecumenical movement, men and women who had inspired two generations of students, were there as speakers. It was time to take stock of all that had been accomplished in the preceding years — the new ecumenical theology, the fresh discovery of the Bible, fellowship in mission among Christians on every continent, work for a responsible society as witness to the transforming work of Christ in the world — and communicate it to a new generation. Lehtonen treats this event with gentle discrimination, but frankly it was a bust. Students wanted to be inspired, but they were not interested in the wisdom their elders had gained from fighting other battles in other decades. The ever-fresh voice of Karl Barth impressed them, but otherwise it was Hans Hoekendijk's apostolate in a radically secularized society and Richard Shaull's radical critique of the institutional church to which they responded.

The result of this, as Lehtonen recounts briefly, was intense soul-searching in WSCF circles, seeking both a new form of the Christian message and a new strategy for reaching the student generation. Christian "presence" rather than Christian mission became the focus. Witness to Christ found its authenticity not in words or truth claims but in actions of solidarity with the world in its own struggles, hopes, and problems. It was a perspective that owed much to Hoekendijk and to

Dietrich Bonhoeffer's earlier call in *Letters and Papers from Prison* for a "secret discipline" of discipleship while sharing the life of the secularized world. Missing from it more and more, however, as events developed, were Bonhoeffer's, and Hoekendijk's, profoundly Christocentric understanding of the world and passionate concern to renew the church for faithful and effective mission. Instead the trend was toward identification with the self-understanding and the struggles of "the people" defined in revolutionary terms, for their own liberation. The focus shifted from mission to power struggle. Its consequences were (1) not just criticism of but scorn for the church as an institution, and the search for other communities that would take its place; (2) definition of discipleship not in terms of grace but law, the law of revolutionary action; (3) rejection of God's transcendence over, and judgment on, human power, plans, and action, which destroyed dialogue in the Student Christian Movement and turned its Christian community into a political battleground.

With this we come to the events of 1968 to 1972, Risto Lehtonen's tenure as General Secretary of the WSCF, when the storm hit in full force. The bulk of this volume describes it in detail. It should be read as dramatic history, in which forces that are still powerful among us clash. Names are named. The issues are clearly stated. Unlike other recently published histories of the Movement, nothing is glossed over or hidden under platitudinous prose. Even thirty years later, it will be surprising if this story does not call forth furious reactions from those who attacked so furiously back then. Lehtonen himself transcends these passions. His account is objective and carefully researched, more that of an investigative reporter than a principal protagonist. Still his concern is deep and his objectives are clear. He fought to defend the integrity of the World Student Christian Federation as Christian, as a community, and as a place of dialogue in a spirit of mutual respect and trust. He did not succeed. Neither did his antagonists, unless the crippling of a movement can be counted success. Since 1973 the WSCF has lost its place in the ecumenical movement and the life of the churches, despite valiant efforts to revive it. This story is a cautionary tale for all who care about the church in mission to the world. It should be read as such.

Why, then, to return to our opening question, does all this matter, thirty years later? What are its lasting consequences? Lehtonen considers these in his final chapter. Let me simply reflect on three of them that are implicit or explicit in his story.

First, a critical source of educated leadership has been lost to the churches and to the ecumenical movement. The springs of faith and action, the pools of prayer and reflection, which grew by lively encounter across confessional lines in universities and colleges across the world, have dried up. Their place has been taken by more sectarian groups. Critical engagement of Christian faith with secular disciplines and with social, economic, and political forces has been weakened.

Second, the backlash, not only among students, against leftist ideology in the Movement has strengthened right-wing organizations and ideologies that call themselves Christian and that exercise power and coercion far more effectively than their counterparts on the left ever did. These organizations are in many ways mirror images of the sixties revolutionaries. They too are anti-institutional, thereby denying their responsibility to the church in any of its visible forms or teachings except their own. They attack and undermine all established church bodies while they try to capture Christian groups or local churches. They appear as mass movements, but tightly controlled from the top. They reject fellowship or correction from fellow Christians who disagree with them, often to the point of using the word "Christian" only as a cover for their own political agenda. All of these are ideologically driven power play, like those on the left in earlier days, but far better organized and financed.

Third, that which was destroyed in the storm that Lehtonen's story describes cannot so easily be cultivated again because what might be called a certain ecumenical innocence has been lost. Christian students had learned to trust one another in the Student Christian Movement, to engage in vigorous and open dialogue because they all confessed that the ultimate reality in whose hands they were was no human program, power, or philosophy but God in Jesus Christ, their judge and their redeemer. That trust has been undermined by the events of the storm. Cynicism and suspicion have poisoned the soil. We shall have to build again, using bruised souls this time, that community of struggle for truth, of love and mutual forgiveness, which is rooted in Christ, that evangelical confidence which only sinners continually judged and transformed by grace can know, that joy in discerning and confessing how Christ is at work in the world which the World Student Christian Federation offered in the years before the storm.

To prepare for this enterprise, read this book.

Princeton   Charles C. West
January 1998

Preface

In 1971, near the climax of the tumultuous events described in this book, I was invited by a group of church leaders in the USA to speak about the circumstances that resulted in the upheaval in the World Student Christian Federation (WSCF) recounted herein. My address, entitled "Story of a Storm — An Ecumenical Case Study," was subsequently published in the World Council of Churches' bulletin, *Study Encounter*.

At that time many persons urged me to provide a fuller account of these tumultuous years in the life of the Federation. For various reasons a detailed study was impossible at that moment. Only in recent years have the archives of the WSCF been systematically arranged. In addition, the obligations of my new work for the Lutheran World Federation (1973-87) and subsequently my responsibilities in the Church of Finland as director of its Finnchurchaid (1988-93) made it impossible for me to undertake the necessary research and writing.

In 1991 the WSCF organized a meeting of "senior friends" in Geneva to prepare for the celebration of the Federation's 100th anniversary in 1995. This included preparation of a book updating the history of the Federation. On this occasion I offered to contribute an account of the years 1968-73. This offer was, however, turned down, and the period in which the direction of the ecumenical student movement was drastically changed was left with little attention in the centennial history undertaking. This stimulated me to undertake my own survey of these years as an independent project.

In the course of my subsequent research I discussed my project with many who had been related to the work of the WSCF in these "revolutionary" years. They included university and seminary professors, church leaders, and executives of church agencies and ecumenical organizations from the USA, Europe, Asia, Africa, and Latin America. The WSCF 100th Anniversary gathering of former WSCF leaders and staff in Berlin in June 1995 provided a unique opportunity to discuss my project with participants, to most of whom the impact of the "stormy" times on the fortunes of the Federation was a common concern.

Throughout my research many former colleagues and current WSCF personnel in Geneva have given me the benefit of their perspective.

It is impossible in this connection to name all those who in the course of my work stimulated and challenged me and encouraged me to plough ahead. There are, however, a few persons to whom I owe special gratitude.

In Finland, archbishop emeritus Mikko Juva, a long-time friend and a leader of the Finnish SCM in the forties and fifties, guided me in his capacity as a professional church historian in the methods of historical research. Philip Lee-Woolf, another long-time friend and a veteran of the British Student Christian Movement and the WSCF, read most of the manuscript and offered many penetrating comments before his death in November 1995.

Two people made an invaluable contribution to the editorial work. The first was Audrey Abrecht, a journalist by training and a WSCF staff member for more than two decades, most of this time as an editor of its publications, who subsequently served as administrative assistant during my period as General Secretary. She helped me with the English language and in checking the correctness of the historical record with the same thoroughness she displayed during the WSCF years and later working with me in the Lutheran World Federation.

The second person was my daughter, Eeva John, of Leamington, U.K., an Oxford scholar of the seventies and a representative of the post-revolutionary generation of students. She took upon herself, with enthusiasm, the examination of the manuscript to help me find expressions and idioms that would be understandable not only to professional church workers but also to the general reader and very especially to the generation that had been bewildered by the ideological turmoil in the decades before their time.

Any errors in the book cannot be attributed to those who offered their assistance and tried to guide me. The responsibility for the result is entirely my own.

I also want to express my gratitude to the faculty members of the Departments of Church History and of Systematic Theology and Ecumenism at the University of Helsinki for their interest in my project, and to the Finnish Society of Church History, which sponsored this book and included it in its series of publications, thus facilitating the publishing of the book in the USA.

Finally, I wish to thank Wm. B. Eerdmans Publishing Company for its kind cooperation in bringing the project to conclusion.

Les Avants, Switzerland   Risto Lehtonen
August 18, 1997

List of Acronyms

AACC	All Africa Conference of Churches
ABFMS	American Baptist Foreign Mission Society
ACER	Action Chrétienne des Etudiants Russes
ALDEC	Asia Leadership Development Center
ANC	African National Congress
ASF	Asia Study Fellowship
CAMECA	Confederation of Argentine Autonomous SCMs
CCIA	Commission of the Churches on International Affairs
CCPD	Commission on the Churches' Participation in Development
CEC	Conference of European Churches
CICARWS	Commission on Inter-Church Aid, Refugee and World Service
CLAF	Communidad Latino-Americana para Formacion (Latin American Leadership Training Center)
CPC	Christian Peace Conference
CSSR	Czechoslovak Socialist Republic
CVN	National Vietnam Committee
CWME	Commission on World Mission and Evangelism
EACC	East Asia Christian Conference
EKD	Protestant Church of Germany
ENI	Ecumenical News International
EPS	Ecumenical Press Service

ESR	European Student Relief
GDR	German Democratic Republic
HAESA	Haimanote Abew Ethiopian Students Association
IFES	International Fellowship of Evangelical Students
IMC	International Missionary Council
IMCS	International Movement of Catholic Students
ISC	International Student Conference
ISS	International Student Service
IUS	International Union of Students
JEC	Young Catholic Students
LMC	Life and Mission of the Church
LWF	Lutheran World Federation
MECC	Middle East Council of Churches
NACLA	North American Congress on Latin America
NATO	North Atlantic Treaty Organization
NCC	National Council of Churches
NGO	nongovernmental organization
NSCF	National Student Christian Federation
NUSAS	National Union of South African Students
OAU	Organization of African Unity
PAC	Pan Africanist Congress
PAIGG	Party for Independence of the African Territories of Guinea-Bissau
PCR	Program to Combat Racism
SASO	South African Student Organization
SCA	Student Christian Association
SCM	Student Christian Movement
SODEPAX	Joint Committee on Society, Development, and Peace
SDS	Students for a Democratic Society
SSPG	Strategic Staff Planning Group
SVM	Student Volunteer Movement for Foreign Missions
SYNDESMOS	World Fellowship of Orthodox Youth Organizations
UCM	University Christian Movement
UEC	Union of Communist Students
UIM	Urban Industrial Mission
UN	United Nations

UNEF	French National Union of Students
UNELAM	Provisional Commission for Latin American Evangelical Unity
UNESCO	United Nations Educational, Scientific, and Cultural Organization
UNISA	University of South Africa
UPUSA-COEMAR	United Presbyterian Church in the USA–Commission on Ecumenical and Missionary Relations
URM	Urban Rural Mission
USA	United States of America
USCC	United Student Christian Council
USSR	Union of Soviet Socialist Republics
WCC	World Council of Churches
WSCF	World Student Christian Federation
WUJS	World Union of Jewish Students
WUS	World University Service
YMCA	Young Men's Christian Association
YWCA	Young Women's Christian Association

Introduction

This book recounts the experiences of the World Student Christian Federation (WSCF) during the peak years of student radicalism. The revolutionary fervor which had spread like wildfire among students in North America and western Europe in the sixties rapidly gained ground in Christian student organizations as well. As a consequence, the Federation became deeply divided and the ensuing turmoil threw this once impressive world organization of Christian students and university teachers into the most profound crisis it had experienced in the course of its history.

The ideological storm of the late sixties and its impact on churches and Christian student and youth movements is now part of the history of the ecumenical movement. It triggered in the WSCF a drama which unfolded in the period from its General Assembly in Otaniemi, Finland, in 1968 to the Assembly in Addis Ababa, Ethiopia, in 1972-73. This study attempts to shed light on what happened in those critical years; how the face of the Federation was transformed; on the role played by political movements, ideological persuasions, and theological views; and on the significance of the WSCF experience for churches and the ecumenical movement, particularly for their social thought. It is an attempt to place the concerns and conflicts within the Federation of those years in a broader historical and theological perspective.

The dynamics of the crisis in the WSCF cannot be fully grasped apart from a consideration of the wider context of university and

1

student life. The breeding ground of the explosive encounters was in the events and forces in the world at large: the escalation of the war in Vietnam, the introduction of the military draft and the shooting of peaceful protesters in the USA, the assassinations of Martin Luther King Jr. and Robert Kennedy, wars of liberation in southern Africa, the Cultural Revolution in China, the May 1968 uprising in Paris, the Soviet invasion of Czechoslovakia, and the heightening agony of many parts of the Third World.

The dramatic unrest among students which culminated in the events of 1968-70 began in the USA but soon spread to western Europe and beyond. The confrontations on hundreds of university campuses, the demonstrations in front of government and military institutions, and the many mass rallies demanding radical change are all part of the chronicle of those years. They electrified student organizations, shook universities and colleges, and almost toppled the French government. The mass events — in Paris, Berlin, Tokyo, Santiago, Chicago, Kent State, and elsewhere — are still alive in the memories of those who participated in them, and for many evoke a mixture of pride, nostalgia, and embarrassment.

Although a systematic analysis of the protest movements among students and the undercurrents in the wider political scene is beyond the scope of this study, their impact on the WSCF cannot be underestimated. The rise of radical political movements among students and the climate of protest affected the members of the Federation and contributed to the turmoil within it.

The ways in which the Federation responded to these movements were an essential part of the cause of its crisis. The capacity of the WSCF to meet the harsh challenges of a politics of power on the basis of its stated aims was put to the test. It was a test of the theological foundations, the multicultural and intellectual maturity, and the political judgment of the Federation and its leadership. What was ultimately at stake was the integrity of its faith.

The WSCF was not the only part of the ecumenical movement shaken by the storm of those years. The same events which stirred students challenged churches and their world organizations, obliging them also to face the ideological, ethical, and political issues involved. The impact of the era was manifest at the 1968 Assembly of the World Council of Churches (WCC) in Uppsala, Sweden, at which new

2

action program emphases emerged. The Lutheran World Federation (LWF) had its share of confrontation over similar issues at its 1970 Assembly in Evian, France, and in following years. Many national church organizations were also deeply affected. Church and ecumenical leaders gave diverse, even conflicting, responses to the revolutionary challenges of the day, thus contributing to a turmoil in the ecumenical movement, the effects of which are still discernible in today's debates and decisions. At stake was their interpretation of the events and forces active in the world, their grasp of ideologies, and their openness to the manifold plights of peoples. The voices of protesting students within their ranks added to these pressures.

The Federation had an intrinsic relationship with the WCC based on its pioneering role within the ecumenical movement since its founding in 1895. Throughout its existence it had served as a testing ground for new ecumenical initiatives and as a training school for the ecumenical leadership of churches and the World Council. Part of the student movement tradition was to be in the forefront of new challenges. Therefore the experience of the WSCF in its stormy years from 1968 to 1973 was significant for the WCC as it faced calls for revolutionary responses.

The "avant-garde" tradition which the Federation had upheld for decades within the ecumenical family was not limited to issues of social and political responsibility. In fact, its pioneering spirit enveloped most areas of ecumenical thought and action, from evangelism to worship and from world mission to relief activity, from encounter with cultural and intellectual currents to dialogue with Marxists and representatives of other faiths.

It was only in the late sixties, under the influence of the rising left radicalism, that questions such as the threat posed by oppressive systems and ideologies to human dignity and freedom, identification with the poor of the world, and the future shape of technologically advanced societies began to dominate the agenda of the Federation. It was a common assumption among ecumenical leaders at that time that the sharp tensions experienced in the WSCF were another sign that the Federation, in line with its avant-garde tradition, had found itself once again on the forefront of the ecumenical movement. At the same time, as a result of the 1966 Conference on Church and Society, the WCC had entered into the debate about the theology of revolution and the role of the oppressed. A kinship emerged between the radical wing of the WCC and the revolutionaries of the Federation.

The origins of several program emphases and trends in the WCC in the ensuing two decades from 1970 to 1990 can be traced back to experiences in this revolutionary epoch. Debates on some of them, particularly those related to ecumenical social thought and to the political role of the WCC, have remained inconclusive to this day. A study of the crisis years of the WSCF may contribute to a greater awareness of the ideological assumptions in Christian thinking and evoke new interest in the role of the church in national and international politics and in the intellectual pursuit of issues involved.

Although the events of the sixties may seem to today's students to be centuries away, their effects are still alive both in the academic world and in churches and ecumenical circles. The experience of that time cannot be erased from the common memory of Student Christian Movements. Nor can it be wiped from the record of the ecumenical movement.

The hundred years' history of the WSCF was recalled at the time of its centennial in 1995. Anniversary celebrations, however, tend to focus primarily on the happy memories of the organization and to play down difficulties and unresolved problems.

It is therefore an appropriate moment to begin dissecting also the phase of which few today are proud and which many would prefer to forget. Some of those responsible for updating the official history of the Federation have indicated that the years in question are too close and the issues too divisive to allow the inclusion of any substantive record of them. Some have even asked, What good can come out of digging up the painful past? Why not concentrate on building the future? It is, however, the experience not only of Christians but of humanity as a whole, that unless you come to grips with the past, including its darkest moments, you cannot cope constructively with the future. Any community or nation which wants to free itself from the hold of its past failures, conflicts, and divisions must face them openly. This is doubly necessary for the Christian community. Unless it is relieved of such burdens, it cannot, in a world full of ambiguities and unresolved conflicts, fulfill its vocation as a messenger of the justice of the kingdom of God and as a carrier of God's unconditional grace. Dietrich Bonhoeffer, himself a participant in

4

one of history's darkest moments, has warned Christians about cheap grace.

The story of the years of crisis in the Federation prompts reflection on the meaning of Christian history, including that of the Christian student movement, and on the pitfalls in presenting it to others.

It is tempting today to glorify the history of the WSCF for its many achievements, its witness through many decades, and the multitude of people whom it has influenced and whose lives it has transformed. From its inception until the sixties, the movement grew and matured and its witness expanded to new geographic regions and to new areas of university life and secondary education. Its impact can be recounted as a sequence of discoveries concerning the role of Christians in public life, especially in situations of national and international tension and conflict. Its story can be told also as the sowing of the seeds of new ecumenical ideas out of which have grown new expressions of common witness and service, and new patterns of manifesting the oneness of the Church.

But all Christian history reflects not only the new life given by God in Christ, but also the frailty and limitations of human beings and the ambiguous role of the church in the world. As long as the divine enterprise is entrusted to human hands, setbacks, wrong decisions, and denials of vocation will remain part of it. The advance of the gospel has never been a smooth process accomplished by a group of reliable people. The message has always been a divine gift, entrusted to women and men, but never placed under their control. To portray the record of the Federation, even of its most spectacular and inspiring periods, as a shining success story would be to distort its real message.

The true significance of the history of the WSCF is its witness to the power of the gospel among university students and teachers. It offers an account of the Federation's role as part of a renewal movement of the church. It transmits the sense of inspiration characteristic of pioneering adventures of witness and service on behalf of churches in unexplored territories. The story of this movement, of its influence on university life, and of its ecumenical and missionary significance is relevant for Christians today as they struggle with current uncertainties and challenges and venture in the name of Christ into the unknown future.

The mission of the church, including its task in society, has been, and continues to be, perceived differently in different religious and cultural contexts and different theological and confessional traditions. What looks like victory from one vantage point may prove to be defeat from another. Similarly the understanding of the social and political responsibility of Christians has undergone many changes, even in the short time span since the Second World War. The effect of the Federation's crisis years on the ecumenical movement is a vivid illustration of this.

History is not simply a chronology, because it always seeks to analyze and interpret events in their social and cultural context. The roots of the Federation's crisis stemming from the past need to be uncovered, and the implications of the experience of the revolutionary years for the Christian ministry among students and also for the whole ecumenical movement need to be evaluated. The positions and decisions taken by Christian students and their leaders have to be considered in light of the options and choices open to them at the time of the crisis, and assessed on the basis of their long-term effects. Such an approach avoids the danger of viewing the past, including positions taken by individual leaders and corporate decisions made at various meetings, in black and white. An assessment of the crisis of the WSCF may help to evaluate contemporary trends in the ecumenical movement and to reach greater clarity about its present, often confused, debates, rash policy decisions, controversial program emphases, and financial crises.

The present study is based on material from a wide variety of sources, including original documentation from the WSCF as well as articles and books by diverse authors. It is also an eyewitness account of the years of crisis, with all the limitations — including my personal views and experiences — which the vantage point of the general secretariat implies. The more than twenty years that have elapsed since the events described have made possible some sense of detachment and given opportunity to view them in the context of personal experiences of the ecumenical movement through the whole post–World War II era.

Chapters 3–14 contain the main substance of the study. Much previously unpublished information is included in them. It has been my intention to base as little as possible on my memory alone and to rely on publicly available documentation. After finishing the work, I turned over the material in my personal archives to the archivists of the Ecumenical Center in Geneva. The archives of the WSCF on this period are extensive but patchy. There are serious gaps, for example, in the documentation of regional programs and the correspondence of regional offices with member movements and churches of their area. Furthermore, some materials were damaged or destroyed by a flood in a storeroom where unsorted documentation of the sixties and seventies had been temporarily stored. It has not been possible for me to explore to what extent member movements have maintained archives covering this period. A list of the sources used is found in the bibliography.

For the sake of historical and ecumenical perspective, I have included a very brief overview of the Federation's history, to illustrate the wealth of pioneering themes and initiatives within its life and its significance for the whole ecumenical movement. A somewhat more detailed account is given of the period of the Life and Mission of the Church program (1956-64) and the years 1964-68, in which the WSCF carried out a series of ecumenical strategy consultations and which saw the rise of radical protest movements among students of North America and Europe.

In the final chapter I try to offer some conclusions about the significance of the crisis years for the student Christian movement, churches, and the ecumenical movement at large, to suggest which dimensions of the Christian faith the experience has helped me to rediscover and what foolishness in the life of the church should be challenged.

Concerning terminology, the names of organizations have been given in full the first time they appear, with their customary acronyms in parenthesis. The acronyms are used as the context warrants thereafter. The World Student Christian Federation (WSCF) is frequently referred to with its normal abbreviated form, "the Federation." The term "Student Christian Movement (SCM)" is used exclusively for Christian student organizations related to the Federation. In other expressions of the Christian community in universities, colleges, and schools, when no specific official name can be applied, terms such as "student Christian movement," "campus ministry," "denominational ministry," "student chaplaincy," and "university Christian community" are used. When the word "Church" is capitalized, it is used in the sense of the Church universal, i.e., the holy catholic Church, with an accent on the theological content of the word. The words "church" or "churches" are used for empirical churches, national or local, as they are structured in various settings. The terms "ecumenical movement" or "wider ecumenical movement" appear frequently, signifying either the movement for Christian unity (also for unity in Christian witness or service) or the family of organizations formed to promote the visible unity of the whole church and practical interconfessional cooperation in mission and service. The organizations include councils or conferences of churches, with the World Council of Churches (WCC) as the most representative, but also ecumenical lay organizations such as the YMCA and YWCA and others.

There was one problem of terminology for which I could find no sufficient single solution: what term should be used to describe the movement which caused the storm? It is evident that no single term, such as "radical," "revolutionary," "new left," "neo-Marxist," or "protest," expresses adequately the character of the phenomenon. In fact, the movement was a conglomeration of several movements, each with its own ideological emphasis. Therefore I have tried to use these and similar words in a way that conveys as accurately as possible the views of the persons and groups as they themselves used them, trying to avoid any derogatory connotations. The word "radical" proved most problematic because it does not arise out of any particular ideology or political view. Nevertheless, it was adopted by most of the student revolutionaries and their supporters of the sixties as an overall attribute of their cause. This usage should not divert anyone from the original and nonpartisan meaning of the word.

CHAPTER 1

Pioneering

1.1. The First Six Decades, 1895-1955

The founders of the World Student Christian Federation (WSCF) shared one passion: to advance the Christian revival which had spread among students in North America, Europe, and the Far East to every university on every continent. They aimed to make it a truly worldwide movement. The title *Strategic Points in the World's Conquest,*[1] which John R. Mott gave to the book in which he described the rationale and task of the Federation, was in itself a striking illustration of the underlying missionary vision and expectations attached to the WSCF.

The Federation was a child of two significant, interrelated Christian movements of the nineteenth century. One was the Protestant missionary awakening which led in 1888 to the founding of the Student Volunteer Movement for Foreign Missions (SVM). The SVM gathered thousands of students in the USA, Britain, and Germany at influential student conferences on missions. Hundreds of students committed themselves to missionary service in foreign countries. By the time the Federation was founded in 1895, SVM had made itself felt even in the Middle East. The other was the nondenominational Christian youth movement which found its main organizational expression in the Young Men's Christian Association (YMCA) and

---

1. John R. Mott, *Strategic Points in the World's Conquest* (New York: Fleming Revell, 1897).

9

Young Women's Christian Association (YWCA). These movements had a significant impact in the Anglo-Saxon world, from which they spread to India, the Far East, and continental Europe.

The names of the key actors in the genesis of the Federation appear repeatedly in the records of the international missionary movement and of the main gatherings of the ecumenical movement in its formative years. These men and women affirmed the significance of a worldwide Christian student movement in deepening and expanding the vision of Christian mission, in breaking barriers between church traditions, and in shaping the modern ecumenical movement.[2]

The first general secretary of the Federation, the untiring John R. Mott, had a decisive influence on the rapid expansion of Student Christian Movements (SCMs) into universities in various parts of the world. Christian student conferences, which multiplied after 1895 and which attracted increasing numbers of participants, laid the foundation for the effective impact of SCMs on the university world and the church. The Federation was no fringe phenomenon. It left its mark not only on students and churches, but also on public life in many countries.

Mott, himself an outstanding evangelist and church diplomat, was the mastermind behind the new world organization. He persuaded key leaders of many nationalities to accept the idea. In August 1895 he brought together the six founders from the American, British, German, and Scandinavian movements and the "SCMs in Mission Lands." Meeting in Vadstena, Sweden, they drafted the provisional constitution of the Federation: a simple document which was later to be revised as the constituency grew and the world situation changed.

The basic evangelical emphasis, stemming from "the corner stone principle of the Federation — loyalty to Jesus Christ as Saviour and as God," stood the test of changing times and moments of disagreement. The statement in the original version of the "Aims" of the

---

2. The following names are engraved indelibly in the history of the founding years of the Federation: Henry Drummond, Martin Eckhoff, Donald Fraser, Karl Fries, Jean Monnier, Dwight L. Moody, John R. Mott, Baron Paul Nicolay, Edouard Graf Pückler, J. B. Reynolds, Ruth Rouse, Ira Sankey, Johannes Siemsen, Nathan Söderblom, Robert E. Speer, C. T. Studd, Robert P. Wilder, and Luther D. Wishard. This is bound to be an arbitrary selection, as many more were among the leaders of the emerging student Christian movements.

Federation, "To lead students to become disciples of Jesus Christ as only Saviour and as God," was first amended in 1920 to read "To lead students to accept Christian faith in God — Father, Son, and Holy Spirit — according to the Scriptures, and to live as true disciples of Jesus Christ." The next significant revision was made in 1960, when "students" was changed to "members of the academic community," the word "lead" to "call," and the reference to discipleship to "discipleship within the life and mission of the Church."

On the one hand, these changes reflected a continuity of commitment to evangelization, mission, and a scriptural basis for the WSCF's work. On the other hand, the changes revealed a clear move away from a nondenominational parachurch or peoples' movement identity for the Federation and toward the acceptance of confessional, cultural, and organizational diversities as an essential element of its ecumenical nature. "Unity in diversity" was emphasized as early as the first decade of the Federation.[3]

The goal of "natives" representing the SCMs in "mission lands" was stated explicitly at the Vadstena founding meeting. This was a departure from the practices of most mission organizations of the era. The main challengers in these matters were not the non-Westerners

---

3. Hans Mayr shows, in his doctoral dissertation ("Einheit und Botschaft, das Ökumenische Prinzip in der Geschichte des Christlichen Studentenweltbundes 1895-1939 mit einem Ausblick bis zur Gegenwart" [Ph.D. diss., Tübingen, 1975]), that Mott consciously introduced a new pattern of Christian unity by making the WSCF into a federation of national SCMs and by encouraging them to shape their own organization and activities according to the particular demands of the situation in each country. With this concept the WSCF parted from the pattern of the YMCA, which was to unite persons in the movement on an individual basis (pp. 14-17). The strength of the American Intercollegiate YMCA and the fact that the leading Asian movements were YMCA-related provided a temptation to model the Federation as an extension of the American movement. Hans Mayr sums up the vision of Mott for the Federation as that of bringing different movements together into one Federation instead of spreading one unified movement to all continents (p. 16). In its quest for unity, the Federation recognized in its early years the theological and confessional diversity of its member movements as a legitimate and potentially enriching aspect in its work. In his general secretary's report of 1911 Mott writes: "Our movement is accomplishing wonders in the direction of drawing together the various Christian communions" (John R. Mott, *Addresses and Papers*, vols. 1-6 [New York: Associated Press, 1946-47], 2:126).

but the Germans, who were worried about the dominance of American theology and organizational style. The WSCF's watchword, "The Evangelization of the World in This Generation," which the Federation had inherited from the SVM, also soon gave way to the motto "Ut Omnes Unum Sint," "That They May All Be One" (John 17:21). An encounter between American and European leaders of SCMs and of the missionary movement about the ecumenical and mission principles contributed to this change.[4]

In parallel with the emphasis on evangelism, the pursuit of Christian responsibility for social and racial justice emerged as a major concern of the Federation. The topics discussed at Federation conferences and meetings of the General Committee illustrate a widening understanding of mission and of the role of Christians in the world. The Federation conference held in Zeist, Netherlands, in 1905, for example, saw the inclusion in the agenda of the Federation of social and economic justice and the need to enlarge the vision of its task, previously dominated by individualistic notions of student evangelism. Part of this challenge came to the Federation from SCM leaders who had been influenced by the Social Gospel movement.

The General Committee in Tokyo, 1907, saw Asian movements become full members of the Federation, bringing to it the challenge of Far Eastern cultures and religions. The Constantinople conference in 1911 was a breakthrough to an ecumenicity in which Christians of the Orthodox tradition took their recognized place. By 1913 the Federation had completed the move from nondenominational evangelicalism to a mission-centered, interdenominational ecumenism. In its first twenty years the Federation probed many basic concepts of ecumenicity which leaders of churches in subsequent years adopted, and which were developed further in the context of the International

---

4. The exchange which took place between the Anglo-Saxon SVM leaders and German missiologists over the watchword "The Evangelization of the World in This Generation" proved significant for the orientation of both the Federation and the ecumenical missionary movement. Mott was influenced by his encounter with the German missiologist Gustav Warneck, who emphasized church planting and the indigenization of mission churches as against the notion of giving all human beings a chance to hear the saving gospel "in this generation." Hans Mayr has documented extensively in his dissertation the Warneck-Mott debate on mission and its impact on the Federation. Mayr, pp. 55-60.

Missionary Council (IMC) and in the Life and Work and Faith and Order movements.

In 1913 the Federation had thirteen affiliated movements, several of which were subregional or otherwise multinational in character. John R. Mott declared in his report to the General Committee meeting in Princeton in that year that the frontier era of the Federation had come to an end and that it had established itself in every part of the world where there were university students. The most recent expansion had been in the Balkan area and in the territory of the Austro-Hungarian empire. Because the political map of the pre–World War I period was very different from that of today, it is difficult to compare the spread of SCMs in those days with the situation in the sixties or the present day. It does seem, however, that in 1913 a higher proportion of university students was touched by the Christian movement of students fostered by the Federation than has been the case at any time since.

The peak event of the pre–World War I era was the WSCF conference held at Lake Mohonk, New York, June 2-8, 1913. With 320 delegates from forty-two countries, it was the largest and most representative gathering of the Federation up to that time. It gave participants an unprecedented opportunity to appreciate what a truly worldwide Christian community can be. It was a milestone in the involvement of the Federation in racial issues: the Americans brought an interracial delegation to a Federation conference for the first time. The proportion of women among the delegates was higher than at any previous Federation gathering. For the delegates from outside North America the conference was part of an extensive training program organized by the American YMCA and YWCA. Ruth Rouse described it:

> At Lake Mohonk the Federation found itself, as a world-embracing student Christian movement — international, inter-racial, ecumenical. We believed that we saw before us the path which God would have us take.[5]

5. Ruth Rouse, *The World's Student Christian Federation: A History of the First Thirty Years* (London: SCM Press, 1948), p. 175.

The role of the Federation took a new turn during and after World War I. Service to refugee students and others affected by wartime hardships led to involvement in ecumenical relief action and to the founding in 1920 of a special agency, European Student Relief (ESR), later International Student Service (ISS), and eventually, through mergers and a broadening of sponsorship, World University Service (WUS).

In the aftermath of World War I, the Federation became a significant forum for Christian students in search of a new identity as they confronted some of the profound changes in the intellectual and spiritual climate of the day. Prewar optimism and its uncritical belief in progress had been buried in the trenches and the ruins of devastated villages and cities. A deep sense of disillusionment about European culture and its values spread among students. Nihilism was more alluring than any faith or ideology. A serious questioning of inherited religious values replaced the evangelical enthusiasm and missionary fervor of the prewar years.

The Federation was drawn into an ardent debate about its own vocation among students and intellectuals who were looking for the meaning of life. Do we preach the same Christ? was the question asked at the General Committee meeting of 1920 at Beatenberg, Switzerland. The quest for common ground, which continued for several years, touched the very foundations of the Christian faith, its place in the university world, and its implications for Christian responsibility in society. The christological question — Who is Jesus Christ? What is his significance for the church and the world? — was the key issue of the debate. In the mid-twenties there was tension between the theological "liberals," for whom Christ was primarily a teacher and an example, and the "conservatives," for whom his sacrificial death and redemption through the cross were of decisive significance and who were closely tied to the heritage of pre–World War I student evangelism.

The period when "the Federation sought its identity," as Suzanne de Diétrich characterized the era, continued from 1920 to 1928.[6] At

---

6. Suzanne de Diétrich, in her history of the Federation, gave the era 1920-28 the title "La Fédération se cherche"; Suzanne de Diétrich, *Cinquante ans d'histoire: La Fédération Universelle des Associations Chretiennes d'Etudiants (1895-1945)* (Paris: Editions du Semeur, 1946), p. 73.

the General Committee at High Leigh, England, in 1924 the conflict between the different views of the task of the Federation reached its peak. Ruth Rouse wrote:

> It came as a shock to them (delegates) to find at High Leigh all manner of unresolved tensions, and views on important questions so divergent as to seem irreconcilable. The hope for unity was far from obvious, and disillusion and profound discouragement threatened not a few. "Threatened." Yes! But did not wreck their faith. The list of delegates shows that many of these very students are to-day well-known leaders in their own Churches or in ecumenical movements.[7]

Although the different perspectives and positions did not lead to any division within the Federation, they may have given additional justification to those evangelical student groups which had already rejected the ecumenical pluralism of SCMs before World War I. They reacted against such "liberal" tendencies and started to form separate student organizations of conservative evangelical orientation.

Keeping the diverse tendencies together and forging from them a more comprehensive ecumenical vision was a major achievement of the Federation in the turbulent twenties. A deliberate choice for racial, national, ecumenical, and theological inclusiveness was made over the alternative of a one-track movement with a sharply defined and closed membership. J. H. Oldham commented on this choice:

> The Federation has realized that fullness of life is found in the tension between opposites, and that when two opposite but complementary principles claim our allegiance, what is needed is not to surrender one of them or to adopt some feeble and half-hearted compromise, but to hold fast to both and follow each as far as it will carry us.[8]

The unity of the Federation was based on the recognition of "the supremacy of the Lord Jesus Christ," which no one contested even if

---

7. Rouse, p. 304.
8. J. H. Oldham, "The WSCF Past and Future," *Student World,* no. 4 (1925): 169.

the meaning of this "first guiding or governing principle" was understood in different ways.[9]

The twenties also brought about a change of style in the leadership of the Federation. John R. Mott resigned as general secretary in 1920 but remained as chairman of the Federation until 1928. The Federation also lost much of the financial support that had been tied to his person. Ruth Rouse, secretary of the Executive Committee and a staff colleague of Mott since 1905, left in 1924. Henri-Louis Henriod of Switzerland succeeded Mott as the general secretary (1920-32) and Francis P. Miller as the chairman (1928-38). W. A. Visser 't Hooft joined the staff in 1929 and was elected general secretary in 1932.

When Francis Miller took over the chairmanship in 1928, he found the Federation in a state of confusion. Together with Visser 't Hooft and Pierre Maury, who was a part-time member of staff, he initiated a "Message Commission," whose work was to become a turning point for the Federation's self-understanding. The commission distanced itself from the theology of extreme liberalism in the Social Gospel movement and also from that of pietistic revivalism. A segment of the evangelical movement had turned to the latter, with which the theological and confessional diversity of the Federation and of the ecumenical movement was incompatible. The commission concluded that the message of the Federation could be nothing but "the one message, forever the same, Jesus Christ." But the meaning of Jesus Christ had to be discovered and articulated anew by every generation in its own context: it could never be formulated in a statement claiming divine authority for all times. The commission also concluded that the Federation should be free from links with any particular ideology or worldview and should not try to impose any specific doctrine or theology on its membership. The heart of the matter was that in receiving the gift of God in Jesus Christ the Federation could become an instrument for God's revelation in the modern world.

The Message Commission also became a launching pad for Visser 't Hooft as he developed an ecumenical strategy for the Federation and became a leading architect in building the ecumenical movement of churches. The thrust of his strategy was no longer the mere geographical expansion of the mission of the church, but the penetration

9. Rouse, p. 305.

of the centers of thought and action with the message of Jesus Christ and moving from the defensive to the offensive in the contemporary arenas of the intellectual and spiritual battle. His leadership was instrumental in the visible return of the Federation to the Bible and to the biblical concept of the one apostolic Church. At the same time he stimulated the Federation to take up the challenge of contemporary political and cultural currents, and particularly the threats posed by rising totalitarian ideologies, most notably communism and fascism.

The WSCF quarterly, the *Student World,* under the editorship of Visser 't Hooft, reflected the main concerns of SCMs and introduced into discussions on its pages many prominent theologians and lay Christian thinkers. It was a particular charisma of Visser 't Hooft to mobilize "the best minds" for ecumenical discussions on critical issues. The topics tackled in issues of the *Student World* in the thirties illustrate vividly the pacesetting influence of the Federation. Among these topics were social and political challenges, including racism and interracial relations; the hotly debated issues of peace and disarmament; the impact of Marxism, nationalism, and particularly the threat of Nazism; the role of the Christian community as a social conscience; the possibility of a new world war — "the next war" (1935) — and the quest for an international order to face the expansion of the German Reich. These issues reflected faithfully the grassroots concerns of SCMs. The periodical's themes, like the themes of Federation meetings and consultations, foreshadowed much of the agenda of the WCC in its first decades.[10] A glance at the lists of participants in

10. The impact of the "Message Commission" and biblical renewal was manifest in the themes of articles in the *Student World* from 1930 to 1939, such as "Do We Believe in a Personal God?" "Can We Know the Will of God?" "What Shall We Think of the Bible?" "The Significance of Jesus Christ — Jesus Christ Our Contemporary," and "The Sermon on the Mount — A King's Speech." Several issues were dedicated to general ecumenical concerns such as the contribution of Eastern Orthodoxy to the Federation, communion and intercommunion, the renewal of the Church and the role of students in it, and to the topics of the 1937 conferences on Faith and Order and on Life and Work. The issues on mission themes reported on the situation in different regions and dealt with such topics as "Christianity and Other Faiths," "The End of the Christian Era? An End — and a Beginning," and "Missions Tomorrow." Themes arising out of the student scene included "A Preface to Christian Morals," "Prayer," "Why Does God Make Things So Difficult?" "The Christian Community in the Modern World," "Women Students," "Men and Women," "The

Federation consultations during that era and of contributors to the *Student World* reveals the significance of the intellectual work of the Federation in the ecumenical movement and its impact on people in public life.[11]

Hitler's coming to power in Germany, the rise of fascism in Italy, the civil war in Spain, Japanese penetration into China, the large-scale liquidation of opponents of the system in the Soviet Union, and the intensifying challenge of Marxism propelled the Federation out of a self-centered debate about its own identity, into a search for the meaning of Christian vocation in the world. Thus the decade before the Second World War was an era of theological renewal and of penetrating intellectual work on fundamental issues of witness and mission. The growing influence of Barthian neo-orthodox theology and a renewed commitment to Bible study set the tone for the Federation's life throughout the thirties. All this happened at a time when the Federation's financial resources were shrinking dramatically.

The pre–Second World War era culminated in the World Christian Youth Conference held in Amsterdam from July 24 to August 2, 1939, sponsored jointly by the worldwide ecumenical youth organizations. The theme was "Christus Victor." This conference of over fifteen hundred youth and students proved providential in conveying a vision and a living hope for the generation of Christian students and their leaders who, in less than a month, were to be separated from one another by war for more than five years. They were to face the collective evils of humankind and be haunted by disillusionment about the inability of the world community to prevent such mass disaster.

During the Second World War WSCF international conference

University — Unity or Diversity?" "The Adversaries of Christianity," and "Christian Students and the Younger Churches."

11. Some of the most widely known among the contributors to the WSCF consultations and the *Student World* were Metropolitan Athenagoras, V. Azariah, Karl Barth, George Bell, John Bennet, Nicolai Berdyaev, Marc Boegner, Emil Brunner, Sarah Chakko, C. Y. Cheng, Yves Congar, Henry P. Van Dusen, Eric Fenn, Francis House, Toyohiko Kagawa, T. Z. Koo, Hendrik Kraemer, Hans Lilje, Albert Luthuli, John Mackay, Robert Mackie, Walter Moberley, Lesslie Newbigin, Reinhold Niebuhr, D. T. Niles, J. H. Oldham, William Paton, Augustine Ralla Ram, William Temple, Reinhold von Thadden, Paul Tillich, Leo Zander, and Stephan Zankov.

activity was reduced to a bare minimum. Nevertheless, Federation staff were able to keep in touch with many movements, both in countries at war and in those not directly involved, and even significantly to expand the Federation's contacts and work in Latin America. The staff consisted of Robert Mackie, as general secretary, based in Toronto, and Suzanne de Diétrich in Geneva. They were helped by workers provided by member movements and senior friends.

The postwar era revealed the undiminished vitality of the Federation and most of its member movements. Many movements had been shattered by the destruction of the war, but their witness had stood the test. New challenges gave added impetus to the life of the Federation. In Asia, for example, India and Indonesia were struggling for independence, and a civil war was being fought in China. The Christian commitment of the Asian movements under such circumstances left its mark on the Federation as a whole. Such themes as "Christians in the World Struggle," "Rediscovery of the Bible," and "The Christian Task in the University" were taken up in Federation gatherings, and the thinking was shared among SCMs with the help of Federation "Grey Books" which were circulated widely.[12] Issues of world mission reappeared on the WSCF agenda, but with the accent on the task in a postcolonial world. In August 1948 the Federation organized a student conference on world mission in Woudschoten, Netherlands, under the title "The Growing Church." Its leaders included General Secretary Robert C. Mackie; K. H. Ting of China, then a Federation staff member; and D. T. Niles of Sri Lanka (Ceylon), all of whom made a strong plea to participants to commit themselves personally to the evangelistic task.

The 1948 victory of the National Party of South Africa, which led to the development of apartheid policies, sent a shock wave right across the ecumenical movement. Its impact was also felt at the Woudschoten conference, and the antiapartheid struggle was rapidly added to the Federation agenda. In addition, it triggered a long soul-searching dialogue between the Federation leadership and the Student Christian

---

12. Volumes entitled *The Christian in the World Struggle,* by M. M. Thomas and J. D. McCaughey, 1952; *The Task of the Christian in the University,* by John Coleman, 1947; and *Rediscovering the Bible,* by Suzanne de Diétrich, 1942, were published in the Grey Books series of the WSCF.

Association of South Africa, which was then organized in separate sections along racial lines.

With the expansion of Soviet influence and the consolidation of Marxist governments in Eastern Europe and later in China, the challenge of Marxism became a major issue for many SCMs and the WSCF. The movements were disbanded and forbidden in the socialist countries with the notable exception of the German Democratic Republic (GDR). The confrontation between the East German SCM and state authorities in 1948 aroused wide interest. Federation contacts with students and universities in Eastern Europe remained minimal until the Federation, under Philippe Maury's leadership, embarked in 1953 on a series of dialogue meetings with the Prague-based International Union of Students (IUS). From the beginning of the Cold War, the Federation refrained from participating in the anticommunist statements or activities which the U.S. government of the McCarthy era promoted openly as well as covertly through international student organizations. This very issue drove a wedge between the World University Service and the Federation in the mid-fifties.

The split between the Federation and conservative evangelical student organizations culminated in the founding of the International Fellowship of Evangelical Students (IFES) in August 1947, in Boston. The first signs of a division had appeared before World War I. Early differences of style and emphasis between the evangelically and ecumenically minded students and their leaders had become gradually more marked. Between the two world wars evangelical groups grew in strength in Britain and the Anglo-Saxon world. The social concerns of the Federation and the alleged sellout of SCMs to liberal theology and the neo-orthodoxy of Karl Barth and Reinhold Niebuhr were the main reasons why the pietistically oriented IFES drew the line at the "diluted Christianity" of the Federation and refused to cooperate with it and its member movements.[13]

The Federation experienced a new wave of expansion in the fifties. Valdo Galland was appointed Latin America secretary, based in

---

13. The IFES made concessions in a few cases and allowed member movements of the WSCF to be associate members of the IFES. The Finnish SCM was one of these. This arrangement was discontinued when the IFES "excommunicated" the Finnish SCM in 1956, without any prior consultation.

Uruguay. The Asia secretaries Kyaw Than of Burma, T. V. Philip of India, and later Kentaro Shiozuki of Japan were based in Geneva, and the first full-time secretary for Africa, Inga-Brita Castren of Finland, who was appointed in 1959, spent part of her time in Africa and part in Geneva. The Federation's presence in the Middle East began in 1961 with the appointment of Gabriel Habib as joint secretary for the Federation and the WCC Youth Department, and with the establishment of a student and youth office in Beirut, Lebanon.

By the time the General Committee met in Thessaloniki in 1960, the Federation's stature among student organizations and within the ecumenical movement was impressive. Its membership consisted of thirty-four affiliated, twelve associated, and some thirty corresponding movements or federations of movements in more than seventy countries. Its latest area of expansion was in Africa, where SCMs were formed in many countries which had achieved, or were about to achieve, political independence. The leadership of the Federation underwent a major change at Thessaloniki when Philip Potter of Jamaica replaced D. T. Niles as chairman and the Uruguayan Swiss Valdo Galland succeeded Philippe Maury as general secretary.

1.2. The Life and Mission of the Church Program, 1956-64

The year 1960 marked the climax of one of the most ambitious undertakings of the Federation, the eight-year program on the Life and Mission of the Church (LMC). Its concept and the overall plan were presented to the General Committee in August 1956 in Tutzing, Germany, where it was received with enthusiasm and approved for implementation. The masterminds whose grasp of the world situation and whose vision of mission were fundamental to the program were the chairman of the Federation, D. T. Niles, a renowned evangelist and strategist of the ecumenical movement, and the general secretary, Philippe Maury of France, a historian who had been active in the French resistance movement. For the seven years following the Tutzing meeting, most Federation activities were focused on this program. Few initiatives since John R. Mott's time had had as wide and tone-setting an influence on SCMs on all continents.

21

The LMC program was an intensive study and teaching program on Christian mission. It was carried out by national SCMs with the aid of study materials prepared by the Federation and stimulated by international conferences which brought into focus the most crucial aspects of the life and mission of the Church in different regions. The program aimed to help the worldwide community of the Federation move into a new era of witness within the mission of the Church in the postcolonial period. Those who launched it had heard the message "Missionary, go home!" from many churches in newly independent countries. They were faced with the crisis of the International Missionary Council (IMC), which revealed that comity arrangements between mission organizations no longer made sense and that a traditional missionary vocation was widely questioned. The aim of the LMC program was to stimulate study of the postwar transformation of the world and the search for a fresh understanding of mission, rooted in Scripture. It was to encourage Christian practice relevant to the modern world.

The ambition of the planners was to transmit to the new generation of Christian students the fresh ecumenical consensus which they saw emerging from the experience of churches during and after World War II. They were convinced that a new postcolonial thrust of mission was already under way in the ecumenical movement and that the Federation should direct it into Christian witness in universities. They reiterated the view that university students were a strategic group for the future mission of the church, and that from among them the leadership for the churches' involvement in the contemporary world would be drawn. They appreciated young people's perception of the forces which would mold societies and the international community. They felt that the critics most sensitive to the failures of churches and their mission enterprise were Christian students who were advocates of renewal in the Church.

The study of the life and mission of the Church caught fire among member movements with surprising speed. Most shaped the program according to their own particular needs and experience. LMC themes appeared on the programs of national student conferences. The Federation published a series of study booklets and bibliographies on the main topics of the LMC program, in English, French, Spanish, and German. In addition, some member movements translated materials from Geneva into their national languages and produced supplementary materials on their own. Thousands of students were involved in the study of mission.

A series of LMC conferences was what attracted most attention from churches and the ecumenical movement. The first major event of the LMC program was an Asian pilot conference in Rangoon, Burma, over the Christmas–New Year holiday in 1958-59, with more than one hundred participants from twenty-five nations.[14] Issues discussed included: the rise of nationalism and ancient religions, the cultural identity of Asian Christians, the challenge to the Church of the Asian revolution (particularly Asian forms of Marxism), problems caused by the minority position of Christians in Asian societies, and the need to restore self-respect among Asian peoples in general and Christians in particular. The conference brought to the surface reactions among young Christians in Asia against Western missionary organizations and articulated their aspirations for church life rooted in Asian culture. It also made a long-lasting impact on the East Asia Christian Conference (EACC), of which the Federation's chairman, D. T. Niles, was the general secretary.

Unquestionably, the center point of the Life and Mission of the Church program was the World Teaching Conference, held July 16-31, 1960, in Strasbourg, France, with some seven hundred participants from all over the world. The idea of the conference was "to bring together some of the best experts on different aspects of the mission of the Church," to awaken the present generation of SCM leaders from apathy and traditionalism, and to provide theological and practical knowledge "without which no one can understand or enter effective service." The conference was also expected to train students and youth leaders for the new type of missionary service needed in the world of the sixties.

The Strasbourg conference was a significant event because of the lectures delivered and the expertise present, but also because of its effects on SCMs, on mission theology, and on the program emphases of the WCC.[15] Nevertheless, the reception among participants of the "teach-

14. *Student World,* no. 3 (1959), reports and evaluates extensively the Rangoon conference.

15. The speakers and resource persons included leading theologians and mission strategists from all continents. Among them were Karl Barth, Kathleen Bliss, Burgess Carr, Kenneth Cragg, Franklin Clark Fry, Ignatius Hazim, Hans Hoekendijk, Joseph

ing" given by the speakers was quite mixed. Many found it merely a repetition of the themes of the "old" prophets of the ecumenical establishment, and as such, outdated. Participants did not perceive the kind of consensus on mission assumed by the planners of the conference, among themselves, among the speakers, or among their churches. Reactions to most of the leaders and speakers were markedly varied, often very critical. Nevertheless, two speakers, the grand old man of the ecumenical movement, W. A. Visser 't Hooft, and the outstanding mission strategist of Asia, D. T. Niles, were reasonably well received, although they, too, had much to ponder over the unexpected turning away of many students from the "ecumenical teachers." The senior theologian who caught the interest of a large crowd of participants at an improvised session was Karl Barth. Among the young, theologically less learned participants there were, of course, many who had not even heard his name before. Despite his representing the grandfather generation, many, including some of the most radical protesters, found him surprisingly near to their own wavelength. However, the production of the play *No Exit* by Jean-Paul Sartre proved, unexpectedly perhaps, the most thought-provoking contribution to the conference and made a substantive impact on the discussions.

Two younger speakers did appeal to this new impatient generation. The first was Richard Shaull, who stirred the audience by claiming that church structures were obsolete, that parishes operated on the periphery of human life rather than at its center, and that mission organizations presupposed a concept of missions no longer valid. In the broken world "the Church is . . . caught with the same structures of worship, thought, program and mission by which it served Jesus Christ in a very different situation." He struck a chord that resonated with the views of those who were already at odds with the institutional church.[16]

Hromádka, Mikko Juva, Jean Meyendorf, José Míguez Bonino, Lesslie Newbigin, D. T. Niles, Richard Shaull, Masao Takenaka, M. M. Thomas, Luther Tucker, and W. A. Visser 't Hooft. "Students and the Life and Mission of the Church," a mimeographed report of the WSCF, 1956-64; also *Student World*, no. 1-2 (1961).

16. Richard Shaull's opening address represented a fairly moderate radicalism compared with his more apocalyptic statements ten years later. Richard Shaull, "Opening Address," in the compilation of the papers of WSCF World Teaching Conference, Strasbourg, France, July 16-31, 1960, WSCF Archives. See also *Student World*, no. 1-2 (1961): 206.

The second was J. C. (Hans) Hoekendijk, the Dutch missiologist. He offered an interpretation of the Christian faith and the nature of mission in a modern secular framework which aroused a positive response. He presented the formula for mission "Christ — world — Church" as a corrective to the assertion that Christ's mission was entrusted to the Church which was sent into the world. For Hoekendijk the Christ-world relationship was fundamental. A related affirmation was that "the coming of Christ is a secular event." The secular world was the stage of God's activity. The coming of Christ and the Christianity following from it "cannot be anything else but a secular movement, a movement in the world and for the world." "We cannot speak about Christ without a clear reference to the world . . . the world cannot be fully understood without testimony to Jesus Christ." To make Christianity a religion was for Hoekendijk a denial of the Christ who was for the world. His position echoed Bonhoeffer's notion of religionless Christianity in a world that had come of age.

Another Hoekendijk theme was the role of "creative minorities" as catalysts for the renewal of faith and mission in churches suffocated by their institutionalism. He referred to Francke, Zinzendorf, and Wesley as pioneers of a relevant mission strategy which was later destroyed by church-centered missions.[17]

Hoekendijk's thought eventually played a role in the sixties in the development of several WCC programs, e.g., the missionary structure of the congregation study and Urban Industrial Mission, later Urban Rural Mission. He was considered the mentor of those who found signs of God's action in the revolutionary political movements in China and elsewhere, in the anticolonial struggle, in Marxist ideology, and in the emancipatory movements of modernization and secularization. The development of contextual theologies became an ecumenical fad in subsequent years. The theology of secularization was followed by the theologies of urbanization, revolution, liberation, and feminism. The slogan "The world sets the agenda for the church"

17. J. C. Hoekendijk's address "Christ and the World in the Modern Age" was published in *Student World,* no. 1-2 (1961): 75-82. His theological and missiological contributions stimulated a wide discussion in the circles of the new WCC Commission on World Mission and Evangelism. His thinking from 1948 to 1964 is presented more extensively in his book *The Church Inside Out* (Philadelphia: Westminster Press, 1966) (original Dutch edition, *De Kerk Binnenste Buiten* [W. Ten Have N.V., 1964]).

summed up the basis for the new contextualism. The term "doing theology," which seemed to exclude any serious scholarly preparation, became a trademark for the concerns of contextualists.

If there was any convergence of ideas at the Strasbourg conference, it was limited to the affirmation that the essence of the Church was mission. Most of the questions were addressed to the structures of churches and their mission organizations, their interpretation of the Scriptures, and the categories they used to express the content of the Christian faith. Many participants felt that the inherited institutions were unable to give an authentic witness to the gospel. Too deep a gulf separated the churches from the world in which the young generation found itself. The sharpness of the protests against traditional theological formulations and institutional forms of the church took organizers and many senior resource people by surprise. In retrospect it is obvious that the planners of the Strasbourg conference and the leaders of the Federation overgeneralized their own convictions and visions about ecumenical convergence in mission and grossly underestimated the sensitivities of students to theological or ideological paternalism.

In evaluating the conference, the Federation leadership concluded that the reaction of participants against the assumed ecumenical convergence was an expression of their concern for mission and for freeing it from institutional self-centeredness and defensiveness, which tended to make churches blind to the real world. They also recognized in the participants' criticisms misgivings about the lack of attention paid to the university world. It became obvious that this reaction, expressed by a majority of participants, had to be taken into account in developing strategies for the future of the Federation's work and for relevant patterns for ecumenical mission.[18]

The Strasbourg conference was followed by a series of regional Life and Mission of the Church conferences held in Bangalore, India (1961); Graz, Austria (1962); Nairobi, Kenya (1963); Montreal, Canada (1963); Broumana, Lebanon (1964); and Embalse Rio Tercero, Argentina (1964). The last world mission quadrennial conference of the National Student Christian Federation of the USA,

18. Philippe Maury presented a summary of evaluative comments in his editorial in *Student World,* no. 1-2 (1961): 1-14.

December 28, 1963–January 3, 1964, in Athens, Ohio, was also in its intention and content part of the same program.

These regional conferences followed the original plan for the Life and Mission of the Church program while taking into account the responses to and reactions of the Strasbourg teaching conference. The themes of the conferences were indicative: "Secularization," "Modernization," "Freedom under the Cross," "Mission in Revolutionary Latin America," and "Relevance to the University."[19] In retrospect it is evident that these conferences, with the enthusiasm that they aroused, stimulated planning for the regionalization of the Federation.

1.3. Search for an Ecumenical Strategy, 1960-67

1.3.1. The Idea

The concern for a comprehensive ecumenical strategy for the Christian community in the university world has been voiced repeatedly with different emphases in the course of the Federation's history. The 1956 General Committee in Tutzing, Germany, had raised the issue with a sense of urgency. The main concern then was to strengthen cooperation among organizations involved in Christian ministry among students for the sake of a united evangelistic witness. However, it was not until 1960 that the theme came back into focus when the WSCF General Committee, meeting at Thessaloniki, Greece, set directions for the Federation's future work and took action on the concerns of the Strasbourg conference.

The Thessaloniki report on "Ecumenical Strategy for Student Work"[20] dealt with trends in the university world, noting the rapid

19. Comprehensive reporting on the whole Life and Mission of the Church program can be found in the eight-year report of the WSCF, 1956-64. The Minutes of the Twenty-Fourth Meeting of the General Committee of the WSCF, Embalse Rio Tercero, Argentina, 1964, pp. 24-25, include a summary report with conclusions for future work. Furthermore, the issues of *Student World,* no. 3 (1959); no. 1-2 (1960); no. 1-2 (1961); no. 3 (1962); and no. 1 (1963), deal with the topics of the Strasbourg and regional LMC conferences.

20. Christian community was the overall topic of the third study commission of the Thessaloniki 1960 General Committee. Its Section B dealt with "Ecumenical

expansion of higher education on all continents, the changes in the status of students in society, increasing specialization, and the impact of science and technology. It gave special attention to the characteristics of the Christian community in that changing context. It emphasized common Bible study, worship, and discussion as nonnegotiable elements of any Christian community in a university trying "to discover what their witness must be in the situation." It affirmed the ministry of Word and sacraments as the foundation of the community, and "confronting the changing university with Christ's Lordship" as its primary aim. Its ministry was to be ecumenical, to reflect its international nature, to be missionary by intention, and to be open to the contemporary world and people of all persuasions.

The report, approved by the General Committee, called for joint efforts by SCMs and churches to develop a common "ecumenical strategy for student work." A series of strategy consultations involving representatives of ecumenical organizations, churches, and missionary societies, to be organized nationally, regionally, as well as globally, was proposed. For the main gathering, a representative worldwide consultation to be held no later than 1961 — an unrealistic timing — was recommended.

The same General Committee made several other decisions which, in hindsight, are of special interest in light of the events of the late sixties. The Federation was to give priority to worship and Bible study. Among the staff was to be at least one person with particular gifts in the life of prayer and pastoral guidance. The report stated "that in order for Christians to 'live in the world' — and particularly in the modern secularized world — a strong personal discipline of worship is absolutely essential."[21]

Political and racial issues also received fresh attention. Involvement in politics was recognized as an inseparable part of participation in the mission of the church. Christian unity did not imply political uniformity, but active dialogue on theologically or politically controversial issues was deemed essential to stimulate a sense of responsibility for

---

Strategy for Student Work." The section reports were integrated into one commission report, Minutes of the Twenty-Third Meeting of the General Committee of the WSCF, Thessaloniki, Greece, 1960.

21. Thessaloniki Minutes, pp. 60-61.

political issues. Topics suggested for consideration within the Federation included the East-West conflict, control of nuclear weapons, race relations, economic imperialism, issues of hunger and the population explosion, aid to developing countries, religious oppression, conflicts in the Near East, and limited wars elsewhere. The General Committee appointed a Political Commission to serve as an advisory body to the Executive Committee and to national movements.

Words of caution about the political role were also voiced. The newly appointed chairman of the Political Commission, Philip Lee-Woolf of Great Britain, warned that "the making of political pronouncements and the taking of (political) action is not the only or the best form of political engagement for the Church; such pronouncements and action may be a form of escape from more relevant and difficult forms of obedience." Warnings about the "profusion of political recommendations" which tended to be immodest and contradictory to authentic Christian witness in politics were also expressed.[22] Such warnings were forgotten in the Federation and in the ecumenical movement at large by the time the decade drew to a close.

Most of the ambitious plans for an ecumenical strategy for student work had, however, to await implementation. Only the Ecumenical Assistance Program was reshaped and expanded to implement a more comprehensive strategy for the systematic sharing of human and financial resources, for the promotion of SCMs in poor or conflict-ridden areas, and for making leadership training available to them. Changes at the top of the leadership of the Federation; the expansion of work in Africa, the Middle East, and North America; and the demands placed on financial and personnel resources by the Life and Mission of the Church program, which continued to mid-1964, slowed down the implementation of other initiatives.

22. The Thessaloniki meeting of the General Committee dealt with political issues in a study commission on politics, divided into subsections on "The WSCF and SCM in Politics," "Peace," and "Racial Questions." The full report of the study commission on politics is found in the Thessaloniki Minutes, pp. 39-51.

1.3.2. "Christian Presence"

The first follow-up to the recommendations on ecumenical strategy was a global preparatory consultation held in May 1964 at Bossey Ecumenical Institute in Céligny, near Geneva. Participants included SCM leaders, university teachers, campus ministers, church executives, and representatives of other ecumenical organizations drawn from different regions. It was referred to as the "wise men's consultation"; although it included women participants, no one was, as yet, objecting to sexist language. Its task was to suggest an approach to the development of an ecumenical strategy, including its theological rationale, to be presented to the 1964 General Committee as the main emphasis for the Federation's work in the next quadrennium. The consultation produced a document entitled "The Christian Community in the Academic World," with presence and participation as its key concepts. It was debated and rewritten twice during the meeting of the General Committee held in July 1964 in Embalse Rio Tercero, Argentina, before being adopted.[23] Although its title remained the same, it became known as the "Christian Presence" document. It quickly became a best-seller within the Federation and was translated into numerous languages and studied widely in member movements and related organizations and agencies. It served as a sort of planning catechism of the Federation for the next three or four years, until the events of 1968 threw it abruptly into oblivion.

The document's theological theme was Christian presence. The main sources of inspiration were the thinking of Dietrich Bonhoeffer and the experience of Catholic worker-priests in France after World War II. It also bore the marks of recent ecumenical discussions on secularization. The term "Christian presence" was used as a contemporary interpretation of "evangelization," "witness," and "mission," and as an allusion to the incarnation and self-revelation of God. It also linked the ideas of wordless witness and anonymous service with the

---

23. The chief drafter of the first version was Philip Zabriskie of the USA, at that time head of the Episcopalian campus ministry, and the chief drafter of the last version was Albert van den Heuvel of the Netherlands, then the head of the WCC Youth Department. The final document can be found in the Embalse Rio Tercero Minutes, pp. 85-97.

concept of presence in the name of Christ. It was chosen because it seemed to offer an alternative to traditional words with their loaded connotations.

> When we try to find words in the living language of today to describe the task of the Christian community in the academic world, we seek to give expression to the same realities as our forefathers knew, i.e. to witness to our belief that in Christ Jesus God has reconciled the world to himself. . . . we use the word "presence" for that reality . . . to express both the center of Christian faith and our response to it.[24]

In retrospect, it is apparent that the idea of Christian presence was developed in two opposite directions. It was used to emphasize God's sovereign action in the world and consequently to describe the task of the Church as tracing signs of God's presence in secular events and political movements, and thus following their lead in its work. Perceiving and following Christ in the midst of peoples' struggles and movements was primary. The gathering of those who acknowledged Christ was secondary. Many of those who wanted to free the Church from its institutional heritage and develop a politically and socially relevant ministry welcomed this interpretation and saw in it the theological rationale for their contextual approaches.

Christian presence had a very different content when it was used as an interpretation of the contemporary meaning of incarnation and the sacramental presence of Christ in the Church. The Church was a vehicle for Christ's presence for the life of the world. The Church had a mission received directly from Christ. This mission made the Church open to all people in all walks of life. Worship as a living encounter with God was a formative expression of Christian community. This view provided a bridge between traditional and experimental approaches to ministry. Although this interpretation of Christian presence did not gain prominence in later ecumenical discussions in the Federation and the WCC, it did stimulate rethinking of the meaning of mission among churches and their mission organizations, and of their participation in university ministry.

24. Embalse Rio Tercero Minutes, p. 88.

The second half of the "Christian Presence" document dealt with ideas and plans for ecumenical strategies designed to draw Christian student organizations and churches' ministries together in a joint ecumenical and missionary ministry to the academic world. At the heart of the strategies was to be the experience of the Federation and its member movements as expressions of the life of the Church, indigenous to the university world. They were also to include plans for the development of leadership for the many new SCMs which had been founded in the late fifties and early sixties in Africa, Asia, and Latin America. Student initiative and leadership and the whole life of the SCM were to be made available to churches as an essential element of Christian community within the university, thus to complement churches' institutional involvement in the academic community. Recognition of the SCM by the churches as an integral part of the life of the Church was to be sought.

The commitment to developing ecumenical strategies in which churches as institutions would participate was a departure from an exclusive SCM-centered approach. The "Christian Presence" document made this clear:

> The call for an "Ecumenical Strategy in the Academic World" . . . is rooted in the transition . . . from interconfessionalism to an "ecclesiastical period" in which the churches themselves have become the bearers of the ecumenical movement. The clearest expression of this was the formation in 1948 of the World Council of Churches. In the light of this development the Federation has been challenged to examine anew its approach to its task. The necessity for this has been made apparent by the growing consciousness in many churches and missionary bodies of the strategic need and desire for a fuller expression of the church in the academic world.[25]

In view of the unprecedented growth of higher education in every continent, the diversity of the academic world, and the variety of Christian responses to it, the document concluded that no single uniform worldwide strategy for the Christian community in the uni-

25. Embalse Rio Tercero Minutes, p. 85.

versity would be adequate or realistic. Strategies had to be developed in local contexts in each region. Furthermore, the document drew attention to the impact of higher learning as a force for social change, especially in developing countries. This, too, had a bearing on ecumenical strategies.

The task of the Federation in the development of ecumenical strategies was to facilitate the coming together of the main partners region by region, to foster discussion of the nature and task of the Christian community in the academic world, and to encourage continued imaginative work on ecumenical programs and structures.

The 1964 meeting of the General Committee approved the recommendation that the Federation launch a series of regional ecumenical strategy consultations. The organizations which were to be brought together with SCMs included university chaplaincies, campus ministries of churches, student YMCAs and YWCAs, denominational student centers, and also evangelical student organizations. The plan assumed participation of the World Council of Churches, especially its Youth Department, and the respective regional ecumenical conferences and councils. The series of suggested consultations were to form the backbone of the Federation's worldwide activities in subsequent years.

Other significant topics were discussed at the Embalse Rio Tercero General Committee meeting. One commission dealt with contemporary questions of ethics under the heading "Called to Be Human." The complexity of issues in the social, political, and personal realms of life, combined with the erosion of inherited moral codes, made this area existential for SCMs. Two motifs stood out in the commission's report. On the one hand, openness to others and solidarity with them should form the fundamental framework for ethical decisions. On the other, solid Christian identity should be the source for openness to others. Such identity can only be found by participating in the life of the Christian community, the Church, and by taking part in personal and communal Bible study.

The commission also pointed to the need for "vicarious expertise" in the church for making ethical judgments in matters requiring technical and expert knowledge, and encouraged member movements to develop such expertise through rigorous study. It called for the formation of disciplined communities — an equivalent of religious orders — to explore possibilities for corporate Christian response in specific situations demanding ethical action and to act as cells of church renewal.[26]

Another commission wrestled with questions of worship, taking into account the experience of the Life and Mission of the Church program and the ideas expressed in the "Christian Presence" document. The report pleaded for a renewed emphasis on "our life as a worshiping community" and for achieving "a new dynamic" in worship and community life within the Federation. The commission made numerous suggestions to member movements and for Federation publications. It also recommended a new policy for Communion services at Federation conferences and meetings. The Embalse Rio Tercero meeting in 1964 was the last major Federation event for at least a decade at which worship practices were taken up as a common concern.[27]

The Commission on Christian Engagement in Politics reviewed the role and the problems of the Federation in its political engagement. It considered the nature, means, and goals of its involvement. Possibilities for cooperation with secular groups, with special attention drawn to the Federation's links with the United Nations Educational, Scientific, and Cultural Organization (UNESCO), with the WCC Commission of the Churches on International Affairs (CCIA), and with the Christian Peace Conference (CPC) were explored. Relationships between SCMs and churches, and theological issues arising out of political engagement, were also considered.

Sober political realism colored the work of the commission. Its report was prefaced with the remark that, with the exception of a letter to member movements about South Africa, it did not see its task as

---

26. The Commission on "Called to Be Human" continued the discussion initiated at the 1956 meeting of the General Committee in Tutzing where "The Call to Holy Living" was the topic of a commission. At Embalse the ethics group attempted to translate traditional Christian concepts, such as sin, repentance, conversion, sanctification, freedom, love, and communion, into language and terminology familiar to contemporary students. The report of the commission is found in the Embalse Rio Tercero Minutes, pp. 54-57.

27. The report of the Worship Commission, Embalse Rio Tercero Minutes, pp. 77-85, is an important document not only from the point of view of the internal development of the WSCF, but also because it touches several points which have emerged at Faith and Order meetings.

presenting statements about particular political issues confronting the world. The commission emphasized that "our action must be based on the political, social and economic realities of national and international life," and that "careful study is required to determine these realities amid conflicting information and hidden facts." The report also drew attention to the need for assessing the expected results of possible political actions.

The use of violence was a major concern for the group. "The change from non-violent to violent action is an ethical problem of major importance." So was the question of order, which some saw as a notion for preserving the status quo, but on which the group recommended further study. "The relation of freedom and stability," "the avoidance of anarchy," and "movements for social justice and peace" needed more attention. The commission noted tensions between SCMs and churches concerning the political responsibility of the Christian community. "Student Christian political action is usually in terms of the political left, an approach not shared by many churches." Tensions, even divisions, within member movements regarding particular political actions were identified. The report stressed the importance of understanding and reconciliation in these matters, but added that reaching unity or achieving a compromise about conflicting positions was not necessarily a goal for Christian community but rather "a mode of life . . . which sees its unity not in ideology but in membership in the body of Christ."

The General Committee decided at the Embalse Rio Tercero meeting to appoint a new Political Commission which should meet annually, and to establish a full-time executive position for its secretary. Topics for its study included violence and nonviolence, the feasibility of the Christian community acting as a community of political action, and the relationship between the Christian gospel and political ideologies.[28]

28. The report of the Commission on the Christian Engagement in Politics, Embalse Rio Tercero Minutes, pp. 68-77. A comprehensive report of the work of the Political Commission of the Federation from 1964 to 1968 can be found in the four-year report of the WSCF, "Christian Presence in the Academic Community," pp. 110-47. For the period 1960-64 the associate general secretary of the WSCF, Elisabeth Adler of the GDR, served as the secretary for the Political Commission. From 1964 to 1968 Bruce Douglass of the USA served as its full-time executive secretary.

In the subsequent years 1965-68 the WSCF China Study Program became the main activity of the Political Commission. Its aim was to understand the nature of the Chinese revolution and its challenge to the rest of the world in general and to churches in particular. The program sought ways to open communication between the Federation and Christian and political leaders of China. The project was carried out by means of a series of consultations and generated a wide range of publications.[29]

1.3.3. Regional Strategy Consultations

Four major regional ecumenical strategy consultations were held during 1966 and 1967. The first, in Latin America, in El Tabo, Chile, January 22-25, 1966, was sponsored jointly by the Federation and the Provisional Commission for Latin American Evangelical Unity (UNELAM). The second, in Africa, in Accra, Ghana, September 1-7, 1966, had the All Africa Conference of Churches (AACC) as cosponsor. The third was the Asia consultation in Hong Kong, November 6-13, 1966, with the East Asia Christian Conference (EACC) as cosponsor. The last and largest was the Europe consultation held in Basel, Switzerland, September 4-8, 1967, with the Conference of European Churches (CEC) as cosponsor. In North America no single regional consultation was held. Instead strategy concerns were taken up at meetings of the Canadian and U.S. ecumenical organizations related to the university world.[30]

29. Three international "working parties" on China were held: July 1966 in Geneva, Switzerland; July 1967 in Hong Kong; and January 1968 in Montreal, Canada. The publications related to the China project included a special issue of the *Student World* (no. 1, 1967), the reports of Hong Kong and Montreal consultations, and several books and articles by Ross Terrill, Richard Hensman, Ray Wylie, Kazuhiko Sumiya, and Leopoldo Niilus.

30. Reports of the three ecumenical strategy consultations of 1966 were published separately. The articles and papers relating to the European consultation were published as a book entitled *A Challenge to the European University* (Geneva: WSCF, 1968). A summary report of the whole series of consultations was included in the mimeographed four-year report on the WSCF from 1964 to 1968 entitled "Christian Presence in the Academic Community" (Geneva: WSCF, 1968).

Each regional consultation attempted to form an overall picture of the university world in its region. A marked diversity in the self-understanding of the university was evident. Recognition of the vast expansion of higher education was the only common factor among the regions. The consultations noted differences in definitions of the nature and function of the university, ranging from "classic" formulations which emphasized the pure pursuit of truth for its own sake to pragmatic ones emphasizing the meeting of manpower needs in society. All reports considered the impact of the different continents' peculiar social, political, and cultural situations on university life. A "revolutionary atmosphere" was noted in Latin America. In Asia the conflict between "modernization" and "traditional values" was of prime importance. The problem of the indigenization of academic life was a major concern in Africa. The Europe consultation focused on the rising student protest. The issues of economic underdevelopment and demographic explosion were taken up in Africa, Asia, and Latin America.

Each consultation tackled questions about the function and structures of Christian community in the academic world. The theological ideas of the "Christian Presence" document were found by all parties to be helpful and interesting, even if they could not fully comply with all their implications. They found inadequate, for example, the assumption that the nature and form of the Christian community within the university world were fully determined by the tasks of that community in its specific situation, as the document seemed to suggest. Being part of the life of the Church implied participation in ministries which were not inherent in the academic scene nor generated within one's own particular context. There was universal criticism of the idea that Christ's work was located exclusively in the world, apart from the Church. Likewise the view that the Christian community — the Church — is a by-product of human responses to Christ present in the world was found to be one-sided.

The Latin American report stated that "the Christian community is the fruit of the Gospel," of "the amazing news that 'God was in Christ.'" The report depicted Christian community as the goal rather than the means of God's work in the world, referring to "the new humanity recreated in the image of God in Jesus Christ." The Church is therefore a part of God's purpose in the world.

All reports underlined worship as an integral element in the life of the Christian community. "This participation (social involvement) is inseparable from participation in the praise of God in his community," said the Latin American report. At the same time they all placed a strong emphasis on the dynamic nature of "presence," using such terms as "involvement," "struggle for liberation," "transforming structures," and "proclaiming reconciliation in Christ," thus repudiating the passive and static connotations of the word.

It was also significant that all the consultations agreed that any theological distinction between the SCM and the Church was meaningless. They affirmed that the SCM was and should be an expression of the Church. This conviction was fully shared by the Latin America consultation, which was well aware of the difficulties of communication between the SCMs and the Protestant churches. The African and Asian reports pointed to the problem that the church in their regions was still considered largely an alien element which had its roots in another culture. The importance, therefore, of the development of indigenous theology was strongly emphasized.

All regional meetings considered themselves just one step in a much longer process of consultation. All recommended that the process be continued through a series of national strategy consultations. It was foreseen that the coordination, planning, and funding of such joint strategy development would be a continued responsibility of the Federation.

The reports indicated that two undercurrents were evident in the Federation. One reflected the new vitality of student movements with a strong emphasis on student leadership, issue orientation, mobility, and minimal structure. The other resulted from the increased involvement of churches through more institutional ministries and structures, such as professional staff and student centers. The reports regarded coping simultaneously with these two undercurrents in the same organization as a positive challenge for the Federation.

The unambiguous rejection, expressed in the reports, of a single-track, single-method pattern for the WSCF, and of a single structure for all its constituency, was a position of far-reaching ecumenical significance. All the reports affirmed that accepting diversity was an inherent ecumenical principle of the Federation, which had most recently been spelled out in the "Christian Presence" document:

[W]e see a great variety of structures and programs. In some places the SCM·is the arm of the churches in the university, . . . in other places a much more independent community confronting and criticizing the denominations . . . in still other places, SCMs may find themselves in the midst of denominational student work and trying to draw into a single conversation students engaged in confessional organizations. . . . Many other possibilities are actually being explored. . . . To choose any one of these as the only possible solution . . . would be to do justice neither to the situation nor to the ecumenical nature of the Federation.[31]

Until the late sixties, there was within the WSCF a high degree of consensus about the Christian presence approach, even if interpretations of its meaning differed somewhat. The regional ecumenical strategy consultations contributed decisively to what became the "regionalization" of the WSCF in the years after 1968, even if many of the recommendations and much of the suggested follow-up were later abandoned.

31. Embalse Rio Tercero Minutes, p. 87.

CHAPTER 2

The Rise of Protests, 1960-68

2.1. Change of Mood

By the beginning of the sixties the prevailing mood among university students in North America and Europe had begun to change. The generation of students who had personally experienced the war had been succeeded by a "silent generation." But by the dawn of the new decade an "activist generation" had entered universities and colleges. Debate about domestic and international political issues increasingly set the tone for existing student organizations. Action groups were founded to deal with specific issues and to launch public campaigns. The increased involvement of American students in the civil rights movement was the most visible sign of the new era.

For students in Asia, the fifties were not as "silent" as they seemed to be in the West. In several Asian countries the struggle for political independence had been won; the war against Dutch colonialists in Indonesia was over, and the People's Republic of China had been established. Students had taken an active part in these national struggles. Many were looking to Marxist socialism as the tool for completing liberation from former colonial powers. By the beginning of the sixties, however, students in Asia had by and large turned from ideological confrontation to nation building, which was widely recognized as the most pressing task ahead. Modernization and national development were the catch phrases of the day.[1]

In Africa the movement for political independence had reached its peak at the end of the fifties and the beginning of the sixties. Although institutions of higher education were still few and far between, and students represented a small elite, they had played a visible role in the struggle for independence. The challenge of building an Africa free from colonial domination was for them a source of contagious enthusiasm, fully shared by Christian students.

African students soon woke up to the wooing of their nations by the American- and the Soviet-led blocs using military and development aid and scholarships. They were not keen to sacrifice their goal of authentic independence, their vision of African nationhood, and their traditional African values to satisfy foreign powers involved in an ideological battle for the soul of Africa. Contrary to the conclusions many in the West had drawn from their militantly anticolonial ethos, African students had little enthusiasm for Soviet-style Marxism. They were not prepared, as one of their leaders put it, "to replace one colonial master by another."[2] Many Western radicals also failed to grasp that African students were not eager to accept any ideological leadership from outside their own continent, however radical or anti-imperialist it appeared.

The emerging political culture of African one-party systems and authoritarian forms of government did not, however, leave much room for public political action apart from that of supporting the ruling powers. The political role of students, therefore, was primarily confined to the intellectual and ideological preparation for the era of independence. The demonstrations with which students wanted at times to voice their apprehension about the ruling powers were usually crushed quickly and brutally.[3]

1. A comprehensive discussion of the cultural, social, and political trends in the post–World War II era up to the end of the sixties can be found in Dick Wilson, *Asia Awakes: A Continent in Transition* (New York: Penguin Books, 1972).

2. José Chipenda at a staff meeting in 1968.

3. Wilfred Cartey and Martin Kilson, eds., *The Africa Reader: Independent Africa* (New York: Random House, Vintage Books, 1970), provide an overview of political and ideological trends on the continent during and after the struggle for independence, and give attention to repression and militarism and also to the role of

Military coups and the repression of democracy were the hallmarks of Latin American political life in the late fifties and throughout the sixties. This had a drastic effect on university students, driving most political activity underground. Since the beginning of the century the whole region had been politically and economically part of the "sphere of influence" of the USA. The expansion of American investment in the fifties and sixties and direct and indirect American support of conservative and military regimes fueled popular resentment and fomented revolutionary sedition among young people. Latin America had a long-standing tradition of student radicalism which had influenced national politics and was tolerated by those in power. Castro's victory in Cuba in 1959 put an end to this toleration. The SCMs, which in the fifties had grown in size as well as in theological depth and social and political awareness, ran into difficulties under military regimes. They also lost the sympathy and support of many leaders of Protestant churches who preferred to lie low and not be identified with the underground opposition.[4]

By the beginning of the sixties students in the West were living in relative affluence compared with their forebears and with students in the rest of the world. This gave them unprecedented mobility and a high level of self-confidence. They could afford to take time from their studies for extensive extracurricular activities and to travel in large numbers to other countries and continents. They could afford to experiment with new lifestyles. The superpower position of the USA after World War II added to the self-confidence of American students, even when they were opposed to American imperialism. Furthermore, the sheer number of university students in North America and Europe made them a potential political force, if mobilized around issues on which their mass action could make an impact.

intellectuals. "Christian Presence in the Academic Community," a report on the World Student Christian Federation, 1964-68 (Geneva: WSCF, mimeographed), includes brief surveys of the situation on each continent, as perceived from the perspective of the Federation.

4. In addition to the report on the WSCF, 1964-68, Irving Louis Horowitz, Josué de Castro, and John Gerassi, eds., *Latin American Radicalism: A Documentary Report on Left and Nationalist Movements* (New York: Random House, Vintage Books, 1969), is an invaluable source of information on the political and socioeconomic state of affairs in the continent and on the ideological forces at work there in the fifties and sixties.

Students in the West involved in political and ideological movements tended, therefore, to claim to represent worldwide movements and to dominate international forums.

As the activist decade of the sixties dawned, student organizations and SCMs around the world found themselves in a variety of contrasting starting positions.

2.2. World Events and Student Radicalism

In retrospect, the rise of student radicalism in the sixties was not just the result of changes in the socioeconomic status of students and developments within the academic community, nor of a subversive propaganda drive conducted from some clandestine revolutionary center. The sequence of world events was an additional major factor triggering student activism. Even a cursory reading of accounts of the upheavals and international conflicts of the decade makes the rise of student protests and engagement in revolutionary activity more understandable.

Fidel Castro and his guerrilla force ended the dictatorship of Fulgencio Batista in Cuba on January 1, 1959, introducing a new element to stimulate radical student movements in North and Latin America. In April 1960 a Fair Play for Cuba Committee was formed in the United States. In the summer of the same year thousands of American students visited Cuba.

In February 1960 black students staged a sit-in against racial segregation at a lunch counter in Greensboro, North Carolina, in the South of the USA. This was the beginning of a new phase in the civil rights movement of black Americans, to be led by Martin Luther King Jr. Many white students joined the sit-in protests, which spread rapidly across the whole country. A major target was the Woolworth department store chain, which had segregated lunch counters in the southern states. In April 1960 a new organization, the Student Nonviolent Coordinating Committee, was formed to recruit students for civil rights action and to relate their efforts to the work of the Southern Christian Leadership Conference and other civil rights organizations. The civil rights movement began to make headlines across the country.

On March 21, 1960, the South African police fired on a crowd of

peaceful demonstrators in the small town of Sharpville, killing 69
blacks, mainly women, and wounding 186. The event caused a massive wave of demonstrations in South Africa against the apartheid
government. On March 31 Prime Minister Hendrik Verwoerd declared a state of emergency and banned the leading political organizations of blacks, including the African National Congress (ANC)
and Pan Africanist Congress (PAC). Thousands of blacks were arrested and banned during the post-Sharpville state of emergency.
Many blacks and whites left the country and joined the antiapartheid
movement in Europe and North America. World opinion turned
decisively against the apartheid regime.

In April-May 1960 thousands of Korean students demonstrated
against the repressive government. The student protest became the
backbone of opposition activities that resulted in the resignation of
Premier Syngman Rhee, on April 27, and in the establishment of a
representative form of government. The parliamentary democracy was
destroyed in the following year by a military junta supported by the
U.S. government, but the student movement could not be brought
to a halt.

In England a demonstration march from Aldermaston to London
to protest against nuclear arms was held at Easter 1960. This was a
breakthrough for the British peace movements and especially for the
Committee for Nuclear Disarmament. Aldermaston marches became
the initial rallying points for student activity from which grew a
broader politically radical student movement with a neo-Marxist
orientation.

In June 1960 Students for a Democratic Society (SDS) was formed
in New York City, and became the most important New Left student
organization in North America. Its pamphlet, issued in June 1962, at
Port Huron, Michigan, became the best-known programmatic guide
for radical political action in America.

On June 30, 1960, the Congo Republic (named Zaire 1971 to 1997)
was freed from Belgian rule and became an independent state. This
event was followed by a prolonged crisis. In February 1961 Colonel
Joseph Mobutu led an armed coup against Prime Minister Patrice
Lumumba, who was later murdered. His death sparked off large demonstrations on various continents against American, British, Belgian,
and French "reactionaries." The Soviet Union cashed in on the event

to promote Soviet-style socialist revolution and tried to attain a leader-ship position among the anti-imperialist movements in Africa. It founded Lumumba University in Moscow for African students. The events surrounding the independence of Zaire marked an intensifica-tion of the competition between East and West for control of Africa.

Events contributing to a mood of unrest among students continued the following year. The Berlin Wall was erected in August 1961. Later in the same year the Soviet Union resumed nuclear testing, which fueled a new wave of peace demonstrations in the West. The U.S. government banned American travel to Cuba in February 1961 and sponsored the unsuccessful Bay of Pigs invasion of Cuban émigrés in April. The military overthrow of President Joao Goulart of Brazil by General Humberto Castelo Branco on April 1, 1964, placed the country under total military control and was welcomed by the USA. American intervention in the Dominican Republic in March 1965 prevented the return to power of the democratically elected social democrat, Juan Bosch. These events were a testimony to the militari-zation of Latin American politics and the determination of the United States to have the final say on the continent to protect American economic interests. The Brazilian coup forced the Federation to move the venue for its 1964 General Committee from Brazil to Argentina.

In 1968 Martin Luther King Jr. and Robert Kennedy were assas-sinated, and in the same year the Soviets invaded Czechoslovakia, putting an end to the "Prague Spring," with its promises of socialism with a human face and democratic governance. These events put the final touches to the political contours of a dramatic decade.

2.3. Student Christians Join Protests

2.3.1. Civil Rights

Civil rights was the issue in the first phase of the American student protests in the sixties.[5] The sit-ins and freedom rides to integrate lunch

---

5. The amount of literature about the American student scene in the fifties and the sixties is overwhelming. I have used, to check my memory of the events, Paul Jacobs and Saul Landau, *The New Radicals: A Report with Documents* (New York:

counters and public transport systems rapidly electrified university and college campuses all over the USA. The charismatic leadership of Martin Luther King Jr. aroused a forceful response not only among blacks but also among students with a strong Christian or liberal background, as well as among ecumenically oriented mainline churches.[6]

The student Christian movement participated already under the umbrella of the United Student Christian Council (USCC) with great enthusiasm in the rising civil rights movement, and continued its involvement after the merger of the USCC, the Student Volunteer Movement, and the Inter Seminary Movement in 1959 as the National Student Christian Federation (NSCF). King, at the 1959 Ecumenical Student Quadrennial Conference on Christian World Mission, challenged participants to live out the claims of the gospel by taking part in the struggle to eliminate racial discrimination. From that event on it was customary for all major gatherings of the NSCF and its member organizations to give ample time to issues of race and civil rights and to brief participants on civil disobedience, nonviolent methods, and an appropriate code of conduct for street demonstrations and for the possibility of arrest. For many students the conferences offered a first experience of joining picket lines in front of government or business institutions which practiced racial discrimination, or of interracial prayer demonstrations in segregated churches. Campus ministers and numerous other clergy took part in these activities, and many of them found a new use for clerical garb on such occasions. By its involvement in the struggle for racial justice in the fifties and early sixties the American student Christian movement became instrumental in creating the framework for a broader activist student movement.

Random House, Vintage Books, 1966); Peter L. Berger and Richard J. Neuhaus, *Movement and Revolution* (New York: Doubleday, Anchor Books, 1970); Carl Oglesby and Richard Shaull, *Containment and Change* (New York: Macmillan, 1967); Bruce Douglass, ed., *Reflections on Protest: Student Presence in Political Conflict* (Richmond: John Knox Press, 1967); Alan D. Austin, ed., *The Revolutionary Imperative: Essays toward a New Humanity* (Nashville: Board of Education of the Methodist Church, 1966); Bruce Douglass, ed., *Trying Times: American Politics in Transition from the Sixties to the Seventies* (Geneva: WSCF, 1971).

6. One of the most important expositions of the objectives and methods of the civil rights movement of the sixties is Martin Luther King Jr., *Why We Can't Wait* (New York: New American Library, Signet, 1963).

Various protest actions drew wide publicity. The demonstrations were risky ventures, especially in the southern United States, where right-wing organizations and the police frequently used violence to try to crush demonstrations, and where state laws provided virtually no protection for the protesters. As demonstrations reached the big industrial centers of the North, violence also spread and took new forms.

The movement soon reached mass proportions. The march on Washington at the end of August 1963, led by Martin Luther King, was a significant breakthrough. New legislation against all forms of racial discrimination was initiated. On July 2, 1964, President Johnson signed the new Civil Rights Act. In 1965 he ordered federal troops to protect civil rights marchers in Selma, Alabama.

Although the movement began to break up into different factions after the first major successes, it continued in the form of the black power movement or black caucuses to be a major factor in the wider student protest movement.

2.3.2. University Protest[7]

Another element of student protest grew out of frustrations over the changing character of higher education and the loss of traditional academic values. Students felt themselves to be mere cogs in the wheels of the education industry. Universities had been replaced by "multiversities," which for students represented a technocratic approach to learning and the replacement of intrinsic human values by those of instrumental knowledge and technological growth. Scientific research, for instance, was serving military and space industries to an increasing degree.

The free speech movement was born on the Berkeley campus of the University of California in 1964, where student enrollment at that time was some twenty-seven thousand. The president of the univer-

---

7. A thorough analysis of the free speech movement, written from a perspective sympathetic to the student protest, is found in Sheldon S. Wolin and John H. Schaar, *The Berkeley Rebellion and Beyond: Essays on Politics and Education in the Technological Society* (New York: Random House, a New York Review Book, 1970).

sity was Clark Kerr, a well-known educator and author of the book *The Uses of the University,* in which he advocated the concept of a value-free, nonideological, and pragmatic university to serve a technologically advanced and pluralistic society. Kerr's approach to the management of higher education was copied from that of industry and big corporations. The campus was in his words a "knowledge factory."

The initial impetus for the free speech movement came from the university administrators' effort to ban student political rallies at the entrance to the campus. They feared that the increased student activism, which had been further boosted by the civil rights movement, would tarnish the image of the university. Unexpectedly, without consulting recognized student organizations, the administration announced, on September 14, that the strip of road used by the students for their rallies was not a city street area but university property. As student political activity on campus had already been banned, no student missed the point of the move. The university administration had expanded its interpretation of the state constitution, according to which "the University shall be entirely independent of all political or sectarian influence . . . in the appointment of its Regents and in the administration of its affairs."

The students responded without delay. They formed a united front, ranging from extreme right to extreme left, to urge the administration to restore a free speech area and to review the university's rules, which in the view of the students did not correspond to the intent of the state constitution. And so the free speech movement was born.

After a series of contestations by students, followed by retractions and revised rulings by the administration, the new movement rapidly gained momentum. The chancellor suspended eight student leaders from the university on September 28, whereupon hundreds of students appeared in front of Sproul Hall, the administration building, for the first mass demonstration, and some two hundred students staged within the building a sit-in which continued into the next day. A faculty group bypassed the chancellor and appealed to the president of the university to compromise. He agreed to negotiate, but first called for a five-hundred-man police force for the campus. Under such a threat, the students called their demonstration off, and the president in turn agreed to restore the privileges of some of the suspended groups and to establish a joint committee of students, faculty, and administration to study the rules.

When the demonstrations had been stopped, the chancellor, with the encouragement of the politically appointed regents of the university, ignored the conciliatory initiatives of President Kerr and resorted to new disciplinary measures. A new series of confrontations followed, which reached a climax when nearly eight hundred students invaded Sproul Hall for a new sit-in and the governor of the state called in six hundred policemen to arrest the demonstrators. As a result, the faculty went on strike. This became the turning point for Berkeley and also for the spread of the movement as a whole.

Because of the reputation of Berkeley and its president, and because of the massive involvement of police force, the events attracted national and international publicity. The protests against authoritarian university structures and for a participatory style of education spread across the whole continent and created problems for hundreds of university and college administrators for several years.

The free speech movement itself started as a moral protest in defense of the traditional rights and values of liberal education. Although stimulated by the civil rights movement, it was, at its inception, conspicuously nonideological. It adopted and represented a new style: its language became radical and its tactics aggressive. It focused on two specific questions. Should the university put restrictions on the exercise of political rights by students on campus? Should the university discipline students for their advocacy of off-campus civil disobedience, such as a sit-in at a hotel practicing segregation? The students assumed that off-campus illegal acts were a matter for the courts and not the university.

As the conflict escalated, the university protest, triggered by the free speech movement, amalgamated into the wider student rebellion which later became identified with the New Left and its umbrella organization, Students for a Democratic Society. At the same time the free speech movement prepared ground also for "the making of the counterculture" which spread much beyond the New Left and lasted longer.

The Christian community on campus became involved in the Berkeley movement at once. Campus ministers played a quiet but recognized role in acting as channels of communication between students, faculty, and President Kerr. Members of Christian student organizations took an active part in the demonstrations and in the free speech movement. The events of Berkeley and the spread of the movement profoundly influenced the NSCF. The pattern of the University Christian Movement (UCM), which replaced the NSCF in 1966, reflected an anti-institutional and antiauthoritarian sentiment directed against the structures of churches, traditional ecumenicity, and higher education, and maintained an uncritical faith in spontaneity and a participatory style.

2.3.3. Antiwar Movement

The third and by far the most influential element of protest arose against U.S. military involvement in Vietnam. The war had escalated in the middle of 1964, with regular bombing of targets in North Vietnam beginning in February 1965. In March the first American combat troops were sent to Vietnam. Draft into the U.S. armed forces was extended in July and again in October 1965. Student reaction was immediate. The first campus teach-in on Vietnam was organized on March 24, 1965, at the University of Michigan, with three thousand students and faculty participating. A little later, the University of California teach-in attracted over twelve thousand. Teach-ins were held at hundreds of colleges and universities. The State Department began to send representatives to interpret U.S. policy.

After the teach-ins, students began to act against the draft. A large number avoided it by emigrating to Canada, and others to Europe. No accurate figures are available, but according to estimates the number of draft émigrés may have reached thirty thousand. Another form of protest was to return draft cards to authorities or to burn them publicly. The hardening of protests was met by tough government and military measures. Toward the end of the decade violence became increasingly frequent. Demonstrations were surrounded by the National Guard and armed police forces equipped for riot control. The killing of four students during a peaceful demonstration at Kent State University on June 4, 1970, was a sad climax to the antiwar movement among American students.

2.3.4. *Latin America and South Africa in Focus*

Brought together by Students for a Democratic Society, the three main streams of American student protest continued side by side with the protest activities against U.S. policy on Latin America, and against apartheid and colonial domination in southern Africa, through most of the decade.

Following the Cuban revolution and the countermeasures of the United States to contain the revolutionary forces in the hemisphere, the departments of Latin American studies at North American universities became centers for academic activity critical of the American government's policy. A group of radical scholars and students founded the North American Congress on Latin America (NACLA), a university-based organization, to provide an institutional base for student protests and to serve as an American forum for work on alternative economic models and development policies in Latin America. The departments of Latin American studies of several leading American universities agreed to sponsor this activity.

The decisions of the John F. Kennedy administration aimed at changing the American image and role in developing countries in general and in Latin America in particular did not convince American radicals of a change in the government's intentions. They considered the founding of the Peace Corps and the launching of an intergovernmental program on economic development, called Alliance for Progress, as a mere cover-up for American imperialism and hemispheric domination.

A parallel development followed the massacre of Sharpville and the subsequent rise of concern for South Africa. What started as spontaneous protest activity against apartheid and American economic involvement in South Africa became coordinated research and advocacy activity within the student Christian movement. Representatives of mainline churches which had mission activity in southern Africa joined the efforts launched by students. Street demonstrations against leading banks and industrial corporations were followed by church leaders' protest speeches at shareholders' meetings and by private and public encounters between representatives of churches and the banking and business community. This activity was backed by consistent study and research. While campus-based committees on southern

Africa mushroomed all over the United States, student activists found a solid support group from within churches. The work continued under the umbrella of the National Council of Churches through the period in which the UCM and related radical student activities began to crumble. The Southern Africa Concerns Group, originally part of the UCM, continued to flourish in the context of the ecumenical church program long after the UCM had collapsed. Similar activity arose in Britain and gradually in continental Europe as well.

2.3.5. Disintegration of the Protest Movement

The Great Proletarian Cultural Revolution in China, which began in 1966, gave an additional ideological injection to the revolutionary aspirations of the Western neo-Marxists. The *Little Red Book* of Chairman Mao became a bestseller among students. It was, however, a romantic courtship from afar, possible only as long as the two ideological partners did not become too intimate. The relationship remained a short-lived, one-sided love affair void of real political significance, but it showed Western students' vulnerability to propaganda.

Ideologically the student protest began to develop a more distinctly New Left orientation from the mid-sixties onward. The California-based German philosopher Herbert Marcuse became the guru of the "movement." His books, especially *One-Dimensional Man,* became bestsellers in the United States as well as in France and Germany. His neo-Marxism drew on existentialism and Freudian psychoanalysis in attempting a comprehensive analysis of late capitalist society. As a result, the student protest movement in North America and, to a large degree, in western Europe developed an anarcho-Marxist direction which appealed to disillusioned liberals in the United States and to the more doctrinaire left in Europe, which was seeking a left alternative to Soviet-style communism. When the movement then began to split, the emerging factions moved in opposite directions, including everything between hippyism and anarchist terrorism or between humanist socialism and established Marxism-Leninism.[8]

8. Peter Collier and David Horowitz, former editorial staff of *Ramparts* magazine, describe in their book *Destructive Generation: Second Thoughts about the Sixties* (New

52

On the American scene the events around the Democratic National Convention in Chicago, August 1968, became a turning point for the New Left and the Students for a Democratic Society. The resorting to provocative violence, to which police responded with force, in order to demonstrate existing "class contradictions" in the USA, to weaken the political influence of liberals and to deliberately incite a right-wing backlash, considered necessary to speed the forthcoming revolution, was a blow to the credibility of the militant leaders and the beginning of the end of broad-based student support of the New Left.

2.4. The Protest Movement and the Federation

The rise of radical protest movements was evident in the life of the Federation through most of the sixties. The American member movement was most directly involved through the civil rights movement, university protests, and the antiwar activity.[9] These protest movements were followed by impressive intellectual work by involved theologians and other scholars. However, by the time the National Student Christian Federation was replaced, in 1966, by a new national organization, the University Christian Movement (UCM), which was to represent a radical form of participatory ecumenism and serve as a platform for the political activism of Christian students, such critical thought had

---

York: Summit Books, 1989) their personal experience as activist leaders of the American New Left and their total disillusionment with it when they saw the deepening rift between its stated goals and increasingly disruptive practice, including the use of violence in internal power struggles. They concluded that the movement was infected by a social "virus," the essence of which was to obliterate the values and structures essential for an organized society, and therefore the whole movement became a negation instead of an agent of humanness and justice.

9. The story of the student Christian movement in the United States, including the history of the short-lived UCM, is recorded in John B. Lindner, Alva I. Cox, and Linda-Marie Delloff, *By Faith: Christian Students among the Cloud of Witnesses* (New York: Friendship Press, 1991), although the writers have not been able fully to avoid a self-justifying, promotional note. A more critical perspective to the history of the UCM and student Christian ministries from 1960 to 1995 is given in the *Journal of Ecumenical Studies* 32, nos. 3 and 4 (1995), with L. Newton Thurber as a guest editor.

little effect on the student leaders of the newly formed UCM, who by then were caught up in the antiacademia, anti-intellectual, and anti-institutional mood.[10]

The first large gathering of the new UCM, the "Cleveland Week of Process '67," at the end of 1967, epitomized the approaching crisis of the organization and its isolation from the rest of the Federation's constituency. The timing of the Cleveland event suggested a desire to link it with the traditional Ecumenical Student Quadrennial Conferences on Christian World Mission, which had played a major role in the student Christian movement of North America as well as in the Federation worldwide. The quadrennials of 1955, 1959, and 1963, all held in Athens, Ohio, had been closely related to the Federation's Life and Mission of the Church program. The Cleveland event, however, bore no resemblance in either substance or style to the quadrennial conferences. It stemmed from the newly approved "organizing principle" of the UCM, which was "to bring about social change through the reformation of the university." The underlying assumption was that universities had a decisive influence on the social, political, and technological aspects of American society and that changing the university was therefore the key to transforming society as a whole. The main emphasis of the UCM for 1967 had been experimental education, which was to be processed by "Depth Education Groups," organized as part of the preparatory process of the Cleveland event. These groups were to form the basis for new patterns of participatory and politically involved education. Cleveland was to draw the process together and to provide an example of the new, more human education that was expected to emerge.

The "Cleveland Week of Process '67" was a free-floating participatory happening, sparkling and spontaneous, with numerous simultaneous activities and several closed-circuit TV programs produced on the spot. Some three thousand students took part. The content was to be provided entirely by participants, with no dictation "from the top." The staff organizers were to function as enablers. No input was provided in the form of lectures or background papers and no

---

10. The story of the UCM from 1966 to 1969 is presented by several of its leaders in four reflective articles and six personal comments in the *Journal of Ecumenical Studies*, no. 3 (1995): 315-83.

plenary sessions were scheduled. Participation could take the form of strolling from one Depth Education Group to another or from one exhibition stand to the next or, even more comfortably, of watching from one's bed a closed-circuit TV debate on U.S. China policy and sending comments in by telephone.

There were only two cohesive moments during the conference. One was a peace march on New Year's Eve from the hotel to the federal building where leaders of the march nailed to the door theses against the war in Vietnam. The marchers sang "Silent Night" while riot police, protected by helmets and armed with sticks, watched. The second was the Communion service during which Richard Shaull preached on the wager of faith and at the end appealed to all those who had received draft cards to place them on the collection plate for return to the authorities. It was an emotionally loaded moment. Quite a pile of draft cards was handed in. Everyone present was aware of the potential cost of the act. The preacher, too, could have been prosecuted for agitating criminal action.

The Cleveland event left many within and without the UCM with mixed feelings. Its high points were mostly for those who were searching seriously for new dimensions of Christian involvement in society. But for the UCM as a whole it was a disaster of massive proportions. It failed to offer any convincing models for education or to stimulate fresh commitment. It simply pooled the confusion of the participants and added to the fragmentation of the ecumenical student movement. As an event it was void of any compelling message or contagious vision about the Christian task in the university and the world.

The new UCM soon ran out of funds. It also failed to build any significant constituency. No membership structure nor patterns for expressing Christian commitment apart from the immediate political issues were foreseen. As the leaders pointed out, the movement was to spread and grow spontaneously. But it did not. Its field staff were hired for "movement building," which was understood as promoting and organizing action-oriented study groups on the political and educational concerns of the day. Many thought that forming ecumenical communities of Christians representing diverse traditions and interests would only inhibit this process, and any attempt to build national programs and staff services "from the top down" was viewed as a denial of the grassroots character of the movement. Churches' campus ministers who were prepared to support the new UCM and act as a bridge from the past to the future and from the movement to the institutional church were deliberately excluded from the UCM. Some of its leaders wanted activist caucuses to form the core of the movement, which as a whole was not expected to be politically or ideologically uniform, while others fought for radical ideological uniformity as the only meaningful option for the UCM.

The latter pattern did not materialize, as separate caucuses succeeded in dominating the national UCM. The most visible of these were the "radical caucus," the "black caucus," and the "women's caucus." They were to build alliances and even merge with secular groups involved in the same causes. Their agendas, however, soon ran into conflict with one another, and some were disappointed that the UCM could not provide from its national funds the subsidies they demanded. Some of the requests were massively out of proportion. Student leaders became paralyzed in the face of these developments. The few experienced senior leaders who saw what was going wrong were either intimidated into silence or ignored. Those who tried fellow traveling as a means to exert influence had no effect on events. In meeting after meeting two questions were repeated by the elected leaders: "Who are we?" and "Where are we going?" The "experimental process" came to its conclusion when the UCM General Committee voted to terminate the organization in 1969.[11]

In retrospect, the most conspicuous failure of the Federation was to allow the UCM to exist in relative isolation from the rest of the WSCF and especially from the European SCMs. As a result the Federation and its European member movements met the student revolution of 1968 poorly prepared intellectually and spiritually, without having benefited from the experience of protest movements, including their pitfalls, within the Christian community in North America.

But the leaders of the American UCM could also have benefited

---

11. The national presidents of the UCM of the era, Charlotte Bunch, Steve Schomberg, and Nelly Sale, as well as a staff member and officer, Poikail George of India, issued soon after the decisive vote statements in which they reflected on the causes and significance of the decision to discontinue the national organization. March 1969, WSCF Archives (mimeographed). See also *Journal of Ecumenical Studies,* no. 3 (1995): 351-52.

from a stronger challenge from the outside, even if listening to one another was no longer "in" among radicalized students at the end of the decade. Perhaps responsible outside voices could have supported the few doubters from among the Orthodox, Lutherans, and Episcopalians who had the stamina to question the significance of the founding assembly of the UCM, described by its leaders in triumphalistic terms as an event comparable to Pentecost. On the whole, such critical contributions went unnoticed in the midst of the ecumenical euphoria of the moment. All denominational student movements related to the former NSCF were supposed to merge into the UCM and give up their own structures and programs. Some participants saw that the UCM had built into its own self-destruct mechanism an expression of institutional suicidal drive. Most nevertheless conformed. Only the Lutheran Student Movement and the Orthodox Campus Commission decided not to close down on the grounds of their doubts about the political movement-theology and ecumenicity of the UCM. At the end of the decade the Lutheran Student Movement was the only organized expression of a national student Christian movement in the United States.

Until 1968 the Federation was surprisingly little affected by the protest movements among students. Nor did the experiences of the UCM create much of a stir among the rest of the Federation's constituency. The view from abroad was one of suspicion rather than appreciation, because of a general apprehension about U.S. influence, the seeming insensitivity of Americans toward other cultures and traditions, and their tendency to generalize their own experiences. Furthermore, SCM leaders in Europe and Asia were bewildered by what they considered an uncritical identification of the UCM with movements characteristic of the American ethos and radical fads.[12]

Signs of a new wave of student unrest did nevertheless appear in other continents in those years. The secretary for Europe, for instance,

12. The correspondence between the WSCF general secretary, Valdo Galland, and the writer, who was then the North America secretary, illustrates how difficult it was from outside North America to grasp the depth of the turn of the ecumenical student movement in the USA. Communication was not made easier by occasional statements from the USA, such as that by Professor Robert Theobold at a WSCF consultation, in which he said that it took European students five days to grasp what Americans had learned in two! Staff correspondence, WSCF Archives.

mentioned in his four-year report of 1964-68 the rise of political activity among students. After Berkeley a wave of protests had touched England, Spain, West Germany, and Italy. Its repercussions had been felt also in Prague and Warsaw. The unrest, which was still embryonic compared with events to come, arose out of disillusionment with traditional party politics. Students looked for liberation from paternalism and authoritarian and hierarchical structures. Democratization of the university and society and some form of socialism were apparent goals. But the socialism of Eastern European countries was bluntly rejected. The "Prague Spring" awakened some positive expectations, and Cuba and the People's Republic of China roused additional hopes. An interest in neo-Marxism was clearly on the rise. Marcuse, J. Habermas, Bloch, and Regis Debray provided the intellectual stimulus. Nevertheless, member movements remained rather quiet about all this until 1968.

Reports from Latin America suggested that among students the tide was turning and that the growing militarization had meant intense preparation for a new stage of struggle against repression. For the SCMs of Latin America this period marked a turn from "conscientization" to training for militancy. This was still more a matter of intellectual activity than a plan for action. The really big change came in 1968.

Consequently the rise of protest movements before 1968 made little impact on either the worldwide or the regional programs of the Federation, the content of the quarterly the *Student World,* or the production of study materials.[13] The only national movement outside the United States which in those years took the American scene seriously was that of South Africa (see chapter 11 below).

---

13. The *Student World* took up themes related to the protest movement, e.g., "Vietnam: A Symposium of International University Opinion," no. 4 (1965); "A New University for a New World," no. 1 (1966); "The Internationalization of the University," no. 2 (1967); and "The Future of Education," no. 1 (1968). Special issues of *Federation News* included an issue on "Presence and Politics," no. 4 (1966), and on SCMs and the war in Vietnam, no. 4 (1967). The WSCF Africa magazine, *Presence,* published an issue on "The Christian Meaning of Revolution," no. 2 (1966). The WSCF Latin America magazine, *Testimonium,* published issues on "Christian Presence in the Latin American Revolution," 10, no. 1 (1965); "Christian Faith and Marxism," 10, no. 2 (1965); and "Political Power," 11, no. 4 (1966). In addition, forty study documents related to the China Study Program were circulated from 1965 to 1968.

CHAPTER 3

1968: Utopias and Traumas

3.1. French Revolution

Each generation has certain years engraved in its collective memory, some more deeply than others. For one whole generation 1968 was such a year — a year of student upheavals and revolutionary utopias and traumas. Political, academic, student, and church leaders were marked permanently by the events of that year.

The epicenter of the political and ideological tremors was in France, where the May Revolution nearly toppled President Charles de Gaulle and his government and sent shock waves all over the world.[1] The events in France were a great stimulus for revolutionary activity and mass protests among students in Western Europe and beyond. Young people were captured by a utopian vision of total democracy, freedom, justice, participation; the fulfillment of a new humanity.

The detonation of revolutionary activity in France did not come out of the blue. The Algerian war (1955-62) had deeply scarred the French conscience. Its brutality and the affliction which it had caused

---

1. There is no shortage of literature on the revolutionary events of 1968. A particularly helpful inside account of events in France is given by Patrick Seale and Maureen McConville in *French Revolution, 1968* (New York: Penguin Books, 1968). Another important source is Daniel and Gabriel Cohn-Bendit, *Obsolete Communism: The Left-Wing Alternative* (London: André Deutsch Limited, 1968). Claire Maury reflects on the meaning of the events in her article "The May Movement in France," *Student World*, nos. 3 and 4 (1969): 271-84.

for the civilian population had caused a trauma among French youth. The longer the war lasted, the more young people joined the protest against it. Some decided to cooperate with the Algerian National Liberation Front, some deserted the French army, and many became draft resisters, ready to accept five-year prison terms. The influence of the French National Union of Students (UNEF) and the Union of Communist Students (UEC) grew dramatically as these organizations became the main channels of student protest.

Another element was the rising protest against the escalation of American military involvement in Vietnam. The experience of the Indo-Chinese war (1946-54), which resulted in the withdrawal of France from the region, meant that French public opinion, and especially that of the political left, was very critical of American involvement. The arrival of American draft resisters and war deserters seeking asylum in France added to this antiwar mood in universities and among supporters of the left. In the midst of these rising protests a rift emerged between the "official" left, which advocated peace in Vietnam, and the militant wing of the UEC, which was opposed to any ideological compromise and endorsed a revolutionary position. As a rival to the peace movement of the Communist Party, the militants initiated the National Vietnam Committee (CVN) with its slogan "FNL vaincra!" (The National Liberation Front will win). Soon after, the militant wing was ousted from the party and its student organization. As a countermove, on April 2, 1968, the militants — some 120 from sixteen French cities — founded a new organization called Communist Revolutionary Youth, which rapidly gained influence among youth and students.[2]

A third element was the mounting frustration of students and

2. Perspectives on the world scene should not be forgotten when the revolutionary activities of 1968 among students are reviewed. Biafra had seceded from Nigeria in May 1967, causing a bitter war that ended only in January 1970. The Six-Day War in the Middle East was fought in June 1967, having profound consequences for Palestinian liberation movements and contributing to further radicalization of Arab students. The election of Alexander Dubček as first secretary of the Czech Communist Party in January 1968 marked the beginning of a political thaw in Czechoslovakia, called the "Prague Spring," and stimulated a vision of "socialism with a human face" inside and outside the country. Nineteen sixty-eight was also the year of the assassinations of Martin Luther King Jr. and Robert F. Kennedy.

many university teachers over the French educational system, which was more centralized and authoritarian than that of any other country in Western Europe. Housing conditions and outdated dormitory rules, combined with educational methods designed more for the mass production of competent manpower than for the education of the whole person, contributed to an atmosphere of confrontation. The blatant insensitivity of university administrators and government authorities toward student grievances fueled the mood of dissent. These elements were tied together by the revolutionary ideology of the New Left, turning French universities into powder kegs. The inevitable explosion came in the spring of 1968.

The drama began to unfold in the early hours of March 18, when a radical left student commando crossed the Seine River and, using a few small bombs, blew out the windows of the Paris offices of the Chase Manhattan Bank, the Bank of America, and Trans World Airlines. The windows of the American Express office were shattered some nights later. In the morning of March 22 the police, determined to stop violent antiwar incidents, arrested five young men, all members of extremist organizations, accusing them of the explosions. In the evening of the same day hundreds of students gathered in the Nanterre annex of the University of Paris to protest against these arrests. A group of demonstrators crashed into the administration building and, after a long and fiery debate, decided to form a Council of Students, or Student Soviet. This event marked the beginning of a new force known as the Movement of March 22.

In 1967, the Nanterre campus had already become a center for radical left activism among French students. It now became the testing ground for "direct action" — a catchword for the tactics of the whole May Revolution — under the leadership of Daniel Cohn-Bendit, a brilliant twenty-two-year-old student of German background.

In the following weeks a massive student revolt ensued. The epicenter moved to the Sorbonne, the pride of French academic life for centuries. After tumultuous events, street battles, the building of barricades, the burning of cars, and fights with the police, students took over the Sorbonne campus and, for more than a month, made it the fortress of the newly founded Student Soviet. For the occupiers it was to be a living illustration of the new society which was expected to emerge and which was to be run on principles of direct democracy.

61

It was interpreted as a resurrection of the Paris Commune of nearly one hundred years earlier. The street battles continued with varying intensity while government and police authorities debated tactics for quelling the insurrection. The use of police and military force, which resulted in escalated violence, alternated with efforts by university and government authorities to negotiate with leaders of the revolution. The war between the French establishment and a liberated Sorbonne ruled by the revolutionary Student Soviet dominated life in the Latin Quarter for several weeks in May and June 1968.

When the large-scale riots began in Paris on May 3, leading to street battles and the takeover of the Sorbonne, the revolution spread almost instantly to other universities all over the country. Demonstrations took place in Aix-en-Provence, Bordeaux, Caen, Clermont-Ferrand, Dijon, Grenoble, Montpellier, Nantes, Rouen, and Toulouse. What had looked like isolated incidents of student unrest turned into a mass insurrection. The climax came when the young leaders of the student revolution succeeded in creating an alliance with the left labor organizations and some ten million French workers participated in a general strike. What had begun as a student protest evolved into a political revolution and the attempted overthrow of de Gaulle's regime by the combined force of students and workers.

The 1968 French revolution was a unique event among the many student upheavals of the sixties. The alliance, though short-lived, between students and workers was its most remarkable achievement. It affected the future development of the ideology of the revolutionary New Left profoundly and contributed to changes in the whole political left of France. Student-worker alliances became a recurring theme in the radicalizing European SCMs in the subsequent years.

Another conspicuous characteristic of the movement was the quality and youth of its leadership and its almost total reliance on teenage supporters, especially during its early stage. Thus the scope and impact of the movement took the establishment, including the middle-class parents of the revolutionary students, by surprise. Nor did the established political parties have any inkling of what was to come. The party most severely threatened by the events was the French Communist Party, the leaders of which were unaware of the ferment in its own ranks and the challenge to come from its own left.

The movement never generated a single identifiable revolutionary organization, although the Student Soviet was an attempt to create a qualitatively new social organization based on direct democracy. The occupiers of the Sorbonne therefore gathered each night for the Assembly, which elected a fifteen-person Occupation Committee for twenty-four hours at a time. Any person who was authorized to take action on behalf of others had constantly to give an account of himself or herself to the whole commune.

The May Revolution was also a very French phenomenon. Its young leaders were knowledgeable about French history and the history of revolutionary movements. They drew heavily on the intellectual heritage of France. Allegations that it was the result of an international conspiracy with its roots in the USSR proved to be without foundation.[3]

The stories of the events of the first dramatic weeks include testimonies about a sense of community and comradeship which was unknown to the impersonal and individualistic way of life in French universities and which had been lost in trade unions as well. For many of those who were in charge of occupying university buildings and factories, providing temporary shelter and food for the strikers, arranging for improvised first-aid and health services, and even keeping the occupied facilities clean and sanitary, all of this was an almost apocalyptic experience. The solidarity, the care for one another under the threat of the armed forces of law and order, and the possibility of enjoying life without the conveniences provided by the bourgeois establishment confirmed belief in the viability of a new, just, and loving order of society. This experience generated a surprising amount of goodwill among the general public during the initial stage of the revolution.

After some weeks of tension and street fighting the mood changed abruptly, however. Divisions cropped up among the leaders. The idealism of the members of the Student Soviet was misused by the underdogs of society and even by criminals. Internal discipline began

3. During the consultation between the delegations of the Student Council of the USSR and the WSCF in 1970 (see chapter 7), and again during my visit to the headquarters of the communist-controlled International Union of Students in Prague in 1972, the student leaders of the Soviet bloc expressed deep suspicions about the New Left and its anarcho-Marxist ideologies. See also Seale and McConville, pp. 40-41, 49-56.

to erode. The original good order and cleanliness of the occupied facilities vanished. An on-the-spot reporter observed that the last days of the Student Soviet were as sad as the first had been heroic. The leaders moved quietly out of the Sorbonne. When the police finally moved in and drove out the last of the students and teachers, they met with very little resistance.

The French elections on June 23 and 30 became the anticlimax of the May Revolution. The Gaullists won with an overwhelming vote and the left was thrown on the defensive. However, the revolutionary ferment could not be destroyed, even though its influence was confined to intellectuals and the shrinking ranks of the remaining anarcho-Marxist elite. The expectation of imminent radical change and the dream of a new humanity and a new society had vanished beyond the horizon. All that remained of the grand utopia was trauma over the revolution which wasn't.

3.2. Repercussions

The May 1968 uprising, without regard to its shortcomings, added momentum to revolutionary student activism all over Western Europe. The signals coming from the French events seemed to be that the revolutionary movement was reaching global proportions. Demonstrations and upheavals were reported from all over the continent. Their message was received with enthusiasm by many and with fear by many more. The shooting of the charismatic radical student leader Rudi Dutschke in Berlin on April 11, 1968, was another spark spreading revolutionary fire to German universities and providing the warning signal of the possible escalation of indiscriminate violence. The defeat of the revolutionaries in France did not quench students' thirst for radical change nor quell their disenchantment with the bourgeois establishment.

The rise of revolutionary activism in Europe coincided with further polarization in America. Out of the civil rights movement had come the black power movement. The Students for a Democratic Society had begun to split and some of its extremists had formed openly anarchist factions. The government decided to meet anarchist force with police force. From April 23 to April 30, students at Columbia University in New York staged a massive sit-in against the war in Vietnam; police intervened and arrested 628 demonstrators. The confrontations grew more violent and reached a particularly unhappy climax at the demonstration in front of the Democratic Party Convention, August 1968, in Chicago. The conduct of the demonstrators mirrored their disillusionment and their loss of vision for a more human society. The brutality of the police mirrored their abandonment of the liberal values embedded in the American ideal of democracy.

In spite of the rapid fragmentation of the French revolutionary front, the ideas and models generated at that time reappeared later in ideological debates in the Federation: interest in the early writings of Karl Marx; distinguishing between Lenin's ideas and Soviet reality; a return to Trotsky's concept of global revolution; the desire to build a united front of students and workers; ideas and concepts drawn from "direct action"; experiencing revolutionary fulfillment in the "politicization of everyday life" and the daily contestation of power structures by a nonbureaucratic style of life.

The May Revolution changed the character of the French SCM, which for some time had been struggling to define its identity under the impact of the Algerian war and the restless ideological debate in the country ruled by President de Gaulle. The leaders of the SCM followed in the footsteps of the leaders of the May Revolution, while its traditional constituency disappeared and its ties with churches were severed.[4]

3.3. The 1968 Assembly of the WCC in Uppsala

Revolutionary winds had rocked the World Council of Churches (WCC) for some time in conjunction with its programs dealing with issues of the responsibility of churches for international affairs, development, and social change.[5] However, only at its Fourth Assembly in

4. The general secretary of the French SCM was Pierre Brenac, whose comments can be found in the WSCF Archives.

5. The theme of revolution came into the limelight in the ecumenical movement particularly at the World Conference on Church and Society, Geneva, 1966, which

65

Uppsala, July 4-20, 1968, did the WCC as a whole have to face the challenge of the revolutionary world, not only as a topic for its program emphases, but as an explosive — even divisive — challenge within its own ranks. This resulted in the most thorough change in its orientation since its founding, a change sealed formally in the Assembly and in the subsequent meetings of the Central Committee. The change was not limited to those programs which were established to deal with the critical issues of society and conflicts of international life, but affected also emphases in mission, evangelization, education, and traditional Faith and Order concerns. The change of direction was reflected in the revision of WCC structures and staff roles. "Prophetic" leadership to complement or even replace "low-profile" serving of member churches became a rising trend. Norman Goodall, the editor of the Uppsala Assembly report, wrote:

> The most obvious and widely acknowledged feature of the Assembly was its preoccupation — at times, almost, its obsession — with the revolutionary ferment of our time, with questions of social and international responsibility, of war and peace and economic justice, with the pressing, agonizing physical needs of men, with the plight of the underprivileged, the homeless and starving, and with the most radical contemporary rebellions against all "establishment," civil and religious.[6]

---

dealt with "Christian Response to the Technical and Social Revolutions of Our Time." Three speakers, D. H. Wendland of Germany, Richard Shaull of the USA, and Vitali Borovoy of the USSR, had been asked to highlight the theme "The Challenge and Relevance of Theology to the Social Revolutions of Our Time." Their presentations and the subsequent discussion were, in retrospect, a prelude to an encounter with revolutionary movements within the ecumenical family itself in the years following. See *Christians in the Technical and Social Revolutions of Our Time,* the official report of the World Conference on Church and Society, Geneva, July 12-26, 1966 (Geneva: WCC, 1967), 232 pages. Ronald Preston gives a compact and helpful analytical summary of the ecumenical discussion on social issues in the aftermath of the WCC Geneva Conference 1966 until the Uppsala Assembly 1968, *Confusions in Christian Social Ethics: Problems for Geneva and Rome* (London: SCM Press, 1994), pp. 24-29.

6. *Uppsala 1968: The Official Report of the Fourth Assembly of the WCC, July 1968,* p. xvii.

The whole tone and temper of Uppsala made it clear that a new age is upon us. The winds of change have become hurricanes. . . . The issues discussed in the following pages (of the Report) and the forces which thrust them, often violently, upon the attention of the Assembly illustrate the startling newness of the Christian task and the largely uncharted territory into which the ecumenical movement moves. Within the domestic life and leadership of the WCC change is no less in evidence. . . . (These changes) become symbolic of what may well prove to be a radical change of direction with consequences which cannot yet be measured.[7]

It is obvious today that the turmoil at the Uppsala Assembly had several roots. First, world events heightened the sense of drama in Uppsala '68. Martin Luther King Jr., who was murdered on April 4, had agreed to give a keynote address. A taped message of his from an earlier occasion was relayed to the Assembly. The so-called Biafran War which was raging in Nigeria caused bitter exchanges on the Assembly floor. The tensions in the Middle East affected delegates. Vietnam peace talks had been launched under a cloud of uncertainty. The progress of liberalization in Czechoslovakia and its vision of a "socialism with a human face" attracted much attention among participants at a time of unabated ideological tension.

Second, the rise of protest movements and student revolts, especially the May Revolution in France, had produced a ferment among the Uppsala delegates in general and among youth participants in particular. Many of the youth who had gathered for a pre-Assembly conference identified themselves with the revolutionary student movement and consequently were keen to interpret the crises of the world and the proceedings of the Assembly from their newly adopted ideological position and their recent experiences of "direct action." Their contribution to the Assembly debates, their dialogue with the leaders of the WCC, and their demonstrations made a tangible impact on the Assembly proceedings.

Third, the WCC had a new general secretary, Eugene Carson Blake of the USA, who epitomized the social activist tradition within American Protestantism. He was known for his uncompromising stand

7. *Uppsala 1968,* pp. xvii-xx.

against racism and his participation in mass demonstrations in the civil rights movement led by King, as well as for his lack of interest in traditional confessional theology, which he was not afraid to reveal in rather blunt terms.

Fourth, trends parallel to those in the ecumenical movement had been observed in the Roman Catholic Church under the leadership of Pope John XXIII. They were displayed at the Second Vatican Council, and they roused new hopes for a rapprochement between the WCC and the Roman Catholic Church. These trends added to the enthusiasm among delegates to Uppsala for opening a new chapter in the ecumenical movement. It was thought that emphasizing contextuality — the world setting the agenda for the church — was the fastest way to bridge the gap between the WCC and the Roman Catholic Church. Plans for a joint Roman Catholic–WCC agency, the Joint Committee on Society, Development and Peace (SODEPAX), to be mandated to deal with issues of social justice, development, and peace, seemed to confirm this view.

Fifth, Uppsala was a turning point in the representation of the Third World, not only numerically but in terms of issues and emphases. The Assembly went all out to rid the WCC, its programs and its image, of any signs of Western domination or of vestiges of colonial attitudes. It thereby discouraged critical discussion and imposed a kind of self-censorship on representatives of churches from the North in all matters of concern for the South.

After Uppsala new programs were initiated. The two best known were the Program to Combat Racism (PCR) and the development program under the auspices of a new Commission on the Churches' Participation in Development (CCPD), whose mandate was to target the causes of poverty and economic injustice, and of the deepening rift between the poor and the rich nations. Gradually a preference for an ideologically predetermined approach in matters of social and economic development crept in, and an open discussion of differing viewpoints was hardly possible. Economists who were critical of ideological oversimplifications became a pariah class for the emerging radical development elite of the WCC.

The unit responsible for international political issues, the Commission of the Churches on International Affairs (CCIA), was restructured and its working style revamped. Previous emphases on quiet diplomacy and the use of professionals in foreign affairs who came

68

from member churches were scaled down, and a "prophetic" role involving the issuing of public statements was upgraded. The new commission was to be a breakthrough for the entry of issues and perspectives of the Third World on the agenda of the WCC and for broadening the representation of different regions on the commission. Inclusiveness overtook competence as a priority.

The unit on Urban Industrial Mission (UIM) was also redesigned and became the coordinator of a network of action groups functioning on the fringe of, or outside, member churches. These were mainly social activist groups, often aligned with movements of the Left. Communication between the UIM (later Urban Rural Mission, URM) and member churches was at best fragmentary.

The once very visible Youth Department was discontinued; only a one-person secretariat was kept. The theory was that youth should be integrated in every function and unit of the WCC. With this decision ecumenical work camps, which had played a much appreciated role in the ecumenical education of youth, disappeared. Instead a few "professional" youth found their way into the membership of the Central Committee and the staff and were confined, almost by definition, to representing the rebellious generation, and were therefore effectively imprisoned by the role of radical dissidents.

The injection of revolutionary elements into the WCC was to contribute sooner or later to some inevitable changes. It stimulated new program initiatives; moved the center of gravity of ecumenical endeavors to the churches of Africa, Asia, and Latin America; and sensitized churches of the North to the voices of impoverished and deprived nations and groups of people. However, the distance between the WCC and its member churches increased as the Council and its staff were tempted to go over the heads of member churches and define in isolation what the world expected from them. As a result some polarity emerged between the staff members who aspired to a clear profile for the WCC on political and social issues and those who treasured a balance between continuity and renewal and for whom emphases on mission, service, and unity were helpful in maintaining close touch with member churches, both weak and strong. Eugene Carson Blake, the general secretary, warned repeatedly against the danger of "polarization" in churches and the WCC.

Despite all the talk about a radically new direction, much of the work of the WCC was carried on after Uppsala in continuity with the previous era. Entire units of the WCC developed their programs on foundations laid before Uppsala. Programs and units such as Faith and Order, Church and Society, Commissions on World Mission and Evangelism (CWME) and Inter-Church Aid, Refugee and World Service (CICARWS), and the Publications Department had been on the frontiers of ecumenical endeavors from the beginning, and therefore did not see the need to allow a new wave of revolutionary enthusiasm to create sudden massive shifts of emphasis in the ecumenical movement.

During the Assembly the Swedish SCM ran a parallel program for the Assembly's youth participants and stewards. Speakers and church leaders were invited to the regular late-evening gatherings for interviews and dialogue. These occasions gave the youth participants some information and insights for preparing their interventions and public demonstrations, and gave the senior leaders a feel for the thinking of the young people at the Assembly. The former general secretary of the WCC and the WSCF, W. A. Visser 't Hooft, appeared on the program, as did Archbishop Martti Simojoki of Finland and many others. Although a few signs of frustration about the church and flashes of revolutionary bluntness occurred, the youth at these evening gatherings appeared moderate, even tame, compared with those who had participated in previous weeks' events in France and elsewhere, and what was to come at the WSCF events following Uppsala '68.

3.4. World Student Conference — Turku 1968 *mid-30 July*

Back in 1965 the WSCF had decided to prepare a World Student Conference, to be held in Finland prior to the next General Committee meeting. The initiative arose, in part, from critical voices at the 1964 General Committee meeting in Argentina which suggested that the Federation was losing touch with the new generation of students. The world conference was to be a genuine student event, planned and led by students. The Planning Committee restricted staff participation to a bare minimum. The committee had two cochairpersons: Betty Milligan, the student president of the Canadian SCM, and Peter Grant of the British SCM, a graduate student at Cambridge University. The

70

staff member to whom the coordination of the planning was entrusted, Bruce Douglass, age twenty-three, was himself a Yale divinity student who had interrupted his studies to serve as the secretary of the WSCF Political Commission from 1965 to 1968. For a year before the conference the implementation of the plans was the responsibility of William Corzine, a member of the national staff of the campus ministry of the Methodist church in the USA. The Planning Committee met October 12-18, 1966, in Commugny near Geneva for its first and only full meeting.[8]

The planning was carried out with unusual thoroughness. The objectives were carefully considered, the quotas and criteria for participation spelled out in detail, and the program, in which a reaction against the felt paternalism of the 1960 Strasbourg Life and Mission Teaching Conference was apparent, was designed to ensure a balance between flexibility and disciplined study.

Turku '68 was to be a *world* conference and a *student* conference. The emphasis on the world meant not only that its participants were to come from all regions, but that the conference was to be about the world and for the world. Participation was to be open to student members of SCMs, and the running of the conference was also to be fully in student hands. Academic and SCM staff were to be invited, but only as expert advisers and speakers. The plans for theological work followed the contextual and functional pattern. There were to be no special, exclusively theological seminars or topics. The theological thinking should arise out of the study of secular problems which formed the topics for the five seminars of the conference. The concept of secular theology as developed in the sixties, as reflected in the

8. The Planning Committee was to include two members, who had to be students, from each of the six regions. The members attending the Cartigny meeting in 1966 were: Betty Milligan, Canada, cochairperson; Gerard van't Spijker, Netherlands; Howard Spencer, USA; Rubens Bueno, Brazil; Peter Grant, United Kingdom, cochairperson; Geoffrey Nwaougu, Nigeria; Dayalan Devanesen, India; Eugene Zau, Hong Kong; Alfredo Bianco, Uruguay; Hanna Guirguis, Egypt; Pares Ditar, Lebanon. Staff members of the Planning Committee were Bruce Douglass, USA; Moonkyu Kang, Korea; Risto Lehtonen, Finland; and Aaron Tolen, Cameroon. Valdo Galland, the general secretary, and Martin Conway, WSCF study secretary, were invited to be present for part of the time. Report of the Meeting of the Planning Committee of the World Student Conference, WSCF Archives.

"Christian Presence" document of 1964 and spreading as a fad in "theologies" of social change, secularization, urbanization, and revolution, was accepted by the Planning Committee as the foundation for its theological reflection.

The structure of the conference was built around five seminars: (1) "Being Human in the Modern World"; (2) "Politics, Power and Social Change"; (3) "Rich Nations, Poor Nations: The Development Dilemma"; (4) "Technological Revolution in the Life of Man"; and (5) "New Universities for a New World." These seminars were to take up most of the available time. They were to draw on the expertise of the invited resource persons from different regions. Toward the end of the conference another solid block of time was to be given to "strategy sessions" which were to convert the ideas from the seminars, region by region, into program emphases and proposals. The conference was to begin with an introductory day and a half during which participants were to become acquainted with one another, with the plans and procedures for the conference, and with the Federation's work as a whole. Jürgen Moltmann, who was well known for his book *Theology of Hope,* was scheduled to give a keynote address for which he had chosen the topic "God in the Revolution." It was also foreseen that every afternoon an hour would be spent on theological reflection, led by a group of involved scholars. Daily worship was scheduled for half an hour at the end of each afternoon, with emphasis on new forms of worship. On Sunday participants were invited to different churches in Turku, where many of the leaders preached the sermon. At the end of the conference reports from the five seminars were to be made available to each participant and the results of strategy meetings were to be pulled together and passed on to the WSCF General Assembly scheduled to begin two days after the end of Turku '68.

Much effort had been put into the planning. Study materials were circulated ahead of time to all delegates. Against all odds, a heavy fund-raising effort had made possible a conference of 261 student delegates, representing all the regions. Together with resource persons, a few speakers, staff, and interpreters, the total number of participants was about 300.

The list of resource persons was quite impressive given the circumstances and financial limitations. They included Jürgen Moltmann of Germany, Paul Abrecht of the USA (a theologian and economist and executive director of Church and Society of the WCC), Ruben Alves of Brazil (visiting professor at Union Theological Seminary in New York), Bola Ige of Nigeria (a lawyer and politician), Robert Jungk of Austria (a renowned physicist and philosopher of science), Laila Shurkyl El Hamamsy of Egypt (an anthropologist and specialist on population problems), Otto Klein of the CSSR (a faculty member of the Philosophical Institute of the Academy of Sciences in Prague), Paul Lin of China (teaching history at McGill University, Montreal), and Ross Terrill of Australia (a scholar on government at Harvard University and a journalist on Asian politics).

Right from the beginning of the conference the reality proved very different from the carefully laid plans and expectations. Delegates who had arrived from the sites of recent student uprisings, some with experience of the barricades and street battles in Paris, and those who had come from Uppsala frustrated about their lack of influence on the WCC Assembly, made it clear that the program and leaders of the conference had to be changed to serve the revolution. The right of the student planning committee to function as a "steering committee," as had been assumed, was questioned. The role of resource persons was restricted, so much so that some were told not to give the papers which they had been asked to prepare for seminars. On top of all this ideological turmoil, the translation equipment broke down. Ruben Alves, who was probably the best-known radical theologian of the Presbyterian Church in Brazil, was booed down as an establishment figure.

After some days of fighting over procedure, an extraordinary evening plenary was called for by leaders of the radical faction, who demanded that a new program be established and new leaders installed for the conference. After a couple of hours of hopeless confusion, an Indonesian delegate was recognized. He made an eloquent-sounding speech in an Indonesian language which totally bewildered the participants. When, immediately afterward, he translated it into English, the message was crisp and precise: Unless the conference returned to the original schedule with its appointed leaders, the Asian delegation would walk out the next morning and arrange its own conference along the originally approved lines. The Asian delegation, he continued, would welcome any other interested participants to join them. This intervention brought the conference back to its seminars and strategy sessions.

The Indonesian student who stopped the takeover effort also reminded the audience that this was a conference of Christian students. This remark was labeled an amusing joke by revolutionaries, who continued to harass and ridicule "conservative" participants. A Norwegian delegate who made a reference to his own Christian conviction was silenced in the same plenary by sneering hallelujah shouts. Hostilities between regional groups continued to deepen and the ideological conflict began to mount.

It was indicative of the time that no comprehensive conference report was prepared. Only an unedited compilation of the reports of seminars and regional strategy meetings was produced in mimeographed form. The texts had not been discussed by the groups, nor had they been officially approved. This summary document makes hard reading because of the repetitive jargon used in most of the reports and the platitudinous quality of much of the argumentation. It comes as no surprise that nowhere in the ecumenical literature is it possible to find references to the Turku '68 report.

The report of the seminar on "Being Human in the Modern World" states the issue at stake:

> The problem of man presents itself today as the problem of the liberation of man from the bondages of the past. This liberating task is a very complex one . . . the oppression suffered by man expresses itself at all levels that constitute social existence. . . . Our task is a revolutionary one.

The report spelled out the group's understanding of revolution as radical change in all realms of social existence and as "liberation from the fossilized complex of oppression" which is caused by the exploitation of the majority of the people for the benefit of a privileged minority. The task, therefore, is to join the struggle against imperialism and socioeconomic injustice. The goal was nothing less than a new man and a new society. The report describes the role of ideologies, which either alienate man and justify oppression or undergird revolution and point to a more human future. On the role of theology the report repudiates concepts of "pure" or "transcendentalist" theologies on the grounds that they are part of the ideological system which justifies oppression. Christian identity emanates from the recognition of the Christ event which enables a person to see himself or herself "as a free man" whose hope is grounded in the coming of the kingdom of God. Hence Christian identity can be perceived only through involvement in the liberation of all people from all dehumanizing forces. The report ends by writing off everything that is related to the "scientific and technological establishment" because of its part in reinforcing colonialism and social injustice. There is a brief reference to racism and the positive example which the peoples of China and Cuba provide.

The seminar entitled "New Universities for a New World," according to the summary report, had four subthemes: (1) the university and the masses; (2) "imperialistic" universities and "depending" universities; (3) different universities in different societies; and (4) universities and permanent education.

The unambiguous perspective from which the seminar considered these issues was that of simplistic Marxist analysis. Accordingly, universities throughout the world, but especially in the capitalist world, are made part of productive structures. They cannot be fundamentally changed "unless the capitalist structures of our society are themselves destroyed." The report left open the question as to whether or not the church is totally and inherently a reactionary institution and whether or not it has some revolutionary potential. The group saw permanent education as a means for students and university teachers to develop "critical consciousness" and to build bridges between socially aware students and other social groups. The report concludes that the struggle for a "critical university" is part of the struggle "for a radical democratic socialism or communism."

The report of the seminar on "Politics, Power and Social Change" chose national liberation and the struggle against imperialism and neocolonialism as the basic framework for its deliberations. A new society and a new type of human being were the ultimate goal. The seminar also considered the question of violence or nonviolence in the revolutionary process. It rejected "a priori dogmatic conclusions." The choice between them was not moral but a question of appropriate tactics in a given situation. The main part of the report deals with strategies required by different regions and national situations. A variety of tactics is considered, such as guerrilla warfare against institutions preventing social change, demasking the brutality of the establishment by direct action, and setting up counterinstitutions.

The seminar "Rich Nations, Poor Nations: The Development Dilemma" took as its point of departure humanization which is to safeguard the full development of a person's potential in his or her cultural and socioeconomic context. Such development includes meeting basic needs, such as food, shelter, education, and human dignity. The imposition of Western cultural values and private or state capitalism was seen as an obstacle to development. The seminar considered the educational needs of developing countries and the problems caused by the excessive dependence of their educational systems on those of developed countries. Suggested methods for reducing the brain drain included keeping closer contact with students studying abroad, establishing teaching and research institutions in developing countries under their own control, and the founding of an international development university. Another area of development discussed was cooperation among developing countries in production and export marketing. The report noted concentration of power in the hands of a few, issues related to foreign exchange earnings, a balance between urban and rural sectors, and the phenomenon of political refugees as problems of developing countries requiring attention. The seminar listed two sets of criticisms, one directed to capitalist systems and the other to socialist systems. The report concluded with points for possible strategies, which included effective use of the UN and its specialized agencies and possible steps toward a more just and equitable international economic order. The group did not reject the value of reform as a means toward authentic development. It emphasized the qualitative difference between developed and developing countries, which is not primarily a question of the economic standards of living but of power: who rules and decides, and who is directed and controlled.

The fifth seminar, "Technological Revolution in the Life of Man," discussed the role of technology in development; the merits and deficiencies of technology in agriculture and industry, and of capital-intensive and labor-intensive technologies; the usefulness of foreign technological aid; the research needs in developing countries; and the role of education in economic development. The group recommended launching "future creating workshops" in which local needs and international expertise could be engaged. Such an approach was felt to be helpful for dealing with population problems, conditions in

76

mushrooming urban areas, health problems, and multinational corporations. The dangers of elitism, of study not leading to action, and of a divorce from reality were seen as points to be taken into account.

The summary document gives the impression that three of the seminars followed clear-cut Marxist or neo-Marxist lines. The report dealing with development was more nuanced in its use of Marxist analysis, and the one on technology did not attempt to use a unified ideological basis as its springboard. It is, however, misleading to draw too far-reaching conclusions from these reports because they reflect only partially what was said in the groups, and because they were not subjected to any democratic control.

In retrospect, only one conclusion can be drawn: The conference was a singular disaster. It failed to produce fresh ideas and to stimulate Christian commitment relevant to the conditions of universities, ideological strife, the problems of the world, and the renewal of the Church. The worship was unable to create a sense of community. Plans for theological reflection missed the point and made no tangible impact on participants. For most delegates the conference was a waste of money and time on a grand scale. This view is confirmed by various evaluative reports. Participants who came with high expectations left the conference disillusioned and disappointed. Revolutionary militants found the conference irrelevant to their cause. African delegates were perplexed by participants who did not want to worship. Asians were dismayed by the attempts of European, American, and Latin American radicals to dominate the conference and to dismiss others as of no value. Latin Americans were disappointed that their intentions had been misrepresented and that they had been misunderstood and dominated by others. Some of the more "traditional" SCM members were offended by the abusive manner in which their contributions were dismissed. The best some participants could say about the event was that it improved their grasp of the situation of students and the problems which SCMs faced and that they had met students from other parts of the world.[9]

---

9. Evaluative letters, reports, or articles by participants are filed in the WSCF Archives. They include: "Criticism of WSCF Summer Conferences 1968," by Eduard von Hengel of the Netherlands (mimeographed); "One-Dimensional Federation," comments by the same writer (mimeographed); "A New Man for a New World,"

At the first joint meeting of Geneva and regional staff after Turku, which was held in Annecy, France, in December 1968, and in which the newly elected chairman of the WSCF, Richard Shaull, also participated, similar criticisms were noted.[10] The conclusions drawn from the Turku experience varied, however, among staff members. While everyone agreed that the time for authoritarian or paternalistic leadership was over, some colleagues alluded to the inadequacies in the preparatory work by staff as an important reason for the failure of the conference. The methods used and the reliance on preparatory documents and on professional resource persons had revealed the planners' insensitivity to the real situation of SCMs and students at large. Moreover, some felt that staff had evaded their responsibility by leaving the show to the students when the going got tough. Out of their own uncertainty, staff may have given the impression that they were open to whatever might happen and thus refused to give indications of what they expected from the conference. Some colleagues believed the conference illustrated the kind of results which permissive leadership produces.

The staff had different opinions about the implications of the student revolution for the Federation. According to Leonardo Franco the failure was not just what happened at the conference, but what had happened to the whole WSCF. The organization was unable to bring together its constituency, to foster real communication between radicals and conservatives or between Western and non-Western members. Turku '68 marked an end of the Federation as it had been

---

World YWCA Monthly, December 1968, by Vivian Lewis, YWCA of Atlanta, Georgia, USA; "Turku '68: A Report on the World Student Conference at Turku, Finland," *Concern* (SYNDESMOS Orthodox Youth), no. 4 (1968), by Serge Schmemann, USA; "Brief Note to My WSCF Friends — What Went Wrong with Turku?" by Paul Abrecht (mimeographed); "A Report," by Eeva Dahl, Norway (mimeographed); "Mini-révolution dans la FUACE," *Convergence* (Pax Romana), by Halina Bortnowska, Poland; letter from Öystein Thelle of Norway to Milan Opocensky, November 6, 1968; translation of an article in *De Bazuin,* by P. van Dongen of the Ecumenical Commission of Pax Romana; "Turku '68 in Retrospect," *World Outlook,* October 1968, by Larry J. Moss.

10. A verbatim record of the comments on the Turku '68 conference made by staff members is included in the Minutes of a Meeting of WSCF Staff and Chairman, Annecy, France, December 9-12, 1968, pp. 6-9.

inherited. In order to find a viable way forward it was necessary to stall the programs so far prepared or proposed. This was, according to Franco, how Latin American SCM leaders experienced the significance of the conference.[11] However, there was no agreement about such an analysis.

When Turku '68 ended on July 30 and the delegates to the Federation Assembly stepped into buses on the way to Otaniemi, it was evident to everybody that the World Student Conference had not generated the kind of vision for the WSCF that had been expected during the two years of preparatory work that went into it. Indeed, for the French SCM leaders, Turku was an anticlimax to all that they had come to share from the French revolution, so much so that they decided to return home and not attend the Assembly at all.

11. Annecy Minutes, p. 8.

CHAPTER 4

In Search of New Directions: The General Assembly in Otaniemi, 1968

4.1. Point of Departure

The 1968 Assembly of the WSCF, held at the Conference Center of the Finland Institute of Technology, in Otaniemi, Finland, August 1-14, 1968, was the largest and most representative decision-making gathering that the Federation had ever held. Of the 254 participants from sixty-nine countries, 133 were voting delegates, 85 nonvoting representatives, and 36 technical and local personnel.[1] According to

1. At the Thessaloniki General Committee meeting of 1960 the number of voting delegates was 118, other participants 76, and technical staff 18, totaling 212, with sixty-six countries represented.

At the Embalse Rio Tercero General Committee meeting of 1964 the number of voting delegates was 100, other participants 55, and technical staff 24, totaling 179, with fifty-eight countries represented.

At the Otaniemi General Assembly of 1968 the number of voting delegates was 133, other participants 100, and technical staff 36, totaling 254, with sixty-nine countries represented.

At the Addis Ababa Assembly of 1972-73 the number of voting delegates was 56, other participants 64, international technical staff 17, plus around 110 registered host committee representatives that included members of the imperial security force, totaling some 247, with sixty countries represented. Minutes of the 1960 and 1964 meetings of the General Committee and of the 1968 and 1972-73 Assemblies.

the revised constitution, the gathering was a General Assembly and no longer a General Committee.

Neither the size of the Assembly nor its modern functional setting in superb Nordic weather could dispel the sense of uncertainty among the participants about the future of the Federation. Questions foremost in the minds of many were: How should or would the Federation respond to the student revolution? How explosive would the meeting be? Would the delegates reach constructive decisions on programs and the proposed restructuring? Or would a frustration similar to that experienced at the Turku conference be the fate of the Assembly as well?

Surprisingly enough, the Assembly opened in a calm and orderly fashion and progressed from beginning to end without any significant procedural hassles. It was as if the mood had suddenly changed from contestation to construction on the road from Turku to Otaniemi. The only breach of order was caused by an unexpected demonstration of children, aged four upward, who broke into the meeting and staged an uncontrollable sit-in around the podium, waving slogans such as "Don't trust anybody over 12."

The report of the outgoing general secretary, Valdo Galland,[2] who had been on the WSCF staff for nearly eighteen years, emphasized that continuity and experimentation, in combination, were characteristics of the Federation. In his view the "continuum" of the WSCF extended from the university community and student scene to churches and international Christian organizations. He emphasized the Federation's pioneering role in the ecumenical movement. He singled out the new stage of relationships between Roman Catholics and other Christians which he saw in the conversations about the possible merger between the Federation and Pax Romana, the Roman Catholic counterpart of the WSCF, and in the founding of the University Christian Movement in the USA and South Africa, both of which Roman Catholics had decided to join. The ecumenical strategy consultations held in 1966-67 were an indication of the "continuum" which the Federation shared with churches and their mission organizations. Galland discussed political responsibility, regionalization, and

2. Minutes of the Twenty-Fifth Meeting of the General Assembly of the WSCF, Otaniemi, Finland, 1968, pp. 8-13.

new long-term patterns of leadership training under the heading of "flexible experimentation," but refrained from placing current expressions of these concerns at the center of the Federation's commitment and from drawing long-term organizational conclusions from them. In the final part of his report Galland discussed "the need for total restructuring." He perceived this to be a need in the university and in its role in society; in the WSCF as a communication network and through regionalization; and in theological thinking. As for the "theological crisis" in the Federation, he pleaded for tolerance and the will to listen: to those who wanted to "abandon out-dated theological language" in order to experiment with new expressions, as well as to those who found it pointless or even dangerous to give up inherited expressions before new language had been found.

The general secretary's report clearly advocated a via media for the Federation in both its theological and political concerns. Unlike the addresses by resource persons at the Turku conference, it aroused no strong reaction.

A whole morning session was given to a panel which reported on the Turku conference. The discussion which ensued did not lead to any immediate conclusions or recommendations. Instead, ideas for the Federation's possible responses to the revolutionary ferment and to the pleas for regionalization were developed further in the four working groups and six regional groups of the Assembly. It appeared that the participants wanted to deal with these issues in some depth, taking into account the different views held by member movements.

4.2. University, Schools, and Permanent Education

The working group on "The Future of the University"[3] wanted to reopen discussion on the task of the university in its political, social, and cultural context. This need arose from the recognition of the potential political power of the university, the impact of new forms of knowledge, and "the global crisis of universities." The group recommended drawing all categories of personnel in universities into the Federation's constituency and launching "a common enterprise of

3. Otaniemi Minutes, pp. 32-43.

study, debate, and action." The Assembly decided to recommend that the new Executive Committee appoint an international commission "representative of the total personnel of the university, and of a number of key disciplines" to guide experimental projects, and that a staff person be appointed to service them.

The same working group recommended a study project on the political uses of the university to scrutinize its role in shaping society: its inclination to undergird political and cultural imperialism, its potential as a politically independent force for creative change, and the danger of it becoming a bastion of conservative ideologies. This project was to be carried out in a similar way to that of the WSCF China project. The recommendation was passed to the new Executive Committee.

A third project proposed by the working group on the university was a study on permanent education. This initiative was based on the understanding of education as "a permanent and continuing process . . . liberating, sensitizing and emancipating" humanity. Such an understanding was important because of the rapidity of social change, overpopulation, and the divisions in the world. The group envisaged an endeavor of "organizing and involving masses in the process of emancipation." It recommended that the Federation "promote a comparative study of Permanent Education in different cultural contexts," linking it with the work of UNESCO and encouraging the WCC to establish an Education Desk with permanent education as part of its mandate.

A paper on permanent education by a group of North and Latin Americans was appended to the report. This paper was an attempt to introduce the work and concepts of the Brazilian educator Paulo Freire to the Federation at large. Permanent education was seen as a method whereby the impoverished masses could become aware of their condition and of their own potential for liberating themselves from the domination of the privileged classes and from the cultural penetration of imperialism.

The working group envisaged further development of the Federation's work among university teachers and foreign and refugee students, and in secondary schools. It suggested launching several additional study projects and leadership training programs, producing publications, and appointing more staff. After a lively discussion in the plenary, the Assembly decided to tone down some of the loftiest ambitions in the report before its recommendations were approved and referred to the new Executive Committee.

4.3. Aims of the Federation

The working group on "Convictions and Questions"[4] plunged into a discussion of the theological foundations and the meaning of faith in the work of the WSCF. The concept of Christian presence, which had been introduced into the Federation at the 1964 Assembly, was considered a valid and fruitful one, even if some of the current tensions within the WSCF stemmed from the diversity of ways in which "Christian presence" was understood. The group observed a greater diversity among the constituency now than four years earlier.

The report provided an explicit analysis of the two different ways in which the concept of Christian presence was interpreted. According to the first, "presence" "means primarily the affirmation of the presence of Christ as God's supreme gift to the world." It can be discovered "through the study of the Scriptures and the Christian tradition." The recognition of the presence of Christ gives Christians a tool for analyzing and judging social structures and proposals to change them. It is "a specific source for the identity of the Christian that is not totally determined by each situation as it arises."

The second interpretation of "presence" meant "concrete and effective action in the struggle for the creation of a new society and a new man." The point of departure was presence in a network of relationships and social structures in order to transform them. The context of struggle for social and political change determined "any meaningful reflection on the ultimate issues of life," whereas traditional theological categories had lost their usefulness. Conceptual tools were sought not in theological systems but in secular disciplines and interpretations of social realities and demands for change. Only theology which played an iconoclastic role was considered helpful, as it opened the way for perceiving new possibilities in each situation by destroying fossilized traditions which blocked change. According to

4. Otaniemi Minutes, pp. 43-50.

84

this interpretation, the future of Christian community lay in its openness to discovering "new ways of relating Christian faith to the contemporary situation."

The report noted that the two interpretations differed not just in the language used by their adherents, but, more significantly, in their understanding of the meaning of Christian faith and commitment. The implications of each needed to be made clear for the constituency of the Federation:

> For the former, Christian students are automatically welcome. While membership may be open to others, the SCM is seen primarily as a Christian community that is bound by some common affirmations about Christ which transcend differences, political or otherwise, among its members. For the latter, the SCM is to be conceived as constituted by those who have a common commitment to change. . . . A certain relation to the community of faith is admitted for the Movement as a whole, but this is not considered the primary principle of selection of those who are to be part of its life. In this sense, certain Christian students may in fact be considered as "enemies."[5]

The report pointed to differences in the political realm. The main dividing line was between those who were committed to a reform of institutions, attitudes, and patterns of social life toward greater social justice, and those for whom disruption of a total political and social system before which justice stood no chance was the foremost task. Among the "reformers," especially in Asia, the necessary change was described in terms of the modernization of institutions. For the "revolutionaries," modernization was a form of power undergirding the positions of privileged nations and social groups against others. Justice, therefore, could only be brought about by a complete change in power relationships.

The report left delegates and member movements in no doubt about the seeds of division within the Federation. While conceding that any basis for unity was "very fragmentary and possibly even superficial," the report did, however, try to outline some areas of

---

5. Otaniemi Minutes, p. 45.

common ground between those holding opposite views. It stressed the need for "being more deeply present to each other" and "not speaking before listening." It asked whether within the current plurality there was still present an element of unity. It suggested that the widely shared affirmation of the presence of Christ in the world, "in whatever way this was understood," might provide some common basis as it pointed to the possibility for the liberation of man and for the realization of full humanity. It also found convergence in "an undefined but very real commitment . . . to be on the side of the oppressed wherever they are in the world," even if the members of the group had disagreed on whether or not such a stand could be expressed in terms of a commitment to a "world-wide ideology of revolution."

The group concluded that it was impossible at that time to spell out explicit aims to which all member movements would be able equally to commit themselves. The Federation could at best provide an international, ecumenical expression of shared responsibility which could enable member movements to challenge each other and help them to transcend regional, national, and ethnic boundaries. It was nevertheless imperative for the Federation to continue to seek to define "its status in relation to faith."

> While it is immensely positive that we have found a new awareness of the indispensability of political involvement, it is equally important that we should develop spiritually, discovering a new awareness of faith, if we are to be new men in a new world.[6]

The group listed issues on which the Federation should focus in the quadrennium ahead:

- the meaning of the "presence of Jesus Christ in the world";
- the relationship between theology and politics;
- is there a Christian understanding of politics and of what can or cannot be achieved through it?
- the influence of cultural contexts on theological positions;

6. Otaniemi Minutes, p. 47.

- the significance of Marxism for our analysis of society and our theological understanding;
- our goals for social change and their validity for all societies.

The practical recommendations were to pursue theological work related to these questions. For the Federation as a whole the group proposed a research project on "The Individual, Religion, and Culture."

The plenary passed the group's recommendations and resolved that the new Executive Committee "be instructed to begin immediate consultation in order to reformulate the aims of the Federation."

4.4. Political Role

"Student Political Action" was the topic of the third working group. This was the group which dealt most explicitly with the challenge of current revolutionary movements. Its report, entitled "Politics and the WSCF,"[7] showed how the perspective of Christian students regarding their social and political responsibility was changing and how this was reflected within the ecumenical movement in terms of the political role of the church in an unjust world.[8]

The report began by stating some of the main convictions out of which the Federation's concern for politics arose. The first was that the Christian faith demands political engagement. Now, more than ever before, politics was an instrument to keep human life human. The report quoted C. Wright Mills, who was said to have asserted that "if one does not become involved in politics, one cannot confront evil and cannot work for good." The second conviction was that the Christian faith demands active opposition to oppression and injustice. In an unjust world mediation and reconciliation were not enough. "We are called to be partisans in the struggles of our day."

A dual perspective on the objectives of the Federation's political

7. Otaniemi Minutes, pp. 50-60.
8. The WSCF Grey Book by M. M. Thomas and J. D. McCaughey, *The Christian in the World Struggle* (1952), provides a contrast to the affirmations of the radical Christian students of the late sixties.

task was evident. On the one hand the Federation was to press for active political engagement of its member movements and of Christian students and teachers all over the world, and to guide this engagement toward opposition to various forces of oppression. The international situation underlined the urgency of this task. On the other hand, the Federation was not to transform the SCMs into political parties or action groups. They should instead provide a forum or context in which "the process of political formation" and the support for political engagement could take place. The political function of the SCM was conceived as that of "critical reflection" and "community support" of secular political movements.

The political work was to serve three types of constituency: (1) politically active SCMs, (2) SCMs which did not show signs of political awareness, and (3) students and teachers outside the SCMs whose political interests coincided with those of political activists in the WSCF.

The report thus contains the first signs of the Federation's parting from an ecumenical pursuit of political responsibility which previous General Committees had affirmed, which had been rooted in Christian community, and which respected confessional and political pluralism. At the Otaniemi Assembly the Federation leaned toward a more uniform political engagement. But while the struggle against oppression was supposed to provide coherence and unity, the articulation of the meaning of Christian faith became increasingly difficult. By conveying a "yes but not quite" approach to the proponents of radical activist ideologies, the report tried to avoid a drastic break with the past. But it also advocated a shift away from appreciating the diverse experiences of member movements toward an almost school-masterly attitude toward politically unenlightened students and SCMs who had to be led to the flock of "the conscientized" or else ignored. Radical political elites were ready to begin separating the sheep from the goats.

The working group listed priorities and criteria for the Federation's political work:

- *"politicization" of the membership of the WSCF* by developing political consciousness; recognizing the problems of the concentration of power; using critical analysis to understand local situations in the wider international context; being committed to change and forming political goals; relating Christian faith to political realities; and preparing strategies for action;

- *development of political communication* among SCMs and between SCMs and political groups by means of publications devoted to political concerns; production and circulation of special papers and bibliographies on particular political problems; exchange of personnel to promote specific political concerns; seminars, research projects, and international task forces; and the establishment of effective ties with emerging new political forces;
- *study and research* to serve the politically committed; to have the highest priority among the political programs of the WSCF; to be directly related to the political concerns of the SCMs; to deal with practical political action; and to involve political activists.

The working group recommended the appointment to the Political Commission for the next quadrennium of members who should "be involved in political action" but also "have experience of and active relation to at least one SCM." It also recommended the continuation of the position of a full-time secretary of the Political Commission.

The working group received a report of the WSCF China Study Project, 1966-68, and recommended, though somewhat halfheartedly, its continuation for another year. The description of the China project presented to the working group reads:

The project was designed as a response to the resurgence of China, its growing importance for other nations and peoples, the separation which had come between Chinese Christians and Christians of other areas, and the need for fresh reflection on these developments. It was shaped in the light of four perspectives:

- It was to be self-consciously Christian. It would draw upon the theology and ethics of the Christian community, and seek to define the challenges to that community posed by the rise of China.
- It was to be university-oriented. It would draw its personnel from the academic world — teachers, students and clergy — and incorporate into its work the relevant resources from academic research.
- It was to be international. It would seek at every stage free exchange across national, regional, racial, and political lines.

89

- It was to be oriented towards the younger generation. It would draw personnel primarily from the present generation of students and younger faculty, and afford at least the possibility of a fresh Christian approach to China — an approach free of direct ties with the events and experiences that produced the alienation of previous generations of Christians from the Chinese Revolution. And it would seek to come to terms with China for the long-term future.[9]

It came as no surprise, therefore, that the working group wanted the new study and research projects of the Political Commission to differ from the China Study Project, which obviously did not fit the one-way activist emphasis.[10]

An outline of two projects, proposed presumably by informal subgroups, was appended to the report of the working group. They were a proposal for a "Power Structures Research Program" and another for a "Europe-Africa Project." Neither of these was formally endorsed by the group, nor were they considered by the Assembly as a whole. Both of them mirrored Marxist undercurrents among the radical activists. The former was later taken up by the new Political Commission. The latter was never accepted by the African regional committee as an interregional effort. It was therefore taken up by the European region alone. (See section 4.6 below and also chapter 5.)

After an intensive plenary debate the sections on the political role of the Federation and its priority tasks were endorsed by the Assembly as "provisional guidelines for the political work of the WSCF." There were four dissenting votes. Furthermore, the proposals to establish a new Political Commission and to extend the China Study Project through 1969 were approved unanimously. The Assembly requested the Executive Committee to initiate a systematic discussion of the Federation's political identity, which should result in a "more complete statement."

---

9. Otaniemi Minutes, p. 56.

10. The minutes state this concern explicitly: "Future study and research programs should differ from the China Study Project in at least these respects, . . ." which included the criteria for the political activist character of the future programs. Otaniemi Minutes, p. 54.

4.5. "The Nature and Function of the Federation"

The overall assignment of the fourth working group[11] was to review the structures of the WSCF to ensure that they would support an effective Christian ministry in the academic world and reflect accurately its constituency. It was to give special attention to the development of regional patterns of work. It was foreseen that moving into decentralized decision making would have implications for the self-understanding and image of the Federation. The working group was expected to (a) draw conclusions from the 1966-67 ecumenical strategy consultations; (b) propose constitutional changes which would reflect the need for regionalization; (c) review the Federation's relationships with other world organizations; and (d) outline a viable financial strategy with criteria for priorities.

The need for fundamental changes in the Federation's patterns of work was acknowledged in the group's report, which referred to new styles of student involvement in political, social, and theological issues. More important than these, however, were the pressures to establish a decentralized structure along regional lines and to allow the Federation to continue to expand. The establishment of regional offices on all continents was taken for granted at that time. A more thankless task for the group was to examine what was financially feasible and to suggest criteria for priorities. Looking back, it is conspicuous how little this working group was influenced by the turmoil of students in Europe and North America, or by current revolutionary ideologies. Its deliberations were guided by the vision for the role of the WSCF which had been made clear at ecumenical strategy consultations.

A subgroup was assigned to consider the concept and implications of regionalization. It recommended that the WSCF remain a federation of national movements and not of regional units. The regional committees which were to be established were to serve in an advisory capacity on matters pertaining to regions, such as the appointment of regional staff and programs of worldwide or interregional character. Responsibility for planning and implementing regional programs and for the financial support of member movements in the region was to

11. Report of the working group on the "Nature and Function of the Federation." Otaniemi Minutes, pp. 61-69.

be delegated to regional committees and staff. The Executive Committee of the WSCF would continue to be responsible for staff appointments, budgets, and general policies, which, however, needed to take into account the recommendations and concerns of regional committees.

The advantages of regionalization over against a centralized pattern were seen to include:

- the potential of regional groups to bring the common concerns of the Federation more effectively to the national movements;
- more opportunities for national SCMs to participate in international Federation activities and a greater sense of belonging to the worldwide Christian community;
- the possibility of national movements forming united fronts to deal with issues which may be common to the region;
- promotion of contextual expressions of Christian faith and discipleship, and increased freedom from domination from outside.

Problems or dangers foreseen included:

- the isolation of regions from one another;
- a weakened sense of responsibility for worldwide concerns and a loss of programs of global scope and perspective;
- unfair competition for funds between regions;
- the formation of regional blocs presupposing conformity of the national movements in the area and leading to a loss of flexibility;
- an increasing distance between member movements and the headquarters of the Federation.

It was foreseen that the new quadrennium would be a period of experimentation with such a decentralized pattern. Each region would have the freedom to develop the kind of structure and style which would best suit its needs. No uniformity would be expected in terms of either structures or programs. Each regional group would be asked to reflect on the experience for itself and for the worldwide Christian community.

In the review of the relationships of the WSCF, cooperation with any organizations and groups which share its objectives was encouraged. Regionalization provided new possibilities for that. The report listed the Federation's established and still valid relationships with a variety of international organizations, including UN agencies, World University Service, and the whole range of Catholic, Orthodox, ecumenical, and evangelical organizations.[12]

The report did mention changes in the current understanding of ecumenism due to a greater emphasis on the unity of humankind in parallel to the traditional affirmation of the unity of the Church. This change was seen as supporting the Federation's concentrating on social issues and concerns of the international community.

The report also noted the proliferation of functional Christian groups around particular issues and tasks. Groups important for the Federation included those of foreign students, political caucuses, informal movements, and groups dealing with highly specialized problems. Some of them were seeking cooperation with the Federation, but because of their ad hoc nature it was unnecessary to formalize relationships with them.

The section of the report dealing with priorities remained fairly inconclusive. Three main categories were listed: (1) programs and projects related to regionalization, (2) communication among member movements and regions, and (3) Federation-wide projects related to student involvement in political action, university and educational concerns, and theological reflection. In addition, the group proposed the creation of an Emergency Fund to meet crisis situations of member movements. Reference was made repeatedly to the concept of the Federation as a "communication network" — a phrase that soon became fashionable in the wider ecumenical movement.

The proposal for a revised WSCF constitution and the amendments made to it by other working groups and from the floor were

12. Organizations listed, and the relationship with them described, were: UN-ESCO and the United Nations; World University Service; SYNDESMOS (an international organization of Orthodox students and youth); Pax Romana and Jeunes Etudiants Catholiques; World Alliance of YMCAs and World YWCA; International Fellowship of Evangelical Students (IFES); World Council of Churches; World Christian Youth Commission; Christian Peace Conference. The report adds that the list is only partial. The regional ecumenical organizations, for example, were left out of it. Otaniemi Minutes, pp. 65-67.

also given to the working group on the "Nature and Function of the Federation" for consideration. The revision of the constitution had been prepared by the officers. It assumed that the Assembly would take steps toward regionalization and recognize an increasing diversity among the WSCF constituency and partner organizations. Only the end result of this work is reported in the minutes under the heading "Restructuring."[13]

The aims of the Federation remained unchanged with the assumption that the new Executive Committee would give high priority to reconsidering them and present its proposal for revision to the next Assembly. The unwillingness of the Assembly to touch the aims showed that they represented an element of continuity which was appreciated even in the midst of theological uncertainty.·

The most significant changes in the constitution were in the articles on the composition of the Federation, the General Assembly, and the Executive Committee. The membership category of "corresponding movements" was eliminated. The two other categories, the "affiliated movements" with full voting rights and "the associated movements" with a voice at the Assemblies, remained. The conditions to be met by affiliated movements were simplified by eliminating clauses stating that, first, "the membership of the Movement shall include not less than 150 students" and, second, that the General Committee had the right to determine the relationship between the movement and the Federation if changes were to occur which would affect the conditions of membership. Interestingly enough, the clause requiring "evidence of stability, strength, and growth" of affiliated movements was left intact in the revised constitution.

The former General Committee consisted of at least one representative of each affiliated movement, of the elected officers of the Federation, and of up to six secretaries, as voting members. It was replaced by the General Assembly in which only the delegates of affiliated movements and members of the Executive Committee had the right to vote. The concept of the old General Committee assumed a membership which lasted until the opening of its next meeting. The new Assembly was a one-off event.

The Assembly would elect the chairman, a vice chairman, if so

13. Otaniemi Minutes, pp. 23-27.

decided, and the general secretary as officers, and sixteen to twenty-two members who, with the elected officers, would make up the Executive Committee. Among the sixteen to twenty-two members "every region and constituency shall be adequately represented," and at least half of them "shall be registered students at the time of election." The phrase "every region" was the only point of the constitution which referred to regionalization. The Executive Committee was to be responsible for electing additional officers from amongst its members — as many as it deemed necessary. In the old constitution the composition of the Executive Committee was left more open and the Committee was in practice much smaller.

The old constitution had stipulated that at least one of the officers should be a woman and that, if a movement had more than one member on the General Committee, it was responsible to ensure "a proper representation of both men and women." In the new constitution all references to the representation of both genders were eliminated.

The approach chosen in the revision of the constitution was that it should ensure an adequate share of students in the decision making of the Federation and provide space for regionalization as an experiment, but not to legislate changes, the value of which had not yet been tested.

4.6. Toward a Federation of Regions

During the Assembly, regional groups, consisting of participants from the region and the regional secretaries, met several times and established specific plans for the Federation's work in each region. They established objectives and proposed plans for the regional programs, committees, and offices. Reports from these groups were presented to the plenary but not debated in any depth. Their recommendations were approved and forwarded to the Executive Committee for action.

Some difficulties came to light because some national movements could not see their place in a regional structure or simply refused to be forced into an artificial unit. The Canadian SCM, for example, was not interested in joining with the U.S. campus Christian organizations in a regional structure which would, by the sheer size of the American movements, be dominated by them. The University Christian Movement of South Africa would be cut off from almost all regional programs because of the country's political isolation from the rest of Africa. The English-speaking Caribbean would have problems in adjusting to a regional program led exclusively by Spanish- or Portuguese-speaking leaders. As a consequence, it was admitted that member movements could relate directly to the WSCF headquarters and be served by it, when there was a special need. The reports of the regional groups display a conspicuous diversity of objectives, methods, and emphases.

Africa[14]

Africans, for example, began their report with a succinct statement:

> We propose the creation of an African region whose raison d'être and objectives will be:
> * to proclaim Jesus Christ as Savior and Lord;
> * to relate Christian faith to daily life;
> * to create and strengthen the SCMs in universities and secondary schools, and to co-ordinate their activities;
> * to improve communication and collaboration between the African Movements;
> * to permit a larger participation of Africans in the life of the WSCF.

The Africa region proposed a Consultative Committee on which the All Africa Conference of Churches would be represented. The main program emphases were leadership training, communication and publication work within the region, stimulation and support of national SCMs, and the development of a strategy which would involve both academic institutions and churches.

Asia[15]

The Asia region had developed its plans sometime prior to the Turku conference and the Assembly. They were ready to nominate members on the Asia committee from among students, university teachers, and

14. Otaniemi Minutes, pp. 69-71.
15. Otaniemi Minutes, pp. 72-75.

SCM leaders and to include three representatives of the East Asia Christian Conference. The program priorities were (1) work among university teachers, (2) training of student and staff leaders, (3) publications, and (4) implementation of ecumenical strategies with national movements and churches. In addition, the regional group recommended several interregional projects such as an Asia–Latin America consultation, a joint project between Canadian and Japanese SCMs on China, and a study project on the American presence in Asia.

The Asia region wanted to focus on the development of higher education, university reforms, engaging Asian theologians in expressing the Christian faith in contemporary Asian terms, and involving itself with students in their struggles for university reforms throughout the region.

Europe[16]

The European regional group proposed the establishment of a six-member WSCF European committee to cooperate with the European secretary. Program and project plans included an annual European Student Conference to deal with such topics as European security, European participation in development aid, and the critical examination of prevailing theological traditions. The first conference was set for early 1969, the year in which the NATO Treaty was to expire, and its theme was to be "A New Pattern for Europe."

The European group endorsed the plan for a comprehensive two-year Europe-Africa Study Project which would focus on West European presence in Africa, which the working group on "Student Political Action" had left open. The topics envisaged for long-term study in the region included the problems of revolution, issues related to "the so-called critical, free, and active universities," and ongoing theological reflection concerning political engagement and action.

Latin America[17]

The Latin American group presented an ambitious plan which had been developed since the Panama conference of Latin American

16. Otaniemi Minutes, pp. 75-77.
17. Otaniemi Minutes, pp. 81-87.

leaders in January 1968. The heart of the plan was the establishment of a Latin American Leadership Training Center (CLAF) for the training of student leaders for the SCMs and as a focal point for theological reflection. It was also to serve as a regional WSCF documentation and information center. The facilities were to accommodate the regional secretariat, which was to have three Latin American executive staff as well as personnel seconded to it from the USA. The ideas for the CLAF were developed in great detail.

The plan proposed a consolidation of the regional structure with a strengthened secretariat and a Student Committee which would consist of the Latin American members of the WSCF Executive Committee and one representative of each of the five subregions into which Latin America and the Caribbean region had been divided. Other elements of the regional plan included the creation of "a true Latin American SCM," which assumed integration of local and national SCMs into a continent-wide grassroots movement led by the regional secretariat and held together "by a critical consciousness of our Latin American situation." The process of moving toward the pattern of an all–Latin American SCM was described as democratization. Its essence was "constant communication between the grass roots and regional structure" so that the regional SCM would become "truly a Movement and not just a structure."

The group used the term "life program,"[18] which had been coined at recent Latin American gatherings and was intended to express the objectives of the Latin American SCM. Its meaning, according to the working group, was:

> to promote the training of students in and for Christian presence, understanding "presence" as concrete and efficient action in the struggle for the creation of a new society and a new man.[19]

The regional plan proposed the holding of SCM conferences in each of the five subregions. Topics suggested for them included

18. Terms such as "life program" and "life project," parallel to phrases such as "critical consciousness" and "authentic process of regionalization and democratization," became a linguistic trademark of many radical Latin Americans in the Federation.

19. Otaniemi Minutes, p. 82.

national development, the new man in the new society, leadership training, and increasing the vision of participants. Compared with other regions and past Latin American SCMs, the absence of any reference to cooperation with churches and the ecumenical movement was conspicuous. The concept of movement as a goal of the envisaged Latin American SCM was defined primarily in political terms with minimal reference to the witness of the Christian community in spheres of life other than the political.

The Middle East[20]

The Middle East group proposed general policies for the WSCF in its region:

The WSCF should continue:
A. To support member and non-member Movements (Orthodox, Catholic and Protestant) in the pursuit of their respective tasks of ecclesiastical and social renewal.
B. To promote further on the national and regional level unity and common action between the Orthodox, Catholic and Protestant member and non-member Movements.
C. To develop communication and exchange between the Middle East Movements and those of other regions, and to promote collaboration between them in pursuing the aims and tasks of the WSCF.
D. To collaborate wherever possible with all churches and ecumenical bodies in promoting church renewal, Christian unity, and common social action.

The group proposed that the regional center be the Middle East Advisory Committee, which would include university and high school students, university teachers, representatives of ecumenical church bodies, and the Middle East members of the Executive Committee. The responsibility for staff and the office would be shared between the WSCF and the WCC Division of Ecumenical Action through a joint secretariat in Beirut, Lebanon.

20. Otaniemi Minutes, pp. 77-80.

The program emphases were to be (1) leadership training: at national levels in Lebanon, Syria, and Egypt; at an interregional level between Iran, Pakistan, and Afghanistan; at the Middle East regional level, an annual course for university students and special training with the help of a scholarship program; (2) a pilot research project in higher education in cooperation with the University Christian Center in Beirut; (3) consultation on higher education and development cosponsored by the Roman Catholic/WCC Joint Committee (SODEPAX); (4) a research project on political power structures in the Near East; (5) ministry to Middle East students in Europe; (6) a regional Middle East youth and student conference; and (7) publication of the bulletin *Al Montada* and study materials on methods and techniques of leadership, and the translation and circulation of documents sent by the WSCF headquarters.

North America[21]

The North America group concentrated on defining and planning the role of the WSCF in North America in the framework of a new ecumenical setting of which Roman Catholics were an integral part. This role referred, however, almost exclusively to the USA. The report stated that "an equal participation of the SCM of Canada and the UCM of the USA through a common regional structure is not possible." Separate national strategies and direct relationships of the two countries with the Federation were inevitable.

The characteristics of the U.S. scene were a new ferment within the student Christian movement, a new style of dealing with social and theological issues, an overwhelming accent on change, and an increasing rejection of structure-oriented patterns of work. The founding of the UCM in the USA was an attempt to give flexible form to an issue-oriented, ecumenical, university-based movement which would free itself from loyalties to the ecumenicity of its inter-confessional or interdenominational predecessors. Ecumenically committed churches were, however, part of the de facto constituency of the WSCF through their campus ministries.

The North America group proposed a plan for a joint ecumenical

21. Otaniemi Minutes, pp. 87-89.

secretariat between the WSCF and the International Movement of Catholic Students (IMCS)/Pax Romana to serve the Christian university community in North America. The group report maintained that there was sufficient common ground between the two partners particularly with regard to social change and theological orientation. Advantages of the new pattern would include the possibility of effective communication of campus Christian groups among themselves and with the ecumenical secretariat, a joint strategy for ecumenical team visits to campuses, increased opportunities for participation in international events by students and campus staff, improved coordination with campus ministries and national church and ecumenical agencies, and increased effectiveness in representing the concerns of the ecumenical university Christian community at the UN. The secretariat should have, according to the group report, four executive staff, of whom two should be provided by the IMCS/Pax Romana and two by the WSCF.

How, in the midst of all the radical unrest, the North America group could present such an organized proposal looks puzzling. Although the plan tried to show openness to the turbulence in U.S. universities and colleges, its main thrust was to achieve structural breakthrough in Roman Catholic–Protestant/Orthodox cooperation and to create a more solid framework for the WSCF in North America than was probable through the UCM. It seems that the radical activists from the USA were too busy in the working groups of the Assembly which dealt with political and educational strategies to have time and patience for the long-term perspectives of the Federation in their region. For the North America group the proposal was evidently a gamble the success of which was not guaranteed. The report ends with the ominous words: "In case the plans for the joint team should fail. . . ."

4.7. Clouds on the Horizon

The election of a new chairperson to succeed Philip Potter was an issue which brought the tension about the future orientation of the Federation to the surface. It was also the only point on which the Assembly became openly divided. The nominating committee presented two candidates for the position: Richard Shaull, a theologian and seminary professor from the USA, and Samuel Parmar, an economist and university teacher from India. The first ballot did not give a clear majority to either of the candidates. Shaull received 66 votes and Parmar 62, with 6 abstaining. A second ballot gave Shaull 71 votes and Parmar 61, and 3 abstentions.[22] In the days preceding the final ballot the atmosphere in the corridors was tense. Undoubtedly, the fact that Shaull was present and Parmar was not was significant. Moreover, those who, earlier in the year, had proposed Shaull as a candidate had also worked hard on a "package deal" which consisted of an academically recognized American radical for chairperson and myself, a Nordic *via media* SCM secretary with a good rapport with churches, for general secretary.

My election as general secretary proved simple and relatively uncontroversial. The nominating committee put forward only one name, following the endorsement of my candidacy by the WSCF officers meeting in January 1968. Votes in favor were 120, against 10, with 3 abstentions.

The uncertainties about the significance of the election results increased at the closing session when the newly elected chairperson of the Federation, Richard Shaull, addressed the Assembly. He began his remarks by welcoming the challenge and promise of regionalization. "Each culture and Christian community in the non-western world has a new occasion to bring its particular gift to the Kingdom of God." The promise would "be fulfilled only as this expression of diversity is accompanied by a new discovery of unity." His message centered on "the new shape of the ecumenical":

> Today, in the ecumenical movement, the institutional church is accepted as *the given,* and the relationship between churches is one of dialogue primarily about their past and present. We tend to forget that the ecumenical movement was not born through such a process. It was rather the work of men and women who did not accept the given forms of the church's life and work, but who dared to step to the front lines of the human struggle of their day, to give individual and

---

22. No one seems to have noted that the total number of votes recorded in both ballots was higher than the number of those registered to vote.

communal expression to a new response, and run all the risks that this involved. The roots of the ecumenical movement . . . lie in the missionary movement, which undertook an urgent and impossible task at the margin of or outside the structures of the church, and in the many lay movements that flourished in Europe and North America. In other words, the paradoxical fact is that the concern for unity and mission which produced the ecumenical movement was the product of what might be called *sectarian* efforts.

Today we face a situation in which dialogue and unity among those who represent the given structures of the church cannot get at the heart of our crisis in church or world. Today our hope lies more in the creation of the new than in the unification of the old.

In the last few days, we have had abundant evidence of this problematic in our discussion. Theology has been at the center of the life of the Federation, but it is now evident that we face a profound theological crisis and that we can move ahead only as we discover the terms for new theological reflection and dialogue. The Federation can fulfil its task only if the university question is at the center of its life, yet we are now clear that traditional concepts of the university and the university itself are in crisis and that any creative work in this area depends upon new formulations and new communities. Our concern for society — for the social structures by which man's life is shaped — has been strong for several decades; but we now know that this concern calls for new politics, which offers a possibility of overcoming the present powers of domination and creating new institutions in a new social order. . . .

Where then lies our hope? *In the possibility we have to make room for the emergence of the new in our midst* — to allow constant experimentation; to work for the creation and strengthening of those new forms which call our thought, structures, and programs into question, and then to confront them in such a way that we will not be allowed to remain at peace with ourselves.

Referring to theology, the future of the university, and the tasks of the Political Commission, he concluded:

I would suggest that . . . we encourage these initiatives, especially in the three areas just mentioned. As this happens, we must avoid

103

all temptations to impose even the new or to force conformity even in experimentation. For us to choose such a direction for our efforts means that we deliberately choose something much more disturbing: we choose to encourage dialogue in the Federation which will constantly challenge what we are, and which will create tension within our own life and in the wider ecumenical movement that may help to move us toward the future.[23]

The Assembly ended with an impressive outdoor ecumenical celebration of the Eucharist which was presided over by a Roman Catholic priest, Colin Collins of South Africa. In spite of the festive conclusion, delegates took away with them more questions than usual about the future of the Federation. The newly elected Executive Committee withdrew to a working-class-district hotel in Helsinki for a two-day organizing meeting. A few days later Russian troops moved into Czechoslovakia.

23. Otaniemi Minutes, pp. 3-4.

CHAPTER 5

Crossroads — Beirut 1969

The Executive Committee of the WSCF met in Beirut, Lebanon, in 1969. Up to that time the ideological conflicts which had surfaced at the World Student Conference in Turku in 1968, and at the subsequent General Assembly in Otaniemi, had not unduly hampered the work of the Federation staff except in North America. Nor did they have much influence on movements in Africa. In Asia, protests seldom broke the social and cultural continuities rooted in Asian traditions. In Eastern Europe, ideologies of the radical left had no appeal for young Christians. Therefore the polarization which the Beirut meeting of the Executive Committee imposed on the whole Federation and its Geneva office took most of those involved by surprise.

The meeting began with an international consultation on student unrest[1] in which several invited experts participated. The two groups in which most of the substantive work was done concluded by endorsing for the Federation's work two sets of ideological assumptions,

---

1. The consultation held on March 30–April 1, 1969, was initiated by the Executive Committee at its first meeting in Helsinki, August 14-15, 1968. The WSCF representative at UNESCO, Dr. Aaron Tolen, was given the responsibility for organizing it. It brought together fifty-three participants, among whom Dr. Pierre Furter and Dr. Michael Huberman represented UNESCO, Professor Tapiomase Ihromi of Indonesia the university teachers work, and Jean-François Marchat of France the secondary schools work. Its full report is found in Appendix 5 of the Minutes of the WSCF Executive Committee Meeting, Beirut, Lebanon, March 30–April 6, 1969, pp. 113-22.

or "options," which were proposed for "serious consideration" by the Executive Committee. The "first option" represented a radical revolutionary line and the "second option" a reformist perspective. While they were perceived as contradictory, the organizer of the consultation, Dr. Aaron Tolen, reporting on the consultation to the Executive Committee, assumed rather optimistically that the Federation would continue an open and public debate on the conflicting issues so that the simultaneous acceptance of the two "options" need not become mutually exclusive.[2] The ideas of the consultation were developed further by ad hoc working groups of the Executive Committee, which also presented a series of practical recommendations.

5.1. The "Two Options"

The working group which formulated the "first option" chose for its report the title "Political Perspective for the Program in the WSCF." It followed in its advocacy of revolution the current neo-Marxist line of argument held widely by the radical student left. The report stated boldly the group's conviction that there is "a convergence of political perspectives among the delegates from the various regions of the WSCF." The activist leadership of the group thus envisaged an active role for the Federation in the global revolution which, in the minds of the group's participants, seemed to be imminent.

Descriptions of the prevailing social situations and current economic and political forces followed a clear-cut, even simplified Marxist teaching. Imperialism was the root cause not only of over-development in "advanced capitalist countries" but also of "structural underdevelopment in the Third World," and, indeed, of social injustice in general. Nothing short of a total change in both developed and developing countries — a global revolution — could alter the power constellation and remedy the situation. The educational system of capitalist countries was a servant of imperialism, as it was geared to mass manpower training for the needs of a technological economy. The university played a key role in training youth ideologically for this role. Also, research in universities of the affluent

2. Beirut Minutes, p. 44.

world was designed to develop and maintain the patterns of oppressive societies.

According to the revolutionary "first option," the strategy for the WSCF, together with the radical movements in the university world, was envisaged as follows:

> Organizing around particular contradictions of university students
> . . . is of central strategic importance in working towards the generalized revolt of the essential productive forces of capitalist society
> and a total change into a socialist society. This means that our work
> in the university is strategic, and any changes we demand there
> must be related to the total change we seek.[3]

In the Third World, the focus of revolutionary leaders in higher education should be on "elite formation and ideological training" since universities had not yet become centers for mass education. The same revolutionary perspective should be brought into the development of primary and secondary education. A "political pedagogy"[4] with its pattern of learning by doing and its context of socialist political theory and strategy should be at the heart of all education in the Third World. The goal was to create "a counter power which can subvert and destroy the present power structures and build a new socialist society."[5]

The Federation was to enable programs in this political perspective. According to the revolutionary group's recommendation, this would imply:

> We see the building of a communications network as a high priority
> in tying together groups in various regions which are working in the
> same perspectives. This will internationalize our regional emphasis in
> projects, as well as contribute to an urgent need for rapid and reliable

3. Beirut Minutes, p. 119.

4. The term "political pedagogy" echoed the thinking of the well-known Roman Catholic leftist educator Paulo Freire of Brazil, whose ideas made a significant impact on the ecumenical movement in Latin America since the sixties and whose approach to education became more widely known through his book *Pedagogy of the Oppressed* (New York: Herder, 1970).

5. Beirut Minutes, p. 119.

political communications between Movements in various countries which are working with the same political focus.

Structures and staff would be developed to fit a frankly project-oriented perspective. If commissions and staff appointments are needed, they will occur in the perspective of the projects elaborated. . . . "Projects" are not to be seen primarily as "academic" study projects, but rather as strategically important projects arising out of . . . political work.[6]

The proposed political communications network was to spread and deepen political consciousness among students, thereby broadening the base for revolutionary change. The political network was to be maintained by means of a political newsletter and occasional papers. The material was to come from those involved in political activity outside the confines of the SCMs, "from the larger movement." The network was also to enable intensification of "personal contact between groups struggling to achieve similar goals." One person in each region was to be made responsible for political communication. The leadership was to be in the hands of the Political Commission secretary and the Communications secretary.[7]

The political network was to be enhanced by establishing a New Experiments Project Fund to provide funding for efforts guided by the Political Commission "to discover, promote, and relate to the new communities, projects and student forces" of radical political orientation, "not now defined as WSCF constituency." The new fund was to help finance meetings across regional lines involving radical activists and interregional travel of teams and individuals who represented particular political settings or new politically oriented communities.

The "first option" group's recommendation for the New Experiments Project Fund provoked a tough debate. The Asian representatives were particularly concerned that the SCMs, which were the proper constituency of the WSCF, not be bypassed, and that an arbitrarily created parallel political constituency not be created. They also found the criteria for the "experiments" too vague and without any explicit reference to principles characteristic of a Christian commu-

6. Beirut Minutes, p. 120.
7. Beirut Minutes, pp. 48-49.

nity. A fear was expressed that acceptance of the proposal and the consequent launching of issue-oriented political projects would lead to a weakening of the actual SCM constituency and create a split in the Federation.

The voice of those who were not happy with the revolutionary option was expressed in an amendment, moved from the floor before the proposal was voted upon, to ensure that national SCMs be consulted before decisions were taken on "new experimental projects." This amendment was defeated. The forming of the fund was then approved, and, paradoxically, the general secretary, who had supported the amendment, was given the sole authority to administer the fund.[8]

The revolutionary "first option" group did state in its report that acceptance of their ideological path would simply release those within the Federation who shared this political perspective to pursue this approach, allowing "those members who do not want to work along these lines to be freed to move ahead with their work." The group assumed, however, that the more dynamic elements of the Federation would naturally be involved in the "strategically oriented projects which unite political, educational and communication aspects."

This pattern of establishing "a new constituency" to the Federation out of activist groups soon found its way to the WCC, in which the Special Fund of the Program to Combat Racism (PCR) was to be administered according to principles analogous to the New Experiments Project Fund. Similarly, the idea of an activist network outside official structures found its place in the WCC as reflected by program units such as the Urban Industrial Mission (UIM) and Commission on the Churches' Participation in Development (CCPD).

The group which elaborated the "second option" represented the political views of "reformists." They favored political pluralism and considered democratic socialism as a concept around which to stimulate open dialogue among member movements in their search for relevant expressions of Christian responsibility for society. The profile

8. The plan for the New Experiments Project Fund was approved by a vote of 10 to 3 with 3 abstentions. The debate and the conclusions on the first group's report appear in the Beirut Minutes, pp. 48-51.

of this group could be described as democratic Christian left.[9] The "second option" group's report affirmed the basic traditional, liberal, and democratic values of university education. The present unrest was caused by distortion and subversion of these values by the impact of technology and by a bureaucratic society. The goal for this group was the renewal of university education. "The main problem was how to bring back these values or how to restore them under changed social and political circumstances in a renewed university."

The group did not claim to represent a consensus about a coherent political strategy for students or for education, or about the role of the Federation. Some of its members even questioned the possibility of such a strategy. The group concluded that

- the university has contributed . . . to the critical questioning of existing social and power structures . . . and could and should serve also in the future as a center of social and political critique;
- the university is still the place where the questions of meaning and value in culture and society can be raised and discussed . . . ;
- the university can and must serve as a place where . . . all professions can be involved during training in such criticism and action towards social change and democratization;
- the university has also served as a place where revolutionary and progressive political action groups could assemble, develop and evaluate their strategies . . . ; its autonomy should therefore be protected.[10]

The group refused to endorse the idea of a global revolution or of a "total change." Instead, it advocated the working out of concrete goals which reflect a more humanized society. The group made it plain that, in its view, the Federation should not endorse "an unhistorical and irrational attitude of protest and revolution as an aim in itself."

The concerns of the second, ecumenically committed moderate left group were picked up by the Executive Committee without much

9. Report of Group II of the Consultation on Student Unrest, Beirut Minutes, pp. 121-22.
10. Beirut Minutes, p. 122.

110

debate or controversy. It approved plans for regionally based study work and a comprehensive regional and interregional communication strategy along the lines endorsed by the 1968 Assembly, with the goal of serving WSCF member movements. The communication program was therefore given two sets of directives. At this point the Executive Committee had apparently either run out of steam or the activists were unconcerned about alternatives to their own proposals. They had, after all, already made certain that the challenges of the radical New Left had set the tone for the meeting.

After a confused and tense debate, the Executive Committee approved the two different ideological approaches in the report of the consultation as a valid framework for the Federation's future. The recommendations following the statements on two ideologies, elaborated by the working groups, were accepted with minor changes. These two decisions had fatal consequences because they effectively sanctioned a division within the Federation.

By appointing Leonardo Franco of Argentina as secretary of the Political Commission and Claudius Ceccon of Brazil as secretary for Communications, both identifying themselves with the objectives of the radical left group, to lead the work on political issues and the development of the new political network, the meeting paved the way for an institutional basis for this division.[11]

In Beirut the majority of initiatives within the Executive Committee were taken by leaders of the radical left group. Even if they made occasional efforts to tone down the high-pitched revolutionary language and to interpret their objectives as integral to the central vocation of Christian community, the basic concept and the proposed methods of work were identical with those of the wider Western European and North American neo-Marxist New Left of the sixties. In Beirut, the most visible leaders of this group were Richard Shaull, Mario Miegge, John Huot, Charlotte Weeks, Mario Yutzis, and Aaron

11. Other staff appointments made were: Peter Musgrove of Australia as priorities secretary in the Geneva office to handle assistance to needy member movements; Placide (Charles-Henri) Bazoche of France as North America secretary, though with some hesitation from the radical New Left representatives of North America; Juan Antonio Franco of Puerto Rico as Latin America communications secretary; and Iberra Malonzo of Philippines, who later declined the appointment, as cosecretary for Asia. Beirut Minutes, pp. 84-85.

Ramos as members of the Executive Committee; Laurence Bright, who as a representative at large from the British SCM was later to become the chief theologian/ideologist of the group; and Leonardo Franco from the Geneva staff.

In retrospect, it is apparent that the militant group advocating the revolutionary "first option" wanted to establish an independent but centrally led global political unit which would create within the Federation a new federation consisting of politically revolutionary member movements and the "new constituency" of political activist groups and organizations, and thereby change the identity and orientation of the whole WSCF.

The reformist group, advocating the "second option," were pushed into a somewhat confused defense. They failed to articulate their alternative vision for the Federation's work in general, and for its political role in particular. They had deliberately shunned proposing global, ideologically uniform programs for the worldwide Federation. Instead they foresaw a period of intense regionally based training and study work ahead. Their most influential representative, Samuel Parmar, the vice chairperson of the WSCF, was unable to participate. Their other strong Executive Committee members who were present in Beirut were Ross Terrill of Australia, Klaus-Peter Hertzsch of the GDR, and Raymond Rizk of Lebanon. Several of the representatives of member movements, who had considerable ecumenical experience, were articulate "moderates." Among them were Jürgen Hilke of Germany, Ninan Koshy of India, and Ghassan Maalouf of the Orthodox Student Movement of Syria/Lebanon. In addition, the majority of Geneva and regional staff agreed, for the time being, with this group.

5.2. The Federation's Theological Task

The theological task of the Federation was the topic of another working group of the Executive Committee.[12] Judging from its report, this group had had a hard time. The net result of its deliberations was a series of questions which did little more than reveal a fundamental

12. Report on the Working Group IV, Beirut Minutes, pp. 56-57.

uncertainty about the Federation's theological task. For example, the group was at a loss about the meaning of Christian unity, expressing the fear that a concern for unity might become entirely separated from political struggles. It looked positively on the critical role of theology as a protection against a "one-dimensional approach to reality." It also wanted to probe the concepts of disruption and continuity as lead themes for theological research. It considered promoting a review of the relationship between Christian commitment and Marxism. The idea which made the group most uneasy was that acceptance of the Christian faith might imply acceptance of political pluralism. On the whole, the report of the theology group gave the impression that all theology, not just "traditional theology," is more of a burden than a help in the political involvement of Christians.

5.3. Regional Plans

Regional reports[13] were an important part of the agenda of the Beirut Executive Committee meeting. They described a wide spectrum of substantive work in member movements on different continents and the many tough issues with which they had had to grapple in their own contexts. These reports, however, failed to inspire the minds of the radical visionaries who wanted to play the first violin and for whom only the clarity and purity of the dominant ideological theme mattered.

5.3.1. Africa

The report on Africa described the state of higher and secondary education in the region and examined key problems encountered by young people. Overshadowing all else were the difficulties of becoming educated to the desired level in the first place and then of finding employment for those who did receive higher education. The number of secondary schools was still inadequate, and the possibilities for entering higher education were even more limited.

13. Beirut Minutes, pp. 9-41.

All this was the result of a low level of national development. Another problem was the high degree of dependence of university education on foreign financing and on expatriate teaching staff; this contributed to the restlessness which was on the increase among African students. The report expressed clearly the goals of the WSCF Africa team. The overriding emphasis was on the strengthening of the basic units, namely, the "SCM or its equivalent in each national setting." Like the church in that region, the SCMs espoused as conscious goals the "three selves": self-support, self-propagation, and self-government. The report underlined the diversity of national situations, the obstacles of communication across the continent, and the difficulties of maintaining contact with African students studying abroad. Angola and Mozambique were still under colonial rule, while Rhodesia and South Africa had white minority governments which pursued policies of harsh racial discrimination. Namibia was under the rule of South African apartheid. These countries were isolated from the rest of Africa. Communication between French- and English-speaking Africa was also very limited. All these difficulties were a practical challenge to the WSCF in Africa. The staff were determined to encourage cooperation between the SCMs and churches' ministries to the university, and to ensure "that the best talents available are put at the service of both Christians and non-Christians in the academic community." Thus the main thrusts for programs in Africa were

- support of national leadership training within SCMs and churches' ministries to students;
- organization of leadership training courses in the subregions of southern Africa, East Africa, French-speaking Africa, and English-speaking West Africa; and
- preparation of an All Africa Youth and Student Conference.

In connection with the report, the Africa consultative group and regional staff extended an invitation to the Executive Committee to hold the next General Assembly for the first time in Africa — in Addis Ababa, Ethiopia, in 1972. The invitation was accepted, much to the disappointment of the Asian representatives, who had hoped that Japan would be chosen.

5.3.2. Asia

The Asia report painted a picture of the complex political and developmental issues in this vast and diverse region. It revealed the difficulty of coping with such a setting in terms of any single model of analysis. Many internal as well as external political forces were at work. The rise of China, the increasing role of the Soviet Union, the emergence of Japan as an economic power, and European and North American interests all had to be reckoned with, while at the same time most countries continued to struggle on under long-standing domestic ethnic, cultural, religious, and ideological pressures. Student political action took the forms of both protest and participation in nation building.

For the WSCF Asia region the basic frame of reference was that of the national autonomous SCMs. Some were large and had a recognized role among students and in churches, while others were small and had the characteristics of action-oriented protest movements. The priorities of the Asia region were

- to knit the movements of the region together;
- to encourage them in political action through study, education, and intraregional activity, and to interpret the Asia region's political stance to the rest of the WSCF;
- to organize an Asian students' conference;
- to draw faculty and students together in the Christian community in order to contribute to the transformation of universities;
- to involve secondary-school teachers in SCM work among their students; and
- to continue the WSCF China Study Project at the Asian level.

Among the planned programs outlined in the report were

- work among university teachers;
- intensification of publication activity;
- joint program with the East Asia Christian Conference (EACC) for theological students;
- work with overseas students;
- a medical students' conference;

115

- ecumenical strategy consultations;
- leadership training in the form of a five-year project of an Asia Leadership Development Center (ALDEC) on Christian ministry in the university.

The revolutionary wave of 1968 was scarcely reflected in the Africa report. The Asia report indicated an effort to evade its impact and instead to respond to the situation in the region's own terms.

5.3.3. Europe

The Europe report gave a brief outline of the main events since the Otaniemi Assembly and of future plans. A European Student Conference and two small consultations had been organized. The challenge of Marxism and radicalism was a major theme at each of them. The plans presented for the future included

- a Europe-Africa project, designed along the lines of European radicalism, and
- a first Protestant–Roman Catholic–Orthodox Student Pastors' Conference.

Acceptance of a radical socialist orientation as the overall emphasis for the region was implicit but not yet spelled out.

5.3.4. Latin America

The Latin America report reflected the difficulties of getting a regional program underway. The reasons given included the repressive political situation, the drastic changes involved in shifting from the concept of autonomous national SCMs to a regionwide Latin American SCM with its own regional profile, and problems and disagreements in giving shape to the leadership training program (CLAF). The tone of the report was all-out revolutionary. Its language was heavily ideological. The first objective for the new SCM in Latin America was "formation of students in and for militant action which presupposes commitment to the transformation of the society and participation as the basis of formation." The issues of the national SCMs did not surface at all in the report. The gap in regional staffing since the 1968 Assembly was reflected in the paucity of ideas and program plans in the report.

5.3.5. The Middle East

The Middle East report described the student and ecumenical scenes in a region in which the Orthodox tradition played a leading role. No sharp distinction was made between students and youth. Christian students in the region reportedly fell into three groups: (1) a "static" group, (2) a group which stressed social involvement and appeared politically activist, and (3) a group involved in the renewal of the church which was seen as a potential force for social change. Future plans for the region included

- research work related to social and political issues;
- leadership training in individual movements;
- work among Middle Eastern students in Europe and North America; and
- a regional conference for youth and students.

An interplay between an ecclesial-spiritual and sociopolitical engagement was conspicuous in the report.

5.3.6. North America

The report on North America was divided into U.S. and Canadian sections. The decision, made on March 1, 1969, to close down the national office and dismantle the structure of the University Christian Movement (UCM) in the USA, and its repercussions for the WSCF, were the main issues of the first part. The reporters did their utmost to prove that the disbanding of the organization was a positive step which would "enable greater experimentation . . . and lead to more vitality among specific ecumenical projects and caucuses." The step

117

was interpreted as a "breaking out of old stifling structures," despite the fact that the UCM had been founded, with great fanfare, only three years previously as an expression of a uniquely new, student-led ecumenism. The report concluded by conveying the wish expressed by various campus ministry and student caucuses that the WSCF appoint one or two staff persons to serve the U.S. scene.

The collapse of the UCM was viewed by most participants, including many of the Americans present, as a major setback for the WSCF in North America. For "moderates" it was a warning signal about the effects of the radicalization of SCMs and of the Federation. Furthermore, the triumphalistic interpretations of the significance of closing the office, in the style of the "institution is dead — the movement continues," did not convince many in Beirut. They felt that for those who insisted on seeing the end of the UCM as a positive step it was clearly an escape into illusion and a desperate effort to defend a failure.

The Canadian part of the report was given by John Huot, a Canadian Roman Catholic and a member of the WSCF Executive Committee, who had begun to lose touch with the Canadian SCM. The report portrayed a Canada harshly repressed by the "USA imperial system," its economy "controlled by USA interests" and "its raw-materials" needed by "the USA military system." The province of Quebec was reported to be the greatest challenge on the Canadian political scene. According to the report, it was still unclear what kind of independence the strong movement in the province was striving toward. Would it be bourgeois independence or socialist independence? The SCM was reported to be in decline because its traditional work was in trouble, and because radical members found it meaningless to work within the pluralistic context of the SCM.

5.4. Observations

The conflict between the determined supporters of the radical revolutionary option and those of the less radical pluralistic option colored the entire meeting of the Executive Committee. It fueled tensions between the regions and also within some of them. This became most evident in the debates and decisions on staff appointments. Candidates for vacancies were weighed not only on the basis of their professional qualifications and in the interest of regional balance, but also to ensure that the influence of the radical wing would be decisive among the Geneva staff.

The Beirut meeting marked the entry of a new terminology, a kind of liturgical language of the radical left, into Federation discussions and documents. It was antithetic to rational argument and to analytical style; it was inherently disdainful of institutions and arrogantly assumed a clear-cut and simple judgment of who was for good and who for evil. "In" words which separated the sheep from the goats included "conscientization," "new lifestyles," "education of the masses," "anti-imperialist struggle," "systems of repression," and the like. Those who did not master the use of this in-language were quickly written off by supporters of the emerging radical left wing of the Federation.

As a result of Beirut, an atmosphere of suspicion took hold of the staff of the Federation and the impact of the ideological division began to break the collegial pattern of debate and cooperation. When the staff met over lunch during the Beirut meeting for an informal discussion to assess the proceedings and to consider possible conclusions for our roles in the follow-up, one colleague expressed constraint about having to attend a staff gathering at all. He made it plain that the staff members were no less divided than the meeting itself. In the future no overall solidarity could be expected from the staff.[14] These remarks proved to be a prelude to the rift that was to affect the whole Federation in the following three years. Not everyone shared such a grim view of their work in the Federation. Toward the end of the meeting one of my Geneva colleagues said: "Mind you, this meeting lasts just a week. The rest of the year we are free to enjoy our work."[15] However, even he changed his mind in the period that followed the Beirut meeting.

The gravity of the conflict, the subsequent breakdown of communication, and the general deterioration of the atmosphere came as

14. Leonardo Franco expressed not only his own view but also the feelings of some others. An internal opposition group among staff emerged as allies of the chairman of the WSCF, Richard Shaull, when the first signs of tension between him and the general secretary began to come into the open.

15. Milan Opocensky in a conversation with the writer.

a shock to most of the participants. Whatever goodwill and mutual respect had existed at the beginning of the meeting evaporated bit by bit, and gloomy clouds of mutual suspicion had set in by the time the participants took their leave of the beautiful Mediterranean city, the center of the ecumenical movement in the Middle East.

CHAPTER 6

Ways Part

6.1. The Situation after Beirut

In 1969, in Beirut, the WSCF Executive Committee had come to the conclusion that two mutually contradictory ideological options should guide the work of the Federation in the next four years. The decision to accept both was intended to be a workable political compromise which would help avoid deadlock. After the difficult days in Beirut the staff was faced with the tasks of completing the change to a regionalized pattern of work, of implementing the plans stemming from the 1968 Assembly, and of responding to those member movements which were in particular need of international solidarity and support.[1] These pressures pushed ideological conflicts into the background for a time.

Furthermore, staff members in Geneva tried to reassure one another that the division was confined mainly to the Executive Committee. The Geneva office should go ahead with its tasks, undeterred by the clouds on the horizon, and attempt to turn differences into fruitful and dynamic cooperation.

However, the ideological rift within the Federation was widening,

---

1. The South African University Christian Movement sent numerous appeals for moral and financial support. The SCM of Argentina asked for help in the face of a division in its own ranks. The East German (GDR) movement wanted to strengthen its ties with the WSCF.

and certain uncontrollable factors became persistent reminders of this. After the dramatic closing down of the U.S. member movement, the most conspicuous development was the rapidly spreading political and cultural radicalization of most of the European SCMs. The result was an increased sense of polarity within these movements and a complete change of orientation in their work. The ferment among these traditionally influential European movements reinforced the position of the radical revolutionary wing in the Federation and contributed to a growing tension between different coalitions and regional emphases.

The leaders of the French SCM had identified themselves wholeheartedly with the French May Movement of 1968. What it gained in fieriness of radical ideas and jargon, it rapidly lost in members and branches. It severed its ties with the French churches and, as an organization, became a small fringe group. Its place among students was taken over partly by the Protestant Student Ministry and partly by a loosely organized Bible study movement for which former members of the French SCM provided leadership. Its material survival as an organization depended on the rental income from the renowned conference center at Bièvres, La Roche Dieu, which it owned.

Although there were signs of serious trouble in the British SCM as early as 1969, the really great changes did not take place for another two or three years. The national SCM began to concentrate on various radical "projects" and "campaigns" and to ignore its branches in universities and colleges. Its magazine, *Movement,* joined the Underground Press Syndicate. The movement adopted a neo-Marxist counterculture style. Initially, the General Council was sharply divided about this new orientation. A major challenge came from Scotland, where the SCM flatly refused to give up its work with local branches. However, such internal resistance was soon phased out with the extinction of local branches. Within a short time span the movement took up an anti-intellectualist stance which was a total departure from the rigorous intellectual discipline that had characterized its past. It began to drift and appeared ideologically and theologically lost. Its constituency shrank rapidly; communication with churches petered out, and various evangelical groups took over much of the Christian student scene.

The real climax came, however, in 1973-74, when, despite the protests of some members of the trustees, the radical leaders sold the old SCM headquarters office building, Annandale, and bought a grandiose rural property in the southwest of England. This was to be used as a conference center and to be managed by a nonauthoritarian "commune" in which all division of labor was to be abolished. The outcome of this was that the movement fell into a deep sleep for at least a decade.

In Germany "die Evangelische Studentengemeinde" (SCM) was a semiofficial arm of the Protestant Church of Germany (EKD). The church provided student pastors for most universities and other institutions of higher education in cooperation with local SCMs. Radicalization quickly strained relationships between church leaders and the SCM. Some farsighted church leaders tried to keep the channels of communication open.[2] Student pastors and SCM leaders pleaded for the patience of church leaders in this situation.[3] During 1968-69 many of the local SCM branches took up the pattern of radical action groups, while others tried to maintain their traditional ministry. Student pastors, numbering more than one hundred, were also divided. Many local branches stopped sending their representatives to the annual national conference of the SCM, which was its key decision-making body but which now had come largely under the control of the militant left. The general secretary of the national SCM, Jürgen Hilke, a "moderate" in this conflict, found the task of managing the national office in this situation desperately difficult.[4]

Parallel strifes were evident in the SCMs of the Nordic countries and of Belgium and the Netherlands. Radicalization among SCM leaders led usually to an anti-institutional stance, which in turn caused a rift between them and church leaders. A particularly dramatic sequence of events occurred in Finland, where the national SCM had been the semiofficial organ for the campus ministry of the Lutheran

2. Bishop Kurt Scharf of Berlin recognized the problem and convened in October 1968 the leadership of British, French, and German SCMs and of the WSCF in a consultation with some senior university and church leaders from his church to discuss the challenge of student revolution and to defuse the explosives inherent in the situation.

3. In October 1969 the writer was invited to interpret the situation within the WSCF to the Bishops' Council of the EKD, together with the general secretary of the SCM and a representative of the student pastors' conference. The unease among the bishops about trends in the SCM was noticeable.

4. Letter from Jürgen Hilke to Risto Lehtonen, May 1970.

church. In November 1969, at the meeting of the synod of the church, the still rather mild symptoms of radicalization of the SCM had aroused a panic reaction. As a result it voted to discontinue the integrated pattern of SCM-related student ministry. The majority of student pastors had to find other employment at short notice.

6.2. Regionalization

The implementation of regionalization thoroughly changed the external face of the Federation during 1969. Until the Otaniemi Assembly, most WSCF staff were based in Geneva. The headquarters were located at 13 rue Calvin in the Old City. The number of personnel in Geneva had grown to more than twenty by the end of the previous quadrennium. Single-executive regional units were located in Kitwe (Zambia), in Buenos Aires (Argentina), in Beirut (Lebanon), and in New York (USA). In the beginning of 1969 the Asia secretariat moved to Tokyo, the main office for Africa moved to Nairobi, and another Africa office was established shortly afterward in Yaoundé, Cameroon. A suboffice for Asia was also opened in Bangkok, Thailand. An expanded Latin America office was established in Lima, Peru. The WSCF Middle East office in Beirut continued to be a joint operation with the Middle East Council of Churches (MECC) and the WCC. The WSCF North America secretary shared an office with the U.S. branch of Pax Romana in New York. Of the regional offices, only the secretariat for Europe remained in Geneva. The WSCF secretariat at UNESCO in Paris, headed by Aaron Tolen of Cameroon until mid-1969, was closed down, and a one-person secretariat was opened at the UN in New York with Louis Simon of India as the staff person.

The number of regional executive staff jumped from six to fourteen while the number of Geneva-based executive staff was reduced from ten prior to the 1968 Assembly to seven at the end of 1969. The Executive Committee in Beirut had made a number of personnel decisions, not all of which were well prepared, but which specified the composition of regional and Geneva-based executive staff for the next two years. (See the appendix.)

Africa was the region in which the work of the Federation expanded most rapidly, with José Chipenda as the chief strategist. Already during the colonial era SCMs had been founded in universities, colleges, and secondary schools in west and southern Africa. The era of independence, beginning in the late fifties, brought a new vigor to expanding higher education throughout the continent. The number of SCMs started to grow rapidly; the Federation was instrumental in this development.[5] The quadrennium after the 1968 Assembly was envisaged as a time for building and consolidating Christian ministry in the mushrooming world of colleges and universities. Having more Federation staff in Africa gave Christian student movements in the region a boost. From 1969 onward, major emphases were the development of African Christian literature and leadership training to equip students and their leaders for Christian witness and social responsibility.

In *Asia* regionalization, under the leadership of Moonkyu Kang, made possible a major expansion of training programs aimed at SCMs and churches' university ministries. At the heart of these efforts was the launching of the Asia Leadership Development Center (ALDEC), which offered an annual three-month course consisting of a two-month seminar followed by one month of in-service training. The seminars were held at the Tozanzo International Youth Center of the Japanese YMCA. The first ALDEC course held in 1970 brought together leaders from nearly all of the Asian member movements. The lecturers included a wide range of ecumenical and academic personalities from Asia and other continents.

Work among university teachers also expanded at this time, building on the pioneering work of more than a decade for which Kentaro Shiozuki had been responsible. Specialized consultations on development concerns were held and publication became an important part of the work, with the magazine *Footnotes,* launched in 1969, as the main medium. The new regional office in the Christian Center in Tokyo provided a solid foundation for the expanded activities of the Federation in this vast region.

The WSCF leaders of Asia reacted to the division experienced at the

5. Prior to the 1960 General Committee the Federation had only two affiliated movements in Africa, while the total number of associated and corresponding movements from the region represented at Thessaloniki was nine. At the 1968 General Committee the number of affiliated movements became six, and the total number of associated and corresponding movements represented there was eleven.

Beirut meeting by trying to dissociate themselves immediately from the conflicts which had erupted from within Europe and North America and which they saw threatening the Geneva office. WSCF African leaders reacted similarly, although somewhat less vocally. Both were anxious to minimize the impact of the radical left on their regions in order to concentrate on building student Christian communities and to continue the regional work of the Federation in their own educational, ecumenical, and sociopolitical contexts. They had no intention of abandoning plans for regional work that had been developed before the events in Paris, Uppsala, and Turku in 1968, nor of making a drastic break with the ecumenical strategies worked out in the previous quadrennium. In their view the student revolution was basically a Western phenomenon. They also felt that Latin America belonged culturally and ideologically to the West, even if the continent was economically part of the Third World. The fact that Latin Americans now looked to the radicals of Europe and North America for allies confirmed this view as far as the Africans and Asians were concerned.

From 1968 onward, the *Europe* office of the Federation continued to operate from the premises of the WSCF head office in Geneva. The annual staff meetings of the European SCMs were replaced by a loosely organized European committee and a series of consultations, conferences, and study projects. The first European Student Conference took place in Gwatt, Switzerland, in 1969. Not surprisingly, the European member movements were turning toward radical socialism. Most of the activist student leaders in European universities and SCMs, with the notable exception of those in socialist countries, behaved like zealous new converts in promoting Marxist ideas. "Christians for Socialism in Europe" was adopted as the overall theme for the Europe program. The Europe secretary, Milan Opocensky, insisted on making theological reflection an integral part of the regional program, even if Marxist ideology did become its dominant contextual framework. The secretariat began to publish the *WSCF Europe* bulletin and "Theological Dossiers."[6] The annual conferences

---

6. The mimeographed "Theological Dossiers," in which significant papers given at WSCF events or published elsewhere were collected, became an important vehicle for the theological work of the WSCF Europe program. This effort continued through 1972. See also below, chapter 12, p. 275, including n. 19.

of European student pastors which had been started much earlier were continued, and many Catholic chaplains began to participate.

The *Latin American region* struggled to formulate a regional program that would be feasible under military dictatorships and the current repression of dissent. Leaders had had difficulty finding a location from which the secretariat could operate with reasonable security. The regional leaders identified themselves with the radical revolutionary vision that was personified by Fidel Castro and Che Guevara of Cuba and Camillo Torres of Colombia. The staff team, once finally together, began to develop plans for the Latin American Leadership Training Center (CLAF) proposed already in Panama 1968 (pp. 97-98), but the shape of which, however, remained blurred for most of the quadrennium. The political conditions on the continent and the heavy-handed treatment of students by the rightist governments undoubtedly impeded the efforts of the staff team. But the vagueness of the whole concept and the lack of definition of the role of the WSCF in this region after 1968 were also conspicuous elements. Meanwhile, many SCMs which had shown such promising beginnings in the early fifties shrank rapidly, and some virtually ceased to exist. Over these years the WSCF lost a good part of its organized constituency in Latin America.

Richard Shaull was the theological and ideological mentor of the Latin American staff team. He and Paulo Freire provided a bridge between Christian commitment and revolutionary social and political objectives. In faithfulness to the teaching of Shaull, the staff team rejected "traditional" patterns of SCM work, thus contributing further to the halting of programs and to the isolation of Latin American SCMs from the rest of the Federation. The sizable funds poured by North America and Europe into the Federation's efforts in Latin America did not heal the paralysis.

The approach of Latin American regional leaders had an affinity with the radicalism of Western Europe, even though the events of 1968 as such did not bring about a drastic change in their ideological leanings. Consciousness of the political repression of students had been growing since the early sixties,[7] and the SCMs had turned deci-

7. The word "revolution" had in Latin American ears not necessarily a Marxist connotation nor the same ring of novelty as it had among the Western European

sively to the left by the time of the right-wing military takeover in Brazil in 1964.

The WSCF *Middle East* office had been integrated into the life of churches and the wider ecumenical movement in the area from its beginning as a regional operation. The office represented both WSCF and WCC programs and became a central part of the MECC during this period. After the 1967 war, however, the Palestinian issue colored all ecumenical work in the region. A strong regional committee coordinated activities in that area, which included leadership training, participation in development, and publication and documentation in English, French, and Arabic. The region also made a distinct theological contribution to the ecumenical debates of the day. The contribution of Orthodox churches gave the entire Middle East program a special flavor. The ecclesial character of the joint ecumenical student and youth ministry of the region was repeatedly affirmed after 1968.[8] Traditional Christianity, as inherited from the churches in the region, was the prime source and guide for political commitments.

The Middle East reaction to the radical revolutionary trend in the Federation and to the resulting polarization was unique. After the 1967 war, most of the young Arab Christians had been drawn politically closer together in their opposition to the Zionist policies of the State of Israel and in their support of Palestinian liberation. They began to seek allies among Christians who showed some understanding of their concerns, and on such grounds found some affinity with the radical revolutionary left in Europe and North America. The alliance was, however, tactical rather than ideological in character because they were as opposed to political and cultural

---

radical left around 1968. It was part of common political jargon in Latin America, used quite loosely about almost any coup or change of government brought about by either the left or right.

8. The affirmation of a clear theological identity, with Orthodox overtones, surfaced in reports of conferences, consultations, and advisory committee meetings held in the Middle East. One of the most thorough expositions of the theological position of the WSCF regional leaders was a paper, "Quelques reflexions sur la 'theologie,'" prepared by Raymond Rizk for the Middle East Advisory Committee meeting, held in Beirut, June 12-15, 1970, and circulated in English also in the European "Theological Dossier" of 1970. Similar emphases appeared in the preparatory documents on the Middle East for the Addis Ababa Assembly. WSCF Archives.

imperialism from the West as they were to the occupation policies of Israel. They were not keen to open the door to Western penetration under the disguise of Western radicalism.

Regionalization proved most problematic in *North America*. First, there was the perennial tension between the Canadian SCM and its counterpart in the USA, which was comprised of numerous Christian student organizations and campus ministry agencies. Second, as we have seen, the University Christian Movement (UCM), launched with great fanfare in 1966, floundered in the midst of campus uprisings and collapsed in 1969 as a result of an internal deadlock. The main task of the secretary for North America was to liaise with the Canadian SCM, the remains of Christian student organizations in the USA,[9] and various American radical campus groupings, as well as with campus ministries and the mission agencies which supported ecumenical student ministries overseas. No coherent regional program apart from such liaison was possible. Father Placide (Charles-Henri) Bazoche served as the secretary for North America from mid-1969 to 1973. Later a cosecretary, Jan Griesinger of the USA, was added to work on women's concerns. After 1969, the American members of the Federation's Executive Committee had no recognized national member organization as their home base.

In this situation the African, Asian, and Middle Eastern WSCF leaders found a new reason to push for regionalization. It served not only as a way of bringing the Federation closer to its grass roots by making its work more contextual culturally and spiritually, but also of protecting them against a new wave of domination from the West, now under a radical ideological umbrella. For the Europeans, the Latin Americans, and the representatives from the USA, regionalization was helpful as a means of destroying centralized power in the Federation and paving the way for a radically different model of power sharing. Therefore, regionalization was not contested by either group in this quadrennium.

9. The two national Christian student organizations in the USA which did not go out of existence when they joined the UCM were the Lutheran Student Movement and the Orthodox Campus Movement. Both of these survived and continued to function after the death of the UCM. Also, some U.S. regional ecumenical student organizations continued, most notably the New England SCM.

6.3. Geneva: A Change of Role

The size and character of the Federation's Geneva office changed drastically as a result of regionalization. The responsibility for the bulk of the Federation's programs was placed on the six regional offices. These also became responsible for channeling financial assistance to member movements in need, formerly handled by the Ecumenical Assistance Program in Geneva. The number of personnel in the Geneva office decreased from about twenty at the beginning of 1968 to fourteen at the end of 1969.

The new Geneva crew was complete by November 1969. New arrivals were Claudius Ceccon of Brazil, an architect and cartoonist, for communications; Leonard Clough of the USA, a minister of the United Church of Christ and a former general secretary of the UCM of the USA, for resource development; Leonardo Franco of Argentina, a lawyer and former Latin America secretary, for the Political Commission; and Peter Musgrove of Australia, a major in the Indian army during World War II, a Methodist minister and former general secretary of the Australian SCM. Those already in Geneva were Nancy Bell of New Zealand, a former secondary school teacher, as the secondary schools secretary; Milan Opocensky of CSSR, a former lecturer of theology at the Comenius Faculty in Prague, as the Europe secretary; and myself as the general secretary, formerly ten years on the Finnish SCM staff and five years as the first WSCF North America secretary based in the USA. Audrey Abrecht, administrative assistant to the general secretary, a WSCF staff member since 1949, with the cooperation of some long-standing support staff, succeeded in maintaining the continuity of the Geneva office operations in this era of change.

From 1969 onward, the main responsibilities of the Geneva office were as follows:

- coordination of the Federation's work as a whole;
- preparation of the General Assemblies and of the annual meetings of the Executive Committee;
- communication programs;
- Political Commission programs;
- secondary schools work;
- various ad hoc consultations and delegation visits;

130

- relationships with other world organizations, especially the WCC;

and last but by no means least,

- the finances of the WSCF.

The Europe secretary, although a regional secretary, participated fully in the life and work of the Federation's Geneva collective.

6.4. From Rue Calvin to Quai Wilson: More Than Just a Move

The WSCF had to vacate its historic headquarters in the debonair patrician house at 13 rue Calvin, in the heart of the Old City of Geneva, where its offices had been located since the 1920s. Colonel Francis Pickens Miller, chairman of the WSCF in the late twenties and early thirties, had been instrumental in finding the house. He had looked for a place worthy of the dignity of the WSCF and its offshoot, the World University Service (WUS), still at that time known as the International Student Service (ISS). Later, more space for the expanding offices of the Federation had been found nearby. The move, made necessary when the descendants of the original owner of the property wanted to put it to more lucrative use, became in itself a symbol of the profound changes through which the Federation was to go. In any case, the urbane archaic elegance of rue Calvin had already become quite impractical as a modern office.

The predecessor of WUS, the ISS, had been formed during World War I as a service arm of the WSCF for relief activities among refugee students. In the course of time, WUS had grown into an independent organization which no longer had a meaningful connection with its original sponsors. The physical separation of the two organizations in 1970 only confirmed the growing distance between them. The two organizations had parted company ideologically already in the fifties under the pressures of the Cold War.[10] WUS moved to offices near

10. WUS established links in the mid-fifties with the Leyden-based International

the airport in Geneva and the WSCF to the John R. Mott House at 1 Quai Wilson, on the lakefront, the headquarters of the World Alliance of YMCAs and the World YWCA, the two oldest world ecumenical lay organizations. However, the Federation's physical vicinity with these two organizations had no noticeable effect on its relationship with them. The WSCF, for its part, had been heading in a different direction from that of the Y's for some time.[11]

The move to John R. Mott House at Quai Wilson was completed without ceremony by the end of 1970. An office Christmas party was held there, but because of the escalation of the ideological conflict among staff it was not a joyful celebration. The atmosphere of suspicion could not be dispelled by Christmas music.

In retrospect the decision not to invest in its own building was a

---

Student Conference (ISC), which had been formed as a Western counterpart to the Prague-based International Union of Students (IUS). The latter organization had come under the control of the communist organizations and governments who also funded it. The ISC received support from the U.S. government for its anticommunist activities. The WSCF wanted at that time to stay out of the Cold War confrontations.

11. The move of the headquarters took place after an interlude. The necessity for vacating the rue Calvin premises was foreseen already in the mid-sixties. Before the 1968 events, Valdo Galland had explored several alternatives, all of which fell through either because of their cost or because of the inadequacy of the space offered. The best practical option became the construction of a new building. The United Presbyterian Church of the USA provided seed money for this purpose and launched the Philippe Maury Memorial Fund to which all supporting agencies were asked to contribute. The fund was also to finance special events under the heading of the Philippe Maury Memorial Lectures. The driving spirit of the new headquarters project was Margaret Flory, director of Student World Relations of the UPUSA-COEMAR, who had a long history of involvement in the life of the Federation. The architect's plans for the new building were complete, the financial details had been negotiated with the banks, and the deed of purchase for a parcel of land from the WCC was about to be signed. A lighthearted ground-breaking ceremony had even been held, when the whole plan had to be called off. Cracks had appeared in the financial foundations of the Federation. Its income had started to decline and the funding drive for the headquarters had fallen short of its target. And coincidentally, news that space would be available at the John R. Mott House had just been received. Not untypically, the decision was reached on very short notice at an emergency meeting of the headquarters committee convened within twenty-four hours. Margaret Flory agreed to leave New York for Geneva directly from her office only a few hours after she received the invitation by phone. The speed of the decision was necessary to avoid penalties for cancellation of the building plans.

signpost indicating the new direction the Federation was to take. Further signposts, in the form of more dramatic events, were to follow before the destination was reached at the WSCF Assembly in Addis Ababa in 1972-73.[12]

6.5. A New Wave of Tension

The Beirut meeting had left a trauma on most of those present. There is much documentation showing that, in the months that followed, Geneva staff were determined not to allow polarization to paralyze work and lead to another deadlock. The procedures of staff meetings from mid-1969 to mid-1970 were exceptionally disciplined. Substantive reports on travels, consultations, and meetings attended were presented. Yet signs of polarization kept resurfacing, first within the communication program and subsequently in the preparations for the 1970 meeting of the Executive Committee.

A focal point of tension which reappeared meeting after meeting was that between the "new" and the "old" in the Federation's work. Leonardo Franco and Claudius Ceccon emphasized that a totally new style was needed if the Federation as a whole, and its Geneva office in particular, were to have any meaning. The new style was described as participatory, nonbureaucratic, and flexible. Individual staff members were to decide for themselves on what areas of work to concentrate, which former functions to abandon, and with whom to work. Staff were to take the lead in developing "cutting edges" for the Executive Committee, which meant creating models of participation in revolutionary action in society and in the church. They often referred to the terms "to do new things" and "to discover new methods and new groups" which Richard Shaull had introduced into the Federation's vocabulary. Shaull and his followers in the Executive

---

12. Twenty-five years after the decision to call off the construction of an office building, it is still obvious that the administrative and financial burden involved would have been excessive for the troubled organization. On the other side, had the construction been carried through, the property would have, for the last ten years, been a gold mine for the financially hard-pressed WSCF of today. The image of a modern office building, though, was unthinkable for the Federation of the seventies.

Committee and staff tended to label the WSCF programs and emphases of the pre-1968 era, the resolutions of the Assembly, and the accountability to the member movements as belonging to the past. All this "old" in the life of the Federation was to be cleared away. History was out and discontinuity in.[13] Advocates of the "new" viewed even job descriptions and budget matters with distaste as part of the old alienating, bureaucratic, institutional heritage. Leonardo Franco frequently used the phrase "monetary Federation" to denote the old order. By that he implied that for the defenders of the old style of the Federation, the principal goal had become fund-raising, which, when successful, gave them a position of power and guaranteed the loyalty of member movements.

What happened in regional committees and member movements outside Europe began to receive less and less attention at Geneva staff meetings. The European region was an exception because the secretary for Europe, unlike all other regional secretaries, was part of the Geneva staff, and also because Europe was the seedbed of the revolutionary left radicalism.

When preparations were begun for the 1970 Executive Committee meeting, Leonardo Franco proposed an internal "cease-fire" in order to avoid a repetition of the ideological deadlock of Beirut. This implied deliberate avoidance of confrontations of an ideological nature. This approach was welcomed by all of us in Geneva, as it seemed to offer the possibility of concentrating on substantive preparatory work. Consequently, the months before the meeting of the Executive Committee held in Cartigny were the last of the quadrennium when a common discipline and a serious effort to communicate across ideological positions prevailed in the Geneva office. The staff meeting minutes of the first half of 1970 with their verbatim reports of all the discussions on current points of controversy reflect the seriousness with which the cease-fire was held.[14]

---

13. Discontinuity was introduced as a key concept by Shaull in several of his statements. A good illustration of his thinking is the article "Liberal and Radical in an Age of Discontinuity," published originally in *Christianity and Crisis,* January 5, 1970, and reprinted in the *Student World,* no. 3-4 (1969): 350-58.

14. The minutes of the meetings of Geneva-based staff on November 13 and 19, 1969, include a verbatim account of the discussion of staff work in Geneva. They convey a sense of serious grappling with the divisive issues and a sincere collective

Whether the cease-fire was intended to allow for the strengthening of positions and preparation for battle, or to prepare the way for long-term peaceful work in spite of differences in emphasis, was a question in the back of the minds of many. However, to have raised it publicly would have meant breaking the rules of the cease-fire. I received the first inkling that a longer-term strategy was in the minds of the revolutionary leftist faction from a discussion with Leonardo Franco only a few days before the meeting of the Executive Committee. He tried to persuade me to make public that I would not run for a second term as general secretary. He implied that such an announcement would make life easier for me in the approaching struggles.

The internal Geneva cease-fire began to show signs of strain in January 1970 when Geneva and regional executive staff met with the chair, Richard Shaull, and vice chair, Samuel Parmar, in Glion, Switzerland. An innocent-looking incident triggered a wave of suspicion. Shaull had invited the Latin Americans present to meet separately at the same time as one of the final plenaries in which plans for the regionalized Federation were to be discussed. He defended his behavior on the grounds that there was not enough time available to discuss the pressing Latin American problems. This was nevertheless interpreted as a partisan action and experienced as treating the concerns of the less revolutionary regions with contempt. The very purpose of the meeting had been to take the pulse of the Federation as a whole, to evaluate what had happened since the Assembly and in Beirut, to review the plans for regions and Geneva-based programs, and to discuss the agenda and procedures for the next Executive Committee meeting.

At Glion the African members of staff raised the question whether the next Executive Committee meeting should not be postponed, since they thought they would not be ready for a major discussion of the Beirut options so soon. Furthermore, they felt that all their energy was needed to get the expanded regional programs off the ground. Diverting some of this energy to addressing the issues causing the turmoil in the

---

effort to avoid a rift. The minutes of the following meetings on December 10 and 17, 1969, and February 26, March 3, March 19, May 14 and 15, 1970, reflect a disciplined pattern of work and a high degree of communication between staff representing very different positions. Substantive reports on travels and meetings attended, and working papers, are appended to these minutes.

Federation was undesirable and unnecessary. Similar opinions were voiced by Geneva staff involved in the Political Commission and Communication programs — those who had also advocated a cease-fire among the staff. They feared that their efforts would come under an ideological assault because they had so little to show for their programs along the lines of the revolution-oriented "options" of Beirut. The officers, who had ultimate responsibility for Executive Committee preparations, concluded that the meeting should be held as scheduled in June 1970 and that in this meeting opportunity should be given to develop ideas for a few crucial concerns facing the Federation, such as the task of the Political Commission and of theological reflection. No extensive discussion of regional programs and emphases would be expected. In addition, the meeting should limit itself to such policy, program, and structural decisions as needed urgent attention.

It was therefore a surprise when a few weeks later Shaull, after receiving more materials on the Executive Committee agenda and program, telephoned Geneva and made an ardent appeal for calling off the Executive Committee meeting. He maintained that a full meeting at this stage would perpetuate the immobilization experienced at Beirut and that the present members of the Executive Committee were not capable of generating ideas which would help the Federation get beyond the impasse which he felt it was in as a result of the sharply polarized meeting at Beirut. He feared that another meeting so soon would lead to further immobilization. He suggested that a select group made up of "some staff, Executive Committee members, and other people who are at the cutting edge of certain particular ideological, theological or communitarian developments" be brought together to prepare a creative role for the Federation. Shaull's plea resulted in a sharp exchange between him and the general secretary. The disagreement revealed the different concepts and convictions which were being brought into play.[15]

---

15. The full record of this exchange is in the transcribed text of the tape of the telephone conversation on February 13, 1970, between Richard Shaull and Risto Lehtonen and in a letter from Lehtonen to Shaull of February 20, 1970. The letter sums up the arguments for and against holding the Executive Committee meeting and illustrates disagreements between the chairman and the general secretary about the function of the Executive Committee.

The main difference at this point was about the role of the Executive Committee. Shaull seemed to dismiss its constitutional functions, emphasizing its role as a radical think-tank, "primarily a place through which new things begin to emerge, new experiments are launched" in line with current ideological and theological reflection. If the presently elected Executive Committee could not function in this way, Shaull did not see any reason for convening it. In its place he wanted to bring together a smaller, presumably more like-minded group which could work effectively together on creative ideas along radical revolutionary lines.

My letter to Shaull was an effort to counter his ideas about the need to bypass the Executive Committee and to suggest ways in which new ideas and initiatives could be not only discussed but encouraged without ignoring the representative decision-making pattern of the Federation. The disagreement centered on the question of who generated creative ideas and initiatives, and where and how they should be developed. Shaull placed the main emphasis on ideologically homogeneous "avant-garde" types of group. He had difficulty with a structure which could absorb conflicting views. If the Executive Committee could not unanimously support the radical revolutionary line with which he was in sympathy, it was merely an obstacle. For me a forum in which different experiences and perspectives were brought together had a positive function. The Executive Committee should be a clearinghouse for a wide range of ideas and views originating from member movements and churches, from the university world, from action groups within society at large, and also from the rank and file of the Federation itself. It should be a forum for critical thinking, in which new ideas were tested before they were converted into programs of action. I tried to emphasize that such an understanding of the role of the Executive Committee would not prevent the WSCF leadership from pursuing specific approaches provided that openness and sensitivity to the diverse constituency of the Federation were explicitly fostered.

Another point of difference arose from conflicting assessments of the state of the WSCF member movements. Shaull thought the SCMs had no future in the form which they had inherited. The two movements closest to him, the former UCM of the USA and the Brazilian SCM, represented the trend of the future for the whole Federation, and for all its member movements. Both of these movements had had to give up their inherited organizational forms and in effect be discontinued, for the sake of the "new" that was about to emerge within the Christian community. For me it was impossible to base the approach of the whole Federation on these two cases. I urged Shaull to recognize the diversity of the situations and the dynamism shown by Christian student movements in numerous countries. "At this point I do not agree with . . . your despair, that nothing useful is happening in most of the Federation. You seem to draw your conclusion too much from what you see or do not see happening in North America and from the difficulties in the Latin American situation."

The exchange touched several other issues as well. The chairman expressed concern about "a bureaucratic mentality," and about proposed visits by members of the Executive Committee to regions other than their own as a form of "ecumenical tourism." He had doubts about proposed ad hoc consultations on specific issues in connection with the Executive Committee because of the presence of unhelpful participants (members of the Executive Committee), and he feared that one region or another would attempt to "take over."

Nevertheless, after this incident preparations for the Executive Committee meeting continued. Shaull's intervention did not divert Geneva staff from observing the ideological cease-fire which they hoped would continue through the forthcoming meeting at Cartigny.

CHAPTER 7

Hope against Hope:
July 1969–February 1970

Shortly after the Beirut meeting several challenging tasks and events came to counteract the divisive trends that had, already then, set in. They prompted some member movements, Executive Committee members, and staff to work together across ideological divisions. The most notable case was the attempt to respond to the University Christian Movement in South Africa, which is reported in detail in chapter 11. The three examples explored in this chapter illustrate that part of the life of the Federation which proved both colorful and inspiring to many member movements as well as to Federation staff who were otherwise absorbed by the follow-up of regionalization and the tensions caused by the growing ideological polarization.

7.1. Mission to Argentina

The first was an international team visit in August 1969 to Argentina to mediate between the National SCM of Argentina and the Confederation of Autonomous SCMs of Argentina (CAMECA). In February 1969 a rift had emerged within the SCM when three of its branches, those in La Plata, Rosario, and Cordoba, had dissociated themselves from the National SCM and had formed a new organization, CAMECA. Both groups claimed to continue the work of the original SCM. The American Baptist Foreign Mission Society (ABFMS) was also involved in the situation; it was sponsoring an Argentine pastor, Daniel Rebasa, who had had his theological education in the USA, for work in the National SCM. The conflict had begun when the leaders of the National SCM protested against the size of the salary of Rebasa, which was paid by American Baptists and was allegedly much higher than what the Argentine SCM could afford for anyone in its service. The conflict soon escalated to include principles of student ministry. Rebasa and the branches which had left the National SCM maintained contact with local churches while the National SCM distanced itself from them. CAMECA seemed to be theologically more traditional, even evangelical, while the National SCM was seeking its identity in radical political activity. Over and above these differences there arose a grueling controversy about revolutionary ideologies.

All the parties involved, including the ABFMS, encouraged the Federation to send a team to Argentina to bring the leaders of the two groups together. The team consisted of Mario Yutzis from Uruguay, a member of the WSCF Executive Committee, and Leonardo Franco and myself from Geneva. For me it was more a plunge into the history and ideologies of Argentina's political left than an exercise in ecumenical strategy as defined prior to 1968.

When the team arrived, the ideological conflict seemed to be the main issue. The National SCM seemed to be committed to the line of the Peronist left and to strong centralized leadership, while CAMECA had opted for a popular revolutionary line with an emphasis on building an active local constituency. Quarrels about relationships with churches and supporting organizations seemed to be of secondary importance. In the past the National SCM had been a partner in the development of ecumenical strategy for student ministry in Latin America. It had strong historical ties with the Union Theological Seminary of Buenos Aires, although more recently it had come to view churches as reactionary institutions. It continued to be the recognized member movement of the WSCF in Argentina and recipient of financial support from the Federation.

The new confederation, CAMECA, had a close relationship with the American Baptists, not least because they had sponsored Rebasa's theological studies in the USA. For CAMECA, close ties with local churches were an asset rather than an obstacle for their revolutionary social and political commitment. CAMECA was also keen to become a member of the WSCF.

As a result of the searching discussions held in Argentina in August 1969, communication between the two groups was established and common ground for their reconciliation was found. However, the healing of the split was reversed only weeks later when Mario Yutzis, a member of the reconciliation team and of the WSCF Executive Committee, identified himself fully with the leadership of the National SCM, endorsing its authoritarian, top-heavy style, typical of the Peronist left, and denouncing CAMECA and Daniel Rebasa.[1]

In the course of a few years the National SCM went out of existence, while CAMECA survived and moved ideologically closer to the left wing of Peronism. The support of the American Baptist mission board probably played a decisive role in consolidating its work.

This, albeit unsuccessful, mission indicates that as late as the middle of 1969 the WSCF was looked upon by many member movements and churches as an embodiment of concern for unity among Christian students. However, the Argentine exercise showed how divisive the uncritical identification of Christians with authoritarian factions of the political left could be. A few months later the unity of the whole WSCF was put to the test under the pressures of similar tendencies.

7.2. The WSCF and the World Union of Jewish Students (WUJS)

Until the tumultuous years at the end of the sixties, the WSCF had had a recognized place among international student organizations for over forty years.[2] The roles and relationships of these organizations

1. The conflict was reported to the WSCF Executive Committee at Beirut, Minutes of the WSCF Executive Committee Meeting, Beirut, Lebanon, March 30–April 6, 1969, pp. 69-70. The failure of efforts of reconciliation is implicit in the nonaction by the 1970 Executive Committee meeting at Cartigny. Minutes of the WSCF Executive Committee Meeting, Cartigny, Switzerland, June 22-28, 1970, p. 6.

2. World organizations with which the WSCF had an active relationship included, in addition to the family of ecumenical world organizations, the WCC and its Youth Department; the World YMCA and World Alliance of the YWCA; the Roman Cath-

changed drastically, however, under the general ferment among students and their leaders. What happened to the relationship between the WUJS and the WSCF in 1969 is a vivid illustration of these trends.

The WUJS and the WSCF had a history of cooperation as sponsors of the international relief and development agency World University Service (WUS). In 1967 social responsibility and interreligious dialogues, contacts and visits became the hallmarks of this cooperation. The organizations sponsored a joint seminar on "People of God and Society," held in Geneva, October 30–November 2, 1967, and the Federation endorsed a two-year Frontier Study and Service project at the Hebrew University in Jerusalem from 1967 to 1969, led by Donna Runnals, a Canadian Old Testament scholar.

When the political tensions in the Middle East grew after the 1967 war and Palestinian youth became radicalized, WUJS suggested that cooperation be stepped up. The atmosphere within the WSCF, then under the impact of political radicalization, was not, however, conducive to any visible joint efforts. WUJS proposed organizing another joint seminar, but the Executive Committee at Beirut could only come up with a halfhearted resolution which authorized the staff to "explore the proposal further with the Jewish leaders" and to report back at the next meeting. An obvious factor in the WSCF's reluctance to pursue this matter was that the Middle Easterners of the Federation were close to Palestinian liberation organizations. They did not want the Federation to be used as a forum for pro-Israeli propaganda, as would, in their view, be inevitable at a joint consultation.

On October 30, 1969, the Federation headquarters staff received a three-person delegation of the WUJS for exploratory talks.[3] It proved to be a difficult day. First of all, the WSCF Middle East secretary, Gabriel Habib, who had been invited to participate and had come from Beirut for the occasion, decided at the last minute not to attend. He was in the

---

olic counterparts, Pax Romana and Young Catholic Students (JEC); World University Service (WUS); International Union of Students (IUS), with its head office in Prague; and the WUJS. The WSCF played in the sixties an active role among the international nongovernmental organizations (NGOs) at UNESCO in Paris and later at the UN in New York.

3. The members of the WUJS delegation were Gordon Hausman, former WUJS secretary for foreign affairs; Josef Bollag, treasurer; and Edy Kaufman, secretary general. Cartigny Minutes, p. 186.

office that day but stayed in another room. His reason for staying out was that he did not want to endanger the trust which he enjoyed among a wide range of Palestinian leaders of different factions. Attendance at a closed and confidential meeting with WUJS would have made him immediately suspect in Beirut. Another difficulty during the day was the WSCF's indecision about holding another seminar with WUJS. The Jewish delegation expressed their disappointment and anger concerning this turnabout of the Federation. They took up other points in which they saw signs of the WSCF bending toward an anti-Israeli, and potentially anti-Semitic, position. They referred to the report of the WSCF consultation on "Peace and Justice in the Middle East" held in Beirut in 1968, to the publication of the Beirut statement in the *Federation News,* and to the dedication of one whole issue of the WSCF quarterly *Student World* to the Beirut consultation papers, deemed by them excessively pro-Palestinian. Although the participants finally agreed on some cautious follow-up steps, the relationships between the two organizations cooled markedly after that meeting.

A postlude occurred a few weeks later. The general secretary of the World Jewish Congress, Dr. Riegner, invited me to lunch in order to interpret the mood among WUJS leaders; to alert me to the diversity of ideological views among Jews, including a non-Zionist tradition; and to encourage the Federation to continue to keep in touch with the WUJS. He refuted as groundless impressions that the organization was identified with the right wing of Israel. He confided how he himself had been a vocal critic of Zionism until 1948. He wanted me to understand how and why, after the founding of the State of Israel, anti-Zionism ceased to exist among Jews in general and within Israel in particular.

These exchanges were followed by a substantive letter from the leaders of WUJS in April 1970. In it the writers criticized the recent actions of the Federation. They charged WSCF leaders with inconsistency in breaking off the dialogue under the pretext that involvement would compromise the Federation ideologically.[4] They challenged the morality of an international Christian organization which

---

4. It was fashionable within the New Left to deny the value of any dialogue with representatives of a different political perspective. Dialogue meant compromising. Common actions or else confrontation were the only acceptable alternatives for a Christian radical group.

refused to talk to Jews for fear of offending Arabs. They accused the WSCF, with its new political orientation, of opening doors to a new wave of anti-Semitism. Finally they spelled out the positions and aspirations prevalent among Jewish students and their leaders and stressed their sense of urgency about Jewish-Christian dialogue.

The WSCF Middle East Advisory Group took up the threads of these WSCF-WUJS contacts at its meeting in Beirut in June 1970 by issuing a succinct statement:

> Christians in all places and in all times are called to be open to other people of any conviction, creed, or nationality. Therefore Christians of the Arab world are not opposed to dialogue with Jewish students. . . . (Such a dialogue) could lead to a deeper understanding of man, his freedom, his dignity, and his liberation. . . .
>
> We make a distinction between Judaism and Zionism, accepting the former but rejecting the latter. More specifically we mean by Zionism, which we reject, the ideology which exploits Biblical texts to justify the existence of the state of Israel e.g. by turning the promises of God to his people as revealed in the Old Testament to a political foundation of a state.[5]

The matter was presented to the WSCF Executive Committee at Cartigny. After a lengthy debate, it was decided to send WUJS some assurances aimed at allaying its dismay about the sharpness of recent Federation statements and showing that the WSCF was not a monolithic organization in relation to the Middle East. It also decided to convey its desire for "informal contacts" between leaders of the two organizations but stopped short of suggesting any practical steps. It also made clear that the WSCF had no reason to label the WUJS a "Zionist" organization.

This resolution cut off communication between the WSCF and the WUJS for many years. No active follow-up of the talks materialized. The need, which Riegner had underlined, to acknowledge and support political openness within the WUJS was ignored in the WSCF; the escalating internal ideological warfare had by then narrowed its perspectives.

5. Cartigny Minutes, pp. 187-88.

144

7.3. The Student Council of the USSR

Another fascinating exercise took place in January 1970. After a series of preliminary talks, the Student Council of the Soviet Union had invited a representative delegation of the WSCF to come to Moscow and Kiev for a joint consultation with the Student Council. The Federation considered this invitation a continuation of the Christian-Marxist dialogue which had been the rationale for earlier IUS-WSCF contacts. A ten-person international delegation was chosen to travel to wintry Moscow. Half of the delegation represented member movements and the other half Geneva and regional staff. The Soviet delegation consisted of nine members and included students, university lecturers and professors, senior staff of research institutes, and staff of the Student Council/Komsomol.[6]

We were received with generous hospitality at the Komsomol hotel. Numerous toasts were proposed for peace and friendship at the rather wet welcoming supper. The hosts fostered a boisterous atmosphere bolstered by daring, even religiously offensive jokes. The Federation delegation stood the test well, with good discipline and a sober sense of humor. The consultation was held in Kiev. In addition to the discussions, the program included a lunch given by the Orthodox metropolitan at his residence; visits to the Ukrainian headquarters of Komsomol, the ancient Orthodox Monastery with its famous relics, and a large textile factory; and an unforgettable evening at the Kiev Circus.

The consultation dealt with such topics as "student action for a more just social order," "the role of students in the elimination of the danger of a thermo-nuclear war," "the role of students in the struggle against

6. The WSCF delegation consisted of Anwar Barkat of Pakistan, Leonardo Franco of Argentina, Gabriel Habib of Lebanon, Bethuel Kiplagat of Kenya, Risto Lehtonen of Finland, Marion Martin of the United Kingdom, Milan Opocensky of the CSSR, Francesca Spano of Italy, Liisa Tuovinen of Finland, and Bas Wielinga of the Netherlands. The members of the USSR Student Council delegation were Igor Blishchenko, professor of international law; Alexander Brytchkow, lecturer in history and sociology; Vyacheslav Gusev, student of radiophysiology; Vladimir Kharlamov, general secretary of the Student Council; Maya Solntseva, lecturer of international relations; Nelly Motroshilova, student of philosophy; Vladimir Ponomaryev, staff of the Student Council; Vladimir Shevchenko, student of cybernetics; and Juri Zamoshkin, professor of sociology. Cartigny Minutes, p. 161.

colonialism and racial discrimination and for development," and "the democratization of the university." The presentations by both sides were carefully prepared. The sessions scheduled for discussion were formal and exploratory. For the WSCF delegation the consultation provided, besides useful information on thinking within the Soviet establishment, a valuable lesson on Soviet procedures and style of debate.

The Federation delegation had previously agreed that they would be prepared to sign a "communiqué" from the consultation provided it was descriptive in character and jointly prepared by both parties. Programmatic declarations would not be acceptable to us. A three-member group from within the WSCF delegation was appointed to participate in the drafting of such a communiqué. The USSR hosts also named their representatives, but they somehow never found time to meet while we were in Kiev, so that the communiqué group did not meet until we were back in Moscow. While in Kiev the WSCF group had prepared a preliminary draft entitled "Working Results." When the full communiqué group finally met in Moscow, it appeared that of the three representatives of the Student Council, only two had been in Kiev, and the third had not participated in the consultation at all. The Soviet group then presented their alternative, entitled "Final Statement (Declaration)." It was marked to be signed by the president of the Student Council of the USSR, I. Starovoitov, who had not been present at the consultation. Several points from the WSCF draft had been included while some had been left out. In addition the Soviet proposal included conclusions which had not been discussed at the consultation proper, for example:

> The participants noted that the struggle for peace, for social progress and just transformation of society in which the dignity of man would be safeguarded and in which oppression and exploitation would be eliminated, is inseparable from the struggle against imperialism and its manifestations: racial discrimination, colonial oppression, fascism and reaction. This makes a concrete platform of uniting actions of Communist and Christian youth.

and

> The participants agreed to do everything possible for strengthening the unity of the progressive student movement. . . .

The WSCF wanted to remove sentences which suggested agreement in areas on which delegations had clearly disagreed in Kiev and also to change the programmatic character of the statement to a description of topics which had been discussed. As the head of the WSCF delegation, I said that we considered the Soviet draft a good basis for developing a final communiqué once we had solved two technical difficulties: first, that the character of the Soviet proposal be changed from a declaration to a descriptive statement, and, second, that the contents be changed to conform with what had happened in Kiev instead of expressing the opposite. This perhaps unduly undiplomatic statement triggered a heated debate. The Soviet side refused to make any substantive changes to its proposal, nor did the WSCF negotiators give in. After a couple of hours of arguing, the general secretary of the Student Council stated that in this situation their delegation preferred not to have any communiqué at all. I said that it was the right of the hosts to propose so, but that this was not the WSCF initiative or wish. It was obviously a serious disappointment to the hosts that they were not able to come out of the consultation with a final statement or declaration in line with the thinking of the Student Council/Komsomol. When I later reported the discussions and the result to the full WSCF delegation, they expressed their agreement with the position taken by the WSCF drafters. The farewell ceremonies turned rather chilly.[7]

A Student Council delegation of three persons, led by the general secretary of the Soviet Student Council, Vladimir Kharlamov, was received in Geneva in May 1971 by the WSCF. Milan Opocensky and I were the main hosts for the visit. However, any serious follow-up of the contacts was no longer viable, because of the internal ideological strife in the Federation.

---

7. A report of the WSCF team visit to the USSR and the two drafts for a final communiqué, which were not approved, are included in the Cartigny Minutes, pp. 160-68.

CHAPTER 8

Cease-Fire That Did Not Last — Cartigny 1970

The Executive Committee meeting held on June 22-29, 1970, at Cartigny was the midpoint between General Assemblies. It had been prepared in the spirit of deliberate cooperation, keeping aside the main ideological conflict. Some staff had hoped that this approach would overcome the deadlock of the previous meeting, while for others it was, in retrospect, a temporary break which was to facilitate the building up of a radical revolutionary program for the Federation.

The Cartigny meeting was preceded by three ad hoc consultations — on politics, on theology, and on the follow-up of the WSCF China Study Project. Their reports formed a substantive part of the agenda, as they were taken up first by subcommittees called "Focus Groups," and then by the full Executive Committee in plenary sessions.

The report of the ad hoc political consultation elaborated ideas which had been expressed by the revolutionary wing of the Executive Committee, under the "first option" outlined in Beirut. One goal for the Federation was to begin to identify, as potential partners in the revolutionary endeavor in industrialized countries, groups which could contribute to changing the international division of wealth and development. The report admitted, however, an ambiguity in the use of the terms "oppressors" and "oppressed," and that in industrialized societies the "traditionally designated agents of change," who belonged to the privileged segment of society, and the internal "oppressed groups," such as the proletariat, the foreign workers, and various minority groups, both functioned as oppressors in an international social perspective. The report expressed the need to evaluate the "historical development of the student movement" and to integrate these experiences into "each new level of political struggle." The group maintained that class analysis needed to be refined in the light of the accumulated experience. The report was permeated by the conviction that the current worldwide revolutionary movement would in due time change international economic and social relationships. The Federation's task was to be part of this movement.

The practical conclusions were twofold: (1) that the Federation should organize a consultation on research into the concentration of power in industrialized countries, and (2) that the Federation's communication program should concentrate on developing alternate media for political education.[1]

The ad hoc consultation on theology defined its main task in terms of Christian reflection which would "look at manifold situations of our personal and social life from the perspective of Christian faith." The suggestion that theological reflection is the prerogative of theological experts was rejected.

The report reflected a shift toward a deliberately contextual approach, the revolutionary struggle providing the main frame of reference for the theological task ahead. The report accepted unhesitatingly the necessity for the Federation to continue dialogue between the biblical heritage on the one hand and the social and ideological context on the other. It aimed to pave the way for the Christian community — the church — to be transformed from being a pillar supporting an inherently oppressive society into a more authentic Christian community, in tune with the new socialist society which the group expected to emerge.

> We came to the conclusion that societies in North America and Western Europe are at present in a profound crisis . . . reflected not

---

1. A detailed description of the background, political purposes, and suggested categories of participants of the consultation of research groups on "Concentration of Power" is attached to the Minutes of the WSCF Executive Committee Meeting, Cartigny, Switzerland, June 22-28, 1970, pp. 68-69.

only in the disintegration of social and political structures, but also in the crisis of concepts and intellectual tools to which we have been accustomed.

Many students and young intellectuals with Christian background have been involved in recent political struggles. Some of them have lost their faith and dropped out. On the other hand, many have been sustained in those struggles by their faith, and from their experience in political engagement they are posing disquieting questions about a new meaning for Christian tradition and symbols. Many of them feel homeless, because they experience both church and political organizations as oppressive and authoritarian institutions. However, they look for some community where they can be confronted with and discuss their experiences of involvements, develop a critical theory, and plan for new actions.

We notice that in different places, new communities and groupings are emerging which are committed in a collective way to social and political work which has a bearing on family, work, leisure, money, new life style. There are communes which clearly come out of Christian tradition, and which draw explicitly on the resources of that tradition. We believe that some of these communities can be very instrumental in helping to shape a more relevant methodology for our reflection and for re-inventing meaning in biblical images and Christian symbols. Such a collective effort, which should include theologians, specialists, and others who are militants, may avoid the temptation of triumphalism or self-deprecation which are common dangers of theologising today.[2]

The consultation suggested that the WSCF should be a meeting place for students and intellectuals involved in the revolutionary political struggles of the day.

The consultation on the WSCF China Study Project — launched by the previous Political Commission in 1965 — became, contrary to the intentions of those involved, the end point of the project in the Federation. Participants in the consultation realized that the project did not have much future within the new Political Commission, which had opted for a course of direct involvement with political movements of

2. Report of the Ad Hoc Consultation on Theology, Cartigny Minutes, pp. 66-67.

the left. The project had been steadily criticized by the left radicals as being too academic and expert oriented. In an open letter to member movements appended to its report, the consultation stated that the China project had now reached a formal close. A series of follow-up steps were recommended and were aimed at making the results available to member movements, churches, and international church organizations. Although the recommendations were approved by the Executive Committee, most of them eventually fell by the wayside because of lack of appreciation for them by the Political Commission.[3]

The trend of resorting uncritically to neo-Marxist terminology, noted already in Beirut, continued. A marked deterioration of language is evident in all the preconsultation reports. The pervasive use of in-jargon which was virtually incomprehensible to outsiders was a symptom of a loss of clarity of thought. Phrases such as "political struggle," "critical theory," "reflection in relation to theory and to practice," "agent of change," "level of social consciousness," "ongoing process," "conscientization," and many others illustrate this trend, a trend that resulted in a form of doctrinaire anti-intellectualism and a disdain of all institutions. George Orwell's analysis of the political language used immediately after the Second World War applies to that used in WSCF and also many WCC reports influenced by the left radicalism of the late sixties and seventies. He wrote:

> The inflated style is itself a kind of euphemism. A mass of Latin words falls upon the facts like a soft snow, blurring outlines and covering up all details. The great enemy of clear language is insincerity. When there is a gap between one's real and one's declared aims, one turns as it were instinctively to long words and exhausted idioms . . . if thought corrupts language, language can also corrupt thought. . . . I have not here been considering the literary use of language, but merely language as an instrument for expressing and not concealing or preventing thought.[4]

3. The Cartigny Minutes include a comprehensive report of the WSCF China project from 1966 to 1970, including a listing of the ten publications produced, pp. 74-81.

4. George Orwell, "Politics and the English Language" (1946), reprinted in George Orwell, *Inside the Whale and Other Essays* (New York: Penguin Books, 1957), pp. 143-58.

The officers and staff had agreed that in Cartigny the time would not yet be ripe for dealing with the larger issues of the identity and orientation of the Federation as a whole. The regional groups, the Political Commission, and the Communication team were to be given more time to develop their work in tune with the current contexts of the Federation. They were not expected to give comprehensive reports as a basis for their evaluation.

The Executive Committee in Cartigny spelled out the role of regional committees and other regional structures in precise terms. In a nutshell, regional committees were to be advisory in character.[5] Final authority on policies, programs, staff appointments, and budgets was to remain with the Executive Committee. Both Aaron Tolen and Moonkyu Kang stressed the need for a high degree of freedom to develop regional programs given their unique cultural and social characteristics, leaving only personnel and budgets to the final authority of the Executive Committee and the Geneva office. In this way the head office of the world organization, with recognized NGO status at the UN, provided, in their view, a protective umbrella for the SCMs and regional staff in critical situations and under pressures from the local political authorities. This concern arose from their experiences with the attitudes and actions of the Cameroonian and Korean authorities.

The regions of Africa, Asia, and the Middle East refrained from presenting comprehensive reports but submitted only brief written or oral summaries of their respective regional meetings and those recommendations which required approval by the Executive Committee.

Contrary to the agreement at Glion, the European region opted to submit a comprehensive report which included an account of consultations, conferences, committee meetings, and extensive staff travels.

---

5. The advisory functions included "(a) to elaborate proposals concerning the strategy . . . in the region for presentation to the Executive Committee . . . ; (b) to advise the Federation staff in the region on the implementation of the programs and policies established by the Executive Committee; (c) to carry out those tasks specifically assigned to the regional committees by the Executive Committee" (Revised By-Laws, Cartigny Minutes, p. 13). The intention was to maintain a balance between greater regional flexibility and the global character of the whole Federation. The next General Assembly in 1972-73 in Addis Ababa opened the doors for a higher degree of autonomy for each region and for reducing the role of the interregional office of the Federation to a bare minimum.

Regional activity in Europe had a clear profile: The European committee had decided that the theme of the Federation in this region was to be "The Struggle for Socialism in Europe." The rationale for this decision was given in these words:

> The most crucial task is to expose and lay bare the centers and mechanisms of power in our societies; only when this is done can we begin to elaborate a revolutionary strategy. We recognize that our analysis must be in political and theological terms.[6]

Two consultations on this main theme had been held. The first, hosted by the Italian SCM, was on "The Anti-Capitalist Struggle in Italy," and participants included not only students and young intellectuals but also workers and trade union and Communist Party representatives. It resulted in the formation of a task force to monitor the anticapitalist struggle in Europe, to organize further education, and to create a platform for militants. The second consultation, held in Lund, Sweden, was a theological consultation. It tried to wrestle with Christian affirmations on the one hand and analyses of society on the other. "Theology is seeing the action of God in any situation. It is not offering an alternative to understanding the situation or to acting to change it at the level Marxism is doing."[7]

The European region also launched a Europe/Africa study project which originated in Britain. Its leader was a Zimbabwean student, Chenhamo Chimutengwende, who was in exile in Britain. The planners of the project had originally suggested that it be made an inter-regional endeavor. However, the leadership of the Africa region rejected this idea and said that it was part of the Federation's European concerns, and that the concept and method of the project were not in tune with the work of the SCMs or of the Federation in Africa. The theme of the project was "Imperialism and the International Division of Labor." It tried to apply the Marxist concept of class struggle to the relationship between Europe and Africa. There were, in addition to the British group, national project groups in West Germany, Italy, and Switzerland.

6. Cartigny Minutes, p. 82.
7. Cartigny Minutes, p. 83.

The European leaders and members of the Political Commission were puzzled by the Africans' lack of enthusiasm for the project. The chairperson of the commission, Mario Miegge, saw in the African leaders the image of his missionary grandparents who brought European pietism to Africa. The Nairobi-based Africa secretary, José Chipenda of Angola, suggested that the current European radicalism represented just another wave of spiritual colonialism to which Africans were immune.

Traditional activities such as work among secondary-school students and the annual European Student Pastors' Conference also had their place in the Europe region, although they received less attention than programs on the "cutting edge," for which Marxist revolutionary slogans provided the main frame of reference.

In the Cartigny Europe report only the member movements which had made their ideological choice clear received positive attention. They included those in Austria, Spain, Portugal, and France. The report regretted the withdrawal of the two Greek movements, both of them with Greek Orthodox membership, from participation in the WSCF programs in Europe. The report was silent about the traditionally large and influential movements of Britain, Germany, and Scandinavia, all of which were torn by internal problems at that time. The Finnish movement was mentioned because of the reaction of the Lutheran church to the radicalization of the SCM. It was obvious that the European region was rapidly becoming an instrument of the revolutionary wing of the Federation. SCMs that were not willing to become "one issue" movements were increasingly being ignored.

The Latin Americans also presented a voluminous report. It dwelt on the shape of the regional staff team and elaborated, in rather abstract terms, the concept of involving member movements in the Federation's work in the region. The second part of the report consisted of ambitious plans for a number of projects and the proposal of an unrealistic regional budget.

The North America secretary had prepared a report on Federation-related activities and organizations in Canada and the USA and a list of suggestions for the Federation's function in the region under the heading of "Strategy."

The Cartigny meeting included a substantive discussion on the membership policy of the Federation. Although this did not lead to

any immediate decisions, it brought into the open many elements of
the current ideological conflict and many allegations used in debating
it. Ross Terrill of Australia had been asked to prepare a background
paper for the discussion,[8] which began by outlining the reasons which
had prompted the Federation to take up this issue. They included the
decline of many traditional SCMs; the emergence of "new Christian
formations" within and around academic communities; the lack of
balance between the financial strength of SCMs and the amount of
funding provided by the supporting community of church and mission agencies; and the ambivalence toward constituencies other than
university students and university teachers groups, senior friends,
specialized Christian groups within the academic setting, and secondary schools movements. He also referred to the current "particularistic
trend" among students and within the political world, which questioned all facile affirmations of unity across national, class, religious,
and ideological lines. Finally, he spoke of a changed understanding of
the ecumenicity implied in the perennial "one country, one movement" policy of the Federation, which, in its heyday, had produced
the National Student Christian Federation in the USA but which now
had lost its applicability in many countries.

Terrill then listed the kind of groups which existed outside the
national movements but which were interested in a relationship with
the Federation. They included foreign students groups; university
teachers and graduates groups; ad hoc "issue groups"; groups reflecting race, gender, or other sociological diversity, such as black, minority,
or women's caucuses; groups reflecting theological, political, or ideological diversity; and church agencies and denominational organizations. He suggested guidelines which should be followed in revising
the membership policy. He excluded the possibility of assuming an a
priori ideology about the nature of the Federation and consequently
the option for a (new) constituency to replace the former (traditional)
constituency. He underlined that the membership policy should be
changed only as far as existing and emerging realities demanded it.
The policy should be basically an expressed "concern about the expansion and renewal of the Federation." Its pluralism must be respected. The policy should not lead to legalism but to a flexibility

---

8. Cartigny Minutes, pp. 226-31.

which allows for experiment. Finally, since the Federation is a Christian organization, the questions of faith cannot be disregarded in dealing with membership issues.

Terrill proposed no quick revisions to the current membership policy. He favored the possibility that groups could be associated with the Federation without becoming part of its decision-making structure. He concluded by outlining a procedure for an orderly reconsideration of the policy with thorough preparation. The paper did not lead, however, to any immediate change of the policy.

It was a new element in the work of the WSCF Executive Committee that special attention had to be paid to fair representation of the two "options" — the parties stemming from Beirut — on each subgroup or subcommittee. So was the continuing erosion of past parliamentary proceedings. This was most blatantly in evidence in the rulings of the Executive Committee, which allowed two of its members to become members of the WSCF project staff without resigning as members of the Executive Committee or renouncing their voting rights. Such rulings were passed at Cartigny with tight margins. Paradoxically, the revised bylaws approved by the Executive Committee stated that no staff member of any category could be a member of the Executive Committee. This policy seems to have been adhered to only partially at the 1971 meeting. These debates and votes also served as tests of strength for the supporters of the two options of Beirut.[9]

Viewed from Africa and Asia, the period from the Beirut meeting in March-April 1969 to the Cartigny meeting in June 1970 was filled with work with SCMs, regional gatherings, and WSCF consultations.

---

9. For the two members who had accepted the invitation to become project staff, the focus group on the decision-making process recommended "that their voting rights be suspended for this Executive Committee." It further suggested that the status of project staff be clarified. The recommendations for the two committee members concerned were voted on separately in the plenary. The minutes read:

> An amendment to the motion providing for separate voting on the two cases was passed. The motion to suspend the voting rights of Mario Yutzis was defeated. The motion to suspend Karam Khella's voting rights was also defeated, with the chairman casting the deciding vote. It was agreed that policy for the future in such situations should be clarified in the revision of the by-laws.

The fact that both persons were supporters of the revolutionary "option" may have been a factor in the voting. Cartigny Minutes, pp. 4-5.

Africa moved ahead with subregional leadership training courses for national SCMs. The program for the development of Christian literature, initiated in 1968 in cooperation with the Christian Literature Fund, reached its full potential. The first three-month course of the Asia Leadership Development Center was organized at Tozanzo, Japan.

Regional programs were also developed vigorously in Europe and the Middle East. In Beirut, the Europe office had been somewhere in between the two paths which diverged from that point. However, the SCMs most vociferously involved in the "struggle" tipped the balance in favor of the "first option," with the result that the Europe office and its programs began to lean toward that direction and joined ranks with the Political Commission–Communication team.

In Latin America there was much soul-searching to find a relevant form for WSCF programs and presence in the region. The characteristic role of Marxist or New Left radical opposition groups did not correspond with the need to develop leadership training and communication programs with a reliable institutional base.

North America was suffering from the collapse of the U.S. national member organization. There was no shortage of local radical caucuses and communities, most of them short-lived. In parallel to them, campus ministries and their agencies formed another potential constituency which the Federation could not afford to ignore. The WSCF office tried to portray a balance between the increasingly fluid radical scene and the liberal-to-conservative church-related agencies, while actively promoting radical causes.

The whole Geneva staff, even with the divergence of views among them, had been determined to bring the impressions and recommendations from all these diverse activities together and take them into account in planning for Cartigny and in the overall work of the Federation. This was done quite apart from the controversies about the role of the Executive Committee, the headaches in the more turbulent regions, and the hassles about the Communication program.

The ideological truce among the staff ended with the Cartigny meeting. The Geneva office and the remaining global programs of the Federation became a battleground for supporters of the two "options" of Beirut. Agendas for action were increasingly developed among the like-minded, and plans were no longer brought together, except for formal decisions when necessary. Any significant exchanges about overcoming the ideological divisions or the deadlock faded away.

The Latin America and North America offices, and later the Europe office, became part of the support network for the radical political orientation of the Geneva office. The Political Commission and Communication program formed the hard core of radical activity.

The role of the Geneva office and of the Executive Committee looked very different when viewed from the less radical regions. The African, Asian, and Middle Eastern offices and groups needed the Geneva office as a global coordination point and as a service center for interregional and worldwide programs and for sharing resources. They suspected that the Political Commission and Communication team in Geneva wanted to force Geneva into serving exclusively those engaged in radical political concerns inside and outside the Federation constituency and to subvert the SCMs and regional activities in non-Western regions.

After Cartigny the secondary schools program was phased out. Efforts to keep the university teachers program alive and to link it to the Catholic intellectual movement failed. The quarterly magazine, the *Student World,* was discontinued and replaced for a short while by Federation Books, which, however, no longer reflected any ongoing dialogue or joint worldwide thinking on issues alive in the SCMs. A political newsletter, *Question,* was launched, and a documentation service to cater to political activist groups was initiated. Both carried a hopelessly amateurish image. Most of the new programmatic functions of the Geneva office took on an ad hoc style. Only the fundraising and supervision of finance remained professionally respectable.

The financial support base of the Federation changed. The contributions of member movements continued to decrease as their constituencies shrank. Backing from church agencies had grown significantly since the mid-sixties until 1970 when the first signs of restraint appeared, although for reasons other than the Federation's ideological problems. Ecumenically minded leaders of American and European church and mission agencies, especially those of a liberal tradition, thought that the latest turn was just another phase of avant-gardism which was characteristic of the very tradition of Student Christian Movements. With few exceptions they failed to perceive the "self-destruct" virus in the ideology of the New Left. Therefore, they, in their liberal innocence, were content to release funds for all causes of "change," irrespective of content. They tended to believe that the current wave of turbulence in the WSCF was the birth pangs of a new generation of committed ecumenical leaders.[10]

Cartigny was also a turning point for the chairman of the WSCF, Richard Shaull. He began to side more visibly with the grouping around the Political Commission and Communication team and the Latin American staff. Their objectives and their style came apparently closest to the vision he had for the future of the Federation and for the new paradigms he was seeking for the ecumenical movement. Shaull's position effectively hardened the positions of the two camps.

10. The income of the WSCF had grown rapidly with the help of American and German mission agencies, with the Methodist and Presbyterian mission agencies taking the lead.

Also the Frontier Internship Program, which the WSCF had co-opted under the name Frontier Study and Service, initiated by the United Presbyterian Church of the USA, channeled and supported several young people of New Left orientation, mainly from the USA, to university and SCM settings in other regions, without adequate consultation with the receiving partners. Such procedures were protested by WSCF regional secretaries and by the Geneva staff.

Mission agencies were alerted to these problems by myself and several regional staff colleagues. Also, my presentation to the Program Board of the Division of Overseas Ministries of the NCC-USA in October 1971 entitled "The Story of a Storm" tried to convey a warning signal to American church and mission agencies.

CHAPTER 9

Constituency Divided

9.1. The General Secretary's Circular

By the end of 1970 it had become quite obvious that the groups supporting the two ideological options articulated in Beirut were on a collision course. I then determined to throw the divisive debate into the open and to try to stimulate a frank and rational discussion about the sore points in the Federation. I did this by sending a circular letter to all member movements as well as to a number of university teachers, chaplains, heads of campus ministry agencies, and senior friends who had been in active touch with the Federation through the sixties.[1]

The letter began with a summary of the trends in the university world, from the vantage point of the WSCF, and of the work of the Federation since the 1968 General Assembly. I revisited the two sets of priorities which the Assembly had approved. The first was a series of worldwide projects and programs, mostly with a radical political orientation. The second was the regionalization of the Federation: the curtailing of global programs in favor of regional programs and structures. I alerted the movements to the danger that the exchange of ideas and mutual challenge across regional boundaries would be diminished if the only global programs to be administered by the Geneva office were those of Communication and the Political Com-

---

1. Risto Lehtonen, "Letter to All Member Movements of the WSCF," February 22, 1971. WSCF Archives.

mission. This could lead, I wrote, to an impoverishment and even a distortion of the work of the Federation as a Christian world organization.

I described the tensions that had been mounting since 1968, particularly among members of the Executive Committee and the staff. In my analysis one pole consisted of those who wanted the Federation to be part of a global revolutionary movement, "radical and leftist" in character. For those committed to it, everything in the Federation's past which prevented identification with this goal was obsolete and irrelevant. A new alliance with the working class would enable the Federation to assume an effective role in the global revolutionary process. This involvement would give the Federation a new identity and restore its raison d'être.

The other pole in my description was represented by those who considered the Federation primarily as an expression of the Christian community — the Church — in the academic world. What united it across cultural, political, and ideological differences was an adherence to Christian tradition. This was the springboard for the specific political involvements of individual Christian students and also of SCMs as organizations. Because of differences within the Christian tradition, and because situations in the different countries and regions varied, such involvements could not lead to a political or ideological uniformity but rather to a diversity of expressions of faith and of patterns of witness in the political sphere.

Trying to find common ground between the two positions, I stated, perhaps overoptimistically, that there seemed to be "remarkable agreement" about the main objectives for the Federation's social and political involvement. Both groups were, I suggested, equally convinced that Christians have to join in the struggle against economic injustice, neocolonialism, racism, authoritarian systems, and militarism, which together blocked the road to a more just society and international order. I emphasized that my characterization of the two poles was a simplified description of two positions in tension and that convictions within member movements were in reality more diverse and more nuanced.

When soliciting responses to the circular letter, I asked for interpretation of the current mood among students, invited comments on the understanding of the relationship between Christian faith and

161

political engagement and on how explicit the Christian character of the Student Christian Movement and the Federation should be, and how far they could opt for one particular political position. Furthermore I raised the question of what should be the desirable relationship between the Student Christian Movement and the church. Finally I welcomed suggestions regarding the task of the WSCF in the university situation. The recipients were informed that the responses would be pooled together and circulated among the constituency.

The thirty-eight written responses to the circular were vigorous and varied.[2] Almost everyone recognized the importance of the issues involved. This was true even of those who disagreed with the way I had dealt with them. In their comments many respondents relied upon their own experience of sharp ideological polarities and acute confrontations within SCMs, within the academic community, and within society as a whole. Some were personally involved in risky political activity. Only a few replies were from persons for whom the issues described in the circular seemed irrelevant.

In what follows, the responses are summed up region by region, beginning with Europe, the region from which the largest number of replies were received, and ending with the Middle East, with its one response on behalf of the whole region.

9.2. Responses from Europe

The fact that almost half of the responses came from Europe was a clear indication that the ideological debate about the roles of Christian community in the university and of politics in the Federation was most intense on this continent. It was also the region in which Marxism played the most visible role among students and SCM leaders. Marxism was either an assumed framework for the reinterpretation of Christian faith or was recognized as a major challenge in practically

2. Out of the responses, 20 originated directly from member movements, 11 from university teachers and chaplains, and 7 from senior friends closely related to the work of the Federation. The regional distribution was as follows: Europe, 18; Asia and Pacific, 7; North America, 6; Latin America, 4; Africa, 2; and the Middle East, 1. Both of the responses from Africa were from white leaders of the University Christian Movement of South Africa.

all the responses. Student and senior leaders often differed in their analysis of the university situation and of the usefulness of Marxism as an ideological tool for Christians.

Italy

The most thorough of the left-radical responses was undoubtedly that written by Marco Rostan, the general secretary of the Italian SCM. His position was not untypical of those of those radical young Christians in much of southern Europe who rejected institutionalized communism and sought a Marxist alternative from further left. He wrote:

> In recent years, more rapidly and profoundly than before . . . the level of class struggle in various countries has had repercussions on all institutions, provoking crises and bringing to light serious contradictions. . . . In particular, thanks to the daily struggle of our Chinese comrades, we have been made aware that class divisions penetrate the very core of the parties, the churches, the institutions, and the trade unions. And these are *the true divisions,* while the others . . . are all fictitious divisions which serve to maintain the power of a so-called democratic and pluralistic society.

Rostan suggested that participation in the class struggle is the central concern for SCMs and the WSCF. He took issue with the traces of Marcusianism which he detected in my analysis in the circular letter. According to him it was totally illusionary to believe that students would form a revolutionary class which would contribute to the liberation of humanity. The student struggle could become part of a genuine revolutionary struggle only if it was led by the proletariat.

Rostan rejected the terms in which I described the polarization within the Federation. The real positions opposed to one another would be unveiled only by means of careful political evaluation of the place occupied by different groups within the class struggle. This was why the first task, according to him, was to make the members of the Federation aware of the real conflicts within it as perceived in the light of the class struggle.

According to Rostan, the two myths which had to be rejected were

163

- that Christian tradition can provide unity across class contradictions, and
- that socialism can be understood as a messianic expectation of global revolution as manifested in the socialism of the USSR.

The socialism Rostan advocated was that of continuing class struggle and continuing revolution, a model of the socialism of the "mass line." For him the most visible illustration of this was the Cultural Revolution in China. His position is in stark contrast with the idea of political pluralism, which, according to him, was a typical temptation for the traditional church and now for the leaders of the WSCF. He concluded that it would be an illusion to think that the WSCF could function as "an international party," because it was not sufficiently linked to the proletariat. He warned that the Federation would end up on the wrong side of the class struggle if it adhered to political pluralism.

Rostan made a number of proposals for the WSCF. At the heart of them all was the desire to help member movements analyze their sociopolitical situation, trace the social origins of their theology, and thereby assume their place in the class struggle led by the proletariat. Some of the practical suggestions included opening conferences up to militant groups, carrying out research projects about the function of the church in society, and changing the working style of the Federation at the international level so that full participation of militant groups in the life of the Federation could be facilitated by the staff.

France

The most castigating reaction to the circular came, not surprisingly, from the French SCM, which identified itself totally with the revolutionary movement of 1968. Pierre Tartier, its general secretary, disapproved of the circular's approach on the grounds that the writer had an "a priori concern for ecclesiastical strategy, for which we couldn't care less." For the French SCM the value of the WSCF was totally different from that of the "traditional" point of view described in the circular.

The WSCF is of interest for us if it can make itself part of a general revolutionary strategy (if it cannot it will collapse, and well ahead of the churches), making possible an exchange of information, discussions between different groups with various ways of working, in order to encourage the maturing of the movement, which for the moment is scattered, divided by the strategy of capitalism.

What does this have in common with a WSCF in the service of the "strategy" of churches, even if, from time to time they admit the necessity of revolution . . . to save the faith. There is always the same contempt for man: the revolution, i.e. the possibility for men to achieve at last their desires without being subject to certain norms, is seen simply as a method of purifying and resurrecting the church. We often have the impression that love for one's neighbor actually means contempt for one's neighbor. This contempt is all the more patent when, under the pretext of ecumenism, the WSCF sets out to make allies of JEC and Pax Romana, those reformist enterprises of the Vatican, in order better to fence in and control all revolutionary inclinations which might be born among its clientele.

After rejecting revolutionary illusions, Tartier put the accent on revolution in daily life, which, according to him, was gaining ground in the French SCM and which was to speed the decay of the capitalist system. The repression experienced in the frustrations of everyday life and sustained by illusions nurtured by the churches had to be overcome. In his view the WSCF would have played a meaningful role if it had provided the soil in which these revolutionary desires could have flourished. However, this it had failed to do, even when it initiated the program "Christians for Socialism in Europe." He concluded by pleading for more openness in bringing together scattered groups with similar aspirations and establishing communication between them:

> The WSCF can be this place. . . . It holds out hope of a maximum of liberty, a minimum of sectarianism, to the extent that it does not seek to establish relationships with other institutions, but with groups which find their self-definition . . . in a revolutionary strategy.

A very different French opinion came from a senior leader and a former general secretary of the French SCM, Professor André Dumas

165

of the Faculty of Protestant Theology in Paris. He pointed to the weaknesses of the analyses offered by Herbert Marcuse and Richard Shaull. They were based more on sentiment than on economic realities.

> In my opinion, the lack of rigor in the analysis has led to lyrical utopianism, in the Fourier style, and not to a political impact à la Marx. . . . A typical illustration is that the Chinese Cultural Revolution has served as a model (after Cuba) for western students. . . . This has resulted in a weakening of political consciousness . . . which is hardly concealed by irresponsible verbiage. Christians, with little experience of political struggle, have leaned too much towards lyricism. They have been new converts to a neo-Marxism lacking any realistic analyses. 1968 was (for them) a Pentecost (but) without any church (resulting), or again, a psycho-drama re-enacting the Paris Commune of 1871, (but) with no party organized to follow it up.

Dumas described how two reactions had become apparent since 1968. Some of the revolutionaries were now joining the orthodox Communist Party, turning a blind eye to Soviet intervention in Prague. Others were replacing politics by individualism, hippie celebrations, and new Oriental religions. In view of this, it was irresponsible and "demagogic" to behave as if politics and the church could function without any institutions.

For Dumas the days of the student revolution were clearly over. He pointed to the resurgence of competition within universities and to a noticeable return of students to their studies and to concerns for career. The student movement of the radical left could no longer be expected to take the lead.

In reflecting on the experience of the revolutionary years, Dumas commented on the relationship between Christian faith and political involvement. He suggested that many young Christians, disappointed and embittered by the institutional church, had gone into politics with undue idealism about being able to make a significant contribution to changing the world. However, a refugee from the church was, in his opinion, "a very bad recruit for (the politics of) this world." Dumas continued:

166

I am therefore definitely in favor of an explicit Christian confession, and this in the interests of politics itself. In my opinion, there are certain irreplaceable contributions which cannot be made without the Christian faith: its witness to God makes the worship of an ideology impossible, . . . its practice of justification by faith makes impossible sectarian self-justification. Finally, in seeking reconciliation, which is the opposite of separation, Christian faith brings freedom from the negativism of terrorists.

Dumas suggested some emphases for the work of the WSCF: to be part of the church, but not too mixed up in church affairs; to work with small groups of students who share a common desire "to hear the hidden word of God," each group of which would assume responsibility for one issue in the social and political world. National SCMs and the Federation should help to link such groups and stop worrying about what churches or previous generations of SCM leaders thought.

Great Britain

The leaders of the SCM of Great Britain and Ireland expressed their unambiguous commitment to Marxist socialism. In their officially signed statement,[3] they rejected the way in which the circular had defined the two positions, contending that since 1968 there was no polarity within the British SCM. Any polarity before 1968 was between those who held to the traditional "open" policy of the SCM, in terms of political neutrality, and those who were trying to express the Christian commitment of the SCM in political terms. After 1968 this tension ended. The response portrayed unanimity not only about socialism but also about a commitment to the newly emerging extra-parliamentary political activity.[4]

3. The signatories of the statement of the SCM of Great Britain and Ireland were David Head, Rakethal Tsehlana, Peter Grant, Carol Barker, and Laurence Bright.

4. The response from the British SCM was very explicit on this: "We never encountered a real clash between Christian and Socialist; in fact, we would probably have said that such an antithesis was a category of mistake . . . we feel bound to emphasize a continuity in political style which reflects a serious concern for Marxist analysis of western society."

The respondents dissociated themselves from the nuances of the "radical" position in my description, in which they detected Richard Shaull's emphases. They saw this as further evidence that the European thrust for socialism was rapidly moving away from the views of the American New Left, which had an anarcho-Marxist slant and whose guru was Herbert Marcuse. The response stated:

> Nor do we necessarily see the link which you seem to discern between political radicalism and the latest thing in reductionist theology in America. The students who attended our Manchester Congress in 1969 were more impressed by Archbishop Camara, who spoke from a frankly conservative theological position, than they were by a good many glib Christian-radical synthesizers, and we notice a general disillusionment with the creed of secular modernism among many of the students who are most politically and theologically aware in our movement at the moment.

As far as the WSCF headquarters was concerned, they expressed their wish that the staff be politically more transparent and more accountable through processes of inbuilt self-criticism. However, they did not want to make their concern for participatory democracy explicit, but left it in the form of an ambiguous suggestion. The response was signed by five persons, including Peter Grant, the chairperson of the SCM; David Head, the general secretary; and some other members of the national staff.

Interestingly enough, only a few days later came another response from Britain, this time from Alastair Hulbert, the Scottish secretary of the SCM of Great Britain. Hulbert addressed his letter to the five signatories of the British SCM reply, challenging the validity of the "official" position they described. He pointed out that the response sent by the leaders of the SCM had not been discussed by its Standing Committee. According to Hulbert, had the statement been discussed at its meeting, there would have been no agreement on it. He questioned the validity of most of the points of the response:

> For you to emphasize "a continuity in political style which reflects a continuing acceptance of a more or less Marxist analysis of British society," is to focus on a small and insignificant minority. And

168

moreover, what of this political style? What is its praxis? What fruits is it bearing? What encouragement is it giving to others?

In policy decisions, the SCM . . . has not faced up to the need for a deep analysis of the student scene or its relation to society. The SCM lacks orientation. Where is . . . coherence in the movement? . . . The last meeting of the Standing Committee was like a left-wing benevolent trust, whose duty it was to allocate funds — for individuals to attend worthy experiences overseas, and for organizations of the left at home which are threatened by extinction because of lack of finance.

Commenting on the question of polarity and on its stated absence from the British SCM, Hulbert accused the signatories of dishonesty:

It (the official response) left me speechless. Were you not aware that the Scottish delegation at the 1969 General Council to a man voted against the Political Stance (of the British SCM)? . . . Have we learned nothing from the response at grassroots level to the decisions of the same Council about the Free University for Black Studies? Have the rumblings and disagreements over staffing policy . . . not registered anything? Even in the discussion . . . at the last Standing Committee about our reply (to the circular letter) there were hot disagreements. Do these things not point for you to a polarity of some kind in SCM?

This exchange demonstrated inherent pressures for uniformity and toward a new authoritarianism of the left in SCMs which had committed themselves to a Marxist option, whether it was a plain revolutionary line or a more sophisticated Marxist Christian approach. The ideology and its supporters came first; the others no longer mattered.

One more response from within the British context came from Martin Conway, a former study secretary of the British SCM and of the WSCF.[5] He wrote:

5. Martin Conway had been one of the chief planners of the Life and Mission of the Church Conference for the Europe region in 1962. At the time of sending his response, he had left the secretaryship for Chaplaincies in Higher Education of the Church of England Board of Education and assumed the position of publications secretary of the World Council of Churches.

Here I can only align myself wholeheartedly with the second of the two poles that you have described on page five of your letter to the movements. . . . If the people presently institutionally caught up in the WSCF wished in fact to choose some sort of basis which is not explicitly Christian, they must as people and as a group be free to do so. But I cannot for the life of me understand how a body claiming the inheritance of the WSCF, let alone its name, can be anything else than based on explicitly Christian affirmations. If the WSCF simply slides away from its earlier basis, then I am sure that in a few years' time there will be as good as nothing left.

Conway joined those who affirmed that the confession of Christian faith — itself a response to God's own action in Jesus Christ — will at all times encourage particular political commitments on particular issues.

Sweden

Two answers came from Sweden, neither of them an official response of the Swedish SCM. One was sent by Karin Rodhe, a medical student who was at that time a member of the WSCF Executive Committee. She was an articulate representative of the "1968 generation" of the Swedish SCM. She, too, had come to the conclusion that Marxism was the most meaningful framework for interpreting the Christian faith today, and that it was pointless to draw a line between a "political" and a "Christian" commitment. Instead she made a distinction between those who identify themselves as within the Christian tradition and those who belong to what she called "the anonymous church" — "people who don't want to consider themselves as Christians but act as if they were." In her view, the SCM and the WSCF could not be built on the latter group. She apparently dissociated herself from the idea of seeking a new constituency for the Federation in political activist groups. Yet she perceived another polarity within the Federation:

The difference between the two poles is really not between a "Christian" and a "radical leftist" approach, but between those

170

who are using a Marxist and those using a liberal model to describe the world and as a starting point for action.

Rodhe was critical of the circular on the grounds that the terms used in it, such as "injustice," "racism," and "neo-colonialism," were "non-political." According to her analysis, this revealed the politically liberal position of the writer. In her view, the appropriate approach would have been to make a clear statement about "capitalism," "imperialism," and "private property" as the sources of social evil. For the WSCF she saw an important, if modest, role. It should define itself in political terms as a community in which the causes of evil in society and the world could be analyzed; it should decide where its political action would be most effective, what instruments for action were available to it, and where it could find its political allies. It should be sober about its potential. It could not represent all "liberating forces" in every place.

So why should we not say very simply: the WSCF is an organization for people who as Christians have agreed that our main task today is to *combat capitalism* and for doing this the Marxist tools are indispensable! We know there are Christians and Christian students who think differently but there are also other organizations. Why should we pretend to represent all? I agree with those who say this might mean a narrowing or limitation, but I think it is necessary so that we can do anything at all.

Another response from Sweden was sent by a former SCM leader and prominent politician, Jan-Erik Wikström.[6] His comments contrasted with Rodhe's views on the mood among students and on the future of the WSCF. In his perception the student uprising was over. The majority of students were concerned with their studies and their future jobs. They had "no time for demonstrations and marches." In view of the changed social position of university students, he raised the question whether a separate Christian movement among students and university teachers was needed any longer. Should not the whole

6. Jan-Erik Wikström was formerly the general secretary of the Free Church SCM of Sweden, and at the time of writing the editor of the Free Church Publishing House and a member of the Swedish parliament.

SCM enterprise be brought closer to the churches and their struggle for unity? But as long as there was an SCM and a WSCF, Wikström's position was clear:

> Either the SCM and the WSCF remain explicitly Christian, or their main and only reason for existence ceases. In any concrete political question they can take a particular position, but they can never affiliate themselves with one political group or party without losing their identity.

The difference between the two Swedish respondents was not about Christian identity but about the political role of the SCM and WSCF as Christian organizations.

Finland

A response on behalf of the Finnish SCM came from Martti Lindqvist, general secretary of the SCM from 1967 to 1970, and, at the time of writing, a staff member of the Research Institute of the Evangelical Lutheran Church of Finland. His comments echoed those of Karin Rodhe, although he was more explicit about the need for a clear Christian identity and about the roles of SCMs and the WSCF as critics of the church from within. However, the political conclusion was:

> Our task is without special reservations to join in a common front with all progressive political forces. It is important, too, that we can show that we have an absolute right to keep our Christian identity in spite of what the conservative forces (within the churches) are saying.[7]

Another Finnish voice was that of Inga-Brita Castrén, a former staff member of the Finnish SCM, former Africa secretary of the

---

7. In the Finnish context the progressive forces to which Lindqvist referred consisted of the left wing of the Social Democratic Party; the People's Democratic League, led by communists; and various left-wing action groups, peace activists, and others. The most influential grouping in general student politics was, however, the "nonrevisionist" wing — the "Stalinists" — of the Communist Party.

WSCF, and, at the time of writing, on the staff of the WCC. The turmoil in the WSCF was for her a sign that the Federation had not lost touch with students. She emphasized that wrestling with questions of the political involvement of Christians was vital for the ecumenical movement and the church as a whole. She expressed a concern that explicit "Christian faith and biblical theology" remain the foundation for the Federation's involvement in political and social matters.

The Netherlands

The SCM of the Netherlands[8] challenged the WSCF leaders in Geneva about the overall orientation of the Federation. The intention of the 1968 General Assembly was to enable the Federation to become fully engaged in the contradictions of society. The Dutch SCM was concerned that, in light of the circular, the leaders in Geneva seemed to want to isolate the Federation from society. While affirming the SCM's solidarity with the left, it stated that the Dutch SCM did not want a radical rupture with its past, for such an intention would be "a romantic idea." Rather the SCM wanted to continue as a movement of "an intellectual élite" which had its roots in Christian convictions. The task ahead was to bring the members of this elite to a consciousness of their political role in society and to stimulate among them a process of solidarity with movements of repressed peoples. The SCM did not recognize the polarization described in the circular. The two poles did not correspond to those characteristic of the historical process within the class struggle. Instead they seemed to be artificial creations used to frustrate a process of change and bolster the concept of a pluralistic society. The statement warned the WSCF leaders against trying to build solidarity with the left from the top. Such solidarity could only be achieved through participation in concrete struggles.

Christian tradition was affirmed as the starting point for the political stance of the SCM. A clear choice had been made for socialism, and this was a choice which Christians had to make, if they were to make any concrete social and political contribution.

8. The statement of the SCM of the Netherlands was presented in the name of its Executive Committee.

The Dutch SCM expressed its hope that the whole of the WSCF would take a similar position. Regionalization was felt to be a good start, but more was needed. The development of a political strategy by the different regional groups and a critical analysis of the political processes were seen as next steps. In addition to having formal ties with one another, SCMs should stimulate the development of common political positions across national and continental boundaries.

There were two other voices from SCM circles in the Netherlands. One came from Dr. C. A. van Peursen, professor of philosophy at Leyden University and a longtime participant in the university teachers work of the WSCF. He analyzed the student unrest as it had touched his own country and university. He saw that its roots were in the social, political, and structural deficiencies of society. The impact of the student protest movement had been only negative, as it had not been able to spell out how to arrive at a better society and what its structure should be. It sought inspiration from distant, almost mythical images of "Maoism" or "Che Guevarism." Efforts to define goals and methods had led to dogmatism, sectarianism, and continued fragmentation of action.

The revolutionary movement tended to appreciate the university merely as an instrument for promoting explosive social revolution, or, if this failed, as a stepping-stone to extra-university revolutionary activity. According to van Peursen, this led only to a hardening of the establishment. Not unreasonably, many Christians in the church were startled by extremist ideologies and therefore clung more insistently than ever to traditional norms. This was widening the gap between those for whom the Christian faith was a source of stability and those for whom it was an inspiration and guide for change and renewal in society. He had observed how the Christian faith had become for many a living but individualistic conviction in the old pietistic way. Both the fixation of traditional values and the individualization of faith tended to "hamper that inventiveness which in a changing world is indispensable for the church, as well as for the university."

Van Peursen pleaded for the development of "a new policy" for the church and the WSCF. Such a policy should facilitate social renewal, a change of attitudes, and the strengthening of a "spiritual outlook." It would necessitate "a cultural strategy" to foster "an inventiveness of an ethical rather than a merely intellectual character."

174

Such a strategy should, however, avoid the approaches of "futurologies" and "utopianism." He stressed the importance of an ethical "no" which implies a functioning relationship with the object being criticized. Such a "no" can never be purely negative or anarchistic. It contributes to a transformation of structures by the incorporation in them of an ethical critique. "The loss of continuity is a loss of self-identity."

As practical measures for developing the "new policy," van Peursen suggested a much closer relationship between the Christian student movement and university teachers, and the creation of special teams as "bridge-groups" between university workers, political leaders, managers of big enterprises, and church leaders. These would serve as "radar posts" of the Federation and the wider ecumenical movement. Finally, student groups should develop an "extrovert productivity" in order to stimulate youth groups in developing countries.

A third response from the Netherlands came from W. Albeida, a professor at the Economic Institute of the Netherlands, University of Rotterdam, and a leader of the university teachers work of the SCM and the WSCF. He assumed that the student unrest was by and large over (in 1971), although the issues it had raised in 1968 were still alive. He underlined the generation gap as a factor to be taken into account. According to him, young people were further than ever from being contemporaries of the older generation. A new mood and a new attitude were more characteristic of this young generation than were new opinions and new ideas. It was obvious that "some rather old ideas" were being presented by young people as new solutions. Some groups of students were ready to accept dogmatic Marxism, while others were drawn by neo-Marxism and neoanarchism. According to him, none of the traditional parties in the Dutch parliamentary system could count on much sympathy from the present generation of students.

Albeida then went into the issues facing the WSCF:

The real fundamental problem should be seen in the question: should Christians take their place within the ranks of the radical left? And if so, do they follow their Christian calling? . . . (What is) the role of Christians in society? Personally I hesitate to see your Federation as part of a global student movement which is

175

radical and leftist. I do not see how your Federation could enter this global movement without reserves. . . . Christians should never enter any (political) movement without reserve.

In his view, the means used and the propagation of convictions which contradict the fundamentals of the Christian faith placed a clear limit for Christian identification with political movements. This left open the possibility of engagement in causes together with secular political groups. Examples which he mentioned were the struggle against apartheid and neocolonialism, criticism of the egoism of rich nations, and exposure of the dangers of polluting the environment. Joining these causes would not, however, imply a rejection of all the elements of Western society, or an acceptance of anarchism as an alternative to the present economic system.

In many cases Christians and neo-Marxists may be allies in the fight against injustice in the present world. But is it possible to find common ideals in the positive sense? Is it possible to disconnect the Marxist or the anarchist view of man and society from the atheist basis of Marxism? . . . I do not see how Christians can swallow Marxist thinking as such and still remain Christian.

Albeida repudiated the idea that the Federation should shift to the right. Instead he proposed that it involve itself in a critical study not only of the existing structures of national and international economy but also of the alternatives proposed by movements of the left. For him the total rejection of present society, with no concern for the details of an alternative, was simplistic, even if it sounded like a "heroic" solution.

The word revolution seems to inspire many young people nowadays. . . . I understand the indignation of many representatives of the present student generation about many aspects of the world economy. This indignation should however not cause us to refrain from fulfilling our duty to study the complicated fabric of society carefully and to look for concrete solutions of concrete problems before throwing over the whole system, without knowing exactly what will be the alternative.

176

He concluded his response by agreeing with those who saw the Federation primarily as an expression of the Christian community in the academic world. This community needed students who refused to restrict themselves to the narrow field of their specialty and who used their student years "to gain and to deepen their Christian understanding of man and society." "We need a new understanding of the consequences of our common faith in a world that poses new questions for us in nearly all respects."

Belgium

The Belgian SCM responded through its general secretary, Paul Van Sichem, who began by reporting the dissociation of one of its branches from the national SCM on the grounds that the latter was too involved in political causes of the left. The response also referred to the tension between the SCM and the Protestant church in Belgium because of the political orientation of the SCM. He then quoted the constitution of the SCM written in 1963, which was still accepted by the national SCM:

> The Belgian SCM responds to its vocation to proclaim the Gospel among students and help them to know and live the Christian life, as revealed to us in the Bible.

The national leaders had affirmed that the political activity of the SCM was an integral part of living out the Christian faith, and that the stand of the SCM on political and other issues was inseparable from its witness to the gospel.

According to Van Sichem, the Belgian SCM was committed to following a pluralistic policy both theologically and politically within its membership. However, the branch which had withdrawn from the national SCM did not accept this kind of pluralism, even though it was such pluralism which allowed it to commit itself to a particular political cause without binding other branches which did not agree to do so. The profile of the Belgian SCM was by and large leftist, but it did not want to exclude from its ranks those with a different political orientation.

Austria

An Austrian response came from Professor Wilhelm Dantine, former general secretary of the Austrian SCM. He wrote:

> In the light of the spiritual and social events of our time, it is not surprising if a movement like ours reaches a serious crisis. . . . Your letter . . . is a very objective and good description of the present situation, and therefore a great help. . . . My own situation as a professor of theology in a central European university reflects all the factors your circular letter describes as significant for the European situation.

Dantine confirmed a trend which was reported in other central European countries: While the elitist minorities took a very keen interest in intellectual and political movements, the majority of students followed traditional lines. The peak of student activism seemed, however, to be over, and a new, strangely resigned attitude had set in. He feared that SCMs were being maneuvered into choosing between a political position and a Christian one. The way ahead for the Federation was clear: It must expect its member movements to take the gospel as the basis of all thought and action. This was not a nonpolitical option. The confession of the Christian faith had political and social consequences. He also emphasized the need for the Federation, its member movements and its regions, to maintain flexibility. The extent to which a uniform position could or should be maintained on particular political issues was in his view an open question. Taking an unequivocal political stand *and* leaving individuals, branches, and movements free to make their own political decisions were not mutually exclusive.

Dantine described the tension which had arisen in Austria between the institutional church and socially involved young Christians. Frustration with the church was widespread among students who were experimenting with new forms of community life. It was vital, therefore, for churches to look toward new forms of life together, and for Christian students to maintain their links with their lifeline, the church.

Dantine welcomed the regionalization of the Federation, because it encouraged member movements to find models of Christian witness and community best suited to their particular cultural and politi-

178

cal situations. He recommended that the Federation leave the responsibility for seeking new models of Christian involvement in society to the regions, and that the Federation, as a worldwide community, place much more emphasis on theological work.

Norway

The Norwegian SCM sent a basic statement entitled "Aims and Goals." It emphasized two characteristics which it considered essential for the WSCF and its member movements — "student" and "Christian." It discussed what the Federation's rooting among students meant, and the danger of national and international student organizations becoming isolated from the grassroots concerns of students. It questioned the wisdom of including the whole of society as the sphere of responsibility and action for the Federation. It expressed concern about the "ideological totalitarianism" which the Norwegian SCM felt was threatening the Federation.

Concerning the Christian identity of the Federation, the Norwegian SCM was not satisfied with references only to Christian "tradition," "heritage," or "background." Faith in the suffering and living Christ belongs not only to the past, but to the present and the future.

The Norwegian SCM considered it inappropriate to assume that every individual taking part in the life of the Federation "should have to confess this personal faith *expressis verbis.*" While recognizing the difficulty of defining the full implications and consequences of the Christian faith, that faith was nevertheless at stake in all SCM and Federation activity and at the center of all Christian community. Distinguishing between the primary affirmations of faith and their implications and consequences in a given historical situation was difficult, and diversities on this point had to be conceded.

The statement warned specifically of an oversimplification of differing opinions presently held within the Federation, alluding to the two poles suggested in the circular letter. A certain theological pluralism is inevitable not so much because of various confessional traditions but because social and cultural situations vary in different parts of the world. As to the function of Christian faith in politics, the document warned against a purely sociological or contextual approach, since different patterns have roots also in basic theological stances. It

179

was not enough to concentrate on an analysis of the role of institutional churches in society. Deeper theological issues, such as questions of authority and motivation for valid modes of action by Christians, needed to be considered.

Finally the document discussed the SCM's expectations from the Federation. The possibility of the WSCF functioning as a political action organization was ruled out because a world organization "cannot be a primary platform for action." The Federation's function was described as "confrontation," although "dialogue" or "encounter" might better convey the intended meaning. "Confrontation assumes a certain pluralism. Such a pluralism could be used as an umbrella for neutralism which we don't want." In the Federation, different points of view and different programs of action should not only be tolerated, but should be studied and made to challenge one another. "Confrontation," as endorsed by the Norwegian statement, should never be allowed to develop into a struggle for influence and power in the Federation.

Poland

The only response from Eastern Europe came from Halina Bortnowska of Poland. She was a member of the Catholic Intellectuals Group and a prominent layperson active in the ecumenical wing of the Roman Catholic Church in Poland. She had participated in the WSCF General Assembly in 1968, in the meeting of the Executive Committee in 1970, and in some European regional events. She pointed out that her response was an answer only to a summary of the circular and also to some of the responses she had seen. She wrote:

> We are at the very first steps of exploring the eventual link between faith and politics. We cannot grasp it in abstract terms but only in our concrete situation. . . . Our group is explicitly Christian. . . . We look for positions inside a generally socialist outlook. In this we are pragmatic and we are beginners.

Germany

The only response from the German SCM (Evangelische Studentengemeinde) was a copy of Jürgen Moltmann's paper on the task of theology in the current political and ideological context. He was one of the main speakers at the WSCF World Student Conference at Turku in 1968. The theses of his paper and his conclusion were very relevant to the issues in the WSCF debate even if they were not a direct response to the latest stage of polarization within the Federation.

According to Moltmann, Christian theology was facing a twofold crisis: that of understanding the world and a crisis of Christian identity. False alternatives were put forward: evangelization and humanization, personal conversion and a change of social and economic conditions, the vertical dimension of faith and the horizontal dimension of love. Such alternatives destroy unity in God and humanity's wholeness. Moltmann underlined the importance of "biblical theology," which alone could point to the liberating character of the kingdom of God. He regretted the diminished interest in contextual Bible study among theologians as well as their preoccupation with philosophical theology and the sociology of religion and anthropology. He advocated the reading of the Bible with a new perception.

> In my opinion, the Bible is the book of the poor, the oppressed and hopeless. It is not the book of priests and lords. It is not a book of laws for the just, but of promises and of the gospel of God to sinners. . . . We must read this book with the eyes of the poor.

He continued by affirming the eschatological dimension of theology, which for him meant acceptance of a creative tension between the old and the new, between law and freedom. He maintained that Christian theology will in the future become more practical and more political as it comes to deal with issues of public life and with the common concerns of all human beings. Its focus will shift from internal church concerns to matters of serving God in everyday life in the world.

Finally he underlined the dialogical nature of all theology:

> (Christian theology) has and reveals its truth first of all in dialogue with other men and other religions and ideologies. Its center lies on their boundaries. Its object is universal and it exists for all men. But because it can itself only be particular, it must discover and spread the universal truth in dialogue with others.

181

It was probably characteristic of the situation of the German SCM that no direct response came from its actual leaders. Once the largest SCM in Europe, known for the strength of its Bible study programs, it was by 1971 torn apart by ever-sharpening ideological conflicts within it and also by the increasing tension between church leaders and student pastors. The majority of local branches refrained that year from sending delegates to the annual national SCM conference because they found its debates irrelevant. Church subsidies to the SCM came under pressure as the traditional ministries of the SCM died out and as student participation in all SCM activities declined.

Thus, the years 1968-71 marked a large-scale transformation of most European SCMs into "one-issue movements." This was followed by a rapid decrease in their membership, by their marginalization in relation to churches as well as to student organizations. The SCMs, which had played such a visible role in the universities and ecumenical and missionary movements in their countries, and which had had branches in most institutions of higher education, shrank, within a few years, to relatively insignificant fringe groups. These were the years of drastic decline for the British SCM, once the most influential member movement of the WSCF in providing leadership for the ecumenical movement. A similar decline hit the Nordic SCMs, with the possible exception of the movement in Norway. The French SCM virtually went out of existence after its leadership took the movement fully into the revolutionary stream and severed its ties with the French Protestant churches.

9.3. Responses from North America

The SCM of *Canada* responded through its general secretary, a former staff member of the WSCF, Donald Wilson. Commenting on the circular's analysis of polarization in the Federation, he found that discussion in the Canadian SCM had followed a similar course. After a spell of "New Left"–type radicalism, the SCM had moved toward an emphasis on Christian identity in the place of wordy political analyses and programs. This had not meant ignoring the "left," "but few now seemed prepared to advocate salvation by political faith alone." According to this response, the Canadian radicals now held a neoliberal concept of the human being and shared a technocratic dream.

> If the marked polarization in the SCM of 1965-69 had gone the way of the most radical, then I think we can say that there would be no ecumenical student-led movement of any kind in Canada today and fewer opportunities for political action or a lay-Christian community. . . .
>
> Perhaps the present and past here in the SCM can be described by Jesus' parable of the man who wished to build quickly, and built on sand rather than the long, hard business of seeking a rock foundation. So far as I can see, change will only come through sustained, disciplined effort.

Five responses were received from the *USA,* three from people directly involved in student or university ministries and two from theological educators. The acute crisis of the ecumenical student movement in the USA was reflected in most of the responses. None of the defenders of the "radical left" in the Christian student scene sent comments.

Henry Bucher, who had been a field staff member of the University Christian Movement (UCM) until its demise, felt that the main tension was between supporters of an "issue-oriented" and of a "tradition-oriented" organization. This, together with the almost total rejection by leaders of the UCM of inherited Christian student organizations and campus ministries, was a major factor in its early death. He wrote:

> The former (issue-orientation) meant working with all those of any faith or doctrine who took the side of the oppressed as generally defined in terms of power. The latter meant conferences, educational meetings, Bible study, etc. with local and regional groups that had formed within the Christian tradition. UCM chose issue-orientation and movement-building, which was one reason for an organizational collapse.

He suggested that

the two are easy to combine, because strong Christian commitment both personally and in terms of the (Christian) community leads to siding with the oppressed in America, Vietnam, South Africa, the Middle East, etc. . . . My hope is that the WSCF will sacrifice neither commitment to Christ nor its commitment to revolutionary change and human liberation. The latter flows from the former, though non-Christians can be just as involved and perhaps more committed to change.

William Webber, president of New York Theological Seminary, described in his brief response the student scene in the United States:

In student circles tremendous insights emerge, new patterns develop, projects appear, with almost no way I see that people moving in kindred directions can learn from each other or even know that they exist. Students with whom I work this year are always going off to some other city just to find out what is going on. They want to know where the action is, what people are into, what they are thinking about. Two areas are prominent: life style questions, as they surface in communes, . . . and strategies for social change. Behind both of these is an intense critique of present educational methods and philosophy, leading to sharp criticism of college and seminary education. But the search for alternatives, for insight is slow, incompetent and frustrating. And underneath it all there is a persistent sense that Christian commitment and stance is possible and urgent, but the institutional expressions be damned.

Associate University Pastor Samuel N. Slie, of Yale University, also voiced the need for communication between centers of initiative. "Where 'the Movement' is going is both ambiguous and difficult to ascertain." He was worried about the self-centeredness of what he called "do-your-own-thing people." He deplored the lack of a concept of Christian ministry which could provide a framework beyond the ad hoc concerns. Contemporary dynamics should not define what the Federation is about. He pointed to the cautionary tale of the American UCM, which "sought such utter immediacy of relevance that its continuity for all other purposes was made to appear irrelevant," and which, with the decision of "a small group of people who felt irrelevant, voted a whole movement out of existence."

Slie strongly underlined the need for an explicit Christian commitment to be the foundation of SCMs and the WSCF:

> Take the word "Christian" out and there are many other names and forms of World Student Federation. Our *raison d'être,* our stance of meaning, our unity is in the Christian tradition; not static, established, Western Christendom, but dynamic, renewing, universal Christian faith and hope.

He also expressed the hope that a worldwide movement represented by the WSCF could help bring Christian campus groups and ministries together into a coherent national campus movement. Such a movement could, in his view, help "overcome increasing generational polarities." He referred to the rapidly progressing divisions not only within the "student left" but in the whole "movement" among students and young people. Students for a Democratic Society (SDS) had proved to be short-lived. So had the Black Panthers and many other militant organizations. The "liberal-to-radical" scene was taken over by "all kinds of radical caucuses, black caucuses, women's caucuses, Indian caucuses, etc." The provincialism of "our own heavy national problems of conscience" had tended to lead the ecumenical movement among the younger generation into a dead end.

Richard E. Sherrell, associate executive director of the Department of Higher Education of the National Council of Churches of Christ, responded on behalf of his unit. The University Christian Movement of the USA (UCM) had, until its death in 1969, been related to it. Sherrell said polarity in society and in the institutions of higher education was leading to schizophrenia. On the one hand, the quest for radical human liberation seemed more than justified. On the other, the "movement" claiming to represent the drive for liberation was in total disarray. Any possibilities for a meaningful overhaul of structures could come only from those working within the institutions.

Sherrell also reported that there were not many signs of explicit Christian student activity outside the nonchurch evangelical groups such as Inter-Varsity Christian Fellowship and Campus Crusade for

Christ. For the ecumenical campus movement, he saw no other possibility than to work at both the theological and the liberation task.

The context of Sherrell's statement was the decline of the national protest movement in the USA and a large-scale return by students to traditional academic work. Only the protest movement against the war in Vietnam was still alive, albeit in its last stages.

In his extensive response, Charles C. West, professor of Christian ethics at Princeton Theological Seminary and a long-standing participant in SCM and WSCF programs, characterized the mood among students in the USA as postexplosive.

> Thirty-five years ago, we learned the hard way — by being used and betrayed by secular movements with whom we threw our lot[9] — that if we were not a Christian movement, we had no basis in existence at all. We learned from the great witnesses of that time how to measure our consciences, not by this or that revolutionary movement or social program, but by the far more searching standard of God's commandment and Christ's calling. . . . I am tempted to suggest that we have come a full circle and lost our nerve again, or perhaps that we are evading our responsibilities.
>
> If the church, WSCF or SCM has any business being and saying and doing at all (in social and political matters), it lies in the capacity to reflect in its words and actions its own response to a power that transcends interests and which often speaks in judgement of the church itself. When the church loses this, it becomes useless even to those movements with which it has allied itself. To put it bluntly, I suspect the WSCF had better decide whether there is a God who has come into this world in Jesus Christ or not, and if not, it had better go out of business so as not to deceive people.
>
> For years . . . the WSCF functioned as the church ahead of the church, as the seed-bed for the theological and social insights which later became the grain which fed the ecumenical movement. I have seen this work on university campuses . . . where there was an active

9. West refers to the rise of fascism, the era of Stalinism, the weakness of liberal Christianity, and to the new vigor of neo-orthodoxy in the mid-thirties, with Karl Barth and Reinhold Niebuhr as its leading theologians.

SCM. I think one ought to make a distinction between church control which the SCM should resist at all costs and responsibility to the church which is one of the basic reasons for an SCM's existence. . . . What is needed is to find the form of the Christian mission to the university, and to focus the responsibility of the academic community for the whole community of the nation and the world.

These responses, unlike those from Europe, showed little evidence of an explicit impact of Marxism. The common point of concern was the failure of the UCM to offer credible alternatives to American political radicalism. The ecumenical student movement had become trapped in its total identification with the protest movements of the sixties. The attempt to build a new identity as a "movement," and even a new "paradigm" for the Christian community, on the basis of ad hoc involvements in a series of political protests, justified as many of them were, proved to be a total mistake. The merging of the ecumenical student movement with a revolutionary protest culture had not saved it from the cultural captivity for which it blamed the churches of liberal or conservative orientation. The American responses also point to the weakness of the theological foundation of churches open to liberal-to-radical causes. When the UCM was formed in 1966 it had virtually no viable theological basis. The heritage of the Social Gospel movement had worn thin, the teaching of the neo-orthodox school of thought had been dismissed by radical prophets, and the heritage of the missionary movement had been left to the evangelicals.

9.4. Responses from the Asian Region

Seven responses were received from Asia and the Pacific: four from India and one each from Indonesia, Burma, and New Zealand. Many member movements with considerable strength in the size of their membership, their sense of purpose, and even their political role did not send any comments. They included those in Pakistan, Sri Lanka, South Korea, the Philippines, and Australia. All of them played an active part in the Asian regional programs of the WSCF.

The general secretary of the SCM of *India,* Ninan Koshy, wrote:

Polarization, the way in which it is described (in the circular letter), cannot be said to be reflected in the Indian Movement. If we give a margin for generalization the Movement more or less reflects the second position outlined.

What is in existence (in the Federation) is a diversity of approaches and stances and there is nothing to despair about. There is diversity in the theological, university and political situations in different parts of the world, and it is neither necessary nor possible to assume that there will be a uniform approach and strategy. The difficulty seems to arise from reluctance on the part of many to accept the fact of such diversity . . . (they want) instead to dominate the thinking and the life of the Movement . . . (and tend to) consider that the other regions are at a lower level of understanding. There is a tendency to demand uniformity and to universalize particular experiences. If the Federation has to live as a Federation, this has to be avoided.

He then referred to the discussion that was under way in the Indian SCM about its constitutional aims and basis. An effort had been made to reformulate them so that they would continue to affirm ultimate loyalty to Jesus Christ and give stronger emphasis than in the past to involvement in the life of the university and in the struggle for dignity, freedom, and justice.

Another response from India came from a former member of the WSCF staff, M. M. Thomas, who at the time of writing was the moderator of the Central Committee of the World Council of Churches. He pointed out that the different regions faced different questions and that the task of ecumenism was to bring these regions into effective dialogue with each other, while responding to the regional issues for the sake of the region itself. He perceived some dangers in the situation of the day. First and foremost, there was the tendency for one region to dominate the thinking of the worldwide movement and to consider other regions as being at an inferior stage.

Second, there was a real danger in assuming that the issues faced in different regions were so unique that there was no point in trying to find common human and spiritual dimensions around which a real dialogue, even confrontation, would be possible. Without dialogue and confrontation the ecumenical movement would die.

He then commented on the relationship between the "exploration of Christ as the center of the life" of the ecumenical student movement and the concern for social and political involvement:

> No ecumenical organization can justify itself as *Christian* unless it is all the time involved in exploring further, as a matter of imperative, the truth and meaning of the person of Jesus Christ. . . . But this does not stand by itself because . . . we are dealing . . . with the meaning of the totality of human existence. Therefore faith must find expression in involvement in society at various levels. I would emphasize the "various levels." Of course politics is rather important especially in relation to the whole question of the liberation of men in society, but . . . politics does not stand alone — political action should be consciously related to the economic, social and even cultural aspects. Therefore, the ecumenical community has to be a community of the committed and . . . this makes . . . the unity of the community very difficult because the commitments (within it) naturally vary and sometimes may even be contradictory. But it is not impossible that the community as such could make a commitment where there is a consensus of common direction. This should be possible without excluding the minority who might have taken the opposite position.

Thomas's conclusion for the role of the Federation was:

> While some of the member movements could go at tangents without the comprehensiveness which I have indicated . . . , the Federation itself . . . has the duty to struggle to remain more or less comprehensive in its approach on the one hand to the regional concerns and the confrontation between the regions, and on the other to its Christ-centeredness and the political commitments.

The third commentator from India was Professor C. T. Kurien, an economist and an active participant in the university teachers work of the WSCF. He wrote:

> Thank God, the WSCF is right in the midst of it all. . . . I mean that we become really effective only when we are fully caught up

189

in the situation and when we feel that we are being torn asunder. And so in the crisis we face today I see the hope for tomorrow.

He made several observations on the situation and the problems of the WSCF:

[W]hat has been happening (in the WSCF) is a deliberate rejection of a long-standing Federation view of the university world which was too academic and too European. This view goes back to the days when the Federation was giving lead in the discussion of the "university question." The intellectual debate about the ideological conflict in the university was quite legitimate . . . but it had two side-effects which have left their mark on the Federation. In the first place the Federation became terribly fond of a kind of intellectualism . . . divorced from the realities around. Secondly, the lead given by the Geneva group to the discussion of the university question was so significant and so powerful that Geneva became excessively the Think Tank of the Federation. Today . . . both of these aspects (are) challenged. . . . I have a great deal of sympathy with the trend of regionalization that you have described in the circular letter. I feel that the rejection of the old intellectualism of the Federation . . . is part of that regionalization trend.

He then described his own impression of the polarization within the Federation. The heresy of those who leaned toward a radical leftist option was, in his view, the result of the heresy of the intellectualism of those who emphasized the role of the WSCF "primarily as an expression of the Christian community in the academic world." He detected a confusion between intellectualism and Christian tradition. He felt that the fallacies on both sides should be admitted. The result would be a radicalism which "springs from Christian understanding of the situation." He concluded that the regionalization of the Federation might help to resolve the problem:

The only way I can see is to reinforce the trend of regionalization. Trouble often begins when the Federation decides, implicitly or explicitly, that it must have a world-wide strategy. But is it necessary? There may be a situation, let us say somewhere in Latin

190

America, where the Student Christian Movement may have to become part of a student movement for liberation. Let the Latin American Movement decide about it without insisting that this must be the strategy for all Movements in all parts of the world. If there are half a dozen patterns instead of two, the Federation will become a real federation of national and regional movements.

He ended his comments with the statement:

I would like to repeat again that in the troubles of today I support the Federation's honest effort to become a truly catholic movement with a sense of purpose and a renewal of mission.

The fourth response from India came from Professor Chandran Devanesen, principal of the Madras Christian College and chairman of the University Teachers Movement, previously national chairman of the SCM of India. According to him, Christian students in India had not yet awakened to a concern for nation and society. The WSCF and the SCM would be relevant only as far as they were explicitly Christian. "The people respect an open and honest Christian in India." The SCM of India cannot opt for one particular political position. Instead its task is to raise the level of political interest among Christian students. Development concerns need more attention in the SCM and the WSCF, and development projects should involve students of all faiths, including those professing no faith.

The general secretary of the SCM of *Burma,* William W. Lay, sent a brief letter which was also a farewell before he became general secretary of the Burmese YMCA. His comment on the orientation of the SCM was:

[T]he Church-centered, religious emphasis and . . . the study of the Bible in the light of the present understanding and interpretation provide the necessary dynamism and security for the continued existence and service of the SCM. . . . The work is expanding and extending to all universities, colleges, and institutions both in Rangoon and the districts. . . . With the help of the Federation and the support of the fellow movements, the leadership training institute is bearing fruits.

Burma, under its dictatorial regime, was at that time one of the most isolated countries. The possibilities for churches and Christian organizations to maintain international contacts were severely curtailed. The SCM was hardly touched by the student radicalism of the late sixties.

The *Indonesian SCM* prepared a substantive document addressed primarily to the Asia committee of the WSCF. It was a response to the two ideological options accepted by the Executive Committee at Beirut and to the initiatives concerning a new, politically radical constituency for the Federation. This document was also submitted as a response to the circular.

In Indonesia the SCM was the only national Christian student organization recognized by the Indonesian government authorities. In terms of membership and number of branches, it was one of the largest SCMs in Asia. According to its own estimate, it served about half of the Christian students, who comprised about 10 percent of all Indonesian students. The principles of national unity and religious tolerance over and against a Muslim-dominated religious society were actively supported by the SCM. The political conservatism of the Indonesian military government was experienced as a constant threat to Christian witness and integrity in social and political matters.

A recognition of the plurality of the Federation, the rejection of an "a-priori attitude" and a "prefabricated ideology" for the whole Federation, and an affirmation of the service which the Federation owed to its membership were the themes of the Indonesian response. It was exceedingly critical of trends which seemed to disregard member movements with their particular traditions and contexts. At the same time, it did not totally exclude the possibility of individuals becoming members of the WSCF without being part of a national member organization.

The document described the characteristics of the Indonesian SCM in its social and religious context, and its expectations of the WSCF. The point of departure was the affirmation of Christian faith as it has been transmitted from the first Christians. The unity of the church was a key concern, but a concept of unity which would imply that Christians alone possess the life of the Church was rejected. Unity which stems from Christian faith is a model and a goal for the whole society, for "all the people of God." The task of the Indonesian SCM, according to the document, was to express all functions of the Church in the university and to assist the university in critical research and in preserving and building human culture.

After describing some difficulties faced by the SCM under the current social and religious pressures, the document affirmed that as long as the perspective of a renewal of society remained a central concern of the WSCF, the Indonesian SCM would wish to be part of it.

The general secretary of the *New Zealand SCM,* Don Borrie, found the links with the Asia region of the WSCF helpful and stimulating. On the question of polarization, he made a brief comment:

> The polarization being experienced by the WSCF is also real for the New Zealand SCM. Some people desiring an action-issue oriented movement have moved out . . . because the SCM continues to maintain the principle of diversity. . . . More effort must be made to spell out the social-political ramifications of Christianity. . . . The WSCF must not flinch from identification with liberation movements but we must be sensitive to those constituencies which contain many socially conservative members.

9.5. Responses from Latin America

Four responses were received from Latin America, two of them from the same movement, the Confederation of Autonomous SCMs of Argentina (CAMECA). This movement was in open conflict with the SCM of Argentina on issues of revolutionary theory and strategy. The two others came from the SCMs of Venezuela and Colombia. Although these did not present a comprehensive picture of the debate within the SCMs of Latin America, they nevertheless were quite illustrative of the ferment and turmoil among students of the whole region. Moreover, they illustrated some of the problems which plagued the regional leaders of the WSCF in Latin America.

The two responses from *Argentina* consisted of a letter from the secretary of CAMECA, Daniel Rebasa, and a formal statement by the leadership team of the same organization. Both emphasized involvement in revolution as an inherent responsibility of Christians based on the revolutionary character of the gospel itself and on the consequent understanding of Christianity as a revolutionary force. They affirmed the principle that the work and revolutionary concerns of CAMECA as a whole needed to originate from local SCM groups, which in turn should form the basis of national and regional SCM activity.

The two responses also affirmed the intention of CAMECA to work within the context of the Peronist left, in cooperation with other organizations such as "Priests of the Third World," Peronist trade unions, and Peronist groups in universities, in the armed forces, and so on. The accent was on cultural rather than economic or social revolution.[10]

The CAMECA statement was explicit on Christian commitment.

> Particularly in Latin America with the national revolutions in which we are living, we need militants participating as Christians in these liberating processes. A negative attitude towards Christianity, in our context, becomes a barrier. . . .
>
> We also share the belief that the point of departure is the Christian faith, though we do not confuse this with Christian revolution. Christians and non-Christians are participating in a national revolution, though we do it as Christians, feeling that our heritage can contribute to the process as such. In our particular context in the words of Peron, the national leader of the popular movement, Christianity is an integral part in the building of socialism ("Socialismo Nacional y Christiano" from "La Hora de los Pueblos").

The two Argentine statements included an open attack on the work of the Latin America staff team of the WSCF. The main points of contention were

1. The WSCF team drew its authority from the world body and not from Latin American national movements.
2. The plan for leadership training represented an imposed educational philosophy which ignored national situations.

10. It is to be noted that in 1969 CAMECA represented a simple popular revolutionary line as against the position of the National SCM, which at that time reflected the views of the Peronist left.

3. The WSCF team based its work on a definition of revolution by leftist liberals and intellectuals which bore no relation to student reality and actual revolutionary movements.
4. The WSCF team represented a secular theology imported from Europe or North America which had negative attitudes toward Christianity.
5. Financial support from other regions for work in Latin America was used mainly for WSCF regional programs and was not shared with national movements.
6. The WSCF team lacked a capacity to relate to people.

The statement questioned the trend toward regionalization on the grounds that it left regional leaders free to develop their own ideas without serving national movements, and to speak for SCMs at world gatherings without any authentic mandate from them. They also felt that the Latin American members of the WSCF Executive Committee were out of touch with the WSCF constituency in the region.

Both statements voiced the desire of CAMECA to be part of the worldwide Federation community, but not in the terms defined by the Latin America staff team:

> Our local and national outlook and even our regional and world view can help to build a new MEC (SCM) in Latin America and to restructure the WSCF on strong local-national-and-regional movements. This does not mean just in terms of numbers. . . . We are in agreement over most issues with Africans and Asians regarding membership in the Federation and the necessity for diversity, since we ourselves have diversity in our national movement.

The conflict between the older but very much shrunken SCM of Argentina with its collective leadership team and CAMECA is reflected in these two responses. The old SCM had opted to follow the Marxist revolutionary line and had lost most of its contacts with churches in Argentina. Its office had been evicted from the premises of the United Evangelical Lutheran Church where it had been located until 1968. By 1969 it had only one local branch situated in Buenos

Aires, while three of its former branches had joined CAMECA. The criticisms by CAMECA of the regional leadership reflected a rejection of the ideas of Richard Shaull and Paulo Freire, which CAMECA felt were being imposed on the whole region.

A response from the SCM of *Colombia* came together with an "Open Letter" addressed to participants in the WSCF Latin America regional meeting held in Chile in May 1971. The response did not deal directly with the points of the Geneva circular but was an even more fiery attack against the WSCF Latin America staff team. It also gave a colorful presentation of another revolutionary position in the orbit of the WSCF.

The open letter described the history of the SCM as a process of liberation from the bondage of North American churches, which in 1965 had begun to finance the office of a national SCM secretary in Bogota, "an indication of the influence exercised in the SCM by the church which, through its financial support, tried to determine the Movement's ideological orientation." According to the letter, the Presbyterian Church was instrumental in preventing the SCM from studying Marx and *Pedagogy of the Oppressed* by Paulo Freire.[11]

> At that time the (SCM) group was clearly the slave of capitalist values, although to the congregation it looked like a subversive element and was regarded with suspicion by the fathers of the church. In the economic life of Colombia, they are magnates and owners of the means of production, but within the walls of the religious community to which they belong they need only the Bible to justify the wealth of the church, and, through violence in the form of ignorance, they keep the church members in a position where their only role in production is to sell their physical strength. . . .
>
> The Protestant Church is nothing more than an underground agent of North American imperialism! The workers are exploited in the factories and also in the place where they live. . . . The Protestant Church preaches the Gospel to these men and converts them to a puritanism which sees their customs as sinful, without understanding scientifically and politically the causes of their situation. The Church

11. Paulo Freire emerged in the early seventies as one of the leading ideologists for Marxist-oriented Protestant Christians in Latin America.

paralyzes them because penitent men do not see the socialist revolution as the way out and they condemn it.

The open letter described the conflict which arose between the SCM and the official church leadership. The topics of the student study groups meeting on the church premises apparently triggered a clash which resulted in the expulsion of SCM members from the Socio-Cultural Center of the Presbyterian Church and in the removal of the pastor who had supported the SCM.

The letter blamed the WSCF for not playing any role in this crisis, although the SCM of Colombia had taken an active part in WSCF world and regional events since 1968.

These WSCF conferences are nothing more than FALSE DEMOCRACY, where what matters is not the people exploited by imperialism but the maintenance of a structure and the distribution of the bureaucratic booty. This means nothing for the revolutionary history of the people.

As a result, according to the letter, the leaders had decided to pull out of the SCM and had finally disbanded the organization. However, they continued in a personal capacity to meet and develop new plans. The open letter reported:

We are coming together again, but naturally with different criteria . . . you will understand that to reject is not to abandon. . . . If that position means that the gods expel us from Olympia, we are ready to break with the WSCF, because we are not working for an institution but for the people, not with a popularist idea but taking the Love of Christ as our stand and Marxism as our Method of Struggle.

The open letter concluded by reaffirming the decision of the SCM not to participate in the Chile regional meeting, which would, in their view, not be open to democratic debates and decisions.

We are not asking for money because we believe that in the process towards socialism . . . new men . . . will rise up out of political

197

theory and practice, ready to fulfil the role which history demands of them. We do not believe we need mercenaries to bring about the revolution.

The WSCF regional team wrote a reply in which it pointed to the political conflicts inside the Colombian SCM, to the tensions with the institutional church from which several students had been evicted, to differing perspectives with other ecumenical organizations, and to changes on the Colombian political scene. It also reported ongoing and attempted discussions with representatives of the different factions of the SCM and different church and ecumenical groups. It repudiated the idea that the WSCF was a monolithic structure and indicated that all doors would be open to further talks about the difficulties.

The letter received from the SCM of *Venezuela* simply expressed appreciation for the WSCF and the ideas and actions generated within it. It mentioned the "dramatic social and political crises" in the country and the conviction of students that the experience of encounter with Christ needed to include an openness to the problems confronted in the "search for a better world." Affirming the validity of the work of the WSCF, the letter stated:

> We believe that similar work, united and motivated by the tradi-
> tional values of our Christian faith, has to serve in the first place
> as an agent for the renewal of the Church today and as a catalyst
> for action in the task . . . entrusted to us.

At the time of the survey most of the organized SCMs in Latin America were in some disarray. The political climate had become increasingly oppressive. The revolutionary forces of the left lacked coherence. Fidel Castro's Cuba and Salvador Allende's Chile were the symbols which kept the revolutionary vision alive. In those years Archbishop Dom Helder Camara of Recife became a leading figure among "progressive" Christians of Latin America. The SCM was plagued not only by the suppression of organized student activities by governmental and university authorities but also by an ideology of "discontinuity" fostered by leaders attracted by the theology of revo-lution. Furthermore, regionalization tended to isolate WSCF Latin American leaders at a time when they were most in need of creative and supportive contacts with SCMs in other regions. The few responses to the circular bear witness to the sad state of the WSCF in Latin America at that time.

9.6. Responses from Africa

The only responses received from Africa came from two white South African leaders of the UCM, in spite of the fact that throughout the sixties Student Christian Movements had been growing rapidly all over the continent. It was evident that the whole discussion about the Federation's Christian identity, its political role, and the ideological tension within it had no meaning for the African SCMs. Furthermore, many SCMs of the region were newcomers to the WSCF and had no experience of participating in its overall concerns. Making distinctions between religious and political concerns was also alien to most of them. In retrospect, therefore, the limited response is not surprising, but it should not obscure recognition of the scope and intensity of the work of many African SCMs among students and their pioneering role in the churches' intellectual and social witness.

The contributions sent by the general secretary of the University Christian Movement of South Africa, Colin Collins, and by his associate, Basil Moore, were significant and substantive. They reacted forcefully against the position which they felt I had taken in my circular by way of formulating two poles. Collins characterized the two "visions" — one as a "radical" vision and the other, with which he (not entirely mistakenly) assumed that I myself identified, as a "conservative" or "umbrella" vision. He felt that the description did not do justice to the people involved:

> You describe the more radical view in largely negative terms and scarcely give any content to what the radical sector is about except by using such terms as "struggle against imperialism and elitist rule." Your description of the more conservative "vision" of the Federation is far more complete and is presented in a far more favorable light. . . .
>
> Secondly, and more important, I object to this division into two so-called "visions." . . . I think the divisions are not as simple as this. . . . Within the conservative (umbrella) division there are con-

siderable differences of stance and opinion. There is, for example, one group of umbrella people who are genuinely concerned with what is going on in the world and particularly with the way that Christianity relates to questions such as the alleviation of injustice. This group is puzzled by the fact that in their own life-style they are not identifying with the problems of the world.

On the other hand there are those within the umbrella group who simply give lip service to change and involvement. They hide behind the fact that Christian involvement is so varied. Temperamentally they have a great need for security; socially they have good salaries and comfortable homes and do not like to be threatened as regards this life-style. I would put many bureaucrats in such a group.

Within the more radical group there are also various gradations of opinion and style. On the one side it must be admitted that there are quite a number of so-called radicals who are arm-chair revolutionaries. If Christians, some of them come to consider socialist models of society with an eagerness that gets them involved in intellectual exercises concerning such models. They frequently get lost in intellectual critique and are unable to find any meaningful actions whereby they can carry out some of their ideas. When radicals are abused by more conservative umbrella people it is frequently this group which is being attacked.

On the other hand there are more genuine kind of radicals. Their critique of society is not one that stems from any kind of doctrinaire outlook be it socialist or capitalist. They opt for total critique of society. . . . Moreover, such genuine radicals manifest in their own life-style their criticism of society. They are involved and committed in acts as well as words. They have frequently to give up any sense of ambition or security. For this they have to live in a constant state of anxiety directed both against police and also resulting from the fact that they are constantly breaking new ground in society. . . . It is this kind of group that I think you have too easily categorized and implicitly dismissed.

I answered Colin Collins, suggesting that he had misinterpreted the points which I had made and ignored my deliberate reference to variations in both "visions." In retrospect I find his position to be very close to my own. I admit that I had in my mind the "genuinely concerned" umbrella people, to use Collins's terminology, when describing the second option, and that I focused too much on a mixture of European Marxist and American Marcusian Christians in describing the first position. He provided an important corrective to my first effort to analyze the undercurrents in the Federation.

Basil Moore's statement was in effect a commentary on Collins's response. He pointed out that radical Christians are not likely to use in any positive sense phrases such as "Christian tradition," as there is so much in that tradition that was being questioned. Secondly, he maintained that radical Christians, whether within the radical or umbrella group, were not prepared to narrow down their commitment to "the academic world." He wrote:

> Where do you place the man for whom Christian commitment necessarily entails a radical political commitment? For him Christian commitment is not merely or even mainly supportive of political commitment. They are facets of each other. At the same time, however, this sort of person is frequently disenchanted by the main-stream Christianity, and is excited by those who without adopting a Christian stance are radically committed politically. . . . Such persons would find it extraordinarily difficult to place themselves in either of your categories, though with strong sympathies for the first position despite its pejorative implications.

Moore went on to underline that the University Christian Movement of South Africa was Christian and that the critical issues testing the genuineness of its Christian commitment were political.

> It wants to remain a Christian unit *in the struggle,* not a Christian unit in the broad amorphous and frequently irrelevant (and therefore un-Christian) Christian "family." It is the ineptitude of broad-stream Christianity which makes the idea of a common identity of Christian allegiance unacceptable.

These two comments came from persons who had themselves taken considerable personal risks in the South Africa of unbending apartheid rule. Both dissociated themselves as well as the University Christian Movement from a doctrinaire Marxist ideology and revolutionary tactics. They pointed in a different direction from those for whom the theory of class struggle provided a normative tool for the reinterpretation of Christian faith.

The heat of Collins's reaction arose partly from a disappointment concerning the amount of financial support the South African UCM had received from the WSCF. In the new regional structure, regional committees had authority to allocate funds which had been earmarked for the region as a whole. The Africa committee felt that the UCM was financially better off than most of the poor SCMs in sub-Saharan Africa. Collins interpreted this decision as a decrease of interest in supporting the work of the "radical" UCM and also as a change in my own views. The part of the correspondence which dealt with this difficulty was not circulated with the responses. The trials of the UCM and the involvement of the WSCF in South Africa in these critical years are described in chapter 11.

9.7. Response from the Middle East

From the Middle East came one response signed by Raymond Rizk for the general secretariat of the Orthodox Youth Movement of the Middle East. It reportedly represented the joint thinking of a widely representative group of young people and adults, students and workers, and all branches of the Orthodox Youth Movement in Lebanon and Syria. The issues had also been discussed with Catholic, Protestant, and Armenian youth movements. It was, therefore, one of the most comprehensive responses.

The nine-page document began with a description of the student mood in Lebanon. There was no consensus about the role of the university in the area. One concept which had survived under the pressure of radicalization and politicization was that of the university as "the locus of rational thinking," although there were differing interpretations of it. The struggle of students in the Lebanese University began as specific protests against its educational policy but turned into a campaign to create a "National University." At the American University of Beirut the student protest against the increase of tuition fees had adopted the broader objective of "Lebanization" of the university. In line with these trends, the debate about the role of students in promoting radical change in society had spread widely, and Marxist analysis had attracted more and more students, especially at the Lebanese university, where students tended to come from the lower classes, in contrast with those at the American University.

The document then discussed some basic issues related to the regionalization of the Federation. It emphasized a need to expand the constituency in each region to include those movements which, while not related to the Federation, "have a real Christian vision, though sometimes perhaps their strategies for action are different from those of the affiliated movements." In regions where Protestants are a minority, in Latin America and parts of Asia, for example, this would mean closer contact with Catholic and Orthodox. Presently, it was maintained, the Federation constituency was far too unrepresentative of the concerns of Christian students and youth as a whole.

Regionalization was considered helpful insofar as it pressed the Federation to approach its task from a broader basis than the merely Western presuppositions, "and to resist the temptation to see problems, their causes and their solutions in the perspective of Western rational pragmatism." For the sake of a truly global vision it was "essential to listen to those who think differently, . . . on the level of the heart rather than only that of the reason, those whose approach . . . remains a loving approach, with respect for the mystery of the person, who adhere to values which, for many Westerners often seem obsolete today, but which remain . . . sources of very rich life."

The document was critical of the idea that the Federation should wish to be a prophetic movement among churches burdened by institutional and political compromises. A fruitful role would imply an active relationship with other movements of renewal in the church, even if they did not have the same approach.

The document's section on the Federation's role in politics breaks refreshingly from the terms set by the primarily Western radical/non-radical arguments, although it starts with a blunt criticism of the work of the Federation's Political Commission.

[T]he work of the Political Commission has not been of much use to our movements, especially because of the extreme polarization of what it does. . . . We approve the concern for political engagement which is emerging in the Federation . . . the struggle against oppression, aggression, racism of all kinds, the struggle for true justice, against poverty and hunger — all this cannot be separated from Christian vision.

What we do not approve of, however is the temptation so often expressed in certain parts of the Federation, to reduce Christian action to political action and to impose a single political option as the only valid one.

The document elaborates the reasons for its criticism:

It is impossible and utopian to expect a uniform attitude to the tactics of political action within the Federation. Would it not be a new form of imperialism to impose at all costs a certain way of looking at things? Isn't the Federation, by wishing to adopt at all costs the so-called radical approach, in danger of falling into a new sectarianism? . . .

We think that different forms of expression can be represented in the Federation without restrictions, without sectarianism. And we criticize the Political Commission for not having acted according to these principles . . . it has made itself a spokesman for a particular ideology.

The criticism is followed by an exposition of a theological perspective on political struggles and the concerns for structures and values which form the fabric of politics.

[T]he Christian life — a life of transforming and defying understanding — is essentially other than structures and values. . . . It is new with the newness of the "world which is to come." It is this eschatological reality which we express in professing that "Christ has risen again." He is present in the world, in his very Humanity, in a new way . . . beyond every structure and every value, beyond every form of death. For in the end, neither structures nor values are a source of life for man, but are rather a constant source of alienation. Changing the structures . . . can be an expression of the will to liberate man, but can by no means . . . liberate all of man and all men. The setting can be changed, but it is the same tragedy which is performed. Our faith as it is lived out is . . . experience of the resurrection of Christ; it is the essential liberation of man. . . .

204

... [I]f it is obvious that our Christian faith must force us to take political structures seriously, it is certain that no social form can be dogmatized, and the gospel does not provide a new political program. "The world which is to come" is not a new structure, nor a new ideology. . . . What we strongly affirm is that the Christian lives his Christian life within politics . . . (which he) tries to transform.

The specific concern of Christians in the political arena is for the wholeness of human beings and of the relationship of structures to the whole human being. This concern finds its ultimate expression in the love that transcends human capacities and has the power to transform individual and common destinies. A conclusion from these reflections is that the fundamental liberation of human beings and the acceptance of the transforming power of the resurrection of Christ, through God's love, leave great scope for the choice of means in carrying out political responsibility.

Therefore, pluralism is possible within the same faith, in fact even desirable, as the method of action in each case is based on "active, inventive love, resolute without expecting total success, and stable within history — but animated by a total vision of the man in Christ, the man who needs bread but also responsibility, friendship, beauty, and eternity" (O. Clément).

The document refers to the analogy between the transformation of the church into the sociological entity of Christendom during the Constantinian era and the desire to create "a new socialist and revolutionary Christendom." Both were alien to the understanding of the church as a mystery. An authentic Christian faith cannot accept any form of "Christendom."

The last part of the document dealt with expectations of the Federation from within an Orthodox point of view. They included

- relations with the Church and awakening the interest of young people in the renewal of the Church;
- respect for the tradition which also carries the ferment of renewal in Christ and the continuity of the Church;
- clarity in distinguishing between the life-carrying tradition

and traditions which include elements of stagnation and distortion;

- moving from one-dimensional involvement in politics into expressing Christian engagement in the world and participation in the life of the Church and the ecumenical movement with a richness of dimensions;
- taking up the Palestinian cause.

The Middle East response is still helpful today for an understanding of Orthodox views concerning social issues in the ecumenical movement.

9.8. Observations about the Survey

The survey revealed that the tension which had appeared among the members of the Executive Committee and staff was part of a widespread turbulence in SCMs. The winds blew strongest in European and North American member movements. The divisive conflict-in-the-making was certainly not an isolated phenomenon of the WSCF Geneva office or its Executive Committee. It was apparent that the ideological storm had a wider sphere of influence than just that of the student world. The Federation's fate was, however, to become the center of that storm.

The survey also showed that the definitions of the poles of tension within the Federation which had been suggested in the circular letter were too simple. The responses offered several correctives to them. For example, a real dividing line seemed to be the question as to what extent the Federation should aim at a unified political profile or whether it should be pluralistic. Many of those who had accepted Marxism as a framework for interpreting the Christian faith and the task of the Christian community advocated a clear-cut choice for the political orientation of the whole Federation. The majority of those who rejected political pluralism on ideological grounds — as a tool used by supporters of oppressive systems — made clear that their political choice arose out of Christian commitment.

Roughly half of the responses from SCMs and the majority of those from university teachers and chaplains did not favor an exclusive and clear-cut political orientation for the Federation. They tended to insist that at least some degree of political pluralism is inherent in the nature of the church and of the Christian community. The church can appear only momentarily and in very specific circumstances as a one-issue movement. In their view, pluralism was inevitable for a worldwide Christian organization. Most of them refrained from proposing simple, one-track solutions but rather welcomed the continuation of the dialogue.

Another point on which opinions were divided was the scope of the Federation's vocation. One group felt that the concept of the academic world was elitist and represented the values of a privileged class of which political pluralism and ideological relativity were characteristic. The Federation's vocation was to serve the movements for justice in the world and especially among the oppressed and deprived. Therefore it should not be imprisoned by the "ivory tower" of the university. Another group was convinced that the primary vocation of the WSCF was among students and in the academic world, which was related to society and the world in numerous ways.

A point most consistently contested by many responders was the implication, which many detected in the circular, that the affirmation of Marxism would obliterate the Federation's Christian identity and lead to a negation of Christian faith. Even several of those who did not subscribe to a Marxist position accepted a Marxist interpretation of Christian faith as an option to be respected.

The survey also showed that the expectations of member movements from the Federation in the midst of their intense ideological search varied a great deal. Most of those who responded had not fixed their position to a definite either-or demand and in fact indicated their willingness to pursue dialogue in the search for common directions. In the light of the survey, in early 1971, member movements showed little interest in a decisive confrontation. It appears, therefore, that the initiatives for a showdown, which surfaced in March-May 1971, came from a group within the Federation leadership.

CHAPTER 10

From Dialogue to Confrontation

In January 1971, by all appearances and despite all the differences, the Federation was set for a promising period. Regionalization was complete. Vacant staff positions had been filled in the regional offices as well as in Geneva. The headquarters — as the Geneva office then was still called — had been established on the fifth and sixth floors of the John R. Mott House on the lakefront of Geneva. Capital for equipping the Federation offices had been raised under the auspices of the Philippe Maury Memorial Fund. Regional leadership training programs were already in full swing in Africa and Asia. Personnel and facilities were provided for in Latin America. The Middle East program, with its unique relationship with the Orthodox churches and the Palestinian liberation movements, was well established. Financial assistance was available for needy member movements, mainly in developing countries. The Political Commission had pursued contacts with other groups interested in radical political concerns and had explored possibilities of serious collaboration with them. Some old Federation programs — work among foreign students, work with secondary schools, and the main publications (the *Student World* and *Federation News*) — had been put on the back burner. Technically, procedures for staff meetings and communication among the staff and with the Executive Committee were in impeccable shape.

There were a few clouds on the horizon, though not particularly threatening. Admittedly, there were financial concerns, but they did not yet cause excessive anxiety. The management of resources was after all now in competent hands. An eye needed to be kept on relationships with churches, which had traditionally been the cornerstone for expansion, as the radicalization of some of the member movements and the increasingly radical image of the Federation was not met with undivided enthusiasm among supporters. Most of us hoped that the radical winds within the Federation could be interpreted as a sign that it was indeed in touch with the young, impatient generation.

So it appeared, at least from the outside.

Unfortunately this rosy picture was far from reality. For those on the inside, each week revealed new cracks foreboding serious division.

10.1. Officers Meeting

The WSCF officers meeting in December 1970[1] epitomized the tensions which plagued the Executive Committee and, to an increasing degree, the staff. Its purpose was threefold: to plan the next Executive Committee meeting, to revise the budget for 1971, and to consider the criteria and preparations for staff appointments, as several positions were to become vacant during the second half of the year. The issue which triggered a divisive debate and further fueled the conflict between ideological camps was the state of the communication program. I had specifically asked for the advice of Shaull and Parmar on how to handle this.[2]

The problems in the communication program, for which Claudius Ceccon of Brazil carried the staff responsibility, had become quite

1. In this quadrennium the officers meetings became more informal in character than before 1968 because the group consisted of only the chairman, the vice chairman, and the general secretary. Other members of staff were invited to participate in an ad hoc fashion. In the WSCF Archives there are no minutes of the December 1970 meeting, although some preparatory documents can be found and there are numerous references to the meeting in the correspondence. The informality was a result of the Executive Committee's decision about the composition of the officers group. The constitutional change in 1968 left to the Executive Committee the decision as to who, in addition to the chairman and the general secretary, should be part of the group. Previously the composition of the officers group had been defined in the constitution.

2. Letter from Lehtonen to Shaull and Parmar, November 27, 1970.

obvious to many member movements and to the Federation staff as a whole. In 1969 a wall poster had been sent to subscribers to the magazine *Federation News* in lieu of the new *WSCF Newsletter,* which was to replace the magazine and was intended to be a frequently appearing house organ. In 1970 only one issue was produced. Moreover, since the last issue of the *Student World* in 1969, nothing had been sent to subscribers, who had been led to believe that two to four Federation Books per year would replace the quarterly. A much advertised innovation, the political newsletter *Question,* of which three issues appeared simultaneously just before the 1970 Executive Committee, and two more before the end of 1970, had already been widely criticized on the grounds that it contained old material already known through newspapers and that it was not helpful either to member movements or to the "new constituency," i.e., radical research and action groups.

The officers had been asked to assess the program. There was a high degree of unanimity among the staff, including its radical wing, that Ceccon was not the person to manage the communication program.[3] It soon became clear, however, that Shaull, a former missionary to Brazil, would support his Brazilian friend Ceccon at all costs and that he was unwilling to consider any personnel rearrangements in order to make the program work. His loyalty to Latin America and Brazil overshadowed all other considerations, even criticisms from outside. As a result, discussions about the communication program turned into another ideological confrontation, and Shaull's position on the competence of Ceccon forced the ideological division into the Geneva office in a way which did not previously exist.

Shaull also took time in the already very short meeting to have a separate consultation with the Latin Americans in the WSCF and with Leopoldo Niilus in the WCC. As a consequence, he was perceived by Asian and African staff members as a staunch defender of the partisan causes advocated by the Latin Americans and as chairman only of the radical revolutionary wing and not of the Federation as a whole. The Asia secretary, Moonkyu Kang, was probably the first to voice such a concern.

---

3. In the office it had become clear that Ceccon was a gifted cartoonist but had no administrative or editorial competence. In November 1970 Leonardo Franco had confidentially volunteered to try to persuade him to move on to another job.

The question of the Federation's constituency was a second issue on which there was a head-on collision between Shaull, on the one hand, and Parmar and myself on the other. Shaull reiterated his view that the traditional member movements of the Federation were dead or dying. For him the paradigms for the constituency of the WSCF were the University Christian Movement of the USA, which had voted itself out of existence, and the Brazilian SCM, which had been extinguished under the repression of military rule in that country. He concluded that the vocation of the WSCF was to accelerate the demise of its inherited organizational constituency and to seek a new identity on the foundation of varied action groups and communes which were united by their resistance to global repression under the old order. These discussions did not lead to any practical conclusions. What they did do, however, was to leave the impression that Shaull was interested in the work of WSCF member movements if and only if they conformed with his paradigm.

The officers had been asked to approve the recommendation for a 15 percent budget cut for 1971, necessitated by a decrease in contributions from churches and mission organizations. Shaull used this fact also to justify abandoning the present WSCF structures and experimenting with nonprofessional staff for the Federation office. Neither the officers nor the majority of the staff responded positively to these ideas.

Debates on these matters took up most of the meeting, so there was no chance to discuss in any depth any of the program and staffing issues to be taken up at the next Executive Committee. Shaull wrote to me in January 1971:

> I regret that my visit to Geneva was so short that it was not possible for us to do more work on a number of items such as the plans for the next Executive Committee, etc. I assume that the staff is well along the way with these plans.[4]

From that meeting on it was evident that neither the officers nor the Executive Committee could be expected to help heal the rift which by then was dividing the whole Federation.

4. Letter from Shaull to Lehtonen, January 26, 1971.

10.2. Two Conferences

Two events at the beginning of 1971 contributed to the hardening of polarities within the Federation. One was the WSCF European Student Conference in Dublin in January 1971. It was the second in a series of three conferences in the quadrennium on "The Struggle for Socialism in Europe," and was attended by some seventy participants from most of the European SCMs.

Reporting on the discussions and their outcome was scant. Faithful to the contextual approach to issues, the conference attempted to interpret the Irish situation in terms of the class struggle. However, none of the findings were included in the official reports. The lack of women delegates to the conference put women's liberation on the agenda of the WSCF Europe region. Following the recent condemnation of six Basque "patriots," the conference also issued a high-pitched statement against the "violent and repressive situation in Franco's Spain."[5]

One of the main objectives of the conference was to draw some conclusions from the consultations held in Agape, Italy, in March 1970, and in Lund, Sweden, in May 1970, on how to relate sociopolitical analysis and theological reflection. Only the preparatory documents shed some light on how these issues were approached at the conference. The main one, written by Laurence Bright of the British SCM, gave some quite clear and provocative signals:

> Any serious attempt to understand and change the human situation must today depend on Marx' work. . . .
>
> The WSCF is now, in general terms, committed to this line. . . .
>
> This implies a rejection of the positivism and empiricism that has so long dominated European thought, which includes Christianity. . . .[6]

In his witty and learned treatment of the enslavement of Christian theology by social and economic systems, he tried to show how the-

---

5. Report on the WSCF in Europe, 1968-72, p. 10.

6. "After Lund, What?" A preparatory paper on politics and theology for the Dublin conference of the WSCF region, by Laurence Bright. WSCF Archives.

ology can and should be developed from participation in the class struggle. His thesis was that the time had come "within the dialectic of history" to allow Christianity and Marxism to correct or corrupt one another. "God is unlikely to wither any faster than the state under socialism." The point of such snappy remarks was probably lost on his audience.

The Dublin conference seemed to draw the whole European program more closely to the work of the Political Commission. Laurence Bright was a key figure in both.[7] It was the first major European event in which the secretary of the Political Commission, Leonardo Franco, participated. The conference strengthened the alignment of European, Latin American, and U.S. groups with the Political Commission and against the constituency and staff members supporting the "traditional," politically pluralistic, regionalized Federation.

It was at the time of the Dublin conference that Opocensky, secretary for Europe, made a U-turn in his loyalties. Until the end of 1970, while coordinating and supporting the program on "the struggle for socialism in Europe," he was known to be an advocate of the work of the Federation as a whole, one who acknowledged the constituency's diversity and the differing theological perspectives within the organization. By the beginning of 1971, he seemed to have changed his mind and began to identify himself fully with the radical left wing of the Federation. He soon emerged as one of the leading figures of this group.[8]

A consultation of research groups held in Andover, Massachusetts, USA, in February 1971 was the second event which consolidated the internal opposition grouped around the Political Commission. The 1968 Assembly had approved a proposal for a Power Structures Research Program.[9] The Political Commission had elaborated plans for

---

7. Laurence Bright was a Roman Catholic priest, a member of the staff of the British SCM. He emerged as one of the chief theologians for the radical Marxist wing of the Federation.

8. The shift is reflected in a change in his role in the staff work in Geneva as evidenced by the minutes of both official and informal Geneva staff meetings in the first half of 1971, in his role at the Europe committee meeting in Rome in late June 1971, and in various memos and letters of that era.

9. Minutes of the Twenty-Fifth Meeting of the General Assembly of the WSCF, Otaniemi, Finland, 1968, p. 59.

its implementation at its meeting in Cinisello, Italy, in November 1969. Staff in Geneva had developed the plans further under the leadership of Leonardo Franco.[10] The approximately fifty participants in the consultation represented some thirty research and action groups in Europe and North America. Participation had been deliberately limited to those personally involved in "radical" research. It was a test case for the concept of the "new constituency" so hotly debated at the Beirut Executive Committee meeting.

The consultation got off to a rocky start. Leonardo Franco reported that participants questioned the Federation's legitimacy to even convene such a gathering. In their minds it represented yet another international bureaucracy which was not involved in radical research or action per se. After such initial maneuvers, the consultation took as its first task a review of the history of the political student movement in the USA and Germany. Second, it tried to clarify how to do class analysis. This led to a confrontation and consequently the question was left open. Third, the group agreed to spell out the need for documentation by the radical research groups represented and to plan for expanded exchange of information and publications activity. Finally it discussed how to find new contacts and organize more homogeneous consultations.

According to Leonardo Franco, the effect of the consultation had been to dramatize the differences among the "radical groups," their goals, methods, and ideological perspectives. In his view, the Europeans, after having gone through an antiauthoritarian anarchist period, were now stressing the need for central direction. The Germans underlined the importance of a clear ideological framework. Cooperation with workers and trade unions was also a joint European emphasis. The Americans, on the other hand, were striving for a participatory collective style of work and tended to reject previous patterns of leadership. They were also more empirical than doctrinaire in their approach. In North America the organizational scene was more fluid than in Europe and "radical" groups generally concentrated on "their own thing" rather than trying to develop an effective "mass organization."

10. The planning stages for the Andover consultation are recorded in detail in the minutes of meetings of Geneva-based staff, e.g., minutes of February 23, 1970.

Leonardo Franco's summary assessment of the value of the consultation was that the personal encounters made there were very worthwhile but that as a study conference it was not successful. The meeting appointed from among its participants a continuation committee "to see what can be done in case the Federation cannot take it up." Nothing was heard of any follow-up work.[11]

There was a marked difference in the openness with which the two events, Dublin and Andover, had been organized and in how their proceedings were reported. The Dublin plans, experiences, and evaluation were never brought to the attention of the staff meetings or the Executive Committee, while the Andover consultation plans and results were presented to the Geneva staff with the same openness as those of any other significant Federation event.[12]

10.3. Opposition Is Organized

From the beginning of 1971, the Political Commission–Communication team in Geneva intensified its radical revolutionary activity. The team wanted to form a new, communitarian style of work which was to be the model for the whole Geneva office in the future. It wanted to respond positively to the criticism voiced in Andover about non-involved bureaucracy. The rationale for the new push was:

> We now know that we are working for involved people. . . . Our aim is not to conscientize people who are not committed to political action. While we are struggling for our existence and autonomy as a team in Geneva, the non-committed people are criticizing us . . . because our production is not relevant to their situation. . . .
>
> In the last six months a new style of work has been developed in which very rigid job descriptions have been broken down and responsibilities are now overlapping. This has challenged all of our hierarchical values and assumptions of personal relationships.

11. Minutes of a meeting of the Geneva-based staff and Moonkyu Kang and Ninan Koshy, February 23, 1971, pp. 5-6.

12. Plans for the Andover meeting were discussed in staff meetings, December 17, 1969, and February 23, 1970.

. . . [W]e see a contradiction between the ideological-theological assumptions of the Federation and its praxis. The intention to work for humanization of society as dictated by our act of faith implies a radical change within our own structure which presently embodies our society's contradictions.[13]

The team's efforts reflected fashionable current countercultures, characterized by the ridiculing of orderly administrative accounting procedures and a marked preference for the sloppy look of publications, and other such antiestablishment images. The increasingly militant posture of the team completed the division of the Geneva office into two antagonistic groups.

Colleagues within the supporting agencies in the USA reported to me that Shaull had made a visit to Latin America in January 1971 and that he had invited the leading Latin America staff member, Edir Cardoso, to the USA in February. Neither of them informed the Geneva office about these visits. News of them added to the atmosphere of secrecy and conspiracy.

Reports and correspondence about the trends in the Federation during this period indicate that after the two conferences, in Dublin and Andover, Leonardo Franco and Milan Opocensky assumed leadership of the internal opposition group which had formed around the Political Commission and Communication offices, and which now received reinforcement from the Europe office and from the presumed support of Shaull.

Nevertheless, in February and March 1971 preparations for the Executive Committee meeting, scheduled for July 2-10 in Japan, proceeded, at least on the surface, in an orderly fashion without any explicit challenges to the methods of joint staff work. On my suggestion, Leonardo Franco prepared the program and agenda. Peter Musgrove and Leonard Clough were in charge of the budgetary work. I was responsible for the recruitment of staff for the positions to become vacant during the latter part of the year. Together, the staff considered all the plans before they were sent to members of the Executive Committee.

13. The position of the team was summed up in a document entitled "Team's Thoughts," signed by six members of the Geneva staff sometime in April 1971. WSCF Archives.

The next round of events occurred during my absence from Geneva. After the preparatory work for the Executive Committee meeting had been completed, I left on March 31 for a six-week tour of regional advisory committee meetings and member movements. Immediately after my departure, colleagues in Geneva who represented the radical wing decided to organize a series of weekly "informal" but selective staff meetings "devoted to preparation for the forthcoming Executive Committee meeting."[14] Most of the meetings were held not in the office but at the home of Leonard Clough. Those executive and administrative staff who were assumed to be in favor of a radical change in the style of the Geneva office were invited, and those too close to me were left out.[15]

The select group prepared a series of working papers which, to a large extent, were in disagreement with the already completed plans for the Executive Committee. Topics included the purpose of the WSCF, the WSCF's constituency, the role of staff in the Federation, two alternatives for planning the next Assembly, and the pattern of decision making in the Federation. Reports on these discussions were marked for circulation to all executive staff. Clough circulated his "position papers" on constituency and on the preparation of the Assembly to Shaull and Parmar as well.[16] These papers did not reach me officially until my return to Geneva on May 8. However, Peter

14. Leonard Clough described in general, even somewhat apologetic terms the purpose of the select staff meetings "in preparation of the Executive Committee" in a personal letter of April 9 to me in Hong Kong.

15. The idea for the meetings of the "informal staff group" was apparently developed by Franco and Opocensky. The members who attended were Ceccon, Clough, Franco, Gilardi, Musgrove, and Opocensky. Musgrove later informed me that he had accepted the invitation, not out of revolutionary persuasion, but in order to have firsthand information about the plans.

16. The papers from the "informal staff group" included papers on "the constituency and purpose of the WSCF" of April 5, and "two alternatives for planning the 1972 General Assembly" of April 13, 1971, by Leonard Clough; a summary of the discussions of the group on April 6, 1971, by Leonard Clough; a paper on "decision-making in the Federation" of April 21, 1971, by Peter Musgrove; a summary of discussions of the group on April 22 and 29, 1971, by Peter Musgrove; a paper entitled "Team's Thoughts," signed by members of the "Pol/Com/Doc Team" (without date), and a dissenting opinion in the form of a memorandum to "members of the Communications Team" from Nancy Bell. WSCF Archives.

Musgrove decided to keep me thoroughly informed during my travels so that I was able to send a first response from Hong Kong on April 17 and to discuss the challenge presented by this "informal group" with the Asian colleagues and with several members of the Federation's supporting community in the USA.

The ideas proposed in the preparatory papers of the group were a rather inhomogeneous collection. The suggestions made by Clough included a quick move by the Federation to become "an international community of communities" which would no longer be limited or even be primarily constituted by national Student Christian Movements. These communities were to be ad hoc groups basically in line with the concept of the "new constituency," that is, radical action groups and communes. He also presented an alternative approach to the preparation of the Assembly, one for which he himself expressed his "strong personal preference" and which would have placed its planning in the hands of a newly selected chairman of the planning group, replaced the representatives of the regions by an ad hoc group representing new trends, and required the recruitment of a new administrative secretary. In this way, the general secretary would be left entirely out of the preparatory process.

The proposals of the group were not followed up. The most visible result was a vocal protest by the Asian leaders against the whole procedure. My messages from Hong Kong may have contributed to the decline in the momentum of the group; I informed the Geneva staff and also Shaull and Parmar that I was planning to participate in the preparation of the Assembly, that I saw no point in including the proposals of the "informal group" in the agenda of the Executive Committee, and that no mailings were to go out to its members before my return.[17]

I was alerted by Peter Musgrove that the "informal group" wanted to meet with me as soon as I was back in Geneva. He also arranged to brief me discreetly at his home on Sunday afternoon, May 9, as to

17. The letters from Peter Musgrove of April 2, 3, 21, 22, and May 3, in which he reported on the ferment in the Geneva office and alerted me on discussions of the "informal staff group," reached me in Nairobi, Hong Kong, and Tokyo. I sent my reactions back from India, April 10 and 11, and from Hong Kong, April 17. WSCF Archives.

his impressions of the group, prior to my encounter with the "revolutionary council" on Tuesday morning, May 11.

Upon my return I received a letter from Milan Opocensky, who wrote:

> Judging from your memoranda I have a feeling that you were under the impression that we were plotting behind your back. . . . I do not wish to go into detail because I am looking forward to participating in a discussion which we may have on Tuesday. . . . My reading of the situation is that there is a sort of cultural and social mini-revolution here and it is up to you to decide whether you wish to be part of it or whether you will fight back from a position of power.[18]

The "informal group" was waiting for me on the morning of May 11 in Leonard Clough's apartment. In hindsight, it is clear that the purpose of the meeting was to pressure me to resign, or, failing that, to give in to the demands of the "team." These demands entailed supporting their plans for staffing and ensuring the continuation of the work of the Political Commission and Communication after Franco's and Ceccon's departure in September-October 1971. As I gave no signs of joining the "cultural revolution," the meeting began to run out of steam, and then, unfortunately, turned into a session of personal accusations about my leadership, to which I replied by challenging the leader of the offensive. The meeting resulted in further entrenchment with no signs of reconciliation.

In the weeks following my return, it became evident that the opposition group in Geneva planned to force the Executive Committee to approve its alternative for running the Geneva office until the next General Assembly. They wanted to make Opocensky responsible for the preparation of the Assembly, thus giving him less time for his responsibilities as the secretary for Europe. They also wanted one full-time successor to the two departing members of the Political Commission–Communication team. The person would be based outside Geneva, thus in their view ensuring the independence of the Political Commission in relation to the headquarters. The

18. Letter from Opocensky to Lehtonen, May 7, 1971.

general secretary's role would be confined mainly to fund-raising. These plans were developed in great secrecy, but their profile became known to me and my closest colleagues when fragments leaked into our hands.[19] After these events communication between the general secretary's group and the revolutionary "team" in the Geneva office was at a low point.[20]

In spite of these sharp tensions, the Geneva staff were able in those weeks to do two things together. First, they continued to discuss proposals for cuts in the central budget and alternatives for cuts in personnel. However, they could not agree on a plan to which all would be committed. Second, they were able to receive a high-level delegation from the Student Council of the USSR and to organize a joint consultation with them. This took place in the latter part of May and was organized by Milan Opocensky, Leo Gilardi, and myself. We succeeded together in engaging our three Soviet guests in a lively dialogue and also managed to keep the uninvited representative of the Soviet mission in Geneva out of most of our program despite the fact that he appeared without any advance notice, assuming that he could participate in everything with our invited guests. Tinged with humor, the cooperation indispensable for the successful handling of such a

19. Half of a key document of June 2, 1971, circulated by Leonardo Franco confidentially to the members of the Political Commission, came to my attention only after the Executive Committee Meeting. It was found among the papers in Ceccon's office after he left the staff. The paper only confirmed the information which was available in the first weeks of June through a variety of channels, including fragments of documents found in wastepaper baskets. WSCF Archives.

20. The general secretary's group consisted of: Audrey Abrecht, administrative assistant to the general secretary; Christine Hubbuck, secretary of the general secretary (she later deserted to the revolutionary group and was subsequently fired); Peter Musgrove, priorities secretary, who was responsible for the financial support of regional programs and assistance to national movements; Christine Griesbeck, accountant; Nancy Bell, editor of WSCF publications (she decided to resign in mid-1971); and Madeleine Strub, translator.

The revolutionary group consisted of Political Commission, Communication, and Europe Secretariat staff: Leonardo Franco, secretary for the Political Commission; Claudius Ceccon, secretary for communications; Dido Wilcox, secretary to the "team"; Leo Gilardi, documentalist; Anne Crane and Jean Collier, volunteers of the "team"; Milan Opocensky, secretary for Europe; Judith Ironside, secretary to the Europe office; and Leonard Clough, resources secretary (he co-opted to the team but chose to leave the WSCF in mid-1971).

sensitive visit proved a welcome interlude in these otherwise tense weeks.

The last staff meeting before the Executive Committee in mid-June gave us one more opportunity to air our internal differences. We had not yet reached a common mind about the budget cuts to be submitted within ten days to the Executive Committee. I thought it was a time to open up discussion about the larger issues which divided the two groups in the office. As an introduction I presented a statement, some of the main points of which were (1) budget and personnel matters could not, in the Federation context, be separated from the basic convictions about the Christian faith, ideological assumptions, and political engagement; (2) an open and public debate was essential for the integrity of the Federation; and (3) it was important for us to understand one another even if we continued to disagree on fundamentals. Referring to the "mini-cultural revolution," the statement underlined the necessity of balance between creativity and technical competence; pointed to the impossibility of organizing the WSCF headquarters on the basis of one person, one vote, because of different accountabilities of executive and support staff, unless the constitution were changed; and finally recommended a thorough study of what would be needed to bring about a deeper sense of justice and participation among the WSCF personnel. I suggested that the whole office take time out for a "soul-session" of mutual criticism and self-criticism as an antidote to the poisoned atmosphere and as a way out of the deadlock in communication.

It may have been a mistake to try to open up the soul-searching with polemical comments on the state of affairs in the office:

> In our discussions there are far too large areas about which we are silent when we really ought to speak out . . . phoney approaches tend to flourish . . . the glorification of the "communication team" approach (has become) unconvincing . . . (as) never before have there been so many paid people involved in the (WSCF) communications effort and so much money invested (in it), and yet the outreach, the amount of original material (published), and the income from publications have never been so low. — Or take the example of "the creative edge" . . . the team has not been able to benefit from the diversity of gifts . . . (or) the way in which the

team has treated those who did not immediately fit into its pattern
. . . a shameful chapter. . . . So I have still to be convinced about
the liberating values of this experience.

A lively discussion ensued. Participants wanted to study my statement overnight. In retrospect, it was obvious that an open discussion
was welcomed by most staff. Only it came too late.

The way the minutes of the meeting were taken was a sobering
signal. Nothing about the content of the introductory statement, nor
about the searching discussion following it, was placed on record,
contrary to the current staff meeting practice of recording all the main
points of discussions. The statement was appended to the minutes,
but the only reference to it in the minutes proper was that I had made
a proposal for the Geneva staff and budget. The secretary, who at this
meeting was Leonard Clough, one of the members of the "team,"
recorded in the minutes in detail his counterproposal which presupposed the acceptance of the one person–one vote decision-making
principle, mentioning the staff positions and persons he wanted re-
tained, despite the fact that the counterproposal had not been considered at the meeting itself.[21] The minutes were not available for
checking before my departure for Japan via the Europe Committee
meeting in Rome. They were formulated so that they could be quoted
at the Executive Committee without informing members about the
content of my proposal and without reference to the content of the
latest staff discussion.

During the months after the awkward officers meeting in December 1970, I was determined to keep open communication between the
opposition and the rest of the headquarters staff and to move the
debate away from infighting to the concerns of member movements
for whom the conflicts in Geneva were of little interest. Furthermore,
I was anxious that the Geneva office not be isolated from SCMs and
from the regional work of the Federation. This is why I myself attended four regional advisory committee meetings held in Cairo,
Nairobi, Hong Kong, and Rome in the months of April-June 1971
and also visited member movements in Egypt, Indonesia, the Philip-

21. "Summary of Discussion and Decisions at WSCF Staff Meetings 15th and
17th June, 1971," by Leonard Clough.

pines, Japan, and Canada on the way. This is also why I wrote the circular letter of February 22 to member movements inviting their responses. I also urged the chairman of the Federation, Richard Shaull, to accept the invitation by Africa staff to participate in the advisory committee meeting of the Africa region in Nairobi in April in order to have a firsthand impression of the concerns of the African SCMs. His coming was a welcome opportunity for the two of us to discuss at length the present state of the Federation. For a moment the healing of the rift which had become ever deeper since the end of 1970 seemed possible.

My colleague Peter Musgrove attended the meeting of the Latin America committee held in Chile in early June and visited SCMs in Mexico, Nicaragua, Puerto Rico, Peru, and Argentina on the way. These visits provided invaluable insights into the situation of member movements in this vast and turbulent region.[22]

On my way back from my Africa-Asia tour in the beginning of May, I had a further opportunity to see Shaull for some hours in New York. It turned out to be a significant meeting in which both of us suddenly became aware of much common ground between us concerning the nature and task of the Church and the Federation. We discussed points of friction between ourselves and between the different parties to the conflicts within the WSCF, and their causes. We took note of our different emphases and main disagreements but concluded that both of us were prepared to do our utmost to avoid further division of the Federation and that this could be possible without denying our basic convictions. Shaull remarked that the two of us were trapped by "too many plotting persons" around us. His concern was that we should expand the kind of discussion which suddenly had opened up between us, to influence the work of the Executive Committee.

In the next six weeks we continued this discussion by correspondence. The letters show vividly that both of us believed in the possibility of a breakthrough at the forthcoming Federation Executive Committee meeting. In the ensuing correspondence we not only touched on the basic issues of faith and trust within the Christian community and between the two of us, but we also discussed in some

22. Travel report of May 29. WSCF Archives.

depth the ground rules necessary for overcoming the polarization in the Federation, our respective positions on such questions as region-alization and the role of the Geneva office, our expectations from the next General Assembly, and future leadership of the WSCF. At this point Shaull's ideas differed drastically from the proposals of the "informal staff group" in Geneva.[23]

In preparation for the Executive Committee in Japan I prepared a report with which I hoped to spark off a discussion about the vocation of the Federation among students, university teachers, churches, and society. I felt this to be all the more important now, as officers and staff as a group were paralyzed by ideological and political division. I was at that time also influenced by discussions with Shaull and by the most recent developments among Geneva colleagues in response to a straightforward dealing with controversial issues, and by the apparent possibilities for rebuilding trust and communication. As we headed for Japan, it was nevertheless clear to all of us in Geneva that the Federation was facing perhaps the deepest internal division in its whole history.

10.4. Showdown at Tozanzo

Tozanzo, the attractive international conference site of the Japanese YMCA at Gotemba, was the scene of the July 2-10, 1971, Executive Committee meeting. It was attended by twenty-one voting members,

23. The tone of the meeting between Shaull and myself in New York in the beginning of May 1971 is reflected in the following letters: Lehtonen to Shaull, May 11; Shaull to Lehtonen (two letters), May 20; Shaull to Lehtonen, May 28; Lehtonen to Shaull, May 28 and again May 29; Shaull to Lehtonen, June 4; Lehtonen to Shaull, May 25. Shaull wrote on May 28, referring to conversations in Nairobi and New York:

> I continue to rejoice in these developments, to accept them as gifts, and to build on them for the sake of the Federation — and especially for the sake of the people for whom the Federation is and can be important. These developments have confirmed two things which I have been sure of for a long time: 1) whatever our differences, we are bound together by a strong common loyalty to the Christian cause and its importance, especially in a time of crisis, and to the Federation; and 2) that each of us has such strength of self-identity, together with commitments to goals beyond himself, that we need not get completely bogged down with our problems or in the defence of ourselves or our positions.

including five proxies for elected members. Most of the representatives of member movements who were entitled to participate without a vote came from the Asia-Australia region. The Japanese setting was amply reflected in the worship and social occasions of the meeting.

The minutes reflect an unusual poverty of discussion following the presentation of reports and program proposals. There was no record of response to the extensive regional reports because the plenary did not go much beyond questions of clarification. Consequently any discussions of substance were confined to the "corridors." Exceptions were the reports on the Communication program and the Political Commission. Their presentations led to a lively exchange, most of which, however, took place only after the Executive Committee had taken decisive votes on the issues at the heart of the conflict.

My report was an attempt to help the whole gathering face the critical issues of the Federation's life and of the reason for its very existence. I said:

> Transition and flexibility have been characteristic of the Federation throughout its whole history. Time after time it has refused to opt for stability as against the risky venture of responding to Jesus Christ in the midst of ambiguities, struggles, and uncertainties of students in rapidly changing societies. Three years ago (1968) strong impulses carried the Federation further in this calling. One came from the wider student movement which at that time had reached one of the peaks of its vitality, and which immersed parts of the Federation in radical political consciousness. Another came from the regions which had enough of Western domination, they demanded decentralization and the freeing of the Federation from Western ways of thinking, believing and doubting, as well as of planning and administering. This is what regionalization is all about. It was to be a step towards a more truly *world* community of Christians whose base is in universities and schools. Because of the two fresh factors, hopes were high in 1968. Many dreams were ventured. A new Federation was to emerge. A new style of work was to be adopted.[24]

24. Report of the General Secretary to the Executive Committee Meeting, Tozanzo, Japan, July 2-10, 1971 (mimeographed), p. 1. WSCF Archives.

The high hopes after Otaniemi had been replaced, my report continued, by a sense of profound crisis. The question to be faced by the Federation was whether or not it had arrived at a turning point. The political dimension of the work of the WSCF needed clarification. What was the meaning of politics of liberation in our time? What should be the role of the Federation with regard to politics? Was our speaking of justice, liberation, peace, education, bread, and human dignity mere loose talk? In-depth analyses and critical study of the complex and controversial issues of international politics and economy had been set aside and a narrow ideological factionalism and repetitive sloganeering had taken their place. In parallel to the political confusion the organizational frame of the WSCF was questioned, but with a notable absence of clear goals for its activity. I continued:

> [W]e cannot deal adequately with our political and institutional crises without facing head on questions of faith, identity and com-mitment. Yet in most of our world gatherings we seem . . . to have evaded this issue. Now . . . we can no longer afford to do so. . . .
> My view is this: Either faith in Jesus Christ is the center and source of our common work, or we have nothing in common. Either we wrestle with our faith and doubts in every concern in which we are involved, or let us stop fooling ourselves that we have any *raison d'etre* as a Federation. Either we agree to be faced with the claims of Jesus Christ and to be open to each other on that basis, or we stop calling our Federation Christian. . . . we have to begin on this issue from where we are personally. . . . I am also con-vinced that unless we begin consciously . . . to make our wrestling with the faith a central and continuing dimension of the whole Federation, we do not have much future together.[25]

I then proceeded to discuss the points of controversy in the Fed-eration. They included

- Christian identity in a political and ideological context;
- regional identities and the world nature of the WSCF;

25. Report of the General Secretary, pp. 2-3.

226

- the identity of the Federation with regard to traditional and "new" constituencies;
- staff leadership and the role of the Geneva office.

Finally, I presented the tasks I envisaged to be necessary in preparation for the next General Assembly. Among them I emphasized the need for clarification of the aims of the Federation, as expressed in the constitution, and the hope of building up a more intensive cooperation between the WSCF, the Roman Catholic groups, and the World Fellowship of Orthodox Youth Organizations (SYNDESMOS). I also proposed that alternatives to Geneva as the site of the central office be studied, in view of the criticism that the Federation's style of work was too influenced by the affluence of central Europe.

The atmosphere of the meeting was apparently too loaded by hidden agendas to allow for a solid debate on my report. Furthermore, the chairman, Richard Shaull, did not encourage plenary discussion on it, nor did he allow time for it. He had arrived late for the meeting and had missed the regional reports. He had no opportunity to read or discuss with me my report before it was delivered. The communication which had been established between us in the previous three months evaporated abruptly. He also refrained at this meeting from giving a chairman's address. Under these extraordinary circumstances, the main significance of my report was that it placed on record many of the concerns of those who were opposed to a neo-Marxist domination of the Federation.

The first half of the meeting proved puzzling. The calm with which the most substantive regional reports were received was interpreted by the radical activist wing as a clear sign that the talk about polarization and crisis had been exaggerated. In retrospect, the tactics were obvious. The activist wing wanted to convince everybody that all was well with the Federation, now that it was on its new, politically "conscientized" path. We agreed on regional diversity. All of us rejected the "status quo" of the past. The critics of my report implied that only the Geneva office had lost touch with reality as evidenced by the fact that its spokesperson still wanted to speak in terms of "a crisis of the Federation" — a crisis which did not exist.

It was conspicuous that most of the substantive program proposals failed to lead to any decisive action by the Executive Committee. A plan for an ambitious Roman Catholic–WSCF project to mobilize Christian intellectuals was accepted with reservations which ultimately torpedoed further work on it.[26] The response to the report on the New Experiments Project Fund was surprising. After all, the fund was to be the foundation for implementing the activities of the "new constituency" of the politically oriented action and research groups. The Executive Committee simply "made no comments or recommendations."[27] The follow-up of the WSCF China Study Project had a similar fate. "No action was taken on the report, but the Executive Committee agreed that every effort should be made to have a representative of the People's Republic of China at the General Assembly."[28] The issue of Chinese participation in the Assembly arose out of the enthusiasm within European and North American radical circles for the Cultural Revolution in China. For them establishing contacts with the Chinese progressives, whom they admired as vanguards of the new humanity, was more important than the pursuit of relations with the Student Council of the USSR, which, in their view, had betrayed the revolution.

The Executive Committee did debate at length the future of the Universal Day of Prayer for Students, which had been celebrated in many churches annually by member movements since 1898. Finding a date equally suitable for all movements had been a perennial problem. In the Northern Hemisphere the day was celebrated mostly on the third Sunday of February, and in the Southern Hemisphere mostly in June. Nevertheless, even without total agreement about a common date, its celebration had given visibility to Christian witness among students and to the pursuit of the visible unity of the church. At Tozanzo the Executive Committee once again opened the question about the date and meaning of the day. The conclusion was that each national movement and each region should arrange for a national day of prayer independently according to its own circumstances, and that the February and June dates should be ignored. The minutes report also a recommendation that "in addition May 1 be celebrated as a

26. Minutes of the WSCF Executive Committee Meeting, Tozanzo, Japan, July 2-10, 1971, p. 9.

27. Tozanzo Minutes, p. 10.

28. Tozanzo Minutes, p. 10.

Universal Day of Prayer for Students," but the committee took no action on it. The debate was another illustration of the ubiquitous impact of the ideological conflict in devaluing the ecumenical symbols of unity in the Federation.

After the reports were over the meeting began to liven up. The discussion of the financial situation and the inevitability of severe budget cuts brought to the surface the different agendas of the opposed groups. The conflict which had been brewing for a long time came to a climax in a closed session which Mario Yutzis of Argentina had demanded at the end of the general discussion of financial matters. The closed session began at 10 P.M. and ended about 3 A.M. It received encouragement from a group of nonvoting participants who were singing the "Internationale" outside the conference room. The meeting began with questions about salary policies and employment practices and moved on to question the role of the Geneva office. Finally, a formal motion was made along lines prepared by the radical left opposition group. It suggested a drastic budget cut; the firing of the priorities secretary, Peter Musgrove; making Milan Opocensky responsible for the preparation of the Assembly; appointing Aaron Ramos of Puerto Rico as the communication secretary; a drastic reduction in the general secretariat; and the limiting of my functions to the technical oversight of the finances and fund-raising. The weakness of the proposal was that it put into one basket budgetary decisions and personnel decisions without any detailed preparatory work. When a vote was taken, after a heated debate, the proposal lost by a narrow margin. A representative of the majority — Anwar Barkat of Pakistan — made an alternative motion according to which the Geneva budget was to be cut by 50 percent, no vacancies were to be filled, and the support staff was to be reduced. This motion largely followed my recommendation, although the cut now proposed was still deeper. It meant that the Geneva office would have to operate with two or possibly three executive staff and that virtually no funds would be available for the Political Commission and its office needs. Only $1,000 was included in the budget for a meeting of the Commission between Tozanzo and the next Assembly. A full meeting would normally cost some $4,000 to $5,000. The door was left open for the co-opting of a staff member which some supporting church or agency would make available. The Barkat motion was passed.

229

A battle ensued over the appointment of a communication secretary. In my preparatory work I had concentrated on finding a competent person with international experience and sensitivity to the aspirations and needs of Student Christian Movements and to the diversity of ideological positions. These screened candidates had to be dropped, however, because their image would have made them too vulnerable in such a sharply polarized situation, even if their personal suitability and professional competence had stood the tests. The Executive Committee decided however to go ahead and act on nominations from the floor. After a confused debate, the committee agreed on a list of three candidates in an order of preference and left the matter to the general secretary for final processing, his decision to be ratified by the Planning Committee of the WSCF Assembly at its meeting in January 1972. The first on the list of the candidates was one of the three Africa regional staff members, Aaron Tolen of Cameroon; the second was Young Bok Kim, a Korean doctoral student of Shaull at Princeton; and the third Aaron Ramos of Puerto Rico, one of the most vocal spokespersons of the radical left group among members of the Executive Committee. This decision was a defeat for the radical opposition group, which had fought for Ramos.

Plans for the General Assembly touched a raw nerve because these plans were intimately related to the power struggle within the organization. The Executive Committee decided to delegate its own authority for the next eighteen months to a Planning Committee which consisted of one representative of each of the six regions and the chairman and the general secretary.[29] This decision, too, marked a clear rejection of the proposal by the radical opposition group.

The defeat of the radical left group's plans for the Geneva office and the Assembly was obviously a serious blow to it. With these decisions, the give-and-take across the dividing lines was by and large finished. The meeting ended on a sordid note. During the closing ceremony someone from the radical left group called for yet another closed session. Its purpose proved to be to launch one final, bitter attack against the majority and especially against me as the general secretary. Andrew Tsehlana of South Africa, who represented the British SCM, accused me of racism and of a typical white man's tactics

29. Tozanzo Minutes, p. 6.

230

to reject a militant (Ramos) and approve an African (Tolen) "because the latter creates less trouble." "In two years' time the African man is ready to give hell to you." After a few other statements Aaron Ramos asked for the floor and requested that his statement be recorded verbatim in the minutes. His message was simply that the winners of the vote represented the dying cause of Western domination and that the future belonged to the militants.[30] This statement marked the end of the Executive Committee meeting. Without any other words participants started moving out of the room quietly as in a funeral procession. When everyone had left, Richard Shaull's parting words to me were that only now did he realize how far apart the two of us were and how disappointed he had been in my report to the Executive Committee.

30. Tozanzo Minutes, p. 19.

CHAPTER 11

The WSCF and the
University Christian Movement
of South Africa, 1967-71

11.1. The Significance of South Africa in the WSCF

Despite its short life span, the experience of the University Christian
Movement (UCM) of South Africa has a distinct place in the history
of the WSCF and the ecumenical movement. Its upswing among the
students of South Africa at a time when apartheid was hardening its
grip was a surprise to many. Its birth and growth under the threat of
repressive legislation and the ever-present security police were little
short of a miracle. Its rise dramatized the aspirations and hopes attached to a radical ecumenical renewal of the sixties.

At the same time the UCM's emerging internal difficulties and its
early collapse revealed not only the ruthlessness of the apartheid regime
but also the untenable ideological presuppositions characteristic of
much of the revolutionary Christian left of those years. In the South
African UCM the ideas of radical ecumenism and intellectual protest
advanced by progressive white Christians failed to meet the aspirations
and convictions of the young black Christians who were rising against
apartheid from the other side of the racial barrier. Consequently, the
movement became deeply divided, and the trust between the radicalizing UCM and the churches which had been sponsoring it was broken.
The sequence of events is a most dramatic display of the influence and

results of the forces which polarized the WSCF. Moreover, the account of the rise and fall of the UCM in South Africa provides an illustration of the problems accompanying the radical ecumenism which draws its orientation first and foremost from activist communities and groups.

Nevertheless, the UCM during its years of existence was a witness to the source of life which could not be exterminated by either the police or the military methods with which apartheid was being imposed. The new movement brought inspiration, at least for a moment, to many church leaders who were concerned for the oneness of the church and the integrity of its witness in a divided society. The premature demise of the organization could not wipe out the impact of its basic witness, which continued in many churches and among groups of young Christians and found expressions in the programs of the South African Council of Churches.

11.2. The Rise of a New Movement

The UCM of South Africa was founded in 1967 to fill the vacuum of ecumenical, interracial Christian ministry in universities and colleges. It succeeded the Student Christian Association (SCA) of South Africa, which had been founded in 1896 but which dismantled its national structure in 1965. The SCA of South Africa had been a member of the WSCF from its beginning to its withdrawal in 1964. The newly founded UCM applied for membership to both the WSCF and the Roman Catholic university organization, Pax Romana, in 1968.

The SCA had had an impressive history as an organization within the old SCM tradition. At its peak it was one of the larger member movements of the Federation, with more than three hundred branches in universities, colleges, and secondary schools, and with a total membership exceeding sixty thousand. From its earliest days it struggled with issues of race and, at times, witnessed boldly to the unity of the Christian community across racial boundaries. The movement played a significant role in the lives of many who became leading opponents of apartheid, including Jan Hendrik Hofmeyr and Alan Paton.[1]

1. The SCA was founded in 1896 in connection with John R. Mott's visit. The Anglo-Boer War and the long-lasting conflict between Afrikaners and English influ-

When the National Party came to power in 1948 and the policy of apartheid was introduced, the SCA resisted formal division along racial lines, although its work, to a large extent, had reflected the prevalent cultural patterns of racial separation. When apartheid was imposed on universities, the SCA gave in and reorganized itself in 1951 in four separate sections: English, Afrikaans, Bantu, and Colored. This decision resulted in permanent internal tensions within the SCA's constituency and caused it to become increasingly isolated internationally.[2]

From the early fifties the movement's position regarding apartheid dominated discussions between the leaders of the Federation and the SCA. The WSCF 1964 General Committee meeting in Argentina voted to send a message to the SCA criticizing it for not dissociating itself from the policy of apartheid, emphasizing the threat which apartheid presented to world peace. As a result the SCA decided to terminate its membership in the Federation.[3]

---

enced the SCA profoundly. Relationships between these groups and the issue of race had always colored the life of the movement. At some of its conferences the SCA demonstrated commitment to racial justice and its disapproval of segregation, even though its everyday practice reflected the prevalent culture of racial separation. For example, in 1930 the African section had invited whites to join in their conference at Fort Hare, which at that time was the only university-level college for Africans. Although laws did not require segregation, the hosts had arranged for separate eating and sleeping facilities. The whites present, some 80 out of a total of 275, voted in favor of common meals. This event proved decisive in bringing the racial issues onto the center stage of the movement for years and causing controversy in churches, especially those of the whites. In his autobiography, *Towards the Mountain* (New York: Penguin Books, 1980), Alan Paton repeatedly refers to the ecumenical significance of the SCA in the twenties and thirties and to its meaning for persons such as Jan H. Hofmeyr. A concise documented summary of the history of the SCA can be found in a document entitled *Student Movements in South Africa,* a study of three student movements illustrating student problems and unrest and the government's response. United Nations, Unit on Apartheid Papers, no. 16/70, May 1970.

2. The SCA tried to evade public discussions of apartheid. Its official position was to accept that its members held different views but that the SCA was not to be a forum for political debate. Nevertheless, some branches left the SCA because they found it too conservative, and some others because they found it too liberal. *Student Movements in South Africa,* pp. 6-7.

3. The disaffiliation was recorded at the WSCF Executive Committee meeting in Cambridge, Massachusetts, 1965. Some SCA sections intended to continue as

The initiative to form a new racially integrated ecumenical student organization came from university and college chaplains of the Anglican, Congregational, Methodist, Presbyterian, and Roman Catholic churches which became its official sponsors. The founding meeting was held in Grahamstown in July 1967. The strong participation of black students overwhelmed the organizers. Dr. Basil Moore, a minister of the Methodist Church, was elected the first president of the UCM.

The goal was to create an ecumenical structure which would bring together Christians — students, faculty, administrators, and chaplaincies — who were committed to an open, racially integrated Christian community and to a nonracial society. Participants in the Grahamstown meeting came from virtually all English and nonwhite universities and colleges of South Africa, and also from Lesotho, Botswana, and Swaziland.

The enthusiasm with which the founding of the UCM was received among black and white students alike showed the need for a university- and college-based Christian movement which would be ecumenical, would bear united witness to the gospel of Christ in the divided society of South Africa, and would mobilize Christian students and churches to oppose apartheid. The new organization's objectives and the methods which were to be used to meet them were right from the outset incompatible with the policies of apartheid.

The founders and leaders of the UCM had no illusions about what would be the government's response to the new movement. The experiences of the National Union of South African Students (NUSAS) left no room for doubt. From the mid-fifties, NUSAS had consistently opposed apartheid. After legislation was passed which sealed the segregation of the previously "open" universities and allowed the government to interfere in their internal affairs, confrontation between NUSAS and the government had hardened. Local student unions of leading English universities openly defied the new laws. Mass antigovernment demonstrations were held at the University of the

---

independent organizations and even considered a possible merger between the English, Bantu, and Colored sections. It soon became apparent, however, that its time as a national organization was over. Some branches continued on local campuses while others joined denominational ministries. *Student Movements in South Africa,* p. 7.

Witwatersrand, in Johannesburg, and at the University of Cape Town to demand academic freedom and free access to teaching and social facilities for all races. As a consequence, most NUSAS presidents were either banned, imprisoned, or expelled from the country in those years. A vast number of students had lost their bursaries, and many professors and university administrators who had supported the stands taken by NUSAS were dismissed. All of them had been followed and harassed by the Security Branch. By the time the UCM was founded, NUSAS had been banned from all nonwhite institutions.[4]

In its first year the main work of the UCM was carried out by the president, the traveling secretary, and five part-time regional directors. Local training courses called "formation schools," regional seminars, and visits to local campuses were the main forms of activity. The magazine *One for the Road* and a newsletter were launched. It was clear from the responses and initiatives of students that the UCM was not to be led and controlled by the institutional leaders of churches but by a movement of committed Christian students of all races whose impatience with the apartheid government and the silence of churches was a revelation to many pastors and bishops. The South African security police followed the new organization closely, although, to begin with, the leaders of the movement tried to avoid provocation. In all their publicity the leaders stressed the "totally open character" of the UCM and its role of service to the university community.

11.3. Stutterheim "Event '68"

One year after its founding the UCM assembled for its second conference and council meeting, "Event '68," in Stutterheim, July 10 to 15, 1968. Among the 167 participants were delegates of twenty-seven local branches and five sponsoring churches, observers from other South African organizations, and a few international visitors. The

---

4. NUSAS received much international attention and support for its opposition to apartheid, and obviously embarrassed the government. One of the peak events was Robert Kennedy's visit to South Africa in 1966, during which he addressed a large gathering of students. However, international pressures did not prevent the government from opting for a hard line.

event was a testimony to the vigor and rapid growth of the UCM. It also signaled troubles ahead: pressure from government officials and mounting tension between students and church leaders.

In his president's report to the council,[5] Basil Moore interpreted the trends and problems of the movement. He pointed to the interest and excitement which the UCM had aroused both within South Africa and internationally, and stressed the importance of international recognition and support at a time when South Africa was drifting into increasing isolation. He referred to the encouragement received from "ecumenically minded South Africans" who saw the rise of the movement as a sign of hope and renewal. The UCM was a significant addition to the coalition of such organizations as the Christian Institute, the Institute on Race Relations, the Inter-Denominational African Ministers Association of South Africa, and the National Union of South African Students. He then discussed the phenomenon of what he called the "authority complex of South Africans," and applied his comments to churches and their leaders:

> The churches in Southern Africa were built into our structure not to invite an authoritative thumb into our midst, but to keep the lines of communication and dialogue between students and churches open. This means that I see UCM basically as a Movement of students, students who are prepared to be free, and in that freedom to discover what commitment to Christ means in this situation; to search for the truth no matter what anybody else claims to be the truth; to accept the responsibility to confront every falsehood with the truth no matter whether that falsehood be in the church, state or society.

He included the UCM among those menaced by the "authority complex." The movement had the right to express opinions and convictions on any matter, but not to assume infallibility:

> No decision we come to can be regarded as an absolute. We have to allow that we may be wrong, and thus open to persuasion even

5. Report of the University Christian Movement of Southern Africa: Event '68, pp. 17-43.

within the structure which has made the decision. Thus we should be careful not to use our decisions to impose conformity on dissentient voices . . . within the UCM.

What specific cases or actions had led him to criticize churches publicly does not appear from his report. It is, however, evident that the unexpectedly strong and vocal contribution of nonwhite students had taken church leaders by surprise and driven some to distance themselves from the UCM. Perhaps already then the security police had played its part in harassing those who appeared to support the UCM.

Basil Moore's introductory remarks ended in a powerful plea for the churches and the UCM to stay together in the search for freedom and truth, in protesting against injustice and immorality, and in affirming the right to associate irrespective of color, class, or denominational differences. He foresaw "a tough road ahead on every conceivable front" and concluded that the churches and the UCM are "going to need each other, and to support each other" in this struggle. This was at a time when the mainline churches were in their practice still racially divided.

Records of the Stutterheim event show that there was a broad consensus of agreement with the UCM president. The sixty-nine formal motions recorded in the minutes of the UCM council dealt with ecumenical affairs; a proposal for a nationwide ecumenical university chaplaincy; the practice of a common ecumenical Eucharist; social concerns such as a minimum wage, literacy, and housing; nonviolent direct action; the study of the Bantu Education Act; publications and promotion of the movement; and constitutional amendments. The council protested against cases of "bureaucratic interference" by the government, including the withdrawal of a residence permit for his diocese from the Anglican bishop of Damaraland, Robert Mize; the denial of entry to a college campus of nonwhite UCM staff members; and the refusal of visas for American visitors to the Methodist Church.[6]

---

6. The movers of each resolution and the votes given were recorded in the minutes. Most of the motions were passed unanimously or nearly unanimously. A significant split of votes occurred only when action was taken on arranging an ecu-

At Stutterheim James Moulder was elected president, and Colin Collins, a Roman Catholic priest and until then secretary of the Catholic Bishops' Conference, was appointed general secretary and treasurer of the UCM. By early 1969, the general office of the UCM was opened in Johannesburg.

11.4. First Tests of the Movement

Not unexpectedly, the difficulties of the UCM began to mount after Stutterheim. The prime minister several times warned that the movement was under observation. Basil Moore's passport was rescinded. On September 6 three hundred students at the nonwhite University College of Fort Hare were suspended after a sit-in. Seventeen of them, all participants in the UCM "Event '68," were not readmitted, on the grounds that they were the cause of unrest. The first edition of the UCM magazine *One for the Road* was banned. So was the UCM branch at Fort Hare.[7] Messages were exchanged between UCM leaders and the WSCF Geneva staff, and procedures were hastily developed to avoid monitoring of communication by the South African Special Branch. Colin Collins alerted the Federation to the tensions which were emerging between some churches and the UCM.

The Federation immediately and confidentially approached member movements and supporting churches and mission agencies in Germany, Britain, the Nordic countries, Switzerland, and the USA for help to students who were expelled from Fort Hare and for funding legal aid to the banned and arrested UCM members. Collins pleaded discretion in all support activities and strongly discouraged

---

menical Eucharist at the conference; when a study of the Bantu Education Act was proposed; when the right of the president to decide the form of opening devotions at council meetings was proposed; and when the official emblem of the UCM was considered. The motions aimed at strengthening structural relations with churches, establishing ecumenical chaplaincies, and promoting cooperation with other Christian student organizations, including the remnant of the SCA, were approved unanimously.

7. Report on "Fort Hare Affair" by James Moulder of September 9, 1968 (mimeographed), and letter from Basil Manning to Risto Lehtonen, September 16, 1968. WSCF Archives.

the Federation and its constituency from acts of public protest at this time. He did ask, however, that the WSCF prepare a plan to launch a worldwide protest campaign in case the South African government were to ban the movement as a whole.[8]

Several church agencies responded positively by sending several thousands of dollars to the UCM in October and November 1968. A small portion of the funds was transferred to the UCM bank account in Johannesburg, but the bulk of the support was channeled through various intermediaries, including church agencies and individuals, in order to avoid drawing the attention of South African authorities.

Bad news continued to flow from South Africa. Two reports received in November informed the Federation that seven Fort Hare students had been arrested by the security police in the early hours of November 3, 1968, and tortured severely during questioning. On November 18 they had been brought to court and fined R 10 each and released. Virtually all nonwhite participants in the Stutterheim conference had been questioned by the Special Branch, some as many as ten times. Students at Turfloop University College had been told by police that the UCM would not be permitted there. During the first half of 1969 all four branches of the UCM at nonwhite colleges were banned.

In April 1969 Collins sent Geneva a confidential report on the situation of the UCM. The old SCA, which had conformed to the proapartheid position of the Dutch Reformed Church and relied for support on conservative evangelical Afrikaners, had begun to discredit the UCM openly. Inside the UCM pressure to become theologically more radical was increasing, especially among white students. The movement faced a choice between remaining a small ecumenical coordinating group and involving "the far larger mass of agnostic truth seekers" in its life. Collins added that in his view the latter direction was more likely, even if it would "cause considerable alarm on the part of churches."

In the same report Collins described the "endless difficulties" of the UCM. It had become almost impossible to organize racially mixed

---

8. Memorandum on the UCM by Colin Collins to Risto Lehtonen delivered at the Otaniemi Assembly, August 1968. WSCF Archives.

seminars or conferences. The venue of the national conference to be held in July was still uncertain because of Security Branch interference. After some particular place had been contacted, the police came and intimidated the church authorities concerned and the site was not made available to the UCM. Meanwhile the president of the UCM, James Moulder, had accepted a position in Australia and left South Africa in January 1969; the vice president had become inoperative because of security police activity and personal difficulties; and the secretary had been sent by his church to a remote site. Nevertheless with vigor and courage plans were being developed for five regional seminars and for a national seminar to be held in conjunction with the council meeting.

11.5. Nanyuki "Happening '69"

The third national conference and UCM Council meeting were held July 12-18, 1969, as a last resort under camping conditions, at Stanger, nicknamed "Nanyuki," some fifty miles north of Durban.[9] Nearly 150 persons attended, including full representation of the five participating churches. This time no participants came from outside southern Africa.[10] The theme of the event, "Power" — a hot topic for the country — was introduced by talks on the biblical concept of power, economic power, political power, and student power. Much time was allotted to interest groups, creative workshops, and regional reports.

9. It is noteworthy that the date and site of the 1969 conference were not revealed in any mimeographed documents, including in the conference report. Nor were they mentioned in the numerous letters from the UCM to the WSCF and SCMs and agencies in Europe and North America from January to May 1968. I found a record of the date only in a brief note to Jürgen Nicolai of Pax Romana of June 12, in which Colin Collins welcomed the Pax Romana representative to the conference. The intention of the secrecy was to make police surveillance of the conference more difficult. This goal proved unrealistic.

10. Outside the territory of South Africa there was a branch in Lesotho which was represented at "Nanyuki." An observer from the WSCF and another from Pax Romana both came from Zimbabwe, at that time Rhodesia. Report of the UCM conference "Happening '69," pp. 33-34.

During the conference there was "an open and frank" confrontation between representatives of the different races. The conference report described it as one of the most valuable features of UCM life. The conference also debated the question of the theological stance of the UCM, but came to no clear-cut conclusions.

The movement elected Justice Moloto, a student at the University of South Africa (UNISA), as president. The choice of a black man had far-reaching symbolic significance.

One of the active participants at this conference was Steve Biko, a member of the UCM from early on, who had also emerged as the leader of the South African Student Organization (SASO), founded at the end of 1968. This organization was intended to be the black counterpart to NUSAS, which had been banned from all black campuses. It was a separate organization of blacks only and, as such, fitted formally into the apartheid structures. Its real significance took the authorities by surprise: It rapidly became a springboard for the black consciousness movement and an influential advocate of black power. Biko, a medical student at Natal University, was a superb organizer, driven by an articulate and contagious Christian commitment. He remained active in the UCM, which advocated a nonracial society and was resolutely against dividing the Christian community on the basis of race. Biko, however, had come to the conclusion that apartheid could not be overcome without creating power centers of black people. An interracial organization would, in his opinion, be unreliable in a situation in which a real, potentially violent confrontation between supporters of the apartheid government and its opponents, led by black militants, would take place. This position disturbed UCM leaders and its white constituency and contributed to its deepening crisis.

Although the resolve of the government to crush the UCM was increasingly evident and there were more signs of tension between the UCM and its sponsoring churches and within the UCM itself, the council's actions continued to reflect the determination of the UCM to pursue its objectives, relying on partnership with churches and the support of international ecumenical organizations, and preparing its members for a nonviolent struggle against apartheid. It expected its momentum to grow with the increase of its membership and the nationwide interest which it had created.

11.6. WSCF Visit

In September 1969 I succeeded in making a ten-day visit to the UCM in South Africa. My visit had been prepared with utmost discretion. A visa was granted on the day of my scheduled departure. The formal invitation came from Lutherans in South Africa who were not official partners of the UCM. The visa application was backed by the Lutheran World Federation, which at that time was not viewed as an actively antiapartheid organization. During the assembly of the All Africa Conference of Churches, September 1-10, 1969, in Abidjan, I had a chance to confer about plans with my African colleagues from Nairobi and Yaoundé who were not likely to receive entry permits. The visit from September 11 to 21 included meetings with national UCM leaders and numerous members and leaders of local UCM branches and university chaplains in the Johannesburg area, in and around Durban, at Rhodes University in Grahamstown, and at the Federal Theological Seminary in Alice, where I was, however, not allowed to enter the adjoining campus of the University of Fort Hare. The journey continued to Cape Town and Stellenbosch and ended with a day in the company of the general secretary, Colin Collins, in Pretoria. I also met several church leaders, including the Roman Catholic archbishop of Durban, Denis Hurley, and the Lutheran bishop of Natal, Helge Fosseus. Justice Moloto and Chris Mokoditoa took me on an unforgettable tour of Soweto, for which I did not have the required entry permit.

Tensions in and around the UCM were evident. My visit was apparently monitored by the Security Branch, as there were unannounced visits and anonymous phone calls to my hosts in Johannesburg and Durban, the callers asking about my program. I had taken extensive notes from all discussions during the whole stay, but I was advised to destroy them before going through the passport and customs control. I had given as my first address in Johannesburg the Hotel Victoria, as recommended by Collins, but upon arrival was taken by him to stay at the house of the Anglican chaplain of the Witwatersrand University. During supper, shortly after my arrival, a strange car appeared in the courtyard and a man introducing himself as a reporter asked to see me. Meanwhile my host had pushed me to a dark storage space and my plate had been cleared away from the table. My host played innocent and said he knew nothing about my arrival. During the visit to Soweto my hosts always first checked whether our car was followed before continuing the journey. I was reminded before every gathering of students which I attended of the likely presence of informers.

The internal tensions of the UCM were revealed most dramatically during an evening gathering at the Medical School campus in Durban. A mixed group of black, Indian, and white students were present. During the rather informal meeting I was introduced to Steve Biko, who was a student at that school. He took me to a lonely room at the far end of the campus and told me about his own background and his involvement in the UCM and SASO. The reason he gave for wanting to talk to me was the lack of trust between whites and blacks in the UCM. There was an urgent need that it be understood outside South Africa that SASO was not turning away from the goal of a nonracial state, but that the struggle of blacks to build up a political force which the whites could no longer bypass necessitated the buildup of a black power base. This was the aim of the new black consciousness movement. In spite of the good fellowship between the blacks and whites, if the white regime were to resort to force, the blacks in the UCM could not be sure of the whites' stand. He was therefore not prepared to reveal the plans developed by SASO to the UCM or to any other interracial group. He pleaded with me for financial support for SASO from abroad through the WSCF. During my visit several white UCM leaders mentioned to me that there was uncertainty among many about who Steve Biko really was. Was he what he claimed to be? Or was he a government informer?

At the end of the tour Collins invited me to join him for an evening in a suburban house in Johannesburg to meet members of the "commune" in which he lived. It was an all-white group of young men and women, who proceeded to have a seminar-type session on the ideological basis for transforming South Africa. Most of the presentations and the ensuing discussion were incomprehensible to me. It sounded like a version of Marcusian-Maoist group dynamics theory. I was told that not only was the group serious about its pursuit of radical ideas, but that it also wanted to express its commitment to total liberation in terms of its lifestyle. Collins mentioned that members of the group had been harassed by the security police and that his car had been damaged in front of the commune's house.

As I left South Africa, my impression was that the blacks and whites within and around the UCM were going in very different directions. To me the white commune epitomized a drift toward the fringe, even toward the absurd: an escape in a situation in which all hope was vanishing. The experience of being rejected by the black consciousness movement had killed their vision of a free and reconciled interracial society and church. They sought a way out in affirming their freedom through denial of the restrictions imposed on them by the conventional white-dominated oppressor society and church. The blacks in the UCM were reserved about this white radicalism. They seemed to prefer a political strategy involving step-by-step tactics for contesting the apartheid rule. They affirmed Christian teaching and counted on the church's continued pastoral and moral support in the midst of the hardships of living in an apartheid society. The church's caring for the arrested, the banned, and their families had brought the church close to them, even though they were frustrated by the conservatism and caution of most black church leaders. The all-out rejection of the church which they heard radical whites advocating did not appeal to them, and wordy ideological debates did not much inspire them. And ultimately, the risks for them were manifold compared with those faced by most whites, however radical their language.

Before departing I shared these impressions with Collins, who saw me off at the airport. I asked him whether he had considered how easily he himself could be discredited in the eyes of black leaders and churches on the basis of participating in activities such as the commune in which he lived and which at best had a fringe value for the struggle against apartheid. It was a disturbing discussion, probably for both of us.

11.7. Plowing Ahead

In the year following "Happening '69," the UCM became more markedly an activist movement. Its role as a "coordinator" of ecumenical student activities among denominational societies diminished. Instead of gathering students committed to the life of the church, it aimed to become a haven for Christian students who were unhappy with their churches, for those who had left the institutional church, and for those searching for religious belief. The leaders of the UCM visited all the branches, whose numbers had continued to increase despite the ban on the organization on nonwhite campuses. Much emphasis was given to the local and regional formation schools. Some of the banned branches and some newly founded, predominantly black groups were active off campus. The growth of SASO caused an exodus of qualified black leaders from the UCM, although blacks continued to be the largest ethnic group within the movement.

Steve Biko, who had become president of SASO, wrote to me elaborating the need for moral and financial support to the black consciousness movement represented by SASO. Significant funding was secured from member movements of the WSCF and from related church agencies.[11]

In November 1969, the general secretary of the UCM made head-lines in the South African press when he announced that he was asking for dispensation from the priesthood. He told the press that the main reasons for his decision were the separation of Roman Catholic bishops and clergy from the real world, the subsequent alienation of the Roman Catholic Church from the people whom it was to serve, its "repellent" attitude toward black people, its preoccupation with its own institutional concerns, and its lack of sensitivity to the problems of laity.[12]

In a letter of November 23, 1969, Collins informed me of his decision to leave the priesthood and also the "commune" with which he was associated and to enter university as a part-time student of sociology of education. He added that he intended to lead a celibate life in spite of leaving the priesthood.

11. In a letter of February 20, 1970, from Steven Biko to Risto Lehtonen, which came through one of the alternative channels established to avoid interference by the Security Branch, Biko repeated part of the information which he had sent earlier by ordinary mail but which had disappeared on the way. He attached a listing of the projects of SASO that included "welfare projects that we wish to tackle almost immediately." This was a reference to students and families hit by arrests and ban-nings. He ended the letter on an almost desperate note: "Try your best to get something. You are our only hope." The visit of the international group to the UCM national conference helped to expand the international support of SASO in the same year.

12. *Sunday Times* and *Rand Daily Mail* gave visible coverage to Colin Collins and his decision to leave the priesthood. He was referred to as "one of South Africa's best-known Roman Catholic priests." Clippings in WSCF Archives.

Two significant theological papers, "A 1970 Theological Point of View from the UCM" and "Towards a Black Theology," written by Basil Moore, were circulated widely within the UCM and beyond. A number of workshops were held on worship, with an emphasis on experimental worship, and plans for a new songbook and a worship manual were developed.[13]

The UCM Department of Social Concerns played an increasingly important role involving students in concrete action programs. Inter-racial work camps were organized to help build or repair schools, clinics, hospitals, and playgrounds in some of the most destitute communities of the country. Communication weeks were scheduled to give groups of UCM members an opportunity to work in parishes prepared to invite such teams. However, literacy campaigns became the most important of the UCM action programs. Within the year after the 1969 conference, more than two hundred literacy teachers were trained in twelve centers in different parts of the country.

Churches continued to support the UCM despite the increasing frequency of critical voices among them concerning its orientation. The main areas of criticism were the ecumenism, politics, religious beliefs, and morality of the UCM. Communication between the UCM and church leaders continued to function, albeit with growing friction. The participation of churches in the UCM probably contributed to the restraint shown by government authorities toward it, although intimidation was steadily increasing. The tension which was brought into the open when church leaders and UCM Executive (committee) members met at Wilgespruit may have weakened the protective role of churches.

11.8. Wilgespruit 1970

Again in 1970 the UCM succeeded in bringing together an impressive national conference, in Wilgespruit, July 10 to 16. Participants included 112 delegates and 9 invited trainers. Among delegates were

13. Alex Boraine had been appointed in 1969 as director of Theological Concerns. After his resignation from the executive group in midterm, Basil Moore took over the department.

nine representatives of the participating churches, and, as a special feature, six representatives of European SCMs.

The planning for international participation was initiated during my visit to South Africa the previous September. Because of the difficulties with visas and entry permits, the plan was carried out with utmost care. A charter flight for a cultural tourist group sponsored by the British University Society of Arts offered an inconspicuous cover for the European group. The names of its members were not sent in advance to the UCM. The "smuggling" of the group into South Africa was a great success. Two participants came from Great Britain, and one each from Denmark, Finland, Germany, and Norway. Officially the group just happened to appear at the Wilgespruit "Encounter '70." Their presence was reported to have been "stimulating and useful" in helping the conference out of a sense of being cut off from the rest of the world.[14] For the visitors themselves the conference and the subsequent two-week stay in South Africa were eye-opening experiences. Both the hosts and visitors agreed that similar visits should be arranged in the future.[15]

The main emphasis of "Encounter '70" was on communication in general and interpersonal communication in particular. "Encounter groups" of twelve persons each brought to the surface conflicting expectations and even dissatisfaction about the program of the conference. Many had thought that in these groups they could deal with deeply felt social and political issues, but they discovered that the emphasis on interpersonal relations made this impossible. Another

14. Letter from Collins to Lehtonen, July 30, 1970.
15. The members of the international group participating in the Wilgespruit conference of 1970 were: Hartmut Barsnick, German SCM (Studentengemeinde); David Currie, SCM of Scotland; Trond Dokka, SCM of Norway; David Head, general secretary of the SCM of Great Britain and Ireland; Jette Holm, SCM of Denmark; and Pirkko Juppi, SCM of Finland. Currie's and Juppi's reports emphasized the value of contact with SASO. Both of them spoke and wrote extensively in their SCMs about their findings. David Head's reporting on the visit was primarily a statement of convictions which followed the general argumentation of the radical left, and in his reporting he revealed the logistics of the visit to such an extent that the organizing of further team visits became virtually impossible. The following year the member of the British SCM who intended to participate in the UCM conference was turned back upon arrival at Jan Smuts Airport, even though British passport holders did not need an entry visa.

objection was that the groups dealt mainly with problems affecting whites and that the working style of the groups was "very white Western." Many blacks found reflection on personal identity and interpersonal communication irrelevant when they were faced with the oppressive social and political situation of the country. Apparently whites and blacks continued to move in different directions.[16]

Another topic which the conference focused on was "advertising." The intention was to help the UCM understand how to get its message across. Because of the difficulties of the "encounter groups," further discussion was limited to two issues: (1) relative merits of socialism and capitalism, and (2) the "image" of the UCM. The groups were quite divided on the first issue. On the second, they concluded that the UCM should have a clearer understanding of itself and its message. It was pointed out that its present image was so bad that it blocked the possibility of any meaningful communication. The UCM had "allowed side issues like drink, sex, and even drugs to form a negative focus so that they drew attention away from its central Christian, social and political 'message.'"[17]

A third element of the program consisted of "spectrum groups" which were formed so that each group had a rather homogeneous attitude to a particular problem. The topic to be considered was sex and sexual freedom. The conference again became quite divided between those who rejected the idea that marriage was the only form for a responsible "contract" safeguarding the value of persons in a relationship which included sexual intercourse, and those who held that marriage was the most adequate form of that contract in which the intention of lifelong commitment is affirmed and mutual responsibility is accepted in a legally binding contract. Another dimension of polarity in these issues was that for one group the affirmation of sexual freedom was an expression of liberation from the rule of a restrictive society and a legalistic church, while for another the focus on sex and the pursuit of sexual freedom were an irrelevant luxury which distracted the UCM from its most crucial social concerns, separating it from its most important allies, the churches, and blurring

16. University Christian Movement Conference Report — "Encounter '70," July 10-16, 1970, Wilgespruit, pp. 16-17.

17. Conference Report, pp. 17-18.

the perspective of the value of sacrifice — even of interpersonal ties — for the sake of greater human issues.[18]

The conference embarked on a thorough discussion of two theological issues: (1) Is Christianity by its essence opposed to black liberation, basically serving white people? Is God the God of white people only? (2) The renewal of worship and reactions to the patterns of worship experimented with at the conference. Again the opinions on both issues were profoundly divided, although the demarcation line this time did not place blacks and whites in opposing camps. There were those among blacks who were profoundly disappointed with the church and the Christianity which it represented. There were also whites who rejected the radical theology and whose point of departure was the inherited affirmations of the Christian faith.[19]

Apparently the most painful part of the conference took place on the last night when the future of the UCM was discussed. Once again black and white members were divided, although not all whites and all blacks stood on opposite sides. The participants could not agree on the continuing value of the UCM as a multi- or nonracial organization. The report stated:

> Perhaps the question that put the steam into the debate was: "Is there any validity in a multi- or non-racial organization in the present South African situation?" An easy answer of "yes" could not be given to this question because for the first time the UCM was described as dampening the militancy of blacks in South Africa, denying them the chance of nurturing their black consciousness. Hence the non-racial UCM was seen as a threat to its black membership. This open hint that blacks were questioning very seriously the validity of a non-racial Movement, and wished to withdraw into all-black organizations raised an immediate, almost angry protest from many white members.[20]

It was pointed out in the course of the discussion that "liberal" whites were politically the least influential group in South Africa. In

18. Conference Report, pp. 19-22.
19. Conference Report, pp. 23-26.
20. Conference Report, p. 27.

order to have any influence they needed the support of blacks. The withdrawal of blacks was therefore an enormous threat for the whites of the UCM. Some of them reacted angrily to being labeled the comfortable, elite, unoppressed people.

The response of many blacks to the question of the validity of the UCM was that they needed a new "black consciousness" which is something very different from black racism. It was needed so that the blacks of South Africa could overcome their sense of inferiority and the whites could be freed from their superiority complex. They expressed appreciation to the UCM for arousing and spreading black consciousness, but they pointed to its limitations as an agent for change in the South African context. They emphasized that the objectives of the nonracial UCM and the all-black SASO were identical: the creation of a truly free nonracial society, but they differed in their strategy and methods of work.

The discussion left many basic questions open. The report concluded that the vision of the UCM as a viable instrument for sociopolitical change was virtually dead. It nevertheless could continue to have a role in keeping the hope for a nonracial society and a nonracial church alive. Also its midwife role for politically effective organizations and for church renewal seemed to have continued validity.[21]

During the Wilgespruit "Encounter '70" a meeting was held between the UCM Executive and church leaders. It entailed a frank exchange in which church leaders expressed their criticisms in no uncertain terms and stated that "the UCM had become an embarrassment to the Churches who were also trying to bring some kind of change in the South African situation." The meeting concluded that continuing dialogue between the sponsoring churches and the UCM was essential and that no changes in the formal relationship between them were to be considered.[22]

The UCM Council reelected Justice Moloto as president and appointed an Executive group consisting predominantly of black members of the movement.

21. Conference Report, p. 30.
22. Conference Report, pp. 32-33.

11.9. New Directions

Soon after the Wilgespruit conference the UCM encountered more difficulties with the authorities, mainly in the form of intimidation. At the end of August 1970, Collins was arrested for a short while but was released when major charges against him were suddenly withdrawn.

In December 1970, the UCM played a leading role at the WSCF southern Africa leadership training course in Malawi. The WSCF regional staff, José Chipenda, Aaron Tolen, and Bethuel Kiplagat, took part in the event. The UCM brought some of the trainers who had assisted at the UCM formation schools and training sessions at the national conferences. They were well versed in methods based on group dynamics. Simulation games were an important tool in the training. The trainers also knew Paulo Freire's educational concepts and tried to apply them to South Africa. Much of this was new to African SCMs outside South Africa and aroused curiosity, even enthusiasm among some. On the whole, however, reactions were quite mixed. Enthusiasm about these new techniques of training and about the concept of "conscientization" was tinged with apprehension about the methods and styles, which were viewed as characteristic of white radicals of South Africa. They were found inadequate for the African cultural context outside South Africa and apparently were not unanimously accepted by blacks in South Africa either. WSCF Africa regional staff, for whom the Malawi training course was their first serious exposure to the UCM and its leaders, came back with critical questions about the movement in South Africa.

After Wilgespruit the UCM developed its work increasingly on the basis of three consciousness groups. The most powerful of them was the black consciousness group, which identified increasingly with SASO. The white consciousness group continued to delve deeper into cultural and personal issues of liberation, developing a white radical lifestyle and distancing itself from churches. Women's consciousness formed the topic of the third significant group. The explosive black and white polarization was tamed mainly by the continued exodus of blacks from the UCM to SASO, while a new ideological tension between the male-dominated white consciousness groups and the rising women's movement grew in intensity. It mirrored the peculiar heritage of South African/Afrikaner double morality, which formally stuck to a strict Calvinist puritanism but accepted the erosion of family structures among the "inferior" races as inevitable and fostered extreme permissiveness and the depersonalization of the sexual attitudes of whites to blacks. The extent to which internal polarization was fed from the outside, by the security police and its informers planted in the UCM, remains only guesswork.

11.10. The Beginnings of Isolation

Cooperation between the UCM and the WSCF Geneva office, which had been very close, suddenly came to a low point in the first half of 1971. The difficulty surfaced in Collins's response to my circular letter of February 22 (see chapter 9, pp. 199-202).

Collins had assumed that the sizable cut of the financial assistance to the UCM from 1970 to 1971 had been made on ideological grounds. He had come to this conclusion on the basis of his conversations with Geneva staff during his visit in November 1970 when he met members of both groups of the escalating conflict there. Presumably stimulated by the views of the opposition group, he found in my circular letter of February 22, 1971, a confirmation of his conclusions.[23]

In addition, he had failed to recognize the seriousness of the financial situation of the Federation caused by the drastic decline of grants from American churches. This, in turn, was mainly a result of their own financial difficulties but partly also of the confrontations between their conservative constituencies and "liberal" leaders, especially in the United Presbyterian Church and the United Methodist Church in the USA.[24]

---

23. Prior to the critical meeting of the WSCF Executive Committee in 1971 in Tozanzo, members of the internal opposition of the Federation circulated Collins's critical letter, which to them was a clear sign of support for their "revolutionary" position. Collins had also circulated his response to a wide circle of SCM leaders and representatives of church agencies. Letters from Collins to Lehtonen, April 7 and June 15, 1971, and from Lehtonen to Collins, April 17.

24. The "Angela Davis case" caused havoc in the United Presbyterian Church. Many local congregations were infuriated by a grant made by the national church

Furthermore, Collins seemed to have ignored the impact of regionalization, which had moved the main responsibility for approving WSCF ecumenical assistance grants to national movements from the central office to regional advisory committees and regional staff. In 1970 the Africa Consultative Committee had come to the conclusion that grants to the UCM had to be brought into line with grants to other African SCMs, which were financially in a more difficult position than the UCM, although not in such global limelight.[25]

The Tozanzo meeting of the Executive Committee eliminated most of the Geneva office's staff and financial resources and hampered its ability to follow the work of the UCM as actively as before. Moreover, the UCM itself virtually discontinued communication with the WSCF headquarters and Africa staff, although the Geneva office tried to maintain contact and encouraged church agencies in Europe and North America to make direct grants to the UCM programs.[26]

The net result was that the UCM ignored the WSCF as an international partner at a time when it was running into increasing difficulties with its partner churches in South Africa and when the South African government decided to resort to ever harsher methods of repression. At that time it also became evident that the revolutionary wing of the Federation had no intention of involving itself in South African concerns. Its interest was limited to seeking support for its own revolutionary stance. In cooperation with the German SCM (Studentengemeinde), several American churches, and the New

---

office for the legal defense of the black civil rights and antiwar activist (Angela Davis), who was known as a leader of the American left and who was said to have no relationship with the church. This case stimulated further the reduction of giving by local congregations to the national and international activities of the United Presbyterian Church.

25. The relative isolation of South Africa and the UCM from the rest of Africa may have led the UCM leaders to bypass the WSCF Africa staff in a manner which some Africans found condescending. Note from the writer's conversations with WSCF Africa secretaries.

26. Information on the programs and the financial situation after the beginning of 1971 came to Geneva mainly through those church agencies in the USA and Germany which continued to provide financial assistance to the UCM in agreement with the Geneva office. These church offices faithfully sent me copies of letters which Collins had sent to them.

York–based Southern Africa Concerns Group, the Geneva office continued to maintain contact with, and provide support for, the UCM. The British SCM also continued its involvement in South Africa, although no longer in cooperation with the WSCF.

11.11. The End

Nineteen seventy-one became the decisive year for the UCM. Concern groups took the place of local branches, which were still in existence on some twenty-five campuses. The shift from a movement with defined membership to an open movement whose only source of cohesion was its commitment to "liberation," in which no formal Christian affirmation or principle was required, had increased the interest of white students in the UCM. At the same time the exodus of black members had accelerated.

The national conference "Freedom '71" at Camp Jonathan, Eston, July 9-16, 1971, marked a turning point. The original concept of the UCM as a multiracial ecumenical student organization and an expression of the life of the Church had been questioned for some time. Now its character as a body providing interracial contact was formally abandoned. Instead the movement had begun to function as a loosely knit federation of different consciousness and skills groups and was leaning toward becoming primarily a movement concerned with Christian adult education.

The theme of liberation was interpreted as an expression of the most fundamental Christian concern. Each group was left to concentrate on its own particular concept and emphasis of freedom. The consciousness groups of the conference included groups on black consciousness, white consciousness, and women's liberation; a married men's group; and a "white unmarried male brigade." The composition of the Executive of the UCM was altered to consist of a director from the three consciousness groups — the black, white, and women's — and three program directors, for literacy, theological concerns, and ideological concerns, as well as the president and general secretary of the UCM. The Executive (committee) was to be a consultative body to facilitate liaison between the various projects and to fulfill the inevitable administrative functions, but was not to be a governing or controlling body. It was explicitly stated that "anyone wishing to participate in any one of the programs will not thereby become a member of a multi-racial organization."

The most painful issue at the conference was the ever sharpening polarization between blacks and whites. It had been a shock to most white participants to discover that blacks no longer accepted them as partners. From the perspective of blacks, whites, whatever opinion they held, were inevitably identified with the oppressors and shared the privileges of those who held power. The debates at the conference seemed to have been dominated by the intellectual, psychology-of-group-dynamics orientation introduced by the white participants. The study part of the program was carried out through simulation games and their evaluation. They were followed by eight workshops which, in addition to the consciousness topics, dealt with urban and rural community development, preventive medicine and nutrition, adult education and ideology. Points of controversy were discussed in plenary sessions under the heading "Current Affairs." The blacks succeeded in threatening the gathering with a walkout unless their terms for dealing with the issues were accepted.

A sizable portion of the black participants were active in SASO, the all-black student organization. In the turmoil of the conference the reports on literacy programs, which had developed into an extensive activity, received little attention, although the budget and personnel approved for them represented the largest segment of resources.

The budget presented to the conference foresaw the formal establishment of a Christian Education Movement with three subunits: the UCM with its branches and formation schools, the black theology movement, and the literacy program.

The only reference in the conference report to the friction between the UCM and the WSCF was in the general secretary's report:

> Of particular significance during the period was a review of our relationship with the WSCF. Frank letters have been exchanged, and it is hoped that the WSCF will be able to have a clearer understanding of what we are doing and where we stand.[27]

27. University Christian Movement Conference Report, "Freedom '71," p. 9.

The discussions at this conference, despite its occasional chaos, did reach unusual depths regarding what was at stake in race relations and how many dehumanizing layers had to be peeled off before any healing could take place. Had the sequence of events after the conference been different, the report would have made an outstanding contribution to the understanding of the complex dynamics of fighting against institutional racism.

Although the conference seemed to make all major decisions together, it allowed the black consciousness, white consciousness, and women's liberation groups to function as semiautonomous movements. The previous council structure of the UCM was pushed aside. No list of participants or delegates was placed on record. Nor was there a record of the response of the participating churches to the changes in UCM's objectives and style.

The conference marked the end of the general secretaryship of Colin Collins. The previous president, Justice Moloto, was elected general secretary; Winky Direko, nicknamed the "People's Mother," was elected the new president; and Basil Moore was made Theological Concerns director.

Soon after the conference the government issued a three-year banning order to the new general secretary. He was arrested by the security police in Johannesburg and taken to Mafeking, where he was to function as a senior clerk under the Tswana Territorial Authority. He was kept in total isolation from his family and his church, and was not allowed to take part in any social, educational, or political gatherings.[28] Chris Mokoditoa, a Roman Catholic layman, was appointed successor to Justice Moloto as general secretary.

A few months later, in February 1972, it was Basil Moore's turn to be banned. He was confined to Johannesburg Magisterial District for a period of five years. He was not allowed to participate in any organization, nor to receive any visitors except his doctor. Anything he had said or written was not permitted to be quoted in South Africa.

Two weeks after Basil Moore's banning a young member of the UCM Executive, Stanley Ntwasa, was banned and put under house arrest. He was a student of theology at the Federal Theological Sem-

---

28. Circular letter of October 14, 1971, from Basil Moore, who had immediately been made acting general secretary of the UCM.

inary and was preparing to become an Anglican priest, but had taken a year off from his study to work for the UCM as director of black theology and as traveling secretary.

Following these actions the government ordered the UCM to be investigated by a select parliamentary committee. The leaders of the movement assumed that this action would lead to its banning as an organization. The UCM Executive decided to dissolve the organization before the investigation began.

The last direct contact between the UCM and the WSCF was the participation of a UCM delegation at the All Africa Youth and Student Conference in Ibadan, Nigeria, in December 1971. The record of the decision of the UCM to be disbanded did not reach Geneva until much later in 1972.

What happened after the disbanding of the UCM? Colin Collins emigrated to Australia for study and research on education. Basil Moore accepted exile rather than being kept in isolation and left with his family for England, where he served as general secretary of the declining British SCM for a short while before moving to Australia. The fate of the black UCM leaders who had been banned was difficult to follow. Steve Biko, president of SASO, emerged as a charismatic leader of the black consciousness movement. He was arrested, tortured, and finally killed in 1977 while in prison.

As a result of my own activity my applications for visas to South Africa and Namibia were refused for fourteen years.

The disappearance of the UCM created a vacuum in Christian ministry to students and in the ecumenical movement in South Africa, but it had opened new paths in the struggle for racial justice and freedom. Its closure was a short-term victory for the government, which had succeeded in dispersing a potentially effective Christian movement within the university community of South Africa and defusing for a little while the explosive ideas which it considered to be a threat to apartheid.

The rapid disintegration of the UCM under all-out repression by the government was not just the defeat of a Christian organization in South Africa but a common failure of the community of Christians and churches in South Africa and worldwide. The UCM had challenged mainline churches in South Africa for their timidity. Too quickly, the five sponsoring churches lost patience with students who were exploring untried paths and embarking on dubious experiments. They also lost their nerve when threatened by the Security Branch for supporting the UCM. As a consequence, the sponsoring churches withdrew their support at a time when the UCM needed it most.

The rapid liquidation of the UCM typified a wider failure of the worldwide ecumenical movement to involve itself in events inside South Africa through churches and Christian organizations of the country there while pursuing antiapartheid activities and supporting liberation organizations outside South Africa. As a result churches in the country were left largely in isolation at a time when they were trying to define a common role in encountering the hardening of racial oppression.[29]

After being intensely involved early on in supporting the UCM and its struggle against apartheid, the WSCF became increasingly paralyzed by its own internal polarization and thereby unable to keep in touch with the UCM and its leaders. Furthermore, the ideological strife within the Federation gave misleading signals to the UCM and perhaps even encouraged it to dive into a self-destructive radicalism. The Federation ceased to be an operative partner to the UCM and failed to provide, in cooperation with the international church community, a protective umbrella of joint action. It also failed to bring global perspectives to the internal tensions dividing the UCM and give effective international support to the students and staff and their families, who were banned or jailed.

In retrospect, it is obvious that there were several causes for the fall of the UCM. The radicalism of the white constituency disabled the UCM from responding creatively to the black consciousness movement and from keeping communications with South African churches open, thus speeding internal erosion. The churches gave in to panic about the radicalism of the whites and the exclusivism of the

29. When launching its Program to Combat Racism, the WCC opted deliberately for an international advocacy of highest possible visibility and placed less emphasis on maintaining broad-based communication with its member churches in South Africa. Consequently it became virtually impossible for the WCC to function as an effective international partner in the agonizing search of South African churches for locally viable joint strategies. For example, from the beginning of the seventies, international ecumenical visits to South Africa were reduced to a minimum for several years.

blacks. The withdrawal of both local and international support, combined with internal ideological dissension, gave the government authorities a free hand to clamp down on the UCM. The end result was that the witness of the Christian community on a strategic frontier was abruptly weakened.

CHAPTER 12

Strategies Updated

12.1. Change of Mood

It was not long after the Tozanzo meeting of the Executive Committee that new plans began to emerge. Before leaving Japan the leading staff members of Africa, Asia, and the Middle East and Pharis Harvey of the Methodist Board of World Mission in the USA met in a Tokyo cafe with Peter Musgrove and the general secretary. Members of the group outlined a series of steps which they believed would help to bring the WSCF out of its current deadlock. The ideas presented included:

- consolidation of the regional programs of Africa and Asia;
- isolation of the Europe region from the rest of the Federation on the grounds that it refused to respect the integrity of SCMs not conforming to its political and ideological orientation;
- the ensuring of adequate financial support for leadership training programs; and
- the launching of a worldwide study of the aims and basis of the WSCF and through such a study stimulating theological work throughout the Federation.

It was felt that apart from these efforts, the worldwide functions of the Federation should be limited until the end of 1972 to a modest information and publication program and to the preparation of the Assembly. Such plans seemed realistic given the reduced budget.

During the meeting Gabriel Habib of the Middle East urged that the Geneva office consider building a "confederation" in which the Protestant-dominated constituency of the WSCF and the Orthodox and Roman Catholic youth and student movements could be drawn together on an equal footing. In his view, such a confederation should gradually replace the WSCF in its current form and thus provide a long-term solution to the Federation's problems. His proposal reflected a strong commitment to ecumenism on the part of Orthodox leaders in the Middle East, although not on terms acceptable to Protestant Christians, who seemed too easily swayed by fashionable political currents and too ready to ignore the historic foundation of the church. These ideas were later echoed in internal Orthodox discussions, at a consultation between the Orthodox youth and student movements and the WSCF, and in the report on the Middle East to the Addis Ababa Assembly.[1]

The informal gathering in the Tokyo cafe heralded a definite change of attitude in the general secretariat and among Asian and Middle Eastern leaders. The African leaders indicated their profound dissatisfaction with events at Tozanzo, but they felt that they needed to give highest priority to the development of their own regional programs and to the support of emerging SCMs. They therefore did not see how, in addition to their own regional work, they could contribute to peacemaking in the context of the ideological warfare within the Federation. However, it was now manifest that the Federation leadership in Africa, Asia, the Middle East, and Geneva formed an alliance within the WSCF. The participants agreed that close communication among them as well as with supporting agencies, especially in the USA, was vital in the coming months. The unifying goal

---

1. The proposal is first described in informal notes from the meeting in Tokyo, and later, more precisely, in the reports of the meeting of Orthodox Student Movements and of members of SYNDESMOS, August 28-30, 1972, Geneva, and of the consultation between SYNDESMOS, the Federation of Othodox Student and Youth Movements, and the WSCF, August 31–September 2, 1972, Geneva. It was also presented to the WSCF Assembly in Addis Ababa as part of the Middle East report; however, it is not included in the printed report but is included in the WSCF Archives as a separate document.

was to safeguard a pluralistic and theologically articulate Federation in which member movements would be respected and listened to.

While still in Tokyo, the group developed a plan for a team visit to North American church agencies and selected university campuses to be carried out in September-October 1971. It was to be part of a strategic approach for rebuilding confidence in the Federation among supporters and American campus ministries. It was also to provide an opportunity to continue the planning initiated in Tokyo. Pharis Harvey agreed to assume responsibility for the overall coordination of the American end of the visit and specifically for contacting American mission agencies and, together with the North America secretary, Placide Bazoche, for arranging visits with campus ministries and groups. A sensitive aspect of the plan was the uncertainty about the sympathies and commitments of Bazoche, who, under normal circumstances, would have been the obvious person to coordinate the whole visit.

The informal meeting in Tokyo injected new drive into the Geneva office after the battles of the Executive Committee, enabling it to implement the immediate but thankless task of terminating several staff positions and of renting office space no longer needed. For participants in this meeting it was evident that the time for seeking a compromise through dialogue with those who did not respect democratic parliamentary procedures was now over.[2]

The radical left group within the Federation had suffered a bitter defeat at Tozanzo. The meeting marked an end to the activity of the Political Commission and the Documentation unit, which had been the stronghold of the radical left activist ideology in the Federation. The leading staff members, Leonardo Franco and Claudius Ceccon, who left the Federation in September-October 1971 as agreed at the time of their appointments, were not replaced. The employment of the rest of the personnel of the Political Commission–Communication "team" was discontinued during the second half of the year. Some rather fruitless efforts continued, however, with the support of the American-sponsored Frontier Internship Program, to ensure staff for

2. No formal minutes were taken of the Tokyo meeting, but the correspondence between Pharis Harvey, Moonkyu Kang, Gabriel Habib, and myself in July-September 1971 provides a substantive record of the plans.

the WSCF Political Commission for a few more months.[3] The search for a new constituency among diverse left radical action and research groups was now over in the Federation. The orientation of the opposition changed from the "New Left" to a more clearly articulated Christian Marxist position, which already set the tone for the European program. This shift also reflected the change of mood among radical student activists in general. After the initial revolutionary wave, some of the militant leaders of the 1968 student uprising in Europe began to look to hard-line Marxism for new direction.

For me Tozanzo 1971 meant a conscious and significant shift in attitude. Until then I had regarded as imperative the maintenance of the most open communication possible with the whole Federation constituency and staff, the pursuit of patient dialogue with the opposition, and the avoidance of statements or actions which would fuel controversies. For me the possibility of building bridges between the two groups in matters of ideology and conflicting ideas came to an end in Tozanzo. Instead I decided to concentrate on stimulating and supporting an ecumenically and ideologically pluralistic Christian witness among students and, while doing so, to draw unhesitatingly on the past tradition of the Federation with all its missionary, intellectual, social, and political connotations. This meant actively contesting tendencies to give the Federation a distinct Marxist Christian profile or to make it subservient to any one political ideology. In my mind advocates of anarchist tendencies were among those to be restrained, as they had nothing to offer but a recipe for total disintegration of the WSCF and the sacrifice of most of what the Christian faith and the Church through the ages had stood for on the altar of confusion and uncertainty.

12.2. Regrouping for New Battles

The conflict dividing the Federation did not end with the Tozanzo meeting. Disagreement within member movements and the Executive

---

3. An American pastor, Keith Chamberlain, who was stationed in Germany as a Frontier Intern of the United Presbyterian Church of the USA, was seconded to the WSCF until the end of May 1972, to function out of Germany. He was, however, unable to reactivate the work of the Political Commission.

Committee concerning the main task of the Federation continued. Redefined demarcation lines separated the Federation's leaders from one another more rigidly than before. Yet within the WSCF constituency there were still many member movements who had difficulty in understanding what the conflicts were all about and who were bewildered by the turmoil among members of the Executive Committee and staff.

The months of July and August 1971 were unusually active ones for the staff in Geneva, for those who met in Tokyo, and evidently also for members of the radical left group in the WSCF. The new phase of confrontation required a regrouping of both camps and a rapid development of new plans of action.

The general secretariat and its allies in the regional offices began deliberate strategic planning to keep the initiative in their hands and to limit the influence of the opposition. Military jargon crept into the vocabulary of the "headquarters," and a combative posture set the tone for much of the office.[4] The discovery of the opposition's confidential plans and the stepping up of security measures added spice to office routines. For the general secretariat the activities of the opposition were naturally of continuing concern, as their intentions unfolded only in fragments. After Tozanzo both sides began consciously to hide their strategies from one another. The sternness of the working atmosphere was pleasantly interrupted by the poetic contributions of Peter Musgrove. One day the following lines were placed on my desk:

There are Marxists at the bottom of my garden.
I wish to heaven that they would go away.

---

4. A professional military touch was added to the office operations by Peter Musgrove, the resources secretary. He had served from 1940 to 1945 in the Indian and British army, participating in war operations in Burma, North Africa, and Italy, and had received counterintelligence training in Ghana for the last stage of World War II. When he left the army to enter a theological college, he had the rank of major. It was at this time that he confided to the writer the history of his military background and how useful he unexpectedly had found it. In fact, a number of his memos to me from mid-1971 on were highlighted with quotes from statements of military strategists. He recommended the works by Clausewitz to the general secretariat as preparation for the 1972-73 Assembly.

They're turning rows of tulips into cadres
and telling all the pansies not to pray.
The ivy is condemned for exploitation,
The columbine — though not without a fight, —
has been pestered and cajoled,
even left out in the cold, to make it
twine towards the left and not the right.
They've divided my tomatoes into classes,
Even rhubarb has to toe the party line,
And the roses in their bed,
if they're white, and won't turn red
have been warned they'll hang —
like grapes upon the vine!

The first task for the general secretariat was to bring to a conclusion the question of the Communication office which the Tozanzo meeting had left hanging and to give notice to those whose appointments were to be discontinued. Upon my return from Japan, I went to meet with the number one candidate for communications, Aaron Tolen, who had left Tozanzo early for Bad Boll, Germany, to attend a WCC meeting on development. He promised to consider positively the invitation by the Executive Committee. He also suggested that the action of the Tozanzo meeting proposing three candidates in a given order of priority was perhaps more a declaration of the Federation's internal political and ideological priorities than an effort to strengthen the communication program. He himself was an advocate of regionalization but shunned supporting Marxist concepts of revolution. The final outcome, which emerged after several intricate maneuvers, was that Tolen agreed to carry out a few global communication functions, mainly related to the preparation of the Assembly, but would not give up his responsibility for the Africa programs nor leave Yaoundé.[5] In January 1972 the Planning Committee for the Assembly, which had been given authority to ratify the choice, decided to leave the Communication position in Geneva vacant and to use the funds saved for the Assembly.[6] By that

5. Letters from Tolen to Lehtonen, September 3 and November 9, 1971.
6. Minutes of the Planning Committee meeting held in Ibadan, Nigeria, from December 31, 1971 to January 3, 1972.

time all support and project staff related to the Political Commission and Communication unit had left the Federation.

The second major task was to carry out a thorough evaluation of the Federation after the Tozanzo meeting and to develop a meaningful strategy for the period until the next Assembly. Various reports by participants helped me to assess the situation, including the objectives of the opposition.[7] The main network of the general secretariat which arose out of the Tokyo group was called — half jokingly — the Strategic Staff Planning Group (SSPG).[8] I put together a seven-page confidential memorandum for the group, outlining five different scenarios for the Federation as it approached the next Assembly. I put forward options for a viable strategy which would renew clarity about the Federation's task among university students and teachers as well as contain the efforts of the opposition.[9]

The third task was to convene a meeting of the SSPG in the USA in conjunction with a team visit to American mission and campus ministry agencies and to selected local campuses. A voluminous pile of confidential correspondence between the general secretariat; the Africa, Asia, and Middle East regional offices; and the university world office of the Board of Mission of the United Methodist Church gives a vivid picture of the intensity and scope of the planning efforts. The meetings took place from October 1 to October 4, 1971, in New York. The most confidential one-day session was held, for the sake of discretion, in the residence of the executive secretary of the Orthodox Campus Commission of the USA, Paul Costapoulos, in the heart of Greenwich Village. Participants included Moonkyu Kang, Gabriel

---

7. Evaluative reports on Tozanzo from the side of the opposition to be found in the WSCF Archives include contributions from Mario Miegge of Italy, Karin Rodhe of Sweden, Rakethal Tsehlana of South Africa/United Kingdom, and other comments circulated by Milan Opocensky to participants in the WSCF Europe committee. A penetrating observer's report (in Finnish) was written by Eeva Karttunen of the Finnish SCM from the perspective of a person who did not want to take sides in the confrontation but who wanted to find out "what is underway" in the WSCF.

8. The SSPG included José Chipenda, Gabriel Habib, Moonkyu Kang, Peter Musgrove, and the writer from the WSCF staff, and Pharis Harvey of the United Methodist Church of the USA.

9. Risto Lehtonen, "Memorandum: An Evaluation of the WSCF Situation after Tozanzo 1971 and Possible Conclusions for a Viable Strategy," August 1971, WSCF Archives.

Habib, José Chipenda, Peter Musgrove, Pharis Harvey, Ruth Harris, and myself.

One more task was to ensure that the wider ecumenical community and supporting agencies of the Federation understood the situation, aspirations, and tensions within the WSCF. An opportunity for this arose when the National Council of Churches in the USA invited me to address the Program Board of its Division of Overseas Ministries in early November 1971. I prepared for this occasion a paper entitled "The Story of a Storm." It received fairly wide circulation, as an ecumenical agency called International Documentation on the Contemporary Church published it in its IDOC-North America series immediately after the meeting, without even consulting me. Encouraged by colleagues in the WCC, I prepared an expanded version of the paper under the same title. It was published by the WCC in its Study Encounter series in early 1972.[10]

"The Story of a Storm" evoked numerous responses from various continents, most of them positive. Asian colleagues in the WSCF wanted to make it an official background document for the WSCF Assembly. Aaron Tolen of the Africa secretariat welcomed the paper but was concerned about its impact on the Federation as well as on the WCC because it dealt with uncomfortable issues. Opposition groups, who tended to label the writer a reactionary, expressed strong resentment about the paper.[11] Richard Shaull discouraged me from publishing it.[12] Some of the more radical left staff members of the WCC disapproved of the theses in the paper and criticized the staff member, Stephen Mackie, who was responsible for including it in the WCC Study Encounter series.[13] Nevertheless, the analysis and the conclusions drawn in the document complemented the SSPG strategy memorandum by spelling out the theological perspectives of the

10. SE/18, Study Encounter, vol. 8, no. 1/1972, World Council of Churches.

11. The written responses of Marco Rostan of the Italian SCM and of Bas Wielinga of the Netherlands represent the Christian Marxist views. Documents in the WSCF Archives.

12. Letter from Shaull to Lehtonen, February 23, 1972.

13. Philip Potter, prior to his election in mid-1972 as general secretary of the WCC, expressed orally on several occasions his unease about the publication of "The Story of a Storm" on the grounds that it was unhelpful to the WCC in its struggle for new directions.

group, thereby undergirding the practical strategy to which the SSPG became committed.

The regrouping of the opposition took a little more time. Milan Opocensky, leader of the Europe office, had been left on his own to keep the radical left flag flying in the Geneva office and to serve as coordinator of militant left causes. The chairman of the WSCF, Richard Shaull, with his controversial, even polarizing ideas about revolution as the model for Christian response to the crisis of institutions, was drifting further from the operational center of the Federation. Quite apart from the distance between Princeton and Geneva, his apocalyptic revolutionary vision and the scarcity of tangible suggestions from him to the WSCF and its member movements made him increasingly remote from the rank and file of the Federation.

Becoming the center of the opposition after the closure of the Political Commission's office had a visible effect on the priorities and style of work of the Europe secretariat. The tone of circulars from the office indicates that, parallel to serving the European SCMs and coordinating the European regional program, it had assumed a wider responsibility, among those member movements which were open to its views, for contesting the measures of the general secretariat. The office also launched the *WSCF Europe* bulletin, which, in addition to serving as an information forum for European member movements, continued the functions and even the style of the political newsletter *Question,* discontinued after the departure of Claudius Ceccon. The first major gathering of the opposition was the meeting of an expanded WSCF Europe committee in Cinisello, Italy, December 10-12, 1971. The commitment to Marxist socialism gave a sense of unity and purpose to the WSCF Europe program.

Even if the influence of Shaull as an ideological leader of the Federation was diminished after Tozanzo, he did not leave the opposition to the advocates of Marxist ideology. This became manifest when, after a silence of several months, he resumed active participation in the discussion about the future of the Federation. He did this in a ten-page open letter, dated November 3, 1971, addressed to members of the Executive Committee and staff. In it he presented an explicit response to the Tozanzo meeting and to the general secretary's report, and a comprehensive picture of his position concerning the course ahead for the Federation. This is discussed in more detail in the next section. At the same time he also distanced himself from the Marxist Christian position becoming prevalent in Europe.

It is still difficult today to determine what detailed planning was carried out among leaders of the opposition group. Documents about it are less numerous in the archives than materials on the activities of the general secretariat. However, the basic theological and political positions of the two opposition camps, and naturally those of the general secretariat and its allies, all of whom regrouped after Tozanzo, can be reconstructed accurately.[14] The regrouping was completed toward the end of 1971.

12.3. Objectives on the Way to the Assembly

12.3.1. Richard Shaull Group

The purpose of Richard Shaull's open letter of November 1971 was to present his views once more to members of the Executive Committee and staff. He now expressed explicitly his disagreement with the approach of the general secretariat and some of the key decisions made at Tozanzo and hoped that his vision would make an impact on the course of the Federation.

Shaull's point of departure was that the Federation was now on its way to adopting new patterns of work and organization. He underlined the roles of the different regions. For him the turmoil of Tozanzo signaled a creative chaos in which the old forms were dying and opportunities for the new to be born were arising. "We are on the threshold of new developments. . . ."

He also drew attention to obstacles which might lead to a failure to grasp the imminent possibilities. Loyalty to the past and uncertainty about new alternatives were the most obvious. Inherited structures blocked creativity. A respect for tradition prevented the Federation from concentrating on what is important today. These obstacles had to be overcome so that the Federation could create for itself a realm of freedom, even if it had to live under the limitations imposed on it

---

14. Some of the issues which have significance beyond the immediate WSCF context are discussed in chapter 15.

by existing social and church structures which could not be readily discarded.

Shaull's "program" consisted of redefining the major issues facing the Federation and establishing new priorities. The main issues which he listed were the vocation of the Federation, the question of its Christian identity, and the definition of its constituency. In the existing situation all of them required a radically new approach.

The maintenance of a pattern of work which was relevant to yesterday's world and its institutional stability made no sense at a time when there was a universal crisis of institutions. The same was true of inherited theological propositions: "The traditional Christian language and world view has lost most of its meaning, and there is no visible community of faith on which we can depend." "Even speaking about the meaning of faith in Jesus Christ has become problematic." According to Shaull, most of theology was a product of the culture and church of the oppressor West and North, and therefore an inadequate foundation on which to build Christian identity. In the same vein other philosophies of the North, such as those of Aristotle, Hegel, or modern existentialism, and even Marxism, had proved inadequate. Moreover, the decline of SCMs, for which Shaull found evidence all over the world, was for him simply an illustration of the universal breakdown of institutions and structures.

He felt that the only meaningful course for the Federation was to take the plunge into an inevitable chaos with all its uncertainties. There it would find a community of persons who shared the same loss of certitudes and who were willing to support each other in a search for new patterns of vocation, new expressions for Christian self-identity, and a new form of horizontal relationships between communities open to the future in a situation in which there were no valid blueprints for faith. They would give the lead to the WSCF at a time of inescapable "floundering."

Shaull summed up his view on what the Federation already de facto was:

> The Federation is no longer the clearly-defined, well structured, prestigious ecumenical organization it once was. It is rather an institution threatened by the disintegration of member movements, plagued by the limitations of its structures, uncertain about

its vocation. But in the midst of this crisis, the Federation is a small, loosely-knit community of men and women around the world who are engaged in the task of creation in a time of transition. As they attempt to participate in the struggle for liberation where they are, they also contribute to the Federation's discovery of its vocation, to the shaping of a new Christian self-identity and to new forms of community.[15]

Shaull warned against a power struggle in the Federation. Such a struggle would deprive the Federation of its creative role at a time of transition. Some seemed to have "a strong desire to establish a power base from which to fight for the preservation of the structure we now have and oppose vigorously all those who do not go along with them." If such efforts were successful, the whole process of searching which he advocated would be delayed or even made impossible. On the other hand, there were those "who want to do everything possible to take power from those who now have it." In Shaull's view such efforts were focused on rival claims for leadership, while the real issues were the vocation and self-identity of the Federation. "If we knew what to do, one group could claim that it could do it better than another." According to Shaull, no such knowledge was available to the Federation.

However, Shaull's open letter offered little guidance for the development of any programmatic approach. For him "programs" were part of the old structures. He did sum up his personal commitments as chairman of the WSCF for the coming year. They were (1) the search for ways in which the WSCF could function efficiently with less money — drawing on the experiences of communities experimenting with new lifestyles; (2) restructuring the Federation according to "emerging patterns of horizontal relationships" as an alternative to the "hierarchical" and "bureaucratic" structures inherited from the past; and (3) initiation of conversations "with a few people I already know" to explore questions of the Federation's vocation and its Christian identity.

Shaull's main recommendation to the staff of the WSCF and the members of the Executive Committee was that regional leaders be

15. Richard Shaull, "An Open Letter to Members of Staff and of the Executive Committee," November 3, 1971, p. 5.

urged to look for individuals and groups whose participation in the Federation would be important at this time and who could contribute to a new understanding of its vocation and of its Christian self-understanding, and to the defining of new criteria for membership. When the efforts of such regional groups were brought together, they would lead, not to a new uniformity, but to a new dynamic diversity, significant not only for the Federation but more widely for the whole ecumenical movement.

It is noted that Shaull had toned down his emphasis on revolutionary politics, on the struggle against capitalism and for liberation and justice, and on the necessity of tearing down all institutions and structures. The open letter placed the accent on internal WSCF matters and on the transformation of the WSCF into a viable international community with a sense of vocation and a Christian identification.

12.3.2. Christians for Socialism — Perspective of the WSCF Europe Group

The main forum for bringing together the ideas and proposals from the Marxist Christian wing of the opposition was the expanded European committee meeting at Cinisello, Italy, December 10-12, 1971. The picture given by its minutes is complemented by the circulars and other materials produced by the Europe office and also by reactions to the paper "The Story of a Storm."

The reiterated priority of the WSCF Europe region was to promote "the struggle for socialism in Europe." The WSCF was to facilitate cooperation between students and the working class, and to promote socialist awareness among SCMs. It should encourage alternative ways of life to the patterns of consumerism. The programs in Europe should center on education. A regional conference was proposed to deal with the economic basis of the educational system. The use of Paulo Freire's educational method, which had been developed for "conscientizing" oppressed people in Latin America to assume responsibility for their own lives and communities, was foreseen as a way to link the European program with liberation movements and other international issues. Documentation on these concerns was to be circulated among member movements. Most of the persons who were asked to select and provide such documentation represented the Marxist left wing of the Federation.[16]

The Cinisello meeting of the Europe group dedicated much of its time to evaluating and following up the Tozanzo Executive Committee meeting. The structure of the WSCF and its Geneva office was criticized, particularly its salary policies which, it was claimed, epitomized the class society. This was considered a major reason why the headquarters was so out of touch with "the new reality of the regions." The question of moving the headquarters out of Geneva was also hinted at.

The meeting tackled several issues raised at Tozanzo, including the question of Christian identity. It was noted that many SCMs experienced bewilderment about the incompatibility of politicized Christian student groups with traditional church and university institutions. The consensus was that the SCMs and the WSCF must continue to live with this tension. Therefore, in contrast to Shaull's position, new constituencies should not be favored at the expense of traditional member movements. Churches were called to help people move away from the inherited concepts of Christian tradition into active engagement in the struggle against capitalism and for a more just society understood in Marxist socialist terms. The need for an international headquarters for the WSCF was affirmed. Its main tasks were to be fund-raising and transregional communication.

The meeting produced a summary of its views on the vocation, tasks, and structures of the WSCF. The rationale of the WSCF as a "mass organization" consisting of "movements, groups and individuals with a Christian background" was reaffirmed. It was also seen as part of the ecumenical movement with a particular calling to be a dissenting element in matters such as Christian witness and expressing Christian identity. The task of the WSCF as a world organization was to provide opportunities for transnational and trans- and interregional meetings. As a partner with the international nongovernmental organizations (NGOs), the role of the Federation was also to protect

16. The group named consisted of Carol Barker of the United Kingdom, with David Head as an alternate, Marco Rostan of Italy, Keith Chamberlain of the United States, and an additional person from West Germany. Minutes of the WSCF European Meeting (enlarged), Cinisello, Italy, December 10-12, 1971. WSCF Archives.

member movements who came under political pressures. However, the test of the credibility of the WSCF was the extent to which it was on the side of "the oppressed and exploited." The style of its work should be consistently "anti-capitalist, participatory and radically democratic." A team of colleagues was envisaged for the headquarters who would "work together on equal terms, dividing the functions of communication, fund-raising and interpretation."[17]

In light of its minutes, the Cinisello meeting looked far less polemical than some of the documents sent out from the Europe office and also some of the European responses to "The Story of a Storm." For example, a paper dealing with the priorities of the WSCF European region, circulated by the Europe office at the beginning of 1972 as a follow-up of the Cinisello meeting, stated:

> We affirm the necessity of a proletarian struggle against capitalism, the bourgeoisie and their allies in all European countries. This struggle demands some immediate and large sacrifices with only small successes. But it is the only basis on which we can patiently build a real alternative to capitalism.[18]

In view of the forthcoming Assembly, it was assumed that the Europe region with its anticapitalist orientation would find common ground with students from countries which had been colonized by the West.

The Europe secretary, Milan Opocensky, continued at this time to encourage theological work in the Federation. Consequently he carried on compiling a "Theological Dossier," which consisted of articles by a variety of authors written from different perspectives, and circulated it to European member movements and also to other regional offices. The dossier aimed to transcend European concerns and stimulate worldwide discussion of the issues at stake.[19]

17. Minutes of the WSCF European Meeting.

18. "Priority Program of the WSCF European Region 1972," a paper circulated by the Europe office, February 1972, mimeographed, author not mentioned, WSCF Archives.

19. The contributors included Richard Shaull (WSCF chairman), Ruben Alves (Brazil), Laurence Bright (British SCM), Staf Callewaert, James H. Cone (Union Theological Seminary, New York), Alastair Hulbert (Scottish SCM), Raymond Rizk

In the covering letter of October 20, 1971, to member movements Opocensky reacted to the Tozanzo meeting and accused some participants of circulating rumors and trying to discredit others:

> It is suggested that non-Christian (perhaps anti-Christian?) forces are trying to seize power in the Federation . . . a handful of the Christian faithful makes every attempt to defend and protect the Federation against irresponsible leftist radicals who put themselves outside the framework of the Christian community.

He then described how he saw the antagonisms and tensions, which he admitted were very real.

> The division reflects the existing rupture within larger sections of the Christian "community" caused by sharply differing views on what social involvement and political action can and should be undertaken by Christians, how to read contemporary history, how to make our faith manifest in an explosive situation.

He maintained that such a rupture was a universal phenomenon experienced in the ecumenical movement and in many institutions of the church. However, in his view, it would be "fatal" to equate politicization with de-Christianization. He also warned against a desire to "excommunicate" or purge members of the Christian community on the grounds of their political views.

The two Marxist Christian responses to "The Story of a Storm," from Marco Rostan of Italy and Bas Wielinga, a member of the Dutch SCM, were most critical.[20] Rostan's paper was circulated among the European SCMs by the Europe office. Both condemned the writer for his separation "from the masses" and for a lack of real local involvement in the struggle against oppressive structures in society and in the church. Rostan maintained that my whole perspective was

---

(Orthodox Church of Antioch), Josef Smolik (Comenius Faculty, Prague), Barbara Troxell (American YWCA), P. N. Williams and Joe Williamson (*Motive Magazine,* USA). In addition some papers produced by consultations of the Europe region in 1969 and 1970 were included. WSCF Archives.

20. The two letters are in the WSCF Archives.

wrong on the grounds that I presupposed that reality is derived from ideas, while correct ideas can only be derived from political "praxis." He also claimed that the concept of Church in my paper was in substance crypto-Catholic, as it seemed to presume that Christ was held as a possession of the church and the church then controlled the gospel and denied its freedom. Third, the paper did not recognize any connection between the crises experienced in the WSCF and the political and economic crises affecting capitalist countries. More specifically the paper bypassed class analysis and therefore did not reach the real issues at stake in human liberation and in the elimination of exploitation and oppression. Moreover, Rostan felt that the writer was condescending with regard to Marxists and Marxist Christians and tried to place himself above political conflicts. Finally, he suggested that ultimately the Federation suffered from an inherited undemocratic institutional structure which had fed a managerial mentality among its leadership. A change would come through a modification of the Federation's structures, through eliminating material inequalities among its personnel, and through appointing staff who would be socially and politically involved and who would work with the proletariat.

The main objectives of the Marxist Christian wing were (1) to defend the right to interpret the Christian faith by means of Marxist categories and within a Marxist frame of reference; (2) to move the WSCF structures in a more egalitarian direction and to eliminate class contradictions within them; (3) to implement cooperation between the WSCF and the working class/proletariat by choosing staff who were personally involved in such cooperation; (4) to promote through the Federation's programs in every region a consciousness of the class struggle and an understanding of socialism as a political approach coming closest to the teachings of Christ.

12.3.3. The General Secretariat and the Strategic Staff Planning Group (SSPG)

The paper "The Story of a Storm" summed up the basic assumptions which undergirded the objectives of the SSPG in preparation for the Assembly. It dealt extensively with the role of the WSCF and of the

Christian community in the political and ideological struggles of the day, an issue which was at the center of the controversy. The SSPG felt it was imperative for the Federation to become clear on its part in working toward a just society, human liberation, and the elimination of exploitation and oppression. The group was convinced that political ideologies should not set the agenda for the whole Federation nor even determine its functions in the realm of political witness. The witness of the Christian community, including the WSCF, among and within secular political movements and organizations which claimed to represent the exploited and the oppressed, was nevertheless an unquestioned part of the divine calling of the church. It was a response to God's own intervention in the world through the life, suffering, death, and resurrection of Jesus Christ. The people of God — the church, the Christian community, or whatever it was called — was, by God's choice, an indispensable part of his action in the world. The group concluded that the main point of the current controversy was, however, not whether the Christian community should be involved in struggles for justice and liberation, but how to judge each situation, how to act, and how to relate to political movements active in the same struggle. These questions were also troubling the waters within the ecumenical movement, including the WCC and the Lutheran World Federation.

The SSPG rejected the possibility that the Federation, as part of the wider Christian community, the Church universal, could redefine its vocation simply through a set of political commitments or through a particular understanding of the causes of social conflicts. Marxist class analysis was one among many tools for interpreting the human situation under oppressive conditions. Nor was the Christian community — the WSCF included — a formless entity floating without direction on the waves of social and political movements and seeking answers to questions of vocation and identity. The confession of faith in Jesus Christ was the source of the commitment in the Christian community. The story of God's saving acts and the confession that Jesus is the Christ were the foundations of the Christian faith. The confession of faith in Christ was also the source of continuity in times of crisis. In this confession, past and present struggles of the Christian community meet. The meaning of God's saving acts had to be interpreted to new generations and to people in new cultural and social contexts in each new phase of history. The Christian community often discovered the significance of its faith also for itself when witnessing to Christ amidst uncertainties and ambiguities.

In line with the preparatory document of August 1971 and the later paper "The Story of a Storm," the SSPG affirmed that confessing Christ in the contemporary world compelled the Christian community to deal with social and political realities and to participate in the struggle for a just society, for human liberation, and for the elimination of exploitation and oppression. But for Christians this was part of a much broader struggle that has gone on throughout the centuries in varying forms, a struggle of which the political aspect was only one dimension, even when the prevailing conditions presented overwhelming political challenges to the church. For the health of the Federation it was essential to tackle not only the political challenges but also the other dimensions of discipleship.

In the same vein the SSPG questioned the possibility of the Federation having a clearly defined political role of its own. Uniformity seemed excluded purely on the grounds of regional diversities. The document recognized nevertheless the positive challenge of contemporary political movements, including those which had shaken the Federation, to a renewed sense of discipleship. It also welcomed the new profile that seemed to be emerging through the contributions of regional groups and through great cultural, religious, and political diversity.

Furthermore, the SSPG emphasized the openness of the Christian community to men and women of other persuasions. It was to be as open to all people as Christ himself was. The confession of Christ was in radical conflict with all political or religious intolerance. The tendency toward intolerance in recent confrontations within the Federation underlined the necessity of affirming radical openness to one another.

The confidential memorandum for the SSPG listed five alternative scenarios for the Federation at the next Assembly. They were (1) a radical takeover which would make the WSCF into a political organization with a Christian history and which would imply a revision of its aims as stated in the constitution and have repercussions for its relationship with churches and the ecumenical movement; (2) a paralyzing conflict about the orientation of the Federation would continue into the next quadrennium with the result that its value to the member movements and also their interest in the WSCF would diminish; (3) a constructive truce would become possible, even if the ideological disagreements could not be resolved, and conditions for a genuine respect of regional and ideological diversity and for a recovery of dialogue would be created; (4) an open split between the extreme radical left and the rest of the Federation would occur, leading to a disaffiliation of some member movements and leaving the question of the identity of the Federation still unresolved; (5) the Assembly would provide a new departure and the emergence of a new identity for the Federation, with a new generation of SCM leaders and students creating a different atmosphere and burying the ideological and power conflicts characteristic of the current quadrennium.

The approach of the SSPG was to avoid at all costs (1) and (2) and to aim for (5), but with an openness to any combination of (3), (4), and (5). It was foreseen that reaching this goal depended upon three regions: Africa, Asia, and the Middle East. Therefore, the regional offices were expected to play a major role in involving member movements in the preparation of the Assembly. In Europe there were several movements which were confused about the conflict and also about the increasing pressure from the European committee to bring all the movements into line with the stated priority emphasis of the region. These movements should be contacted by members of the SSPG. The Latin America region seemed to be strong in words but weak in work. Therefore, the regional leaders and, where possible, the movements should be approached with a combination of patience, understanding, and frankness. In North America the two remaining national student movements in the USA, i.e., the Lutheran and the Orthodox, and the Canadian SCM were likely to support the approach of the SSPG. Contacts with them and with campus ministry agencies prior to the Assembly were foreseen. The All Africa Youth and Student Conference being prepared for the Christmas season of 1971 and the next sessions of the Asia Leadership Development Center were considered to be significant events which were likely to inspire member movements and help them face decisions about the future of the Federation. Possibilities were explored for inviting some key participants from Europe, North America, and Latin America to these events. Finally it was agreed that the support community in North America and Europe should be kept informed about developments and problems in the WSCF.

There was one significant point of agreement among the three groups after the Tozanzo meeting. The regionalization of the WSCF was unanimously reaffirmed, not only as a matter of conviction, but in light of the progress of the work in four of the six regions. Even if the reasons for welcoming it varied from region to region, this agreement proved to have a major impact on the planning of the Assembly.

CHAPTER 13

The Final Stretch, 1972

In 1972, the last year of the quadrennium, the life of the Federation had at least three different faces. Many member movements continued to plow on steadily, paying little attention to what was happening outside their own region or in Geneva. The WSCF programs in Africa, Asia, and the Middle East served them effectively at a time when the Federation as a whole was divided by ideological conflict. New students were drawn into the Christian community, participation in the life of the WSCF stimulated SCMs and churches' ministries in their witness to the university community and in their search for new ecumenical expressions of commitment to the renewal of the church and to social justice and development.

In Europe, Latin America, and North America both the constituency and the regional leaders of the Federation were captured by the vision of an anticapitalist struggle which they believed was to transform the world, and of which they wanted the WSCF to be a part. They failed to recognize that the momentum of the radical revolutionary movement had already died, and that the just society to which they were aspiring had proved to be a deceptive mirage. In these regions most SCMs were rapidly shrinking and their political and theological programs were losing all appeal.

The Federation was heading toward its first Assembly in Africa. Preparation for this was almost the sole function of the Geneva office of the WSCF in that year. Once more the task stimulated some sincere, even desperate, efforts to heal the division within the Federation, involving persons from both sides of the conflict. But it also became the main battleground in the war between the two factions among the constituency and staff.

13.1. Regions

In Africa extensive visits by the three WSCF regional secretaries, José Chipenda, Bethuel Kiplagat, and Aaron Tolen, to member movements in more than twenty African countries began to bear fruit. The training courses for SCM leaders and university chaplains held in Dahomey (Benin), Zaire, Malawi, and Tanzania had been well attended, with participants from fifteen African countries. New movements were organized and drawn into the fellowship of the Federation. Bible study and attention to local, national, and continental issues which affected students and universities were the programmatic pillars of the national movements and of the Africa regional work as a whole. The regional staff described the characteristics of the Africa program:

> While Student Christian Organizations in other parts of the world are searching for modern political theories to justify their action, SCMs in Africa remain Bible-centered. As in the previous quadrennium, the Bible was again extensively used, each time occasioning real excitement among the students and generating living connections between the message and the meaning of the text and the contemporary situation in Africa. It may be a passing phase, but for the moment this still seems to be the case.[1]

Cooperation with churches had been visibly strengthened since the establishment of regional offices in Nairobi and Yaoundé. The All Africa Conference of Churches (AACC) was represented on the regional committee. The year 1972 saw considerable consolidation of the SCMs and the WSCF in Africa.

The All Africa Youth and Student Conference, held from Decem-

---

1. Africa Regional Report, 1968-1972, p. 8. Most regional reports were printed in the Minutes of the Twenty-Sixth Meeting of the General Assembly of the WSCF, Addis Ababa, Ethiopia, December 28, 1972–January 9, 1973. However, the Africa and the Middle East reports were mimeographed separately.

ber 20 to 31, 1971, cosponsored by the AACC, was the climax of this era. Its theme, "In Search of a New Society," set the overall tone for the WSCF Africa region as it prepared for the Assembly of the Federation at the end of 1972. It injected new vigor into the SCMs and gave them an increased sense of belonging together as they sought to define their role in the postindependence era of Africa. At the same time, the conference became an African prelude to the last phase of the Federation's crisis in this quadrennium.

The conference was held on the campus of the University of Ibadan, Nigeria. It brought together some two hundred delegates from twenty-six countries in Africa, and some observers from Europe, Latin America, and North America, of whom a group of African-Americans made the most vocal and controversial contribution. The first all-Africa WSCF conference in Nairobi, nine years earlier, at a time when most of the countries had just reached political independence, had radiated contagious enthusiasm for a free Africa and confidence in its future. The 1971 event was overshadowed by a sense of the failure of national development endeavors and by disappointment with both national leaders and the world community. Gone was the sense of hope of the 1963 conference which had made such a strong impact on the whole Federation.

Furthermore, the conference was influenced by the change of mood in the Federation and in the ecumenical movement as a whole. It had been planned as a thoroughly participatory event, with few plenary addresses. The main topics were development, education, and African identity and personality. African delegates saw in the radicalism of the North a sign of fading global solidarity and a tendency to abandon Africa as a politically insignificant continent. The clash between African delegates and some of the radical African-American visitors proved symptomatic. "You are not African enough," proclaimed one of the American "soul brothers," when telling about his "coming home" to Africa. The response of the African chair was chilly: "Our American guests may not quite grasp what Africa is."[2] Representatives of African liberation move-

2. It was an awkward exchange in a plenary, after which most of the African-American group withdrew to meet by themselves. The atmosphere was not improved by their reaction to the food at the student dormitory. They somehow found their way to the faculty club of the university, where the food was more acceptable to them. Personal notes of the writer.

ments made the most profound impact on the conference. They impressed participants with their commitment, their high level of education, and their vision. Their idea of liberation contrasted with that of "black power," which, especially in its American form, found little resonance. The conference concluded that

> Almost everywhere and above all in the USA the success of the black man will not come out of a racial confrontation but will be the result of carefully selected social, economic and political objectives which can be mobilized by different racial groups for the attainment of a truly just society.[3]

The consolidation of the Africa region did not proceed without difficulties and setbacks. The South African University Christian Movement was discontinued. A wave of student unrest on campuses shook most universities and caused disruption, although no single unifying concern or political position could be detected in them. Communication between African SCMs and the rest of the WSCF remained rather sparse. The Federation as a whole seemed to lose interest in the problems of Africa and seemed to have become preoccupied with issues and concerns foreign to it. The confrontations within the Federation were incomprehensible to most Africans, who were thus poorly prepared to cope with the politics of the WSCF when finally forced to face it at the Assembly in Addis Ababa.

In Asia most SCMs had had a much longer history. Cultural and religious diversity was a significant characteristic of the region. Also, political systems varied from country to country. The movements in India, Sri Lanka, and Indonesia, with their numerous branches and large membership, represented continuity and stability. Those in Korea, Singapore, and especially the Philippines had to cope with harsh dictatorial regimes that dealt with dissent by repression. In Pakistan, Thailand, Burma, and Hong Kong, Christians were a tiny minority among adherents of strong religious traditions.

The Asian student population was not dominated by any single political ideology, unless a general anti-American or anticolonial sentiment is so considered. Japan was rising rapidly from the ranks of the

3. Africa Regional Report, 1968-1972, p. 8.

developing countries and knocking at the door of the club of economic big powers. China, most of Indo-China, and Burma were still isolated from the rest of the world. Only in Burma was there an SCM, indeed a lively one, able to function under the umbrella of the Baptist Church.

The WSCF had made long strides in Asia between 1968 and the beginning of 1972. The Asian Leadership Development Center (ALDEC), which had been launched in 1970 after intensive preparation, soon became the backbone of the regional program. The courses held in 1970 and 1971 took place at the Tozanzo training center of the Japanese YMCA, from where field trips were made to Tokyo and other sites in Japan. The 1972 course was brought for part of its duration from Japan to the Philippines so participants would experience personally the contrast between a multicultural, socially and economically under-developed part of Asia and the rapidly industrializing part.

On each occasion nearly all Asian SCMs sent their present or potential leaders to ALDEC to be trained together for Christian witness and service in Asian universities. In addition several campus ministers and young university teachers attended. ALDEC made on Asian SCMs an impact which was felt over many years, even decades. The materials which were produced in preparation for the courses became a testimony to the outstanding intellectual and theological work in which the Asian leaders of the Federation of this quadrennium involved the region's students and teachers.[4]

The enormous scope of university education, academic pressures, and large-scale poverty in much of Asia and the physical distance between its countries and subregions, from Afghanistan to New Zea-

---

4. ALDEC stimulated the production of study documents which were first used at its seminar sessions and later published as WSCF Books and as pamphlets of the Asia Study Fellowship (ASF) Series. Many more were circulated by the WSCF Asia office in a mimeographed form and can be found in the WSCF Asia office archives in Hong Kong. The titles of the ASF publications of the 1968-73 period are *The Secular and Secularization,* by Emerito P. Nacpil; *Pressures on University,* by Chandran Devanesen; *The Domination of Technical Knowledge and Its Effect on Values,* by Yung Hak Hyun; *Development Planning and the Economic Situation in Asian Countries,* by Tsuneo Nagauchi; *International Politics and Social Change in Asia Today and Tomorrow,* by Ross Terrill; *Ideology in the Modern World,* by Anwar Barkat; *Developmental Challenges in Asia and Our Responsibilities,* by Saral Chatterji. The WSCF Books *China, the Peasant Revolution* and *The Modern Idea of Revolution* included materials produced in conjuction with ALDEC, both edited by Bruce Douglass, 1972.

land and from Sri Lanka to Japan and Korea, had always made it difficult to bring the leaders of the various movements together, to develop an all-Asian identity for the student Christian community, and to enable its members to challenge one another over substantive issues. By its success in creating a regionwide community of SCM leaders and university pastors ALDEC was a breakthrough in expanding and deepening the work of the Federation in Asia.

Most leaders of the WSCF Asia region came at times under ideological sniper fire from the radical left. This was especially true of the Asia secretary, Moonkyu Kang, who seemed to be immune to any intimidation in defending the purpose and integrity of the Asian program. The customary allegations by left radicals about bureaucratic mentality or authoritarian decision making did not succeed in perturbing the work of the Asia office. The meetings of the Asia committee provided for regular evaluation in which criticism from both inside and outside was considered. As a result of the 1972 evaluation of ALDEC, the regional committee concluded that in the case of Asia the Federation should go further in decentralizing its programs by organizing its training activities in the subregions of its huge territory.

The Middle East program of the WSCF, which was part of the joint WSCF and WCC youth and student program, had developed rapidly after a consultation in Nicosia, October 1969, on ecumenical youth and student work. The consultation had resulted in the formation of an advisory committee for the entire WSCF/WCC youth program in the region. Its members represented a wide spectrum of Christian youth and student organizations active in the Middle East, including the Near East Council of Churches.

At its last meeting, in November 1972 in Beirut, the advisory committee reviewed the work of the whole quadrennium. New elements had been added to the overall program in late 1971. They included an ambitious effort to involve Christian youth and students in regional concerns for society, development, and peace. Teny Simonian of the Armenian Orthodox Church in Lebanon had been invited to the staff in Beirut to coordinate this work. Another addition was the program on sociopolitical commitment under the leadership of Tarik Mitri of the Orthodox Church of Syria and Lebanon. This program sought to combine study and action and to keep them within the circle of the churches' responsibility, while relating also to the radical student and youth endeavors on other continents. Besides the new emphases, the regional office was heavily engaged in promoting Christian education. The tenseness of the political atmosphere caused by the Israeli occupation of Palestinian territories in Jerusalem, the West Bank, and Gaza was naturally felt in all these activities.

In the period when the relationship between SCMs and churches was deteriorating in Europe and Latin America, churches in the Middle East were joining with vigor in the work among youth and students. The charismatic ecumenical leader of students and youth, Gabriel Habib, himself a member of the Orthodox Church, played a decisive role in bringing ecumenical youth and student movements in the Middle East together and opening doors for youthful ecumenical cooperation both in the ancient historic churches of the Orthodox and Catholic traditions and among Protestants. At the end of the quadrennium a merger of the expanded ecumenical youth and student office and the Near East Council of Churches into the Middle East Council of Churches was already being negotiated. The new regional body was to represent all the main Christian traditions of the region.

Latin American regional work suffered from paralysis. Only a modest training event, a "mini-CLAF" (Communidad Latino-Americana para Formacion), was organized in conjunction with relief and reconstruction efforts in rural Peru after the devastating earthquake in 1970, and a continental consultation was held in Chile in 1972. Meaningful as these events were for their participants, virtually no information on them was communicated in writing to the national movements or to the Federation. The WSCF regional program had suffocated in the repressive atmosphere existing under military governments and in the internal weakness of the ecumenical student movement in Latin America.

The central event of the year for the Europe region was the European student conference in Strobl, Austria, October 30–November 3, 1972. It concentrated on preparations for the forthcoming WSCF Assembly, dealing with future plans for the Europe program and the overall politics of the Federation. The anticapitalist struggle and its theological foundation continued to be the main issues pursued.

In North America concern for women's liberation was on the regional agenda more visibly after Jan Griesinger was added as a project staff member in late 1971. The WSCF constituency continued in some disarray through the whole of 1972. The SCM of Canada was the only affiliated member with voting rights. The rest included two U.S.-based associated organizations — the Lutheran Student Movement and the Church Society for College Work — and a variety of American campus groups and caucuses. In addition an advisory group on WSCF–Mission Board relations functioned backstage to keep the Federation concerns alive in churches and ensure their financial support. These groups were assumed to represent the presence of the WSCF on the continent.

The North American constituency gathered in Toronto on December 9-10, 1972, for a consultation between the Canadian SCM and USA representatives. It dealt almost exclusively with organizational questions, listing future program possibilities, establishing a new WSCF regional committee, and finalizing technical preparations for North American participation in the Assembly.

Throughout the year the Federation became increasingly dispersed, and awareness in the member movements of being part of a worldwide Christian community diminished. Particular regional concerns, some well thought through and some rather fragmented, filled the minds of most delegates as they prepared for the Addis Ababa Assembly.

13.2. Preparation of the Assembly

In the last year of the quadrennium the preparation of the Assembly, scheduled for December 28, 1972, to January 9, 1973, in Addis Ababa, rose to the top of the agenda of the Federation as a whole. The preparatory work was guided by the Assembly Planning Committee, appointed at Tozanzo, which in the interim, until the meeting in Addis Ababa, was also to act on behalf of the Executive Committee on all pending matters, including staff and budget. The preparation for the meetings of this committee and the implementation of its decisions was the most important task of the head office in 1972.

In addition to the inevitable organizational and technical tasks, the preparatory work for the Assembly presupposed extensive consultation with member movements and regional offices about suggested changes in the constitution. Moreover, efforts had to be made to generate a working vision for the Federation to help rid itself of the ongoing devastating ideological war. It was vital to promote discussion among member movements in every region about the future task of the Federation so that they would be equipped to make informed decisions at the Assembly. The deadlock in communication between opposing groups made this preparatory task exceptionally demanding.

The Planning Committee met for the first time from December 31, 1971, to January 3, 1972, at the Church and Society Institute, Ibadan, Nigeria, immediately after the All Africa Youth and Student Conference; and a second time from June 10 to 14, 1972, in Annecy, France. The committee consisted largely of staff members.[5] The host movement for the Assembly, the Haimanote Abew Ethiopian Students Association (HAESA), was well represented at both meetings in an advisory capacity.

The first big task was to establish the quotas for member movements, Executive Committee members, and representatives of the supporting community, following the principles approved at Tozanzo that each affiliated movement was to have one voting delegate, that associated movements would be invited only if additional earmarked funds were to be available, and that each region was to name two of the members who represented it on the Executive Committee to participate. The constitution stated that all members of the Executive Committee had the right of vote at the Assembly. The voluntary restriction was prompted by the tightness of the budget and to avoid overrepresentation of the old guard in relation to the reduced number of delegates from member movements. It was evident that the WSCF was on the way to becoming a federation of six regions instead of a federation of member movements. No way could be found out of the situation in which the influence of small, even marginal movements, once granted affiliation, was increased out of proportion to that of movements with numerous branches and a large membership. The Europe committee, for example, proposed the affiliation of two small movements which hardly met the criteria of full membership.

5. The members of the Planning Committee were Aaron Tolen, Africa secretary; Moonkyu Kang, Asia secretary; Milan Opocensky, Europe secretary; Edir Cardoso, Latin America secretary; Tarik Mitri, student, Lebanon, Middle East region (unable to attend); Beth Hutchinson, student, Canada, North America region; Richard Shaull, chairman; Risto Lehtonen, general secretary. José Chipenda was present in staff capacity. Minutes of the Meeting of the Planning Committee for the WSCF General Assembly, Ibadan, Nigeria, December 31, 1971–January 3, 1972.

The Planning Committee agreed at its first meeting that the Assembly program should reflect the Federation's de facto regionalization. The first days should, therefore, be given to thorough regional exposure and discussion of regional programs. The second focal point was to be the change in the constitution which was expected to give some expression to this regionalization. In contrast with previous meetings, no plans were established for a discussion of fundamental convictions and concerns. The only space for stimulating such discussion would be provided by the addresses and reports of the chairman and the general secretary and those regional groups which found such considerations important.

All members of the Planning Committee had read "The Story of a Storm," but by a ruling of the chairman it was not taken up in the formal sessions of the Ibadan meeting. It was, however, discussed, perhaps all the more intensely, in the corridors. My hope to stimulate the Planning Committee to take up the issues involved and to plan for a discussion of them at the Assembly proved unrealizable.

The Planning Committee solved the controversy about the position of the Communication secretary by deciding not to fill the vacancy but to strengthen the communication role and capacity of regional offices for the purposes of Assembly preparation. It also decided to provide only one thousand dollars to wind up the Political Commission, thereby excluding the possibility of a full meeting.

The civilized tone of the first Planning Committee meeting was completely opposite to that at the last meeting of the Executive Committee. This led the chairman to suggest that the tension so far experienced had been overcome and that prospects for a constructive Assembly were good. The Africa secretary, José Chipenda, however, made the sobering remark that nothing had changed since Tozanzo, that the fight would have continued unabated had the same people been in Ibadan and Annecy as had participated in the Executive Committee six months earlier.[6]

6. A most thorough evaluation of the Ibadan meeting of the Planning Committee was given by Moonkyu Kang in his paper "Confidential Report of the First Planning Committee of the WSCF Assembly," January 1972. He expressed his basic satisfaction with the direction toward further regionalization. The alternative, in his view, would be fruitless continuation of ideological polarization. He also rejected in no unclear terms the ideas of "complete liquidation of the world headquarters" and "the Federation as another experimental tool for those who believe in small communities." Another source

291

The second meeting of the Planning Committee in Annecy concentrated by and large on constitutional change, based on proposals received from regional groups and some national movements or groups.[7] These reflected the desire of each region to ensure that no one from outside could interfere with its priorities and programs. The main responsibility for programs, financial support of member movements in need, budget and regional staff would be moved from the Executive Committee to the regional committees and groups. No one seemed any longer to imagine a complete control or takeover of the Federation by any single ideological group. In retrospect, it was as if each region and interest group was seeking to build fortifications or trenches around its own position in the Federation and thus prepare itself for another quadrennium of coexistence and power contestation.[8]

The question of future leadership of the Federation was touched upon at the Annecy meeting. I myself proposed that a nominating committee be appointed and an orderly procedure be launched to screen candidates for the positions of chairman, vice chairman, and

---

of interpretation of the Ibadan meeting is my own reporting letter to the vice chairman of the Federation, Samuel Parmar, of January 24, 1972, which reflected some reemerged optimism about the Assembly and the Federation's future. WSCF Archives.

7. Proposals for constitutional change had been received from Africa, Asia, Europe, the Middle East, the SCMs of Canada and Finland, and an informal group in the USA related to the Federation. The Europe region presented some additions, and different alternatives for Article II — Aims. For example, it had three alternatives to the first paragraph:

1. "To call its members to faith in God — Father, Son and Holy Spirit — according to the Scriptures"; or
2. add to the above: "and within the world-wide community of the Church" or
3. "to call them to the Christian faith questioning the way in which Christian witness is carried out and seeking a new expression of Christian identity."

It also proposed inclusion of such phrases as "a style of work which is radically democratic" and "struggle for the elimination of any type of exploitation." All regional groups proposed that the Executive Committee should have twelve members, two from each region. WSCF Archives.

8. The minutes of the two Planning Committee meetings provide a record of only the decisions and do not give any account of the preceding discussions. Therefore, information on the content and tone of the meetings can be found only in various confidential memoranda and correspondence about the planning work.

general secretary, as had been done prior to previous Assemblies. Chairman Richard Shaull, however, was totally opposed to this, and the Planning Committee was divided. The formal excuse for not appointing a nominating committee was that the outcome of the constitutional change would be decided only by the Assembly, so why nominate persons for positions which might no longer exist? As a consequence, formal preparations for the election of leaders were abandoned and the matter was left to informal, regional, and political caucuses. This inaction did not reduce political tension in the Federation.

The future of the general secretariat and the question of leadership after the Assembly were naturally consequential issues for me. The continued sharp conflicts within the Federation and the excessive concentration on ideological and organizational concerns had an alienating effect on me. With the division in the ranks and twenty years of full-time involvement in student work behind me, it was obvious to me that I should prepare to leave the Federation to move on to another field of work. In late 1971 I made my first soundings about a possible return to Finland after the Assembly. I did not, however, want to spread the impression that I was giving up and leaving the battlefield clear for the utopian revolutionaries. After careful consultation with my colleagues in the "strategy group" (SSPG), I decided to refrain from revealing my personal plans to a wider circle. The political objective was to keep the opposition in the dark and make its leaders uncertain. After all, I had not lost my conviction about the validity of the ecumenically and politically pluralist concept of the Federation and of its biblical and missionary tradition. It was therefore important to try to strengthen the ranks of those who shared this concept and to look for new leaders who could pursue such a vision in the years to come.

When the Executive Committee refused to establish an orderly search procedure, the "strategy group" began to make discreet investigations about who among competent and theologically balanced WSCF or SCM leaders would be both available and able to muster enough support to be elected as my successor. At the same time we wanted to make it as difficult as possible for those to be elected who in our view advocated a wrong cause. This part of the Assembly preparation was the most worrisome.

293

The second meeting of the Planning Committee took note of the voices of protest, emanating mainly from European movements, which questioned the choice of Addis Ababa as the venue for the Assembly. They felt that it was not proper for the Federation as a progressive organization to meet in territory controlled by such an extreme reactionary government as that of Emperor Haile Selassie, and that it would hardly be possible in such a setting to have an open discussion about the real concerns of the Federation for Africa and the world. The African leaders were particularly irritated by such criticism. They felt that Africans in the Federation were not considered as adult members by the critics and that their attitude was a symptom of perennial European arrogance which caused them to make decisions on African matters without listening to Africans. The regional advisory committee was asked to prepare a response to be circulated to all member movements. The statement, entitled "Welcome from Africa Region," written by Aaron Tolen on behalf of the regional group, began by describing what had happened during the years of decolonization and the first decade of African independence. It pointed to the unfinished task of political liberation of southern Africa and to the work ahead in independent countries. It stated that the Africa which was organizing itself with much difficulty wanted now to welcome the Assembly. The paper then continued:

We know that many of you have asked questions about our choice. Let us tell you frankly that Ethiopia comprises today almost all the features of contemporary Africa. You will have no need to visit several countries to perceive the sum of the efforts and the complete array of problems which are the fate of all Africans today. Look at the organization of power, question the social stratification, be impressed by the wealth of the few compared with the misery of the many. At the same time though, you should visit the O.A.U. [Organization of African Unity], talk with the representatives of the Liberation Movements, drink coffee with some civil servants of the U.N. Economic Council for Africa. Then you will realize the struggle, the contradictions, but also the possibilities which exist in Africa today. It is our conviction that the message of salvation as proclaimed by Isaiah and in our Lord Jesus Christ must be made flesh in our true context. . . . Do not look for a place where things would be easier, where work would be less handicapped, where your efforts would be less restricted. There are none.[9]

The statement silenced vocal criticism, although some murmurs continued throughout the Assembly.

The host movement, HAESA, named three persons to follow the international preparations of the Assembly. Two of them were well known through Federation activities in the previous years, and one, the chairman of the host committee, was a newcomer. It gradually became known that the chairman served also as the chief liaison person between the Assembly organizers and the government. The closer the time for Assembly came, the firmer was the grip of the host committee over technical arrangements. There were no problems with visas to Ethiopia. Accommodation was booked promptly in two hotels, with the host committee insisting on assuming responsibility for deciding on who stayed in which. Furthermore, strict rules were communicated to the office staff about the production and distribution of Assembly documents. Nothing could be mimeographed without the authorization of the general secretary. Finally, we were told that the host committee would make available a large number of its representatives, who were not registered in advance, to help with room assignments, transportation, and distribution of documents. In the months prior to the Assembly it dawned on us that the Ethiopian government and its security agency had followed the preparations much more closely and with greater professional competence than we had expected. Consequently preparations on the spot went much more comfortably for the Geneva office than had been foreseen.

It was the Orthodox members in the Federation who had the courage to take up fundamental questions of the Christian faith and witness and who tried to give some theological depth to the discussions of the vocation of the Federation. They had organized a meeting of Orthodox student movements related to SYNDESMOS, from August 28 to 30, 1972, in Chambésy, Geneva, which then continued as a consultation between SYNDESMOS and the WSCF, from August 31 to September 2, 1972, at Foyer John Knox, Geneva. The first meeting reviewed the situations of Orthodox student movements,

9. Addis Ababa Minutes, p. 32.

analyzed trends in the university world, and issued a statement concerning the role of Orthodox movements.

The SYNDESMOS statement began with an affirmation of basis:

> Jesus Christ is the life of the world, the real solution to all problems, . . . revealed to us by the Holy Spirit through full participation in the life of the Church.
>
> The Church, a major sign of God's presence in the world, is a community of life where men and women meet and are sanctified together in community around Christ, a community where clergy and laity, young and old, black and white meet through a permanent "Metanoia" or movement of repentance, . . . in the royal priesthood of service and teaching to which every Christian is called in the Church and the world.
>
> Full participation in the Church involves participation in the Eucharist and the community of the faithful, participation in prayer and discovering God's word in the Bible, and service to our fellow man, in whom we find Christ, whether it be only on the personal level or on *other levels*.
>
> Christ calls every member of the Church, and therefore us as students, to continually renew ourselves in Him and renew our Christian communities in order that the Church becomes through us in the world the true witness of Christ's love. Our mission, then, is to meet this need of renewal and witness.[10]

The role of the student movement was described as that of a dynamic unit of change in the Church, and through the Church in the world; as a place of freedom of thought where different points of view for expressing Christian witness are accepted; and as a place where leaders for the Church are recruited and trained.

The SYNDESMOS/WSCF consultation reviewed the past and present involvement of Orthodox Christians in the WSCF and then gave special attention to the "crisis of the last few years." It discussed the loss of identity in the Federation: "some members of the WSCF" reject all forms of institutions, including the church, which according to them

---

10. Report of the Meeting of the Orthodox Student Movements — Members of SYNDESMOS, August 28-30, 1972, Geneva, Switzerland, p. 5.

is "compromising with the oppressor," and reject the traditional values of the Christian faith, "even questioning the use of the word Jesus Christ." Political crisis was a result of the intolerance by "some members of the WSCF" of anything other than radical political engagement. The report emphasized the importance of continuity against the sense of discontinuity introduced by the Protestant Reformation, and the sense of belonging to a community that was in but not of the world. The report criticized Protestant activism which assigned more responsibility to human avant-gardes than to God for shaping history.[11]

The consultation placed a big question mark on the continued participation of Orthodox Christians in the ecumenical movement and stated three fundamental objectives which should be met to enable them to be part of the WSCF:

- There must be a "positive pluralism" — tolerance for other points of view.
- There must be personal renewal in Christ as the important root of WSCF activity.
- Neither closed individual pietism alone nor social activism alone can be the answer. The spiritual and the social involvement for justice and peace are two fundamental and inseparable dimensions of the Christian faith.[12]

The report then listed organizational proposals addressed to the Federation. The most far-reaching was the proposal that a permanent consultative body be formed as "a three-fold confessional group" made up of the WSCF (considered to be mainly a Protestant organization), the Roman Catholics, and SYNDESMOS, with the intention that this would lead ultimately to a confederation which would replace the WSCF. The other proposals aimed at facilitating Orthodox participation in the present WSCF. The report concluded with a list of proposals which sought to strengthen the ecumenical role of SYNDESMOS.

Sadly, these significant meetings had virtually no impact on the Assembly. Had they taken place before the second Planning Com-

11. Report of the SYNDESMOS/WSCF Consultation, August 31–September 2, 1972, Geneva, Switzerland, pp. 1-2.
12. Report of the SYNDESMOS/WSCF Consultation, p. 3.

mittee meeting there might have been at least a small chance for the issues to have been discussed in Addis Ababa.

The preparation of the Assembly included a review of the salary structure of the Federation. The Executive Committee had appointed a three-person committee at Tozanzo, July 1971. It did its work mainly by correspondence and met only once, on November 4, 1972, at Strobl, Austria, and then without its only member who had any experience of living and working in Geneva. The goal of the review was to bring the salaries of executive staff close to those of parish pastors in Geneva, but without provision for housing. It was foreseen that in the next quadrennium the staff in Geneva would be closer in age to students, and consequently the possibility of longer-term staff assignments and the emphasis on professional experience would be reduced. The most radical proposal, however, was modified in a more realistic direction when presented to the new Executive Committee in Addis Ababa. It was nevertheless fairly obvious that the new salary policy was likely to lead to a complete turnover of WSCF staff after the Assembly.[13]

On the whole, the year prior to the Assembly included fewer explosions than the three previous years. The only open confrontations took place in the meetings of the Europe committee and the European pre-Assembly conference at Strobl, Austria. The plan to isolate the Europe office from the rest of WSCF activities and from the functions of the headquarters led, as expected, to several unpleasant exchanges between the Europe secretary and myself, mostly in the form of written messages from the Europe office. It was a state of conflict in which personal trust had mutually been lost. I hope that such situations will never arise again.[14]

---

13. The members of the salary review committee were Mario Miegge, chairperson, WSCF Executive Committee, Italy; Karin Rodhe, WSCF Executive Committee, Sweden; and C. I. Itty, WCC staff, Geneva (India). The committee wanted to base the calculations on salaries paid by local churches and organizations in the Geneva area and ignore the salary patterns of international ecumenical organizations. In the 1969-72 period the salaries paid were slightly below the salaries of WCC staff with comparable responsibility.

14. The warfare can be glimpsed in communications such as the letter from Opocensky to Philip Lee-Woolf, December 21, 1971, regarding my role at Tozanzo; from Opocensky to me, January 28, 1972, regarding my letter to Mauri Wahlroos on high school work in Europe; cable from me (from Helsinki) to Opocensky, February

Besides involving myself in the work for the preparation of the Assembly and in the remaining communication tasks of the headquarters, I traveled extensively during this year, visiting SCM branches, head offices, and supporting churches and attending student conferences and WSCF regional meetings. The main issues during these visits were the ministry to students and its support, and the possibilities for the Federation to serve these causes. Meetings with leaders naturally gave opportunities to discuss the internal politics of the Federation.[15]

27, 1972, regarding my visit to the IUS in Prague; cable from Opocensky to me (to Helsinki), February 28, 1972, regarding the same visit; note from me to Opocensky, May 19, 1972, regarding my findings in East Berlin; letter from Opocensky to Klaus-Peter Hertzsch (GDR), July 28, 1972, regarding participation in the Assembly and information received from me; cable from Opocensky to me (to Tokyo) regarding publication of Wielinga's letter to me; memorandum from Opocensky to me, October 23, 1972, regarding the lack of communication; memorandum from Opocensky to me, November 9, 1972, regarding staff recruitment and various Assembly matters; letter from Heikki Palmu (SCM of Finland) to me, November 3, 1972, agreeing with my interpretation of Finnish SCM to Wielinga; letter from Opocensky to Heikki Palmu, December 18, 1972, questioning my honesty.

15. My own travels in 1972 included Ibadan, Nigeria, All Africa Youth and Student Conference and the Planning Committee of the WSCF Assembly, December 22, 1971–January 6, 1972; visit to the British SCM, London area and Belfast, January 24-31; visit to SCMs in Norway, Sweden, and Finland, February 20-29; visit to IUS headquarters, Prague, CSSR, March 1-2; WSCF Europe committee, Zurich, April 3-4; visit to SCM and government authorities, East Berlin, GDR, May 16-17; Assembly Planning Committee, Annecy, France, June 10-14; Lutheran Student Movement conference, Valparaiso, Indiana, USA, July 31–August 5; Mission Board of the Disciples Church, Indianapolis, Indiana, USA, August 6; WCC Central Committee, Utrecht, Netherlands, August; Nordic SCM conference near Kristiansand, Norway, August; meeting of SYNDESMOS and Orthodox leaders, Chambesy, September; Local Assembly Planning Committee, Addis Ababa, Ethiopia, September; visit to SCMs of Pakistan, India, and Burma (Lahore, Karachi, Bombay, Bangalore, Madras, Rangoon), September; visit to SCM of Korea, ALDEC at Tozanzo, and Asia office in Tokyo, October; visit to mission agencies, New York, USA, October; WSCF European Student Conference and meeting of the Europe committee, Strobl, Austria, November; meeting of the Middle East Advisory Committee, Beirut, Lebanon, November; seventy-fifth anniversary of the SCM of Finland, Helsinki, November.

CHAPTER 14

Assembly without Communion

14.1. The Beginning

The Africa Hall of the headquarters of the UN Economic Council for Africa, beautifully designed and purpose-built for inter-governmental and other international conferences, located in the heart of Addis Ababa not far from the Imperial Palace, provided a festive setting for the Twenty-Sixth Assembly of the Federation. The opening ceremonies were solemn. The prayer of invocation was offered by His Holiness Abune Tewoflos, the patriarch of the Ethiopian Orthodox Church; His Excellency Ato Akalework, the minister of justice and president of the host movement, the Haimanote Abew Ethiopian Students Association (HAESA), welcomed the Assembly on behalf of the government. A message from His Imperial Majesty Haile Selassie I was read to the Assembly. The chairman of the host committee, Ato Agdew Redie, principal of a large high school in Addis Ababa, welcomed the participants. An Ethiopian Orthodox choir presented several sacred songs. The chairman of the WSCF, Richard Shaull, responded to the several messages of welcome on behalf of the Federation. The text of this was delivered to the emperor. Many present who were committed to giving the WSCF a new face looked somewhat lost in this setting, which at that moment embraced the whole of the deeply torn Federation.

There were 56 participants entitled to vote. They included 42 delegates of affiliated movements, 12 members of the Executive Committee, and 2 ex officio members. There were altogether 136 participants from outside Ethiopia. The host country provided a large number of local advisers and staff as well as numerous observers, mostly part time, from many branches of the HAESA and from Christian youth organizations and churches, totaling 110.

At the opening session, robust men bearing name tags marked "Host Committee" were everywhere: at the doors, around the podium, and taking pictures of participants row by row. I was later informed that altogether some one hundred of these highly conspicuous "Host Committee Members" had been provided by the government security force.

In order to avoid large quantities of air freight, the Geneva office had sent by airmail stencils of documents to be run off by local staff at the Africa Hall in an office provided for the Assembly. When we arrived, nothing had been done, because a part of the mimeographing machine had vanished. Once the proper personnel to authorize duplication of documents had arrived, the missing part suddenly reappeared.

All delegates of member movements and most other young participants were housed in the Hotel Afrique, which was guarded by four armed military. The senior participants were placed in the slightly more comfortable Wabe Shebele Hotel, which was guarded by two soldiers. Originally we had thought of having all the Executive Committee and Standing Committee members in the same hotel. The host committee was totally uncooperative on this matter. Some Federation staff members succeeded in transferring to the hotel where the younger participants stayed, closer to the revolutionary cadres. It later transpired that two "members of the Host Committee" from the Ethiopian security force were lodged on each floor of the Hotel Afrique.

14.2. Proceedings

Once the work of the Assembly began in the plenary hall and in the committee rooms, everything seemed to run smoothly. The presentation and discussion of regional reports took several days. Some of them were more substantive than others, some had been distributed ahead of time, some were made available in writing only when the minutes had already been printed.

The Latin America report gave an account of the WSCF regional leaders' views on the political, economic, social, and cultural realities of the continent. It contained page after page of all-too-familiar Marxist jargon — the presence of foreign colonizers, the establishment of economies of extraction, the creation of national consciousness, the consolidation of imperialist domination, the era of monopoly capital, the class struggle, the populist period, the failure of Christian democracy, the future of the mass struggle, the guerrilla experience, the pedagogy of life, paradigms for action, and so on — but failed to provide a single word about the actual work of the WSCF and the SCMs in Latin America. Plans for the future were given orally, but nothing was included in the report submitted for the minutes.

The North America report was in two parts. The report on Canada described trends in universities and society at large as well as the work of the SCM locally and nationally. The province of Quebec received special treatment. The report on the USA provided a neo-Marxist interpretation of the American political scene and separate reports on women's liberation, theological developments, and the black movement, concluding with an account of the situation of student movements, campus ministries, and the work of the North America office.

The Europe report began with a summary of regional programs and events in the past quadrennium and went on to discuss trends in education in Europe, giving primary attention to the democratization of education and to "permanent education." The report included separate sections on the experience of the Cinisello commune in Italy, the women's liberation movement, the situation of migrant workers, "the new praxis of the SCM" in the socialist GDR, the Europe/Africa research project in which the Africa region had refused to participate, and the collision between the radicalized SCM and the conservative church establishment in Finland. The report concluded with an "Attempt at a Synthesis" by the general secretary of the Italian SCM. He aimed to spell out a contemporary understanding of the confession of faith in a Europe for which the SCMs foresaw a socialist future. He referred to an "incarnate" reading of the Bible — with a consciousness of the class struggle — and to the necessity of repudiating "all bourgeois values of well-being." According to "the synthesis," it

was possible in the midst of the inevitable political struggle to rediscover the meaning of love between people "who are not brothers
today." In a separate session the regional group presented a summary
of emphases and program plans for the future of the WSCF Europe
region. The familiar concepts and words reappeared once more:

> [W]e stay together because we want to support each other in our
> study and action, wherever our faith in Jesus Christ manifests itself
> in practice. In our view there is a dialectical relationship between
> insights arising from our Christian tradition, our study of the Bible,
> and our political involvement.
>
> . . . we commit ourselves to a style of work which is participatory,
> radically democratic, and against the capitalist division of labor.
>
> In our work . . . we are related to churches and the ecumenical
> movement. Out of loyalty to our Christian heritage and to the Fed-
> eration tradition, we aim at being critical and — if necessary — a
> dissenting element, examining the ways in which Christian witness
> is carried out and seeking new expressions of Christian identity.

The projects envisaged included Bible study in light of a class
analysis; theological research into the marginal groups and sects in
Christian history; and the study of class contradictions in the educational system, of imperialism and international division of labor,
migrant workers, an alternative style of living, students and trade
unions, women's liberation, racism, building of socialism in the GDR,
ecological issues, and European security and cooperation. By the time
of the Assembly, "old hands" in the Federation could recite lists of
this kind by heart. Their expectations of serious work on any of these
issues were rapidly diminishing.

The report from the Africa region was also in two parts. The first
part, which was left out of the minutes, included a careful analysis of
political, educational, and spiritual trends in Africa and a summary
report of WSCF activities in the region.[1] The second part, which was
discussed in the regional group of the Assembly, concentrated on plans
for the future. It began by highlighting the weaknesses experienced

---

1. The first part of the regional report from Africa is filed in the WSCF Archives
separately from the Minutes of the Twenty-Sixth General Assembly.

in leadership development, in poorly functioning SCM branches and in the failure of the region to generate adequate financial support for the student ministry. It commented on the theme of "Liberation" proposed for the Federation in the new quadrennium and then outlined the regional programs and the composition of the Africa Consultative Group. Despite the African venue of the Assembly, the issues and problems of the region as they were presented by African students and leaders — clearly, thoughtfully, and with a touch of refreshing realism — seemed to arouse little enthusiasm among delegates from other continents.

The Asian report reflected the region's vast extent and its social and religious diversity. It included analytical sections on "Asian Realities — and Our Hopes," "University and Society in Asia," "The SCM and Its Raison d'être in Asia," and "Issues Related to Indo-China." In addition, the main project of the region, the WSCF Asian Leadership Development Center (ALDEC), was dealt with in detail. The objectives of ALDEC were twofold:

> to develop leadership for the Student Christian Movements among the rising generation; and to provide a new forum for young Asian Christian intellectuals to engage in a common search for new theological, educational and political perspectives.

The plans for Asia regional work included the continuation of ALDEC, work with university teachers, communication, and support of national SCMs. The war in Vietnam and Cambodia prompted the group to make peace a major concern of the regional work. Other issues were theological self-reliance, the role of women in Asia, racism and pluralistic societies, and several others relating to the social and international situation of Asian countries, such as the need for a "new diplomacy," especially in relation to China; students' contact with workers and peasants; issues of land, population, and poverty; and the influence of foreign presence through aid, trade, investments, and military involvement. The group responsible for the report and the plans deliberately refrained from suggesting a unified ideological frame for the work of the Federation.

The Middle East regional leaders had prepared an extensive analytical, even scholarly, report of more than fifty pages, but it, too, was somehow not included in the minutes.[2] This report is a valuable source of information on the political and religious history of the region, the church situation and theological emphases characteristic of the region at the time, the rise of developmental concerns and the role of Christians in them, and the ecumenical and confessional youth and student work. The Palestinian issue and the contemporary role of historic churches, especially the Orthodox, gave a distinctive flavor to the report. In the presentation of plans for the future, the proposal for a worldwide confederation between the existing WSCF and the Orthodox and Roman Catholic student and university constituencies was reiterated. It was indicative of the mood of the Assembly that the Middle East report received least attention and that the distinct theological elements and the far-reaching proposals on ecumenical policy were virtually ignored.

This whole sequence of reports and the presentation of future plans for regional work left the impression of an inevitable formal necessity which, however, made no serious impact on the Assembly as a whole. The triumphalistic comments which had been heard since the Tozanzo meeting of the Executive Committee, suggesting that the real dynamism of the Federation was in the interplay between strong regional programs and units, proved illusory. There were no doubts about the meaningfulness of many regional programs for students, university teachers, and even for churches. But the interaction and mutual challenge had vanished. The Federation had lost its global identity.

The validity of these impressions was confirmed by the response to the reports on the Federation's global operations. The joint report by the chairman and the general secretary gave a factual account of the implementation of the resolutions of the 1968 Assembly, the work of the Executive Committee, and the activities of the Geneva office. Peter Musgrove, secretary for priorities and finance, gave a report in which he analyzed in depth the Federation's support structure and pointed to the causes of the deterioration of the financial situation. Aaron Ramos presented an oral report on the Political Commission, and I presented a general secretary's report in which I tried to outline

2. The Report of the WSCF Middle East Regional Group is filed separately from the minutes in the archives of the WSCF.

ways out of the current polarization. In it I affirmed the strategy of regionalization and tried to redefine the Federation's overall objectives and articulate the meaning of the gospel, an explicit witness to Christ, and commitment to the Church. None of these reports made any difference to the course of the Assembly. Responses to them both in plenary sessions and working groups were platitudinous.

14.3. Revision of the Constitution

The Assembly dealt thoroughly with the revision of the constitution on the basis of the proposals put forward by the Planning Committee. Each regional committee was given an opportunity to express its views. The most significant changes were (1) the recognition of regional structures as part of the composition of the Federation, with significant responsibility for regional budgets, the appointment of regional staff, and decisions on membership; and (2) the reduction in the size of the Executive Committee, which was to become strictly representative of the regions.

The initiative to replace the position of general secretary by an interregional staff team did not receive the required two-thirds majority. Consequently it remained the responsibility of the Assembly to elect both the chairman and the general secretary as well as appoint two members from each region to the Executive Committee from regional nominees.

14.4. Working Groups

The Assembly then established five working groups to deal with various emphases and areas of concern.

The group on *Christian Identity* underlined the importance, and also the difficulty, of the issue and concluded that its pursuit meant for the Federation "an effort to develop a new Christian consciousness that can more usefully contribute to the process of liberation." It also recommended that the issue be pursued primarily on regional levels in the spirit of "theological self-reliance," and that some provision be made for interregional communication.

The group on *Various Forms of Liberation Struggle*[3] recommended that the Federation make liberation the main theme of its work in the new quadrennium. This was accepted by the Assembly. The group defined "liberation struggle" as follows:

> Liberation struggle is one which is to be found in all our societies and regions. Although it has various forms — for example the struggle against sexism and racism — we suggest that these are all interrelated in the common class struggle against capitalism and its psychological/cultural consequences.

The report recommended that the Federation initiate a study program to identify interrelationships between various forms of oppression, investigate the dynamics of liberation and oppression within the Federation itself, encourage the development of liberation movements "in all regions and countries," and spread information on such movements. It made suggestions concerning several specific situations, such as those in Indo-China, Angola, Mozambique, Namibia, Zimbabwe, South Africa, Guinea-Bissau, Chile, Puerto Rico, and Palestine. The problems of exiled and political prisoners in Latin America, the role of NATO, and possibilities of cooperation with various secular and religious international organizations were also discussed. The group seemed to have gotten carried away by the drama of the situations from which some participants came and to which all had been exposed by TV screens and the press. Consequently the tone of the report resembled more that of the UN Security Council or some other powerful political forum than that of a weak and divided ecumenical student organization.

We request that:
- Immediate contact be made with students and representatives in the Democratic Republic of Vietnam.
- Immediate support be given to political prisoners, especially students in South Vietnam. . . .
- The Asia Regional Committee be especially involved in this issue.

3. The Report of the Working Group on Various Forms of Liberation Struggle, Minutes of the Twenty-Sixth Assembly of the WSCF, Addis Ababa, Ethiopia, December 28, 1972–January 8, 1973, pp. 18-20.

or

> The WSCF should identify with and establish formal contact with
> the PAIGG (Party for Independence of the African Territories of
> Guinea-Bissau).

> The WSCF should send a representative to Guinea-Bissau on the
> day in 1973 when formal independence is declared.

As for Latin America, the WSCF was requested to "give support
to the Chilean Popular Government" (of President Salvador Allende)
and to oppose the imperialist blockade and other efforts to disrupt
Chilean development; and in the rest of the continent to defend
human rights violated "by the oligarchical governments" and deal with
"the problem of exiled and political prisoners."

On the whole, it made no difference whether or not the Federation
had had any previous contact with the country concerned, its students,
or any Christian community in it. The Assembly addressed itself as
freely to governments and political organizations as to member movements, churches, and ecumenical organizations.

The group on *Education*[4] presented a lengthy report which discussed the problems of educational institutions and programs, especially in the developing countries, and suggested directions for educational reform. The report as a whole expressed openness to the
diversities of the educational contexts on different continents. It was
refreshingly devoid of militant jargon and did not propose solutions
through quick action. It reflected a sophisticated version of current
radical Marxist thought. Nevertheless, the group was not untouched
by the epidemic of grandiose organizational triumphalism. In making
the first of its final recommendations it seems to have forgotten that
it was not UNESCO but the WSCF which was speaking:

> The WSCF should get more involved in the educational systems
> in member states. It should have a clear-cut structural policy on
> education to offer to governments of member states.

4. Report of Working Group on Education, Addis Ababa Minutes, pp. 20-23.

In the rest of its recommendations the group affirmed the WSCF policy on liberation; advocated interregional cooperation on education; encouraged national study projects; issued a warning against educational reforms "carried out by national bourgeoisie, supported by international imperialism" promoting neocolonialism; suggested the creation of a permanent fund to study the influence of mass media in developing countries; encouraged meetings between students and young nonstudents; and urged SCMs to admit nonstudent members.

The working group on *Regions*[5] simply pulled together the discussion carried on at the Executive and Planning Committee meetings and presented the basic questions which had arisen. For example: How far should the WSCF be a federation of member movements or regions? Is the "one country, one movement" policy still valid? What are the criteria for defining regions? It also pointed to the need for further work on the aims and basis of the Federation, which this Assembly left untouched.

The fifth working group, on *Publications and Communication,*[6] expressed in three brief recommendations its wish that the Federation continue publishing books related to its main concerns; that regional publication work be consolidated; and that a WSCF newsletter be published.

14.5. Resolutions

After the group reports the Assembly considered proposals for resolutions and passed nine. Most of them stemmed from the Working Group on Various Forms of Liberation Struggle and seemed to have been prepared in an ad hoc fashion. The statement on Indo-China condemned the bombing of North Vietnam, supported the peace plan of the Provisional Revolutionary Government, and demanded a total withdrawal of the United States from the region. The one on Puerto Rico expressed solidarity with its independence movement. The resolution on the WCC Program to Combat Racism stated that the

5. Report of Working Group on Regions, Addis Ababa Minutes, p. 23.
6. Report of Working Group on Publications and Communication, Addis Ababa Minutes, pp. 23-24.

WSCF was "in full support" of the program, and in the same resolution hailed the position of the WCC against American aggression in Vietnam. The resolution on Australian aborigines, which expressed the Federation's concern for "the conditions under which many Australian aborigines are living and its full solidarity with their demands at this time . . . for land rights, adequate nutrition, housing, medical and legal services," was to be sent to the Australian government. The rest denounced French colonialism, Zionism, and the sports relations between New Zealand and South Africa; deplored the absence of any representation from the People's Republic of China at the Assembly, instructing the new general secretary to initiate "official contacts with Chinese students"; and, the final one, welcomed the process of socialist transition in Chile, condemned the imperialist actions of the United States and the multinational corporations against the government of President Allende and hailed "the exemplary action taken in solidarity by the people and government of Cuba who have decided to support Chile materially."[7]

The amateurish issuing of such a multitude of resolutions about which little follow-up action was possible was an innovation for the Federation and stood in sharp contrast with the style of previous Assemblies and General Committee meetings.

14.6. Elections

The issue which occupied delegates most intensely was the choice of future leaders for the Federation. The tension was focused on the election of the chairperson and general secretary. The Assembly had to start the process from scratch, because none of the customary preparatory work by a search committee had been done. The vacuum was filled by several small and select caucuses.

During the early part of the gathering, the only available information on candidates came through corridor conversations. Three persons appeared to be candidates for general secretary: Feliciano Carino of the Philippines, Milan Opocensky, and myself. For chairperson, Richard Shaull's name was reintroduced while African dele-

7. Addis Ababa Minutes, pp. 24-27.

gates soon put forward the name of Mercy Oduyoye of Nigeria and Ghana.

Carino was more or less a "dark horse" from outside the current leadership of national movements or the Federation. He had had SCM experience in the Philippines, where he had in his younger years served as general secretary, and had been involved in the ecumenical student movement in the USA. He had achieved some fame as the person who had moved the termination of the American UCM in 1969. Currently he was known in WSCF circles as a frequently used resource person at Asia regional events and as the newly appointed executive secretary of the university world office of the mission section of the United Presbyterian Church in the USA, succeeding the long-time pioneer and supporter of the American and the worldwide ecumenical student movement, Margaret Flory. Furthermore, Carino was known to have been a student of Richard Shaull during his doctoral studies at Princeton Theological Seminary. He was perceived by many at the Assembly as outside the ideological battles of the WSCF, but with sympathy for the radical student movements in North and Latin America and his home region, Southeast Asia.[8]

On January 3 the Assembly appointed a Nominations Committee for which the establishing of a list of candidates for the Executive Committee was unusually easy because it was done on the basis of the nominations from the regional groups. On January 7 I announced my withdrawal from candidacy for the general secretary, expressing the view that the Federation needed new leaders in order to free itself from the polarization of the recent past, and that it was the turn of non-Western persons to lead the organization. The Nominations Committee had a rough time — involving even a flash of physical violence — before it was able to announce the nomination of Mercy Oduyoye for the position of chairperson and Feliciano Carino for the general secretaryship.

There was a problem with the candidacy of Oduyoye because she was not present in Addis Ababa — she was attending the world

---

8. Actually Carino had done his doctoral work under both Charles West and Richard Shaull. The assumed link with Shaull helped to dispel any doubts which his ties with church establishment could have raised among the Latin American radicals and the "New Left" supporters in North America and Europe.

assembly of the WCC Commission on World Mission and Evangelism in Bangkok, Thailand, where she could not be reached. The Assembly was informed about this difficulty, and Richard Shaull ruled from the chair that her candidacy should be maintained. A second problem was the candidacy of Shaull, who was present. This was resolved when he informed the Nominations Committee that he was no longer available. Latin Americans especially, but also others from the radical camp, had stood behind him. In the end, Carino was elected by a vote of 53 to 0 with 2 abstentions, and Oduyoye by 28 to 3 with 23 abstentions.

14.7. Highlights and Thrills

Peter Musgrove, the finance secretary of the Federation who also supervised the technical running of the Assembly, had to work closely with the chairman of the host committee, Agdew Redie, who it became clear was a member of the Ethiopian security services. What the state authorities feared most was that radical leftist students from abroad would get into contact with Ethiopian students opposed to Haile Selassie's government, and that the Assembly would fuel student demonstrations in the city. Therefore the mimeographing office and the distribution of documents were under strict surveillance. Being so closely watched provided some color to the otherwise stark proceedings.

My WSCF Asian colleagues polled a number of delegates and found that I would not be reelected if I remained a candidate, and subsequently came, with much embarrassment, to inform me of their findings. It later turned out that the Ethiopian security agents had arrived at more or less the same estimate!

Another incident occurred around the election process. Immediately after I had made the announcement of my withdrawal, I received a message from the minister of justice that he wanted to see me in the lobby outside the meeting hall. When I met him he told me in no unclear terms how dissatisfied he was that I had made such a decision. He said that I should have informed him if I was in difficulty regarding reelection and that he could have helped me. As I walked back to the meeting, I tried to imagine what shape his help would have taken: that of a police van or army truck collecting a few Latin American delegates to be held in custody until the end of the Assembly?

Other absurdities occurred. When I learned that one of the most influential leaders of the Asian delegates' group, Anwar Barkat, had to leave before the end of the Assembly, it occurred to me that with a minor delay of his departure he could probably still participate in the election of the chairperson. With the tight voting situation it was important that the moderates' position not be weakened at a critical moment. Perhaps the minister of justice could now help? I went to him to ask whether the departure of the Ethiopian Airlines flight which Barkat was to take could be delayed, to ensure his presence in the decisive session. After a short while the minister reported that the plane would be slightly delayed, but he did not want too many passengers to miss their connecting flights. He said that he would have his government car ready to take Barkat directly to the plane at the latest possible moment. He would be given a signal in the meeting hall when he should leave. The plane took off one hour behind schedule.

There were also more innocent highlights which every participant could enjoy. The most spectacular was the reception by the emperor in his imperial palace. It was my task to introduce every participant, giving their name and their country. When the Italian delegate — one of the leaders of the radical left — came, he bowed deeply and said: "Your highness, forgive us!" An African-American student pastor was caught by a security guard leaving the palace: He had put a champagne glass into his pocket to take home as a souvenir. When he explained, with some embarrassment, the motive of his crime, the guards donated the glass to him. No one wanted to stay out of the party. No one felt prompted to stage a protest.

The Assembly was over before the Ethiopian Timkat celebration. This is the equivalent of Epiphany and, for the Ethiopian Orthodox, a more important feast than Christmas. Nevertheless, some of the participants had a chance to attend the worship services of the ancient and unique Orthodox rite in churches of Addis Ababa. Sadly enough, these experiences did not seem significantly to penetrate the life of the Assembly nor to make any impact whatsoever on the overall mood of the gathering. Daily worship had been planned and conducted by representatives of the Africa region, primarily the Ethiopian host movement. Despite the dedication of the leaders to devotions, the Assembly participants seemed to remain distant from its worship life, almost as indifferent outsiders. It became, in effect, unique in the series of international ecumenical events as a nonworshiping gathering. No one had the strength to insist on a celebration of the Eucharist to draw participants together as a community, at least for a moment. It was an Assembly without Communion, in stark contrast to the 1968 gathering at Otaniemi, which had ended in such an unrestrainedly joyful open-air ecumenical celebration of the Holy Communion led by a Catholic priest.

14.8. The End

The newly elected Executive Committee met for two days after the others had left for home. When that meeting also was over, the Chinese, whose Cultural Revolution was a source of inspiration to the Federation's radicals and whose absence from the Assembly they had deplored, did appear in imperial Ethiopia: The Chinese ballet troupe from Beijing arrived to mark the opening of direct flights between the empires of Haile Selassie and Chairman Mao by Ethiopian and Chinese airlines. The spectacular performance to the Addis Ababa audience — by an elite group from the land of the radical Cultural Revolution to people of the imperial establishment — was a visible reminder of the character of the real world as it was with all its ambiguities, and not as utopians wanted it to be, with clear demarcation lines drawn between the just and the unjust.

During a day off when most of the participants had left for home, Peter Musgrove, our Ethiopian security friend Agdew Redie, and I pondered the future of the country. Agdew Redie was quite candid: The misery and corruption had grown beyond anyone's control. What could be done? The liberals, among whom he counted himself, were too weak to make any difference. My own bet was that there would soon be a military takeover. Apart from the privileged few, the soldiers represented the best-educated segment of society. They knew what discipline meant. My guess was that the coming revolution would be carried out by well-educated military leaders who had studied in the

314

West and that the country would gradually develop a liberal orientation. We agreed that whatever happened, a big change would come soon.

On June 29, 1973, less than six months after the end of the Assembly, the army took control of Ethiopia. A few weeks later the minister of justice, together with fifty-eight other ministers and civil servants, was executed by the new revolutionary regime of Haile-Mariam Mengistu. Our friend Agdew Redie became a refugee. The military did step in. But when their one devil had been evicted from the imperial palace, seven or more, so it seems, had already come in. The repression of students was soon multiplied.

14.9. Assessments

The reactions of participants to the Assembly varied from deep disillusionment to somber realism, with surprisingly similar conclusions being drawn by both extremes of the divided constituency. No one suggested that there would be a rapid strengthening and healing of the Federation. Most thought that regional cooperation was at this stage the only viable pattern of survival. Whether or not the WSCF had any real future was an open question for several.

Louis-François Caude, the delegate of the French member movement, wrote about his disappointment, not with any particular point of the meeting, but with the whole Assembly and its significance for member movements.

> There is no point in dwelling on the permanent scandal of the surroundings — glorious — during the ten days of our Assembly: hippopotamuses, guarded residence in a three-star hotel, feudal ecclesiastics and ambassadors squeezing into the hall, not to mention His Majesty, the Emperor of palaces and shanty towns, his demagogic ministers. . . .
>
> As far as the actual Assembly goes, I have the impression that during the debates we never worked clearly and constructively. . . .
>
> [W]e were too hampered by our guilty consciences (at being Europeans in Africa) to see debates close in and be reduced to confrontations between two opposing blocs. . . . Far from seeing the

"enemy" troops divide and break up, we saw our own give way on different fronts.

He left open the question whether the WSCF as a world organization would have any useful role in the future. For him, only the local and regional European functions made sense any longer.[9]

Haakon Hansen, the delegate of the Norwegian SCM, himself a convert to radical socialism, wrote:

> [T]he General Assembly in Addis will not be remembered as one of the great moments in the life of the Federation. On the other hand, it cannot be evaluated totally negatively. Some common concerns in political as well as theological matters still exist, but I doubt that we can expect any common actions within the next few years. Projects of this kind . . . must grow slowly in accordance with the needs of regions. The hope that this can happen makes it still reasonable to keep the WSCF together as a world-wide organization.

Hansen listed several problems which he had observed during the Assembly. They included bad communication between participants; a tendency to move from regionalization to regionalism; and a sense of alienation of some groups from the Federation and the consequent lack of interest in an effective world organization. He found the level of political discussion in Addis Ababa meaningless for those who took their political involvement seriously. "It is not possible or fruitful to discuss world imperialism on such a general level. . . . Better modestly relevant than greatly irrelevant." His recipe for the Federation was a new, antibureaucratic structure and style of life, which seemed possible in the Europe region.[10]

Ann-Catrin Jarl of Sweden wrote a report entitled "To Play a Side Role" (in the ecumenical movement) in which she saw the Assembly as a battleground between progressive and reactionary Christians. She

9. Louis-Françoise Caude, "Report and Views on the 26th General Assembly of the WSCF" (mimeographed), WSCF Archives.

10. Haakon Hansen, comments on the WSCF General Assembly, Addis Ababa, March 1973, written for the WSCF Europe committee.

found greatest promise for the Federation among the Latin American delegation as a whole and in the growing radicalization of some of the Asian movements, most notably those of the Philippines, Singapore, and South Korea. She blamed "some conservative African leaders" for having scared the whole regional delegation into a clear-cut reactionary stand against "a democratic pattern of world program." She accused them of sowing seeds of mistrust in the Federation. She appreciated Richard Shaull's vision with its emphasis on a "faith freed from glamour" and saw potential in a Federation reduced in size and influence, active as a consistent ecumenical dissident, to keep perspectives of hope and love alive.[11]

Paul Costapoulos of the Orthodox Campus Commission in the United States wrote a lengthy report on the Assembly. He pointed to the size of the Orthodox delegation; with twenty members it was "the largest Orthodox delegation ever to attend a WSCF international gathering." He referred to the increasing difficulties which Orthodox movements experienced in trying to participate in a radicalizing WSCF. A new mood, manifested already at the World Student Conference, Turku '68, had been breeding "enmity, passion and discord." This mood "again beclouded the deliberations (of the Addis Ababa Assembly) by a nimbus of hostility, diatribe and conflict." He described the sense of expectation, even enthusiasm, with which the Orthodox delegates had arrived, viewing "ecumenism as a natural concomitant toward living in Jesus Christ" and being ready to learn from the WSCF, confident of having a contribution to make to it. He continued:

> By the end of the Assembly, however, we felt defeated and disillusioned; uncertain that we had learned anything; more certain that we had offered less; and most certain that at future Assemblies Orthodox participation would be kept at a minimum unless the present reality of the WSCF is modified.

He expressed his satisfaction that the "conference radicals" did not succeed in closing totally the door to the Orthodox, as they did not

---

11. Ann-Catrin Jarl, "To Play a Side Role," *Kristet Forum* 1 (1973): 21-22 (in Swedish).

muster the two-thirds majority required for "excising the constitutional heart of the Federation and transplanting it with another one." In his report to the Orthodox movements he appealed to them not to leave the Federation but to continue to pursue the proposal to form a threefold confederation which would comprise the present Federation and strong Catholic and Orthodox sections. He also made it clear that the Orthodox "must become more informed and better prepared to understand the problems and challenges" of contemporary student ecumenism and that "they must lose neither their faith nor courage, nor must they allow themselves to be intimidated into withdrawing from the picture by the non-Orthodox constituencies." He pleaded that the Orthodox become educated "into the language of the Federation," even if it had no Christian base, in order to participate more effectively in dealing with social and political issues "as an integral part of our commitment to Jesus Christ."[12]

Milan Opocensky commented in the editorial of the bulletin *WSCF Europe* on the diverging opinions about the Assembly. He took issue with the Orthodox views:

> I have to challenge the underlying assumptions expressed in that critique. If the SCMs in Europe are not interested in rediscovering a new meaning of faith, the Bible, and Jesus Christ himself, I wonder why they should have bothered to discuss these issues constantly throughout the last quadrennium. . . . We have agreed to continue looking into the question of anti-capitalist struggle and how to participate in it, but we have also agreed to study the dimension of faith and love in that struggle.
>
> . . . [O]ur direction seems to lie somewhere between an a-political pietism à la "Kein anderes Evangelium," IVF or "Jesus People" on the one hand, and political radicalism in a Christian disguise on the other. It seems that church leaders still prefer the former heresies to the latter. Student groups are — in conformity with an obvious conservative backlash — expected to become neutral, church orientated, docile and obedient.

12. Paul Costapoulos, "Addis Ababa 1973; A Report on the World Student Conference" (mimeographed), February 6, 1973.

He continued his assessment:

The Assembly in Addis rejected the WSCF "cardinals" and other self-imposed "defensores fidei." The election of a new staff was a clear indication that the experiments have to continue.

Of course, it will be up to everybody to show whether all the talk about liberation, self-reliance, education within the context of one's own culture was just empty rhetoric.[13]

In June 1973, Gabriel Habib wrote a circular to Orthodox student movements, schools of theology, and the leaders of SYNDESMOS in which he discussed the implications of the Addis Ababa Assembly for Orthodox participation in the Federation. He referred to the indifference with which the Assembly had received the Orthodox proposals for forming a confederation, and stated:

At this stage . . . almost every Orthodox student movement is raising fundamental questions about its membership in the WSCF . . . in particular the A.C.E.R. in France (Action Chrétienne des Etudiants Russes, i.e. the Russian SCM outside Russia) has informed us of its tentative decision to withdraw from the Federation.

Habib wanted to discourage Orthodox movements from hasty decisions and, instead, to organize another consultation in conjunction with the meeting of SYNDESMOS.[14]

There was little echo of the Assembly in the ecumenical press. The American *Christianity Today* had a column about the events, in which the reporter deplored the direction which the WSCF had taken.

Personal comments were more numerous. Visser 't Hooft remarked that the Addis Assembly marked the most drastic break which had ever occurred in the ecumenical movement. Philip Potter, the

13. Milan Opocensky, an editorial entitled "1968-1972 + 1973-1977 . . . ," *WSCF Europe,* no. 6 (March 1973).

14. Gabriel Habib, general secretary of World Fellowship of Orthodox Youth Organizations — SYNDESMOS — to Orthodox student movements, schools of theology, members of the Executive Committee, June 25, 1973.

newly elected WCC general secretary, made his view plain to me when I went to report to him on the Assembly: The damage was caused by incompetent handling of a tough situation. He himself seemed to expect a new momentum for the WCC to come from the radicalism which was spreading through various activist groups into churches.

In the early months of 1973 the WSCF Geneva office of the crisis years was dismantled. The overhaul was complete: Peter Musgrove left for Australia to become the pastor of a Methodist congregation; Audrey Abrecht, administrative assistant to the general secretary, was dismissed; Christine Griesbeck, the accountant, resigned; and I moved to the Lutheran World Federation. The regional secretaries of Africa, Asia, and the Middle East also resigned one by one within a year of the Assembly. Milan Opocensky, who had been invited to continue for two more years as secretary for Europe, received an abrupt call from the government authorities to return to the CSSR in June 1973.[15]

It was the end of one era and the beginning of another, still confused but very different.

15. Letter from the Ministry of Culture of the CSSR to Milan Opocensky, June 27, 1973, signed by the secretary of church affairs, Fr. Jelínek v.r.

CHAPTER 15

Looking Back

15.1. A Last Look at the Storm

It was indeed a storm. Few would deny that today. The revolutionary wind which first struck North American students soon shook universities and colleges, teachers and students on every continent. It stirred up fierce controversies in churches and in the ecumenical movement. Its impact was felt by governments and political parties. It produced intense debates, mass demonstrations, and acute social-ideological tensions, occasionally accompanied by violence. The storm drew thousands of students and young scholars into its vortex with irresistible power, giving, for a moment, the impression of a rising political mass movement and imminent radical social change. However, the storm reached its peak rapidly and then, almost as suddenly as it had come, receded, leaving much wreckage in its wake.

The storm itself has become part of the history of political movements, the university world, the church, and Christian student organizations, and it is now possible to ponder its origins and assess its consequences with some dispassion. Some came to regard the left radicalism of the late sixties as an epidemic disease. Although its major impact was soon spent, it continued to weaken academic institutions and theological seminaries, and especially Christian youth and church organizations, debilitating them and reducing their ability to restore themselves to health. Whatever the metaphor, an analysis of the events of those years in the organizations most directly affected can help

321

identify the nature of the forces — the germs that caused the epidemic — which even today affect the ecumenical movement.

The storm had its origins in the convergence of several factors: the evolving social status and new affluence of students in the industrialized world; the changing nature of the university; the grievances and frustrations of students; the multiple impact of many dramatic political events and military actions in which the superpowers were involved; and the sudden upsurge of ideologies of the left, offering a vision of a new world and avenues of direct action to reach it. To these must be added a genuine religious and moral awakening among young people who found the growing gap between rich and poor in the world intolerable and who watched on their television screens what happened to the civilian victims of aggressive military operations. Side by side with political, economic, sociological, and psychological factors, an unpredictable spiritual element, usually present at the turning points of history and inexplicable by rational analysis, made itself felt in the advent of this storm.

The force of the storm took almost everyone by surprise. Inevitably it was met with suspicion or hostility by most authorities in both capitalist and socialist societies. A notable exception was Mao Tse-tung and his government in China, who absorbed it into their Cultural Revolution.

Assessments of the storm's impact are likely to differ according to the vantage point of the commentators, their convictions, and the depth of their participation in the events. Whether or not the radicalism of the sixties resulted in any positive changes in the world of higher education, in the church, or in society at large, is obviously a debatable issue. Its long-term effects, including the reactions it invoked, were inevitably different in different societies and institutional contexts. What can be said, however, is that much in the world has gone in a direction which is totally opposite to that envisaged by activist leaders.

Many socially involved Christians originally considered the student uprising as a healthy unrest and a positive challenge to the establishment. However, its turning to a new political dogmatism and authoritarianism alienated numerous sympathizers within churches and academic institutions. Only die-hard liberal optimists and radicals remained totally uncritical of the revolutionary movement and thought its emphases and working methods could be integrated into the programs of churches and the ecumenical movement. Subsequent events have made it increasingly difficult to uphold such a view. For the ecumenical student movement the devastation wrought by the storm leaves little ground for nostalgia.[1]

The ideological heritage of the revolutionary student movement of the sixties proved mostly disruptive. Only its contribution to the end of American military action in Vietnam and the increased popular sentiment against "imperial" wars can be listed as positive achievements. Confrontation and fatigue with left radicalism, which claimed to be the only effectual answer to the plight of the world's poor, spread cynicism about the movement's concern for the deprived and ultimately diminished popular interest in development and human rights. In many countries all idealism has subsequently become suspect. No movements or major international initiatives of any intellectual or political significance have since surfaced which have made greater international justice a primary goal. Few politicians today dare to promote ideals which socialism once contributed to political thought beyond party affiliations.

As far as churches are concerned, the influence of the revolutionary left ideologies has proved more tenacious. After the initial stage of protest movements which increased awareness of questions of social and economic justice among Christians in a healthy way, the detri-

---

1. In 1985 the Chinese Christian leader K. H. Ting, once considered an ardent defender of Chinese Marxism, gave an unequivocally negative reply to my question in a personal conversation as to whether he could see any positive outcome from the Chinese Cultural Revolution from 1966 to 1982. "It was all-out destructive, in every conceivable respect." Two well-known leaders of the American left in the sixties who were editors of the radical magazine *Ramparts,* Peter Collier and David Horowitz, described in their book *Destructive Generation: Second Thoughts about the Sixties* (New York: Summit Books, 1989) what made them leave the revolutionary movement in the USA: the turn to violence; the discrepancy between stated goals and the methods used; an increasingly ideological interpretation of social reality; a conscious refusal to face facts and arguments contrary to the radical position; and a disillusionment with what happened in Indo-China after the American defeat in Vietnam. A leading figure of the radical left in Finland, at the time the youngest elected member of the Finnish parliament, Terho Pursiainen, has stated repeatedly in recent years that he was wrong in believing in the goals of the radical left and that his choice at that time represented a serious misjudgment.

mental effects of the ideological orientation of the sixties became more marked. New Left ideologies continued to appear in the thought patterns, language, and theological views of many ecumenical leaders, causing tensions within the ecumenical movement and distancing the constituency from its leaders. The current crisis of confidence of the ecumenical movement, which is felt acutely in many member churches and which is reflected in the recurring financial problems of the WCC, stems significantly from the influence of these ideological "germs."[2]

15.2. The Impact on Christian Ministry in Universities

The storm made the WSCF a different organization. Although this book is not the place to review its history beyond the Addis Ababa Assembly, some long-range consequences of that meeting may be noted here.

a. In Addis Ababa the Federation rejected the ecumenical vision which had inspired its members from its beginning. It turned its back on the concerns for explicit Christian witness and for the unity and renewal of the church. Class analysis and the search for a new identity by abandoning the past became the normative guidelines for the Federation's work. The insights and experience of past generations were regarded as incompatible with this new direction. By taking this course the WSCF lost most of its value for the churches. At the time of writing there are few signs of any creative contagious vision being transmitted by the Federation to its member movements and to the leaders of the worldwide church.

b. The WSCF turned away from its missionary vocation, which had been renewed generation after generation up to the era of the Life

---

2. An informative presentation of the development of Christian social teaching in the ecumenical movement and in the Roman Catholic Church from the thirties to the present decade, including some penetrating criticism of the trends manifested in the WCC program of Justice, Peace and the Integrity of Creation (1986-90), is presented by Ronald H. Preston in *Confusions in Christian Ethics: Problems for Geneva and Rome* (London: SCM Press, 1994).

and Mission of the Church program, 1956-64, and of the Christian presence emphasis. Conveying the gospel to students was no longer the driving force of the Federation, even if the article on aims in its constitution was left intact in Addis Ababa. The mission of the Church was no longer a Federation concern. This contributed to a vacuum in the ecumenical student ministry in universities and schools. The Federation left the responsibility for evangelism to the churches' more heavily institutionalized ministries and to a number of evangelical student organizations.

c. The Federation sacrificed Christian responsibility for intellectual and academic work in favor of a doctrinaire anti-institutionalism and a disregard for research and study which were not politically and ideologically oriented. This in turn made many university teachers and scholars leave the SCM communities and contributed to a weakening of lay Christian witness in the rapidly expanding world of higher education. Ecumenical communities of Christian scholars were deprived of an important avenue for pursuing dialogue with one another about their Christian vocation in the academic world.

d. The conflict within the Federation over political responsibility proved to be a defeat for Christian involvement in the complex social and economic issues characteristic of the present world. Not only were the problems of poverty, underdevelopment, and oppression in the Third World unsolvable by the ideological panaceas of both the doctrinaire and the anarchist radical left, but the revolutionary student and youth movements, themselves rapidly shrinking, inoculated with their tenacious slogans the next generation of students against any serious concern for the unresolved and increasingly urgent social and economic issues.[3]

e. The Federation's rejection of the church and the organized ecumenical movement deprived the World Council of Churches of one of its major sources of growth: committed critics and courageous

---

3. Ans van der Bent points out in his book *Commitment to God's World: A Concise Critical Survey of Ecumenical Social Thought* (WCC, 1995), p. 197, the damaging effects of the ideological struggle between 1969 and 1973 on the WSCF. He writes: "As a result, the influence of the Student Christian Movement as an active contributor to international ecumenical social thought, which had been substantial for many years, virtually disappeared."

young leaders. After 1973 the WSCF became uninteresting and irrelevant to the wider ecumenical movement, though some ideas promoted by student radicals found their way into WCC programs and,
by their ideological slant, contributed to an alienation of member
churches from the Council and to a turning away from ecumenical
commitment. Some of the undercurrents which had led to disastrous
results in the WSCF were thus kept alive and even nourished by the
WCC in the ensuing years.

f. The most pertinent example is the fate of the once-flourishing
Youth Department of the WCC. Those responsible gave in very
quickly to advocates of a reorganized Youth Desk which would facilitate the entry of "radicalized" youth and counterculture groups into
the WCC. When recruiting leaders, more attention was given to satis-
fying such concerns than to the expressed desires of member churches
and their youth. Thus the radicalism of dissident youth on the WCC
staff was given an institutional sanction. It is not surprising that such
widely appreciated programs as ecumenical work camps were sacrificed in favor of activities in line with the new revolutionary mood.

g. In the late sixties the WSCF and many of its member movements
introduced the idea of exclusive student leadership as the key to
renewal and dynamism, thereby eliminating most senior leaders and
severing ties with graduates, faculty, and senior friends. This trend
was a reaction against the increase in the average age of WSCF leaders
following its institutional expansion and the emergence of new patterns of cooperation with churches and ecumenical organizations. The
need to bring the Federation's Executive Committee and staff into
closer contact with the current student generation had been felt from
1964 onward. But the restructuring approved in Addis Ababa 1972-73
swung the pendulum to the extreme, thus minimizing continuity in
the work of the Federation.[4] The emphasis on student leadership was

4. The terms of office for both Executive Committee members and WSCF
Geneva staff were drastically shortened and frequently did not last even a full quadrennium. For an international organization like the WSCF, this meant that its leaders
were no longer in a position to become acquainted with the Federation's worldwide
constituency and consequently were unable to develop effective leadership. Regional
offices followed suit: Staff appointed after Addis Ababa in many cases left just when
they had had their first exposure to their own region and only a preliminary feel for
the worldwide organization.

a handy method for pruning the Federation of the elements of continuity, which for the revolutionaries were undesirable excess baggage. The ensuing heightened "short-term mentality" has only recently been recognized as a weakness rather than a strength for the WSCF.

All in all, this era created a dogmatic anti-institution, antichurch, antihierarchy attitude in the Federation which inevitably alienated church leaders and those who had supported student work in the past. The short-lived attempt to define "a new constituency" for the WSCF based on ad hoc interest groups and activist caucuses, to replace the constitutional member movements, and to promote this pattern as a new paradigm of creativity heralded a Christian "self-destruct" mentality. However, in spite of its recognized destructiveness, the same idea appeared later in some WCC programs which sought to rely on "people's groups" outside the formal constituency of the Council, as well as in the emphasis on a "new paradigm for the ecumenical movement."[5] The heresy which considers all structural forms of both church and society as instruments of injustice and repression is still alive and discernible as part of the heritage of the radical left.

The Addis Ababa Assembly was followed first by an "anti-structure" period when the WSCF sharply reduced its organized relations with churches and ecumenical organizations. After it came a period of Euro-Marxism which lasted until the early eighties and in which Marxist socialism was expected to provide the basic framework for the "inter-regional office."[6] By this stage, however, few member

5. Konrad Raiser, the general secretary of the WCC since 1992, discusses in *Ökumene im Übergang, Paradigmenwechsel in der ökumenischen Bewegung* (München: Kaiser, 1989), pp. 45-48, the significance of "basis groups" for the ecumenical movement. He suggests that they took over the social and political avant-garde function in the ecumenical movement from the disintegrating Student Christian Movement at the end of the sixties. He is more confident about their contribution than the WSCF experience would lead one to expect, although he does admit occasional problems about their Christian identity and their generally rather short life span.

6. Feliciano Carino, general secretary, 1973-77, gave his report entitled "Advances and Contradictions; 1977 — Evaluation of a Changed WSCF" to the WSCF 1977 Assembly in Colombo, Sri Lanka, of which an abbreviated version is in *World Student Christian Federation: Memoirs and Diaries, 1895-1990,* ed. Elisabeth Adler (Geneva: WSCF, 1994), pp. 199-208. In his report Carino questioned the ideological and political assumptions of the Marxist-oriented members of the Federation and also the main emphases of the former chairperson, Richard Shaull. He emphasized the need

movements any longer sought or expected inspiration or guidance from Geneva and each regional program tended to go its own way. Only at the end of the eighties did signs of a new consolidation of the Federation's work begin to appear, with a new Geneva leadership indicating a desire to be freed from the slogans and theories which had entangled the WSCF since its crisis years.

Looking back on the stormy years of the Federation, it is difficult to see any way in which the radical left strengthened Christian student ministry. The awareness of social injustices and of the snares of an advanced technological society had existed long before. So had the determination to make the Federation more of a global community by providing space within it for the diversity of regional settings and socioreligious contexts. Similarly, the accent on the openness of the SCM to people of other faiths and of no religious belief as a characteristic of a missionary community was much older in the Federation than the left radicalism of the sixties. As far as the ideological leaders of that time were concerned, however, a "new" Federation was born in 1968, when "the New Man and the New Society" — the heavenly Jerusalem — would be realized with the coming revolution of which the Federation was to be a forerunner.[7] But what the glorious promise produced was bitter conflict and the sharpest decline the Federation had ever experienced.

Several of us who were involved in the SCMs and the WSCF during this stormy period have agonized for many years over the question of whether the damage to the WSCF could have been

---

of the diverse membership "to stay together" and to look more at the basis, "at the very root on which the Federation is anchored," to give renewed attention to the Federation's relationship to the churches and ecumenical movement as a whole. A paper by Emidio Campi, general secretary, 1977-83, entitled "Crisis and Hope: A Perspective on the Present State and the Future of the WSCF," *WSCF Dossier*, no. 12 (August 1977) gives an overview of Campi's thinking in the year when he became general secretary. The ensuing period did not bring about any signs of serious responses to Carino's farewell report. At least until late eighties the best efforts of the leaders of the Federation were unable to draw the ecumenical student movement together.

7. The last issue of the magazine *Federation News* put out by the new WSCF communication team in 1969 was a poster with the phrase "The New Man and the New Society" in several languages as its sole content.

avoided. Even if we admit mistaken decisions, misjudgments of situations, and failures to understand the intentions of others, the answer nevertheless can only be negative. The Federation, and, more widely, Christian ministry to students, was caught up in an ideological storm beyond the control of any thoughtful Christian student leaders and, ultimately, even of radical activist leaders. The failure to provide a more dynamic response to it reflected the thinning of the theological foundation of the Federation as well as the vulnerability of representative democracy in the face of populist-totalitarian movements. It is time to ask: Is the Christian church today — its old and young members — any better equipped theologically and politically to confront rising political and ideological movements than before 1968?

A profoundly disturbing weakness in the recent efforts to consider the lessons of the history of the WSCF has been the unwillingness of those involved in its history project to touch upon the difficulties and the causes of the weakening of the Federation during the turbulent sixties and seventies.[8] The vision — the "Pressure of Our Common Calling," as Visser 't Hooft called it[9] — vanished from the Federation in those years. Temporarily? Or permanently? How can a movement live without a vision? The Federation needs its history for its search for a way ahead. Turning a blind eye to what went wrong in the WSCF in the revolutionary years closes rather than opens doors for a meaningful future. What is at stake here is not just a conflict between generations but a lack of serious reflection on the ideological heritage of the revolutionary era.

Whether the Federation will fully recover from the damage caused by its internal insurrection and conflict or whether it will remain an ecumenical invalid for years to come is yet to be seen. In any case,

8. The paramount example of the unwillingness of senior ecumenical leaders to touch the painful aspects of the WSCF history is the treatment of the critical period 1964-77 in the volume on WSCF history by Philip Potter and Thomas Wieser, *Seeking and Serving the Truth: The First Hundred Years of the World Student Christian Federation* (Geneva: WCC, 1996).

9. W. A. Visser 't Hooft, *The Pressure of Our Common Calling* (London: SCM Press, 1959), was a programmatic book which spelled out also much of the vision of the WSCF and was much used by the WSCF and SCMs during the Life and Mission of the Church program.

what happened to it is a relevant warning signal for churches and the ecumenical movement today. A vaccine against the virus of self-destruction in the ecumenical movement has not yet been discovered. But perhaps something has been learned.

If the Federation — or its possible ecumenical successor organization — is to have a meaningful future and serve a global ecumenical community in the university, it must return to its roots. Bible study, worship, intellectual integrity, respect for theological and political diversity within its ranks, alertness to what happens in society and in the world were hallmarks of the communities which made up the Federation in the past. The ecumenical student movement should, also in the future, be an inspirer of such communities and a testing ground for the mission of the Church in the next century. Christian students and scholars should find in such a movement a spiritual home and a source of inspiration for their witness and service within the academic community and in the world.

The tendency among many SCMs after the revolutionary years has been to join ranks with various advocacy communities to defend minorities in the church and society and to play a dissident role in discussions of social and ecological concerns. Such groups, especially when they drift into isolation from the wider life of the church, are unlikely to resume a significant role in bringing together the Christian community in the university or to generate contagious vision for the ecumenical movement. For any such group to be cut off from the wholeness of the one holy catholic and apostolic Church means that it becomes an obstacle for an open encounter with the mystery of Godhead, for carrying the gospel in its fullness, and for witnessing to the Church, which crosses boundaries between minorities and majorities, between different cultures and generations, even between time and eternity.

Surely one-issue groups have their place in the church, for they are bound to create controversy. They must not be harassed by those in charge, but they will not be treated with tolerant indifference either. However, the Church also needs in its midst communities that are committed to a comprehensive, ecumenical vision of the Church, even when working on particular concerns and even when running into tension with the church establishment. Such communities are the real carriers of the SCM tradition.

330

The Federation used to affirm that it was an expression of the life of the Church universal. An unswerving commitment to Jesus Christ meant a commitment to God's People, the Body of Christ. The Church existed for the life of the world. Will these commitments be renewed among Christian students and their leaders in the coming decades? Such an affirmation would imply humility and patience to bear with the imperfections of churches and to guard against messianism in any engagement with social and political concerns.

15.3. Ecumenical Repercussions

The WSCF used to be a pioneer of the ecumenical movement. In the past it has addressed many issues which later became part of the agenda of the WCC and other ecumenical organizations. This kinship continued unbroken until the early seventies. The events of the stormy years of the Federation still drew much attention among senior leaders of the ecumenical movement until communication was abruptly broken in 1973. Consequently, no serious examination of the WSCF experience and its repercussions for the ecumenical movement has since been pursued. The fact that the WSCF crisis touched upon many sensitive, even controversial, issues being debated in the WCC in those years contributed to the silence about the Federation. Interestingly enough, the secular world and "academia" seem to be more ready to evaluate the heritage of the revolutionary years than the church.[10] The time might now be ripe for the ecumenical movement to return to the lessons of that era. The issues are not yet dead.

The desire of ecumenical leaders to be in the front line of the church's witness to the world and a partner in its renewal has been an appreciated characteristic of the WCC. Its architects wanted it to

10. Recent books give evidence of an evaluation which by and large is still missing in the ecumenical movement. They include Stephen Macedo, *Reassessing the Sixties* (New York: Norton, 1996); Ray Connolly, *In the Sixties* (Pavilion, 1996); Paul Berman, *A Tale of Two Utopias* (New York: Norton, 1996); and David Burner, *Making Peace with the 60s* (Princeton, N.J.: Princeton University Press, 1996). The *Economist,* October 19-25, 1996, reviewed these books and the discussion which they generated.

be both a meeting place of churches in their own right and a forum for ecumenical renewal movements. They believed that continuity and renewal belonged together and were dependent on one another. This inevitably implied tension, but also an interplay between different aspirations and trends. The late sixties, however, brought about a drastic change. Continuity and renewal came to be viewed as mutually exclusive options. Structures and traditions were viewed as enemies of renewal and change. The emergence of theologies of revolution epitomized such views. Anyone who was not "for radical (revolutionary) change" was labeled as a supporter of the evil of evils: the "status quo." "Change" became a sacred word for the young generation. A wave of anti-institutionalism ensued.

The parallel change of attitude toward ideologies came as a surprise. It is bewildering that the ecumenical movement, which advocated the renewal of the social witness of the Church, so readily fell under the spell of the increasingly authoritarian political ideologies of the New Left and of neo-Marxism — and all this only some twenty years after churches and the ecumenical movement at the founding Assembly of the WCC in Amsterdam 1948 and also the WSCF in its conferences and publications had taken a clear stand against any compromising of the Christian faith in the face of ideological pressures. That stand had been directed against all ideologies with totalitarian claims, especially Hitler's national socialism, but also communism, nationalism, and capitalism.[11] Suddenly, after 1968 a surprising number of church and ecumenical leaders, together with the radical student generation, were willing to welcome totalitarian ideologies and to accept their claims to provide a normative interpretation of reality, including that of the Christian faith. This experience points to the ongoing vulnerability of the church to becoming a vessel for ideologies which are in basic conflict with the Christian view of human nature and history.

The move of social and political concerns to center stage in both the WSCF and WCC did not generate greater clarity about the political

11. The preparatory papers for and the report of the WCC 1948 Assembly in Amsterdam, the issues of the *Student World,* and the Federation "Grey Book" *The Christian in the World Struggle,* by M. M. Thomas and J. D. McCaughey, spell out the dangers of ideological coloring of Christian witness.

role of the church. Instead, considerable confusion prevailed, most visibly in the Federation but also in the senior ecumenical movement. Activist pressures contributed to a failure to seriously study and discuss the principles involved. The contribution of the Federation at that time was to illustrate what the political role of the church should not be rather than what it should be. The experience showed once more that a church cannot, without denying its own foundation, base its political role on ideologies, political parties, or action organizations. The church is also mistaken if it strives to achieve political power and thereby turn the Christian faith into a political ideology. Furthermore, the experience of those years confirmed, in spite of what the Vatican may occasionally claim, that no one church or ecumenical organization has superior or final answers to the political problems of the day. The best the church can do is to be informed by its theology, try to clarify its position on social and political issues, and offer possible solutions, whenever it can. The authority of its statements, however, depends on their quality and integrity, in the same way as do the positions and solutions of professional politicians or people of good-will in general. In Addis Ababa the WSCF exemplified in numerous ways how an ecumenical organization can deviate from a sound political role.

Numerous Christian organizations have succumbed to the temptation of issuing "ex cathedra" statements on every conceivable international or national issue. Even the Lutheran World Federation (LWF) jumped on the bandwagon after the mid-eighties.[12] Quickly drafted pronouncements have been frequently issued under the name of the chief executives of the organizations, often with minimal consultation with the churches most concerned. Many of them have been simple

---

12. From the mid-eighties on the LWF Executive Committee and especially its general secretary felt compelled to issue public statements on political situations at a moment's notice. On only a few of them had serious preparatory work involving theological study and political analysis been done. The quality of these statements decreased as their frequency increased. Such statements were addressed to governments, to the UN, and to liberation movements. The governments of South Africa, Israel, Haiti, USA; the liberation movements in southern Africa; the factional leaders in Afghanistan, Liberia, and many other places as well as the UN received their share of advice and appeals from the LWF executive leaders (*Lutheran World Information,* 1986-92).

applications of a preconceived ideological position. The authors have thus relieved themselves of the necessity for careful scrutiny of the underlying, complex facts and from further theological or ethical considerations on which churches could be expected to have something to say. Such a misconceived political role of the church is a disservice to all concerned, and can easily result in a distortion of the Christian message.

The same trend can be discerned in the fields in which the ecumenical movement has the longest history of involvement. From the beginning the WCC became engaged in public witness on issues of social and economic justice, peace, and human rights. The Life and Work movement and other expressions of ecumenical cooperation since the first decades of the century were the precursors to this involvement. In the early seventies a new emphasis on the "prophetic" role of the WCC emerged which mirrored the rising anti-institutional attitude fueled by the revolutionary left. Accordingly, ecumenical leaders felt compelled to take an a priori stand against anything resembling "establishment," including the governments of most industrialized countries, UN agencies, large and wealthy churches, and, very especially, multinational corporations. Under the influence of the "prophetic" emphasis, critical discussion of social and economic issues, involving serious analysis and examination of alternatives to the policies and practices of "the powerful," was diminished. Such a posture seemed to suggest that no government and no industrial or business enterprise could be a worthy partner for churches and the ecumenical movement.[13] Such a confrontational attitude persistently echoes the theologies according to which all institutions of the old order, including organized churches, are inherently obstacles to justice.

Since the WCC is an organization of many different churches, such ideological tendencies did not lead to the kind of catastrophic confrontations experienced by the WSCF. Their influence was

13. During the visit of the South African minister of education, Dr. Sibusiso Bengu, to Finland in March 1996, he asked why churches and the ecumenical movement seem to be lost in a situation in which apartheid as a system has been dismantled. He emphasized that national reconstruction and reconciliation cannot be carried out without the moral strength which the Christian message promises. "To repeat revolutionary slogans no longer makes sense in South Africa," said this freedom fighter.

nevertheless not marginal in the seventies and eighties. Some WCC programs which traditionally had been in the center of member churches' interest and colored much ecumenical social ethics were visibly dominated by such ideological trends.[14] One consequence has been a decline of interest in the ecumenical movement and in the WCC programs among many member churches. Many of them no longer regard the WCC as an instrument accountable to them, but instead, as an independent organization run by an in-group, which wants to speak for churches but which turns a deaf ear to the concerns of churches which do not coincide with its interests.[15] All this has resulted in recent decades in a decrease of knowledge about the world-wide ecumenical movement in local congregations, dioceses, and synods. The most tangible sign of this decline is the series of financial crises which has confronted the WCC in recent years.

Today it is clear that most of the social issues which came to the fore during the sixties and seventies are still largely unresolved. In addition new problems have emerged since the collapse of communism. The list of today's issues is even longer than it was then: overcoming the growing gulf between rich and poor; the promotion of greater international economic justice; the search for viable alternatives for the world market economy; dealing with new expressions of ethnic and racial hatred; respect for human rights; the reconstruction of former communist countries; facing threats to the global environment; and many others. The recipes of the radical left were not helpful. Many of them have become counterproductive.

From where will churches and Christian students find a vision

14. Evidence of the positions and program emphases and the controversy created by them in member churches can be traced in the minutes of the Central Committee of the WCC, the official reports from the WCC subunits, and also the *Ecumenical Review*. Ronald Preston gives a summary of controversial elements in the programs of the WCC related to social responsibility in the book mentioned above in note 2.

15. The constitution of the WCC allows that up to 15 percent of the voting delegates to an Assembly can be named by the Central Committee in addition to those who have been chosen by member churches to represent them. In practice the delegates invited by the Central Committee are chosen by the WCC staff. The original purpose of this clause was to ensure adequate balance between different confessions and geographical regions. It can also serve the purpose of safeguarding critical support for policies and positions advocated by the staff and challenged by member churches. A similar clause in a political organization would be considered undemocratic.

for the mission of the Church for the days and years ahead? A hard look at the history of the ecumenical movement in general, and the heritage of the stormy years in particular, is essential so that pressing ecumenical tasks may find their proper place in the lives of all churches and the WCC regain its role as a significant instrument of its own constituency.[16]

15.4. Reflections on Repentance

The WSCF experience stimulates further reflections. One line of argument frequently expressed at ecumenical gatherings is that the primary arena of God's action is the world in general, and the struggle for and with the poor and oppressed in particular. According to this the church has at best only a secondary role, if any, in God's design for the world, and that is to discern and follow God's action in political struggles. Furthermore, the redemptive action of God, the salvation brought by Christ, is expected to take place outside church structures. The ministry of Word and Sacrament is viewed as rather irrelevant to God's action in the world. Moreover, the institutional church is viewed as an enemy of God's action when it is perceived as part of the oppressive system and appears to be a defender of the "status quo." Only those who renounce the "status quo" and commit themselves to radical political action, with the poor, for change, and against oppression, can, according to this view, identify themselves with God's purposes, the coming kingdom. *Intra ecclesiam nulla salus* (there is no salvation inside the Church).

According to this reasoning, revolutionary action programs for the poor and God's design for the world become one. Who is on God's side and who is against him is revealed by one's political stand.

16. In this connection a study tour into the ideas of the theologians and thinkers whose influence on the ecumenical movement has been formative could provide some surprises concerning their contemporary significance. The work of Walter Rauschenbusch, Karl Barth, Reinhold Niebuhr, William Temple, W. A. Visser 't Hooft, and Pope John XXIII has an astonishing relevance for today's debates. Many others should not be forgotten either: Nicolas Berdyaev, Dietrich Bonhoeffer, Joseph Hromadka, Toyohiko Kagawa, Dom Helder Camara, Martin Luther King Jr., Julius Nyerere, and more. Nor is the influence of the encounter between the Catholic, Lutheran, and Calvinist positions since the Reformation by any means over.

God is no longer a hidden God whose essence is revealed in the suffering Christ. The gospel of the cross is replaced by political and ideological triumphalism.

For the WSCF liberationist the correct political praxis was the condition of a credible Christian witness. It was emphasized that, unless the church rejects capitalism and its system of oppression, its message will have no credibility in society in general and among the poor in particular. Thus the message was made dependent on ethical purity achieved by commitment to the anticapitalist political struggle and by withdrawing the church and its agencies from any bonds with financial and business institutions promoting the market economy. In theological terms such demands represented a clear-cut return to justification by works and a denial that the credibility of the church rests ultimately on nothing but the unmerited gift of salvation in Jesus Christ.

The storm of the sixties became a test case for the validity of theological and confessional traditions of the church. The teaching on God's creation and on the meaning of God's law in the universal moral consciousness has proved once again helpful and relevant. Social justice is not the monopoly of Christians. The church is called to witness to it together with all those who thirst for it, with the deprived and the poor and with all people of goodwill. The goal is not a particular "Christian" social order, but a *more just* society. In practice it is a search for the path of least evil. The pervasive presence of sin makes it meaningless, in fact blasphemous, to speak of a "just society" as a politically achievable goal. But the obligation to work for justice — for a *more* just and *less* evil society — is absolute for the church.

Another important lesson of the WSCF experience was that its conflict and crisis did not originate from evil intentions. Strong ethical convictions, indeed a passion for justice, drove the wedge which divided the Federation and damaged the ecumenical movement. There is nothing unique about this in the history of the church, although it was a new experience for our generation in the Student Christian Movement. Just causes carried to extremes once again proved more dangerous than evil ones, because evil hidden behind half-truths is more deceptive than plain, unmasked evil. The scope of the damage inflicted on institutions and individuals by a passion for what proved to be a half-truth was unforeseen in the case of the WSCF. The language of ecumenical prophets does need watching.

Some clues for unraveling problems which arise from a passion for justice are given by Saint Paul. He speaks of the "law," which in itself is right, but which is at the same time a destructive power. This paradox makes sense to those of us who went through the WSCF experience. He continues in his letter to the Romans to speak about the gospel as a vehicle of God's grace which frees us from the powers of destruction, including sin, death, and also the law. What is characteristic of the destructive grip of law is that it does not tolerate ambiguity. It justifies enmity. It permits no weakness. It kills laughter. Only God's grace can break its suffocating grip and show that everyone without distinction is in the same boat, allies and enemies alike.

In the same vein, according to Saint Paul, the justice and grace of God — undeserved gifts — enter fallen humanity and make possible what no political programs can guarantee: the exposure of evil within and outside the Christian community, among allies and enemies, making reconciliation and love possible against all odds. The revelation of goodness in fallen humanity both inside and outside the church is beyond human mastery because it is a miracle of God, transferred as a gift.

15.5. Final Remarks

Each crisis in corporate or personal life raises questions about the foundation of faith. Most of the creedal and confessional formulations of the Christian faith have arisen in response to external pressures on the church and controversies within it. This is also what happened during and after the storm in the Federation. What was left of the World Student Christian Federation was forced to examine its foundations. For some the question marks grew bigger. For others the meaning of many old affirmations became vital to the contemporary context. The rethinking of the meaning of the Christian faith and the role of the church in the world must continue both in the Federation and in the ecumenical movement as a whole to prepare for new situations and to meet new crises.

At a time of sharp conflict the value of the inner freedom which stems from the gospel is heightened. It equips one to face complex social and political choices without being threatened by them. Political opponents can be seen not as enemies but as human beings created by God and as neighbors who are objects of God's love. The gospel frees persons to transcend political and ideological boundaries without compromising God's truth, and to challenge the interests of any party or group which threaten the humanity of others.

The continuing weakness of the worldwide ecumenical student ministry is a cause for concern. There is still nothing equivalent to a functioning SCM in Britain and in the Netherlands, and only a fragmented one in Germany and the USA, although before 1970 they were leading movements in the WSCF. Similar weakness prevails in many other parts of the world. The remaining well-organized movements, mainly in Africa and Asia, have ended up in relative isolation. The once-flourishing SCM in secondary schools no longer exists. The absence of the generations of the seventies and eighties was conspicuous in the 1995 centennial celebrations of the WSCF in Berlin, Vadstena, and Ivory Coast. The vacuum is very real.

The question remains open as to whether a revival of the ecumenical movement can once more emerge among students and in universities, as happened one hundred years ago. This much-needed renewal may come from unforeseen directions. The preservation of the heritage of any single period, including that of the revolutionary years, as normative for the movement is clearly not a solution. It is hard to imagine how those who long for vital manifestations of the Church universal for the next century could do without the evangelicals and the Roman Catholics. It can also be expected that in the next phase of the ecumenical movement, religious issues will return to center stage and that the reduction of faith to the likeness of social and political ideologies will recede. The call for personal discipleship and responsibility is likely to sound with a new urgency. The future of the ecumenical movement will be interesting.

Finally, this story, sad as much of it is, should give no comfort to those who would seek to ignore the lessons of the revolutionary era. Without regard to the different vantage points and to the different experiences of those years, this history must be faced together. Errors must be admitted so that doors can be opened for the renewal of the Church and its mission. Ultimately, the hope for this to happen has no other ground than the promise of God to those who repent and long for new life.

Appendix

WSCF Executive, Administrative, and Project Staff, 1969-72

Head Office — Geneva

Audrey Abrecht, Canada/USA, Editorial Assistant, then Assistant to General Secretary, 1949-73

Alice Austin, Finance and Personnel, 1969-70

Kees Baans, Netherlands, Finance, 1961-69

Nancy Bell, New Zealand, Secondary Schools, Publications, 1972

Claudius Ceccon, Brazil, Communication, 1969-71

José Chipenda, Angola, Foreign Students, 1968; Africa, 1968-73, see below Africa Office — Nairobi

Leonard Clough, USA, Resources, 1969-71

Ann Crane, USA, Project Secretary, Political Commission/Communications

Leonardo Franco, Argentina, Latin America, 1969; Political Commission, 1969-71

Leonardo Gilardi, Italy, Documentation, 1970-71

Christine Griesbeck, Germany/Switzerland, Finance, 1970-73

Risto Lehtonen, Finland, North America, 1968; General Secretary, 1968-73

Peter Musgrove, Australia, Priorities/Ecumenical Assistance, 1969-73

Inga Stauffer, Switzerland, Personnel, -1970

Europe Office — Geneva

Milan Opocensky, CSSR, Secretary for Europe, 1973

Africa Office — Nairobi

José Chipenda, Angola, Secretary for Africa, 1968-73
Bethuel Kiplagat, Kenya, Secretary for Literature, 1968-71

Africa Office — Yaoundé

Aaron Tolen, Cameroon, Secretary for UNESCO, 1969; Secretary
for Africa, 1969-73

Asia Office — Tokyo

Moonkyu Kang, Korea, Secretary for Asia, 1973
David Swain, USA/Japan, Publications, University Teachers, 1973
Kentaro Shiozuki, Japan, University Teachers, ALDEC, -1972

Asia Office — Bangkok

S. N. Sugunanthan, Sri Lanka, 1970-71

Latin America Office — Lima

Edir Cardoso, Brazil, Secretary for Latin America and CLAF, 1969-
Juan-Antonio Franco, Puerto Rico, Secretary for Latin America,
1969-
Alan and Stephanie Olivier, USA, Publications, 1968-72
Pablo Zavala, Peru, Secretary for Latin America, 1969-72

Latin America — Project Secretary, Buenos Aires

Mario Yutzis, Argentina, Project Secretary, 1971-73

Middle East Office — Beirut

Gabriel Habib, Lebanon, Secretary for Middle East, 1960-73
Adele Manzi, Italy, Project Secretary for Communication, 1971-
Teny Simonian, Lebanon, Project Secretary for Development,
    1972-

Middle East — Project Secretary, Hamburg, Germany

Karam Khella, Egypt, Project Secretary for work among Middle
    Eastern students in Europe, 1969-72

North America Office — New York

Placide (Charles-Henri) Bazoche, France, Secretary for North
    America, 1969-
Janet Griesinger, Women's Concerns, 1970-73

Office at UNESCO Headquarters — Paris

Aaron Tolen, Cameroon, 1969; see Africa Office — Yaoundé above.

Office at UN Headquarters — New York

Louis Simon, India, Secretary for NGO Relations at the UN,
    1970-73

Bibliography

Books

Adler, Elisabeth, ed. *World Student Christian Federation: Memoirs and Diaries, 1895-1990.* WSCF History Series, vols. 3-4. Geneva: WSCF, 1994.

Austin, Alan D., ed. *The Revolutionary Imperative: Essays toward a New Humanity.* Nashville: Board of Education of the Methodist Church, 1966.

Bent, Ans van der. *Commitment to God's World: A Concise Critical Survey of Ecumenical Social Thought.* Geneva: WCC, 1995.

Berger, Peter L., and Richard J. Neuhaus. *Movement and Revolution.* New York: Doubleday, Anchor Books, 1970.

Cartey, Wilfred, and Martin Kilson, eds. *The Africa Reader: Independent Africa.* New York: Random House, Vintage Books, 1970.

A Challenge to the European University. The report of the WSCF/CEC European Ecumenical Strategy Consultation. Geneva: WSCF, 1968.

Christians in the Technical and Social Revolutions of Our Time. The official report of the World Conference on Church and Society, Geneva, July 12-26, 1966. Geneva: WCC, 1967.

Cohn-Bendit, Daniel, and Gabriel Cohn-Bendit. *Obsolete Communism: The Left-Wing Alternative.* London: André Deutsch Limited, 1968.

Coleman, John. *The Task of the Christian in the University.* Grey Book of the WSCF. Geneva, 1947.

Collier, Peter, and David Horowitz. *Destructive Generation: Second Thoughts about the Sixties.* New York: Summit Books, 1989.

Conway, Martin. *The Undivided Vision.* London: SCM Press, 1966.

Diétrich, Suzanne de. *Cinquante ans d'histoire: La Fédération Universelle des Associations Chretiennes d'Etudiants (1895-1945).* Paris: Editions du Semeur,

1946. In English, *World Student Christian Federation: 50 Years of History, 1895-1945.* WSCF History Series. Geneva, WSCF, 1993.

Diétrich, Suzanne de. *Rediscovering the Bible: Bible Study in the WSCF.* Grey Book of the WSCF. Geneva, WSCF, 1942.

Douglass, Bruce, ed. *Reflections on Protest: Student Presence in Political Conflict.* Richmond: John Knox Press, 1967.

Freire, Paulo. *Pedagogy of the Oppressed.* New York: Herder, 1970.

History's Lessons for Tomorrow's Mission: Milestones in the History of Missionary Thinking, an Anthology. Geneva: WSCF, 1960.

Hoekendijk, J. C. *The Church Inside Out.* Philadelphia: Westminster Press, 1966. Original in Dutch, *De Kerk Binnenste Buiten.* W. Ten Have N.V., 1964.

Horowitz, Irving Louis, Josué de Castro, and John Gerassi, eds. *Latin American Radicalism: A Documentary Report on Left and Nationalist Movements.* New York: Random House, Vintage Books, 1969.

Jacobs, Paul, and Saul Landau. *The New Radicals: A Report with Documents.* New York: Random House, Vintage Books, 1966.

Kennan, George. *Democracy and the Student Left.* Boston: Little, Brown, 1968.

King, Martin Luther, Jr. *Why We Can't Wait.* New York: New American Library, Signet, 1963.

Ledger, Christine, ed. *World Student Christian Federation: A Community of Memory and Hope.* WSCF History Series, vol. 1. Geneva: WSCF, 1992.

Lindner, John B., Alva I. Cox, and Linda-Marie Delloff. *By Faith: Christian Students among the Cloud of Witnesses.* New York: Friendship Press, 1991.

Mackie, Robert C. *Layman Extraordinary: John R. Mott, 1865-1955.* London: Hodder and Stoughton, 1965.

Marcuse, Herbert. *Eros and Civilisation.* Boston: Beacon Press, 1955.

———. *Five Lectures: Psychoanalysis, Politics, Utopia.* Boston: Beacon Press, 1970.

———. *One-Dimensional Man: The Ideology of Industrial Society.* Routledge and Kegan Paul, 1964.

Marty, Martin E., ed. *No Ground beneath Us: A Revolutionary Reader.* National Methodist Student Movement, 1964.

Maury, Philippe. *Evangelism and Politics.* Geneva and London: WCC & Lutherworth, 1959.

Mayr, Hans. "Einheit und Botschaft, das Ökumenische Prinzip in der Geschichte des Christlichen Studentenweltbundes 1895-1939 mit einem Ausblick bis zur Gegenwart." Ph.D diss., Tübingen, 1975.

McCaughey, J. Davis. *Christian Obedience in the University: Studies in the Life of the Student Christian Movement of Great Britain and Ireland, 1930-1950.* London: SCM Press, 1958.

Mott, John R. *Addresses and Papers*. Vols. 1-6. New York: Associated Press, 1946-47.

———. *The Evangelization of the World in This Generation*. New York: SVM, 1900.

———. *The Future Leadership of the Church*. New York: Association Press, 1911.

———. *The Present World Situation*. London: SCM, 1915.

———. *Strategic Points in the World's Conquest*. New York: Fleming Revell, 1897.

———. *The World Student Christian Federation: Achievements of the First Quarter-Century of the WSCF and Forecast of Unfinished Tasks*. WSCF, 1920.

Oglesby, Carl, and Richard Shaull. *Containment and Change*. New York: Macmillan, 1967.

Orwell, George. *Inside the Whale and Other Essays*. New York: Penguin Books, 1957.

Potter, Philip, and Thomas Wieser. *Seeking and Serving the Truth: The First Hundred Years of the World Student Christian Federation*. WCC Publication, 1996.

Preston, Ronald. *Confusions in Christian Social Ethics: Problems for Geneva and Rome*. London: SCM Press, 1994.

Rouse, Ruth. *The World's Student Christian Federation: A History of the First Thirty Years*. London: SCM Press, 1948.

Seale, Patrick, and Maureen McConville. *French Revolution, 1968*. New York: Penguin Books, 1968.

Shiozuki, Kentaro, ed. *The Relevance of Social Sciences in Contemporary Asia: University Teachers in Dialogue*. Tokyo: WSCF, 1968.

Tatlow, Tissington. *The Story of the Student Christian Movement of Great Britain and Ireland*. London: SCM Press, 1933.

Thomas, M. M., and J. D. McCaughey. *The Christian in the World Struggle*. Grey Book of the WSCF. Geneva, WSCF, 1952.

Visser 't Hooft, W. A. *Memoirs*. London: SCM, 1973.

Wilder, Robert P. *The Great Commission*. London: Oliphants, 1937.

Wilder Braisted, Ruth. *In This Generation: The Story of Robert P. Wilder*. New York: Friendship Press, 1941.

Wilson, Dick. *Asia Awakes: A Continent in Transition*. New York: Penguin Books, 1972. First published by Weidenfeld & Nicolson, 1970.

Wolin, Sheldon S., and John H. Schaar. *The Berkeley Rebellion and Beyond: Essays on Politics and Education in the Technological Society*. New York: Random House, a New York Review Book, 1970.

345

WSCF Books, 1970-73

Derr, Thomas Sieger. *Ecology and Human Liberation: A Theological Critique of the Use and Abuse of Our Birthright*. WSCF Book No 7. Geneva: WSCF, published in collaboration with Church and Society, World Council of Churches, 1973.

✓ Douglass, Bruce. *The Evolution of the Modern Idea of Revolution*. WSCF Book No. 6. Tokyo: WSCF, 1972.

Douglass, Bruce, ed. *Trying Times: American Politics in Transition from the Sixties to the Seventies*. WSCF Book No. 1. Geneva, WSCF, 1971.

Hall, Douglas John. *Hope against Hope: Toward an Indigenous Theology of the Cross*. WSCF Book No. 3. Geneva, WSCF, 1971.

Smolik, Josef. *The Fourth Man and the Gospel*. WSCF Book No. 2. Geneva, WSCF, 1971.

Tolen, Aaron, ed. *A New Look at Christianity in Africa*. WSCF Book No. 5. Geneva: WSCF, 1972.

Wylie, Ray, ed. *China: The Peasant Revolution*. WSCF Book No. 4. London: WSCF, 1972.

WSCF Periodicals

Federation News, a quarterly news magazine of the WSCF, discontinued in 1969.

Footnotes, WSCF Asia magazine, published 1967-74.

Presence, WSCF Africa magazine, published in Kitwe, Zambia, and later in Nairobi, Kenya.

Question, a political newsletter of the WSCF, published in 1970-71.

The Student World, a quarterly review published by the WSCF; the last issue was numbers 3-4, 1969.

Testimonium, WSCF Latin America magazine, discontinued in 1968.

WSCF Europe, a bulletin published from 1970 to 1977 in Geneva, Switzerland.

WSCF Newsletter, an occasional news bulletin of the WSCF published from 1970.

Reference to specific issues of these publications is made in the notes.

WCC Reports and Publications

Christians in the Technical and Social Revolutions of Our Time. The official report of the World Conference on Church and Society, Geneva, July 12-26, 1966. Geneva: WCC, 1967.

346

Dictionary of the Ecumenical Movement. Geneva: WCC, 1991.

Minutes of the Meetings of the WCC Central Committee, 1969 and 1971.

Releases of Ecumenical Press Service (EPS), replaced by Ecumenical News International (ENI), issues of *Ecumenical Review, Anticipation,* and *Study Encounter.*

Uppsala 1968: The Official Report of the Fourth Assembly of the WCC, July 1968. Geneva, 1968.

Specific Sources

Minutes of General Committee/Assembly Meetings

Minutes of the Twenty-Second Meeting of the General Committee of the WSCF, Tutzing, Germany, 1956.

Minutes of the Twenty-Third Meeting of the General Committee of the WSCF, Thessaloniki, Greece, 1960.

Minutes of the Twenty-Fourth Meeting of the General Committee of the WSCF, Embalse Rio Tercero, Argentina, 1964.

Minutes of the Twenty-Fifth Meeting of the General Assembly of the WSCF, Dipoli Conference Centre, Otaniemi, Finland, 1968.

Minutes of the Twenty-Sixth Meeting of the General Assembly of the WSCF, Africa Hall, Addis Ababa, Ethiopia, 1972/73.

Minutes of the WSCF Executive Committee Meetings (mimeographed).

Cambridge, Massachusetts, USA, August 1965
Prague, Czechoslovakia, April-May 1967
Helsinki, Finland, August 17-18, 1968
Beirut, Lebanon, March 30–April 6, 1969
Cartigny, Switzerland, June 22-28, 1970
Tozanzo, Japan, July 2-10, 1971

Minutes and Reports of WSCF Staff Meetings (mimeographed)

Minutes of a Meeting of WSCF Staff and Chairman, Annecy, France, December 9-12, 1968.

Minutes and Reports of Meetings of Geneva Staff:

1969: November 13, 19; December 10, 17

1970: February 23, 26; March 3, 19; May 14 and 15; June 4; July 27; August 4, 27; September 4

1971: January 6; February 2-3, 11, 23; April 23, 29; May 4; June 15, 17; September 29

(The collection of minutes and reports in the WSCF Archives is so far incomplete.)

WSCF Documents and Reports

"The Christian Community in the Academic World." A statement issued by the General Committee of the WSCF at its meeting at Embalse Rio Tercero, Argentina, July 15-31, 1964, a separate edition. Geneva: WSCF, 1964.

"Christian Presence in the Academic Community." A report on the WSCF, 1964-68. Mimeographed.

"Consultation on Ecumenical Strategy in the Universities of Asia" (EACC/WSCF). Hong Kong, November 6-13, 1966.

"Report of a Consultation (AACC/WSCF) on the Christian Community in the Universities of Africa." Legon Hall, Accra, September 1-6, 1966.

"The Report of the Meeting of the Planning Committee of the World Student Conference." Commugny, Switzerland, October 12-18, 1966. Mimeographed. WSCF Archives.

"The Reports of the Seminars of the Turku 68 Conference." A compilation of unedited reports. Mimeographed. Geneva, 1968.

"Students and the Life and Mission of the Church." A report on the WSCF, 1956-64. Mimeographed.

"Study Documents on China." Related to the China study program, 1965-68. Mimeographed. WSCF Archives.

"Towards an 'Ecumenical Strategy' for the University Work in Latin America." Report of the consultation held in El Tabo, Chile, January 22-25, 1966. Mimeographed. WSCF/UNELAM.

Evaluative Reports on the Turku '68 Conference

Abrecht, Paul (USA/WCC Geneva Staff). "Brief Note to My WSCF Friends: What Went Wrong with Turku?" Mimeographed.

Bortnowska, Halina (Poland). "Mini-révolution dans la FUACE." *Convergence* (Pax Romana).

Dahl, Eeva (Norway). "A Report." Mimeographed.

Dongen, P. van (Belgium). Article in *De Bazuin* of the Ecumenical Commission of Pax Romana.

Hengel, Eduard von (Netherlands). "Criticism of WSCF Summer Conferences 1968." Mimeographed.

————. "One-Dimensional Federation." Mimeographed.

Lewis, Vivian (USA). "A New Man for a New World," *World YWCA Monthly*, December 1968.

Moss, Larry J. (U.K./WCC Staff). "Turku '68 in Retrospect," *World Outlook*, October 1968.

Schmemann, Serge (USA). "Turku '68: A Report on the World Student Conference at Turku, Finland," *Concern* (SYNDESMOS Orthodox Youth), no. 4 (1968), by USA.

Thelle, Öystein (Norway). Letter to Milan Opocensky, November 6, 1968.

Report of the meeting of the Planning Committee of the WSCF General Assembly. Ibadan, Nigeria, December 31, 1971–January 3, 1972.

Staff Correspondence and Staff Reports. WSCF Archives.

"Theological Dossier." Compiled by the WSCF Europe office, 1969-72.

SCM Reports, Magazines, and Other Publications

Journal of Ecumenical Studies. Perspectives on Ecumenical Christian Presence in U.S. Universities and Colleges, 1960-1995. I-II. Vol. 32, nos. 3 and 4, 1995.

Reports of member movements, including those prepared for WSCF meetings, their responses to circulars and reports, and documents addressed to regional consultations and meetings. Mimeographed. WSCF Archives.

WSCF Archives has also an uneven collection of magazines of member movements. Those used in this study included those of the SCM of Britain *(Movement)*, India *(Aikya)*, Finland *(Etsijä* and *Ad Lucem)*, and South Africa *(One for the Road* and *Newsletter)*.

Other magazines dealing with WSCF concerns in the sixties and early seventies include *Christianity and Crisis* and *Christianity Today* (USA), *Kristet Forum* (Sweden), and *Vartija* (Finland).

Statements by Charlotte Bunch, Steve Schomberg, Nelly Sale, and Poikail George on the causes and significance of the discontinuation of the national organization of the UCM, March 1969. Mimeographed. WSCF Archives.

Index

351